www.wadsworth.com

wadsworth.com is the World Wide Web site for
Wadsworth Publishing Company and is your direct
source to dozens of online resources.

At *wadsworth.com* you can find out about
supplements, demonstration software, and
student resources. You can also send e-mail to
many of our authors and preview new publications
and exciting new technologies.

wadsworth.com
Changing the way the world learns®

The Wadsworth College Success™ Series

Santrock and Halonen, *Your Guide to College Success: Strategies for Achieving Your Goals* (1999). ISBN: 0-534-53354-X

Holkeboer and Walker, *Right from the Start: Taking Charge of Your College Success*, 3rd Ed. (1999). ISBN: 0-534-56412-7

Petrie and Denson, *A Student Athlete's Guide to College Success: Peak Performance in Class and Life* (1999). ISBN: 0-534-54792-3

Van Blerkom, *Orientation to College Learning*, 2nd Ed. (1999). ISBN: 0-534-52389-7

Wahlstrom and Williams, *Learning Success: Being Your Best at College & Life*, 2nd Ed. (1999). ISBN: 0-534-53424-4

Corey, *Living and Learning* (1997). ISBN: 0-534-50501-5

Campbell, *The Power to Learn: Helping Yourself to College Success*, 2nd Ed. (1997). ISBN: 0-534-26352-6

The Freshman Year Experience™ Series

Gardner and Jewler, *Your College Experience: Strategies for Success*, 4th Ed. (2000). ISBN: 0-534-53415-5

Concise Third Edition (1998). ISBN: 0-534-53749-9

Expanded Reader Edition (1997). ISBN: 0-534-51898-2

Expanded Workbook Edition (1997). ISBN: 0-534-51897-4

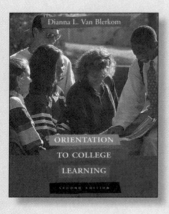

Study Skills/Critical Thinking

Longman and Atkinson, *CLASS: College Learning and Study Skills*, 5th Ed. (1999). ISBN: 0-534-54972-1

Longman and Atkinson, *SMART: Study Methods and Reading Techniques*, 2nd Ed. (1999). ISBN: 0-534-54981-0

Sotiriou, *Integrating College Study Skills: Reasoning in Reading, Listening, and Writing*, 5th Ed. (1999). ISBN: 0-534-54990-X

Smith, Knudsvig, and Walter, *Critical Thinking: Building the Basics* (1998). ISBN: 0-534-19284-X

Van Blerkom, *College Study Skills: Becoming a Strategic Learner*, 3rd Ed. (2000). ISBN: 0-534-56394-5

Kurland, *I Know What It Says . . . What Does It Mean? Critical Skills for Critical Reading* (1995). ISBN: 0-534-24486-6

Your College Experience

STRATEGIES FOR SUCCESS

Fourth Edition

John N. Gardner
Executive Director, University 101 and The National Resource Center
    for The First-Year Experience and Students in Transition
Professor, Library and Information Science
University of South Carolina, Columbia

A. Jerome Jewler
Professor, Journalism and Mass Communications
University of South Carolina, Columbia

Wadsworth Publishing Company
I(T)P® An International Thomson Publishing Company

Belmont, CA • Albany, NY • Boston • Cincinnati • Johannesburg • London • Madrid • Melbourne •
Mexico City • New York • Pacific Grove, CA • Scottsdale, AZ • Singapore • Tokyo • Toronto

Publisher: *Karen J. Allanson*
Development Editor: *Alan Venable*
Senior Editorial Assistant: *Godwin Chu*
Marketing Manager: *Jennie Burger*
Project Editor: *Christal Niederer*
Print Buyer: *Barbara Britton*
Permissions Editor: *Bob Kauser*
Production: *Cecile Joyner/The Cooper Company*
Copy Editor: *Jennifer Gordon*

Designers: *Ann Butler, Carolyn Deacy, 17th Street Studios*
Illustrator: *John Nelson*
Cover Design: *Stephen Rapley*
Cover Images: *PhotoDisc and Dick Luria/FPG International*
Compositor: *New England Typographic Service*
Printer: *Banta*
Cover Printer: *Banta*

Printed in the United States of America
3 4 5 6 7 8 9 10

Wadsworth Publishing Company
10 Davis Drive
Belmont, CA 94002

International Thomson Publishing Europe
Berkshire House
168-173 High Holborn
London, WC1V7AA, United Kingdom

Nelson ITP, Australia
102 Dodds Street
South Melbourne
Victoria 3205 Australia

Nelson Canada
1120 Birchmount Road
Scarborough, Ontario
Canada M1K 5G4

International Thomson Editores
Seneca, 53
Colonia Polanca
11560 México D.F. México

International Thomson Publishing Asia
60 Albert Street
#15-01 Albert Complex
Singapore 189969

International Thomson Publishing Japan
Hirakawa-cho Kyowa Building, 3F
2-2-1 Hirakawa-cho, Chiyoda-ku
Tokyo 102, Japan

International Thomson Publishing Southern Africa
Building 18, Constantia Square
138 Sixteenth Road, P.O. Box 2459
Halfway House, 1685 South Africa

Library of Congress Cataloging-in-Publication Data
Your college experience : strategies for success / [edited by] John N. Gardner, A. Jerome Jewler—4th ed.
    p.   cm.—(Freshman year experience series)
    Includes bibliographical references and index.

ISBN 0-534-53423-6
    1. College student orientation—United States.   2. Study skills—United States.   3. Critical thinking—United States.   4. Success—United States.   I. Gardner, John N.   II. Jewler, A. Jerome.   III. Series.
LB2343.32.Y68   2000   98-52103
378.1'98—dc21

Just as first-year students everywhere are forever learning new ways to succeed, so we are discovering new ways to help them. Each of us began college not knowing if we were going to make it through. Our beginnings were shaky, yet by using common sense and relying on the advice of others we did succeed. Not once during our college years did we realize what a powerful effect our college experiences would have on the rest of our lives. We dedicate this fourth edition to those of you who are just beginning this journey. We believe much good advice lies within these pages, advice we wish we had been privy to during our college years. All we ask is that you strive to follow as much of it as you can.

Brief Contents

Contents

IMPROVING CLASSROOM AND ACADEMIC SKILLS

Foreword to the Instructor

By Vincent Tinto
Distinguished University Professor
Syracuse University

I have been involved as a researcher and consultant in studies of student retention and retention programs for nearly 30 years. In that time, I have come to learn four important lessons about the character of successful retention strategies.

First, retention is the result of successful education. Students who learn, stay.

Second, becoming a successful learner takes time and skills, both academic and social. It is not easy, but it is doable.

Third, environment matters. Students who are involved, both academically and socially, are not only more likely to stay, but are more likely to learn while staying.

Fourth, the first year of college is a critical period for student learning and persistence. It is a period of transition and adjustment, both academically and socially, during which students acquire important skills that furnish the foundation for subsequent learning. It is a period when involvement matters most, and when learning is most readily shaped by educational programs designed to provide students with learning experiences that are motivating, challenging, and involving.

In this regard, I have also discovered that few individuals are more qualified to speak to the needs of new students and the first-year experience than Professors John Gardner and Jerry Jewler. They have been working with new students and with faculty who teach those students for more than 25 years. In that time, they have acquired knowledge that few can match of what works and what doesn't.

That knowledge is contained within the pages of this book and in the programs their work has inspired. The first section introduces students to the goal-setting process, provides them with a set of "keys to success" that are noted throughout the book, stresses the benefits of collaborative learning and the value of a liberal education, and explains the process of thinking critically.

The second section provides students with the basic academic skills they will need to survive college: time management, note-taking in the classroom, reading textbooks for information, studying for exams, using the library and technology to gather and organize knowledge, speaking with confidence in the classroom, a problem-solving method for math and the sciences, and choosing academic majors and careers.

The final section deals with matters of a more personal nature: values clarification, appreciating diversity, developing relationships, managing stress, sexual decisions, alcohol and drugs, and money management.

At the end of each chapter are numerous exercises instructors may assign at will. Annotations in the Annotated Instructor's Edition suggest other activities for classroom use, and the Instructor's Resource Manual provides additional ideas for teaching each chapter of the book.

I can't imagine a more comprehensive introduction to the college experience. So, as I have recommended to students, let me also recommend that you take Gardner and Jewler's advice seriously and use it as a guide to your own thinking about the education of new students on your campus. As I have found in my own institution, where I teach our version of the first-year seminar, their advice works.

Foreword to Students

By Vincent Tinto
Distinguished University Professor
Syracuse University

So you're just beginning—or returning to—college. What now? Well, if you feel a bit unsure of yourself, unsure of what to expect and what to do, take comfort in the fact that most of your peers feel the same way. More to the point, you should take comfort in the fact that you are beginning a path that has been trod by thousands of others before you. Their experience and the lessons they convey will prove invaluable to you as you begin or resume your college career.

This book, edited by two of the nation's leading authorities on the college experience, represents the accumulated wisdom of those students who preceded you. Through the authors' words, these students speak and share their wisdom about what you can do to make the most of your college experience.

So my advice to you is simple. Read this book and take its advice seriously. Ask yourself how you can apply the lessons learned by former students to your college career.

Pay particular attention to the Keys to Success in Chapter 1. If you can follow them, you should have no difficulty surviving college. Indeed, you will flourish.

In the first section of this book, Chapters 1, 2, and 3, you'll find help with the goal-setting process and a set of "keys to success" in college. You'll learn about the benefits of collaborative learning and the value of a liberal education, and you'll explore the process of thinking critically.

In Chapters 4 through 13, you'll find the skills essential to being a successful learner: time management, learning in the classroom, how to read a textbook, how to study for exams, how to use the library and the Internet for research, and other important information, including a comprehensive look at career planning.

Finally, Chapters 14 through 20 introduce you to the personal side of college: developing values, appreciating diversity, making friends, managing stress, managing money, and dealing with sexual decisions, alcohol, and drugs.

As you read this book, be aware that your college has a variety of specialists whose job is to help you adjust to the academic demands you will face. Most students require some form of help during the first year of college. It's quite normal, because college presents different challenges from high school.

Colleges are gold mines of knowledge and information. Tap into that information. Don't let your college years go by without exploring the many wonderful resources and knowledgeable people on your campus.

Explore the library and discover how it links you to knowledge well beyond the boundaries of your campus and your nation. Get to know faculty, not just from your program, but throughout campus. Choose a few courses that sound interesting, that intrigue you, and attend them not for the sake of your academic program, but for yourself! Treat yourself to knowledge. It's low in fat and high in vitamins and minerals.

And don't worry if you're not sure about your major. Most students are either undecided about a major when they enter college or change their minds at least once. Being undecided is actually more common than knowing what you want to do for the rest of your life. So if you don't know, don't panic. But don't be passive. See the specialists in your career center. Get involved with activities that take you beyond the classroom and perhaps beyond the college. Seek summer internships in areas that might interest you. Many students have discovered their careers during such internships.

College is also a time of personal growth. Although this makes the college experience wonderful, it can also make for stormy weather. But storms pass, so hold on. And when times are stormy, reach out for help. Stay connected to other people, and remember once more: you are not the only one going through this.

You will have few other times in life when you can explore and learn as you can do in college, so take advantage of the next few years. Be sensible. Be smart. And above all, enjoy.

Preface to Instructors

■ THE KEYS ARE ESSENTIAL

As founders and dedicated supporters of the First-Year Experience movement for nearly thirty years, we have always kept two ideas foremost in our minds:

- All students can succeed in their first year of college.
- As educators and scholars, it is our responsibility to provide the best possible support for their efforts.

Research by scholars at the National Resource Center for the First-Year Experience at the University of South Carolina and at other institutions continues to show that first-year college students are most likely to succeed and continue in college if they

- Get to know at least one faculty or staff member on campus
- Make friendships and form groups that support their college goals
- Learn ways to define and accomplish goals for academic and career success
- Manage their time to best effect
- Master the fundamental learning skills required in college
- Pass beyond "survival" thinking to an attitude of critical thinking and intellectual growth
- Master basic writing skills as an integral tool of college learning

The *Keys to Success* that you see listed on the inside front cover of this text are still the book's guiding principles, as they are for outstanding college success courses across the country. Every chapter of this book begins by letting the student know how studying the chapter and completing its activities will help them acquire and master specific key skills.

From its first edition, this text has been based on these keys to success, which in turn are based on the most reliable research into the foundations of success in college. With extensive input from adopting instructors, exercises have been created and continually improved to broaden students' experience and skills in self-assessment, goal-setting, critical thinking, use of digital technology, collaborative learning, class discussion, journaling and other forms of writing, and classroom presentation.

We view this fourth edition as a major advance over previous editions. We think you'll agree!

■ NEW IN THIS EDITION

A Shorter, Crisper Text

With this edition we have consolidated the contributions of dozens of experts from around the country into a shorter format and a completely unified voice. By combining some topics and streamlining others, and by other changes mentioned below, we have reduced the length of the book while at the same time expanding the coverage of several important topics. One great strength of *Your College Experience* has always been its reliance on a multitude of experts in their fields. With this new revision, we believe we make that expertise more accessible to student readers.

Unified Text and Expanded Activities

Following the advice of numerous reviewers, we have changed the chapter format by moving the exercises to the end of each chapter. Marginal callouts beside the text show where and how each exercise applies to implement the ideas of the text. One advantage of this new arrangement is that students can now read the chapter text without interruption. Another advantage is that we have been able to expand the number of exercises and make clearer how they build on one another. New also to the comprehensive edition is a special full-page *Resources* activity at the end of each chapter as well as a journal page that allows students to write their responses to the journal questions.

Internet and InfoTrac College Edition

Also new to this edition are *Internet* activities for every chapter, allowing students to practice multiple uses of the Internet, from e-mail, to chat groups, to using the World Wide Web for personal and academic research. In addition, each chapter ties into the unique resources of *InfoTrac College Edition*, an extensive, professional Internet database of over 600 journals with full-text articles. By using this text, your students have 24-hour access to comprehensive and up-to-date research information for all their course work.

New Chapter on Critical Thinking and Writing

Prior editions have integrated William T. Daly's four-phase approach to critical thinking in discussions and exercises throughout the chapters. In this edition we add to that a full chapter on critical thinking and writing early in the text, to provide a broader context for Daly's approach and more discussion and activities to introduce critical thinking as a key objective for first-year students. We also make explicit the crucial role of writing as both a tool for critical thinking and an effective method to reinforce learning.

New Chapter on Alcohol and Other Drugs

Every instructor in college success knows how difficult it is to address this issue realistically and positively with traditional-age first-year students. This edition offers a new approach that focuses primarily on binge drinking, now recognized nationally as the most serious public health issue on American campuses.

Expanded Chapter on Math and the Sciences

This redesigned chapter emphasizes the importance of scientific thinking and mathematical skills and logic, not only for majors, but for all students.

It connects the ability to master such skills with the ability to land a good job after graduation and reminds students that most employers require skills involving words and numbers. Entering students whose mindset is, I can't do math, will be encouraged by the approach this chapter takes. Using word problems, the chapter encourages students to work logically through the steps of arriving at the right solution.

New Focus on Collaborative Learning

Research increasingly indicates the importance of collaboration for student learning and retention. In this edition, Joe Cuseo of Marymount College, whose research specialty is collaborative learning, has added special text and activities throughout the chapters to enable students to work effectively in teams. Collaborative learning has been linked to higher levels of student comprehension and success in math, science, and technology. It helps students to develop their speaking and writing skills and encourages independent, self-directed learning. Collaborative college learning also prepares students for the teamwork required in today's workplace.

■SUPPLEMENTS AND SUPPORT

A complete resource package for instructors accompanies this text.

Instructor Resources

Toll-Free Phone Consultation: 1-800-400-7609 For helpful advice on information about our products and services.

Instructor's Resource Manual Includes background on the college success course; background on book-specific features; an overview of the six learning themes emphasized throughout the text; academic research-based material supporting the six learning themes; teaching strategies based on the six learning themes (including strategies for encouraging active involvement from students, effective questioning strategies, effective assignments); chapter-by-chapter teaching tips; test items and transparency masters.

World Class Testing Tools A fully integrated collection of test creation, delivery and classroom management tools! You can generate tests randomly, select specific questions, and write or import your own questions. You can also choose the method to deliver the tests—via diskette or local hard drive, LAN, or Wadsworth's Internet server. The tutorial feature allows students to answer sample test questions and receive immediate feedback as to why a particular answer was wrong. The test management software allows you to automatically extract and track data from online tests, practice tests, and tutorials. For more information and a demonstration, visit *http://www. worldclasslearning.com.*

College Success PowerPoint This cross-platform CD-ROM contains text and images to illustrate important concepts in the college success course. Use this CD in conjunction with your own PowerPoint program for the additional flexibility of adding your own slides, making changes or deleting existing slides and rearranging the slide order.

College Success Transparency Acetates 50 color transparencies featuring helpful checklists, charts, and key points about college success topics to help organize your classroom presentation.

The Keystone The exclusive newsletter of the Wadsworth College Success program. Published twice during the academic year, the Keystone brings you ideas and information about events and resources from colleagues around the country.

The Wadsworth College Success Course Guide This helpful resource covers a range of subjects, from building support for a first-year course to administering the course and reshaping it for the future.

Workshops and Training

College Success Workshops Wadsworth offers multiple training options to best meet your needs, including regional workshops, customized on-site workshops, and workshop offerings by authors Gardner and Jewler. Call 1-800-400-7609 for more information on creating a workshop just right for your program!

Teaching College Success: The Complete Resource Guide An *exclusive* to Wadsworth, *Teaching College Success* is the perfect tool to create your own tailored training program for college success instructors! Designed as a stand-alone resource or as a reference, this training package focuses on faculty development and common issues related to teaching the first-year seminar across institutions. Contains a complete set of training modules and a PowerPoint CD-ROM. *Teaching College Success* includes a blend of content information (the nature of the college success course, relevant theoretical approaches, and current national data) and experimental activities for trainers to try with training groups and later with students. Sampler package 0-534-53644-1. Full product 0-534-53640-9.

Video Resources

CNN Today: College Success *Exclusive* to Wadsworth, this innovative video program presents segments on key topics in college success, produced by the award-winning educational team at CNN. Perfect for "lecture launchers," these tapes are updated on a yearly basis.

Your College Experience: Strategies for Success Video Series This twelve-part video is designed to teach and stimulate lively group discussions. Based on the nationally acclaimed University 101 first-year seminar course directed by John Gardner at the University of South Carolina.

A World of Diversity A powerful two-video set on communication and conflict resolution between cultures. Reviewed by African-American, Asian-American, and Latino-American and other multicultural scholars for language authenticity and content accuracy.

Wadsworth Study Skills Videos *Volume 1: Improving Your Grades* features students talking to students and involves viewers in the issues that contribute to their success. It is divided into five parts designed to help students get what they want out of college: Choosing an Approach to Learning, Making Decisions About Your Time, Learning in Your Classes, Making Sense of Textbooks and Taking Tests. *Volume 2: Notetaking* features a series of college lectures which provide students with the opportunity to practice their notetaking skills and instructors with the opportunity to assess student skills.

Wadsworth College Success Video Series An extensive selection of videos from Films for the Humanities and Sciences on stress management, reading improvement, time management, healthful eating and nutrition, substance abuse prevention, AIDS, maximizing mental performance, and many others.

Internet Resources

InfoTrac College Edition Designed to help your students make the best of the Internet, Wadsworth's *exclusive* InfoTrac College Edition provides them access to full-length articles from more than 700 scholarly and popular periodicals, updated daily. Four-month subscription free to adopting instructors.

World Class Course The easy and effective way to create your own dynamic web site! Post your course information, office hours, lesson information, assignments, sample tests and links to web content, including student enrichment materials from Wadsworth. Updates are quick and easy and customer support is available 24 hours a day, seven days a week. More information is available at *http://www.worldclasslearning.com.*

Success Online
http://www.success.wadsworth.com
This new web service provides current and helpful professional resources including:

- Training information for instructors of new and established college success courses
- Course Tools to easily create a web site for your own course
- InfoTrac College Edition—online access to more than 700 popular and scholarly periodicals, updated daily
- Online Instructor's Manuals and PowerPoint slides
- The ability to create your own custom textbook online, by selecting individual chapters or sections from Wadsworth texts and combining them with your own campus materials
- Additional student resources

College Success Internet-at-a-Glance This handy one-page laminated pocket reference for students has a host of URL addresses related to college success topics such as study skills, learning styles, health, financial management, and career choice—to give your students a guided tour of the Internet! Available free when packaged with Gardner and Jewler's *Your College Experience,* 4th Edition.

College Success Guide to the Internet Written especially for college success students, this practical guide includes step-by-step instructions and tips for learning to use the Internet and a substantial collection of sites grouped by key topics discussed in the college success course, such as health issues, study skills, time management, test taking, and more.

Time Management Resources

Franklin-Covey Day Planner, Collegiate Edition This ultimate daily planner—consisting of a binder, 365 daily pages, 12 monthly tabs, a personal information section, a zippered pouch, and much more—is designed to help students manage their college and professional careers! Includes a training audiotape for students that explains time management principles and how to use the planner. Available at an *exclusively* low price when packaged with Gardner and Jewler's *Your College Experience,* 4th Edition.

■ACKNOWLEDGMENTS

Although this text speaks through the voices of its editors, it represents major contributions from many others. We gratefully acknowledge those contributions and thank these individuals whose special knowledge has made it possible to introduce new college students to "their college experience" through the holistic approach we deeply believe in.

Preface. Vince Tinto, Syracuse University, for his pioneering research on leaving college.

Chapter 1. Thorne Compton, University of South Carolina, for his thoughts on the value of a liberal education.

Chapter 2. Joseph Cuseo, Marymount College, for his contributions on collaborative learning as well as his authorship of the instructor's resource manual for this textbook.

Chapter 3. William T. Daly, The Richard Stockton College of New Jersey, for developing a clear formula for critical thinking. Carolyn Matalene, University of South Carolina, for her observations on writing. Alan Venable, our development editor, for making the critical thinking section—as well as the rest of this book—work.

Chapter 4. Johanna Dvorak, University of Wisconsin—Milwaukee, for her recommendations on time management.

Chapter 5. Steven Blume, Marietta College, for his detailed explanation of learning styles.

Chapter 6. Donald Jugenheimer, Southern Illinois University at Carbondale, for stressing the importance of listening in the classroom. Harry C. Payne, Williams College, for "Listening: The Neglected Art."

Chapters 7 and 8. Mary Walz-Chojnacki and Johanna Dvorak, University of Wisconsin—Milwaukee, for providing an approach for reading textbooks and studying for tests and exams.

Chapter 9. Marilee Birchfield, University of South Carolina, for demystifying the campus library for new college students.

Chapter 10. Kenneth C. Greene, Claremont Graduate School, and Steven W. Gilbert, American Association for Higher Education, for underscoring the significance of the computer in this age of information and technology.

Chapter 11. Constance Courtney-Staley, University of Colorado, Colorado Springs, and Robert Stephens Staley III, Colorado Technical University, whose strategies for successful speaking can help students gain confidence before a group.

Chapter 12. Mary Ellen O'Leary, University of South Carolina, for explaining the importance of math and the sciences in every student's life.

Chapter 13. Linda Salane, Columbia College, and Viki Fecas, University of South Carolina, for their detailed advice on career planning. Mary Stuart Hunter for the important information on catalogs and advising.

Chapter 14. Richard L. Morrill, University of Richmond, and Deborah Ritter-Williams, South Carolina Educational Television, for their discussion of values and academic integrity.

Chapter 15. Tom Carskadon and Nancy McCarley, Mississippi State University, for their extensive look at relationships. David Janes, Coordinator of Community Service Programs, University of South Carolina, for urging students to be involved in service learning.

Chapter 16. Joan A. Rasool, Westfield State College, for new perspectives on diversity. Monita Johnson for her stirring article on being a minority on campus.

Chapter 17. Kevin W. King, Counseling Psychologist, for his advice on reducing stress. Danny Baker, University of South Carolina, for explaining how to avoid becoming a victim of campus crime.

Chapter 18. Lisa Ann Mohn, Mind/Body Medical Institute, for sharing her extensive knowledge about sexual decisions. Tricia H. Phaup, Office of Sexual Assault Services, University of South Carolina, for educating us about sexual assault on and near campus.

Chapter 19. James Turner, M.D., University of Virginia, for straightforward advice on alcohol and drugs. Michelle Sutherlin for "The Police Got Me Drunk."

Chapter 20. Ray Edwards, former financial aid officer, University of South Carolina, on managing your money.

We would also like to thank Daniel J. Kurland for providing Internet exercises throughout the text which are both useful and imaginative.

Special thanks also to reviewers whose wisdom and suggestions guided the creation of this text:

Fourth Edition Reviewers

Pamela S. Backes, Keene State College
Lynn Carlson, University of Wisconsin—Parkside
Dena A. Deanovich, Purdue University Calumet
Linda J. Dunham, Central Piedmont Community College
Sheri Cranston Fraser, University of Maine at Augusta
Sharon Gagel, UNC Charlotte
Michael Edward Harris, Guilford Technical Community College
Bonnie J. Henrie, Utah State College
Kathryn K. Kelly, St. Cloud State University
Alice Lanning, University of Oklahoma
Evelyn J. Leggette, Jackson State University
Kathy L. Matthews, Kennesaw State University
Cheryl Notari, Seton Hall University
Dwight M. Patterson, Central Piedmont Community College
Bruce Peterson, Sonoma State University

Louise C. Rosenberg, University of Hartford
Voulynne B. Small, Guilford Technical Community College
Betty Smith, University of Nebraska—Kearney
Leon J. Van Dyke, University of Wisconsin—Parkside

Third Edition Reviewers

Mona J. Casady, Southwest Missouri State University
Kathy Jones, University of California—Riverside
Frances M. Kavenik, University of Wisconsin—Parkside
Molly M. Thacker, Radford University
Esther J. Winter, Northwest Missouri State University

Previous Edition Reviewers

Peter Biegel, Purdue University
Mary Jo Boehms, Jackson State Community College
Sandy Darnell, Rappahanock Community College
David Entin, NYC Technical College
Barbara Greenstein, The College of New Jersey
Elizabeth Hall, Texas Tech University
Michael Johnson, Western Kentucky University
Wendy J. Palmquist, Plymouth State College
Lauren Pernetti, Kent State University
Nancy Sonleitner, University of Oklahoma
John Steingoss, University of Toledo
James Stepp, University of Maine at Presque Isle
Michael Stoune, Texas Tech University

Thanks to the following reviewers for their close scrutiny and good advice for Chapter 3, Critical Thinking and Writing, and Chapter 19, Facing Up to Alcohol and Drugs:

Lynn Carlson, University of Wisconsin—Parkside
Leon J. Van Dyke, University of Wisconsin—Parkside
Sheri Cranston Fraser, University of Maine at Augusta
Cheryl Notari, Seton Hall University (New Jersey)
Pamela S. Backes, Keene State College (New Hampshire)
Bruce Peterson, Sonoma State University (California)

Thanks also to the many focus group participants and survey respondents for past editions.

All of this could not have been possible without the Wadsworth team that supported our text, guided us through the writing and production, and worked hard to make *Your College Experience* one of the most popular texts in its field. Our special thanks to Susan Badger, president; Karen Allanson, publisher; Alan Venable, development editor; Godwin Chu, senior editorial assistant; Jennie Burger, marketing manager; Christal Niederer, project editor; Bob Kauser, permissions; Cecile Joyner/The Cooper Company, production; and Jennifer Gordon, copyeditor.

John N. Gardner

A. Jerome Jewler

CHAPTER

College Makes the Difference

KEYS TO SUCCESS

- *Learn what helping resources your campus offers and where they are.*
- *Understand why you are in college.*

" I just stood in line for two hours and spent over a hundred dollars for two books. And I realized I have three exams during the same week in October. First week of college and I'm already stressing out. At least I've met a few interesting people. Wish I had time to talk to them! "

I t used to be that college teachers and administrators made some big assumptions about new students. Among other things, they assumed that by the time students got to college they would know how to manage their time, how to handle stress, how to do research, and how to choose a major. In most cases, they were wrong.

How do we know they were wrong? We know because we were the new students then, and we didn't really know how to do any of these things. Eventually we discovered how to do them—more or less—on our own. We learned the hard way, and often too late.

In the 1970s things changed for new students with the introduction of the first contemporary "college success" course. These courses are designed to help new students learn more about themselves, their college or university, and higher education in general. Their goal is to eliminate as many of the barriers to success as possible through readings, discussions, group exercises, writing assignments, and relationships with teachers and other students. And they have succeeded for the most part in lowering the high dropout rate in the critical first year.

If you're reading this book, chances are you're a new or returning college student. And, depending on your age and situation, we suspect you're having some of the following thoughts:

- This is the first time someone has not been there to tell me I *had* to do something. Will I be able to handle all this freedom? Or will I just waste time?
- I've never been away from home before, and I don't know anybody. How am I going to make friends?
- Maybe college will be too difficult for me. I hear college teachers are demanding. Will I be able to understand them?
- Not only do I miss being at home, but I hope I won't disappoint the people I care about.
- In high school, I got by without working too hard. Now I'll really have to study. Will I be tempted to cheat?
- I have responsibilities at home. Can I get through college and still manage to take care of my family? What will my partner think about all the time I'll have to spend in classes and studying?
- Will I like my roommate? What if (he, she) is (White, Black, Asian, Hispanic, and so on)? I've never known anyone like that before.
- What if I don't pick the right major? What if I don't know which major is right for me?
- Can I afford this? Can my parents afford this? I wouldn't want them to spend this much and then have me fail.

LESS TODD/PHOTO COURTESY OF DUKE UNIVERSITY

- Maybe I'm the only one who's feeling like this. Maybe everyone else is just smarter than I. Maybe everyone knows I'm a misfit.
- Looking around class makes me feel so old! Will I be able to keep up at my age?

This book will help you find the answers to such questions. Each chapter will take you one step closer to your goal of making it through college. But first, think about why you wanted to go to college in the first place. Was it because everyone else was going? Was it to make enough money to support a family or to start a new midlife career? Also, have you wondered what college is really like and how you will change as you travel through your college experience?

THOSE WHO START AND THOSE WHO FINISH

In 1900 fewer than 2 percent of Americans of traditional college age attended college. How different that is from today! At the end of the twentieth century, new technologies and the information explosion are changing the workplace so drastically that few people can support themselves and their families without some education beyond high school.

Today more than 50 percent of high school graduates go on to college, with over 3,600 colleges serving more than 14 million students. More than half of those enrolling in college begin in two-year institutions. Adult students are also enrolling in record numbers. As the century turns, over one-third of college students are over age 25.

SEE EXERCISE 1.1
INTERNET ACTIVITY

Half a century ago, most college students were White males. Again, what a difference time has made. Today, women outnumber men, "minorities" are making steady gains in numbers, and college has become financially possible for nearly everyone, regardless of income.

Greater access to college for everyone—this is the bright side. The not-so-good side is that 40 percent of students who start in four-year programs never finish their degrees. In two-year colleges, half or more of the entering class will drop out by the end of the first year.

First-Year Questions of Freedom and Commitment

The first year—that's when the highest dropout rate occurs and not simply because students haven't earned passing grades. Of those who quit, the majority were in good academic standing.

What is it, then, that causes so many students to drop out of college? There are two major reasons affecting two fairly distinct groups of students.

For those fresh out of high school, the overriding problem in the first year of college often involves newfound freedom. No more do teachers tell you exactly what to study, how, or when. No more do parents get you up in the morning, govern what you eat or when you sleep, monitor whether or how well you do your homework, or remind you to allow enough time to get to campus. In almost every aspect of your life, it suddenly all depends on you.

For returning students, the opposite is true: a daunting lack of freedom. Working, caring for a family, and meeting other adult commitments and responsibilities compete for the time and attention it takes to do your best or even simply to persist in college. And the easiest thing to do is quit.

SEE EXERCISE 1.2

SEE EXERCISE 1.3

SEE EXERCISE 1.4

Whichever problem you are facing, what will motivate you to overcome it? And what about the enormous investment of time and money that getting a college degree requires? Are you convinced that those investments will pay off? Having a clear sense of what a college education can do for you in the long run is critical for students who not only have begun their college studies but who will see them through to completion.

■ EDUCATION, CAREERS, AND INCOME

Will you earn more money with a college degree? Facing a job market that places a high premium on education and technology, men and women with only a high school education will make less than their contemporaries who earn college degrees.

The gap in earnings from high school to college is widening. In 1996 men with college degrees were earning an average of one-and-a-half times the salary of high school graduates; in 1970, the difference was only one-and-a-quarter times as much. In 1996, women with college degrees were earning nearly twice as much as women with high school diplomas. One probable reason for the growing disparity is the sudden spurt of jobs in technology and information. Whatever the reason, it becomes more evident each year that a college education is truly worth its cost.

In the past several decades, college-educated women's wages have increased more quickly than the wages of college-educated men. However, much of that gain has come from working longer hours. As Table 1.1 shows, college-educated men still earn substantially more than college-educated

Table 1.1 Earnings of Men and Women by Educational Attainment and Age

Educational Attainment	Men		Women	
Some high school	$13, 961		$7,674	
High school diploma	$20,870	(+$6,909)	$13,075	(+$5,401)
Some college	$23,435	(+$2,565)	$17,157	(+$4,082)
College degree	**$32,708**	**(+$9,273)**	**$26,043**	**(+$8,886)**

Source: U.S. Department of Education, 1993

women. But these are averages, of course, and many women with college degrees have earnings equal to or higher than those of many men.

In addition to higher earnings, according to the Carnegie Commission on Higher Education, as a college graduate you will have a less erratic job history, will earn more promotions, and will likely be happier with your work.

The commission also notes that you will be less likely than a nongraduate to become unemployed. Critics of higher education occasionally point out that some people with college degrees are unemployed or underemployed, but you have only to look at the unemployment rates of high school graduates and dropouts to see that the better educated you are, the better your opportunities. As the saying goes, "If you think education is expensive, try ignorance."

■ LIBERAL EDUCATION AND QUALITY OF LIFE

Of course, college will affect you in other ways. No matter what your major, you will emerge from college with a liberal education. Liberal, as in "liberate" or "free," signifies that a well-rounded college education will expand life's possibilities for you by steeping you in the richness of how our world, our nation, our society and its people came to be.

Liberal education is about learning to learn, discovering how to think for yourself, on your own and in collaboration with others. The result of a liberal education is that you will understand how to accumulate knowledge. You will encounter and learn more about how to appreciate the cultural, artistic, and spiritual dimensions of life. You will be more likely to use integrity in decision making and to realize how our lives are shaped by global as well as local political, social, psychological, economic, environmental, and physical forces. You will grow intellectually through interaction with cultures, languages, ethnic groups, religions, nationalities, and social classes other than your own.

The evidence from many studies suggests that as a liberally educated college graduate, you will

- Know more, have more intellectual interests, be more tolerant of others, and continue to learn throughout life.

- Have greater self-esteem and self-confidence, which helps you realize how you might make a difference in the world.

- Be more flexible in your views, more future oriented, more willing to appreciate differences of opinion, more interested in political and public affairs, and less prone to criminal activity.

- Tend to delay getting married and having children, have fewer children and share child-care and household responsibilities with your partner, and devote more energy to child rearing.
- Have a slightly lower divorce rate than those who did not graduate from college.
- Have children with greater abilities who will achieve more in life.
- Be an efficient consumer, save more money, make better investments, and spend more on home, intellectual, and cultural interests as well as on your children.
- Be able to deal with bureaucracies, the legal system, tax laws, and advertising claims.
- Spend less time and money on television and movies for leisure and more on continuing education, hobbies, community and civic affairs, and vacations.

SEE EXERCISE 1.5

- Be more concerned with wellness and preventive health care and consequently—through diet, exercise, stress management, a positive attitude, and other factors—live longer and suffer fewer disabilities.

Financially and otherwise, a college education can indeed be priceless.

■ KEYS TO SUCCESS

Researchers have identified what you can do to succeed in college. Many of these keys to success may strike you as common sense, and many of them are. Nonetheless, you will benefit from a careful reading of them. We've organized these keys into two major groups for all students—academic and personal—and followed these with additional keys that are specifically for minorities and returning students. Why are both academic and personal keys important? If you take care of yourself, you'll be in better shape to succeed academically. Conversely, if you practice the academic skills we list, you'll feel better about yourself. Sounds simple, doesn't it? It is. With a pencil, check (✓) every key that you think will be challenging for you. Later in this course as you determine you have mastered them, come back and convert the checkmark into an X. Throughout this book, you will learn how to master these keys.

Academic Keys

1. **Show up for class.** Not just most days, but every day. When you're not there, you're missing something. You're also sending your instructor a message that you don't care. If you know you are going to miss class because of an appointment, sickness, or an emergency, contact your instructor as soon as possible and certainly before the next class meeting.

2. **Have your work done on time.** Not only may you face a grade penalty if you're late, you will most certainly incur the wrath of some of your teachers if you are perpetually late with assignments. Some instructors may have a policy of not accepting late work and grading it with a zero. Ask if you are uncertain. Submitting work late won't lead to success in college or in your career after college. If your work must be late because of illness or an emergency, let your instructor know. Your thoughtfulness may earn you an extension without penalty.

3. **Set up a daily schedule and stick to it.** Learning how to manage your time can make the difference between success and frustration. Get an appointment calendar from your campus bookstore now and start using it.

4. **Assess and improve your study habits.** Learn how to read a textbook, how to take notes in class, how to study for an exam, and how to use information sources on campus. Find out about your preferred learning style. If your campus has an academic skills center, visit it when you're having difficulty with your studies.

5. **Study with a group.** Research shows that students who collaborate in study groups often earn the highest grades and survive college with fewer problems.

6. **Choose instructors who actively involve you in learning.** The more you can participate in class, the more you'll enjoy learning. Ask upper-class students who these instructors are.

7. **See your instructors outside class.** You are encouraged to do so, and students who do tend to stay in college longer. Your instructors have office hours because they expect you to visit them.

8. **Improve your critical thinking skills.** Challenge. Ask why. Seek dependable information to prove your point. Look for unusual solutions to ordinary problems. Never accept something as fact simply because someone tells you it's true or allow your emotions to interfere with your logical thinking powers.

9. **Know how to find and work with information on your campus.** That means not only knowing how to use the library but being able to handle a computer for a data search.

10. **Be the best writer you can be.** The more you write, the better you write. Instructors—and employers—want people who can think and write. That's why this book provides many writing assignments and suggestions.

11. **Find a great academic advisor or counselor.** This should be someone to whom you can and will turn for guidance and support.

SEE EXERCISE 1.6

12. **Visit your career center.** A career counselor can help you learn more about your academic major or find another major that suits you better. And if you cannot decide on a major immediately, don't worry. Instead, talk about your options.

13. **Learn what helping resources your campus offers and where they are.** Academic and personal support services are usually free and confidential. Successful students use them. See "Where to Go for Help," p. 9.

14. **Learn from criticism.** Criticism is healthy. It's how we all learn. If you get a low grade, ask to meet with your instructor to discuss what you should do to improve your work.

15. **Understand why you are in college.** Identify your goals by using the goal-setting process on page 11.

Personal Keys

16. **Get to know at least one person on campus who cares about your survival.** It might be the teacher of this course, some other instructor, your academic advisor, someone at the counseling or career center, an advisor to a student organization, or another student. You

may have to take the initiative to establish this relationship, but it will be worth it. Remember: In college, as in life, you become like those with whom you associate.

17. **If you are a full-time student, try not to work more than 20 hours a week.** Most students begin a downhill slide after that. Need more money? Consult a financial aid officer. If you must work, look for a job on campus. Research indicates you'll enjoy greater success in college when you work on campus, too. Visit your college career center for career counseling as well as leads on jobs during and after college.

18. **If it is difficult for you to stand up for yourself, take assertiveness training.** Your counseling center probably offers workshops that can teach you to stand up for your rights in a way that respects the rights of others.

19. **Get involved in campus activities.** Visit the student activities office. Work for the campus newspaper or radio station. Join a club or support group. Play intramural sports. Most campus organizations crave newcomers—you're their lifeblood. Even joining one group will raise your odds for success in college.

20. **Take your health seriously.** How much sleep you get, what you eat, whether you exercise, and what decisions you make about drugs, alcohol, and sex all contribute to your well-being and how well you will do in classes. Find healthy ways to deal with stress, too. Your counseling center can help.

21. **Try to have realistic expectations.** At first you may be disappointed in the grades you make, but remember that college is a new experience and things can improve. Also, remember you are not alone. Thousands of other students have faced the same uncertainties you may be facing. Hang on to that positive attitude. It makes a difference. Keep telling yourself, "I can do it."

Additional Keys for Minority Students

22. **Take advantage of minority support services.** If your campus has centers for minority students, visit them and introduce yourself. Ask for help. Take advantage of mentoring programs.

23. **Maintain connections with your home base, but be aware of the changes you may be going through and the impact of those changes on family and friends.** They may put pressure on you to stay the same or accuse you of selling out if you are successful in college. Use e-mail, phone calls, and letters to stay in touch with parents as well as friends at other schools.

24. **Be proud of your heritage and culture.** In college you may hear ugly remarks and witness or be the target of bigotry caused by ignorance or fear. Stand tall. Be proud. Refuse to tolerate disrespect.

25. **Immerse yourself in your culture as you learn to interact with people of other cultures.** Take courses in African American, Hispanic, and Asian studies, women's studies, and other cultural, ethnic, and gender studies. Help other minority students. Make friends with students from different backgrounds. Get to know minority faculty and administrators. Get involved in sensitizing others to cultural diversity.

Where to Go for Help

College support services are not always located where you might think or named what you might expect. If you're not certain where to look for a particular service, there are several ways to begin. You might ask your academic advisor or counselor; consult your college catalog, phone directory, and home page on the World Wide Web; or call or visit the office of student services (called student affairs at some schools) for assistance. The majority of these services are free.

- **Academic Advisement Center**
  Guidance about choosing classes
  Information on degree requirements

- **Academic Skills Center**
  Improve study skills and memory skills
  Help on how to study for exams
  Individual tutoring

- **Academic Computing Center**
  Minicourses and handouts on campus and other computer resources

- **Adult Re-Entry Center**
  Programs for returning students
  Supportive contacts with other adult students
  Information about services such as child care

- **Career Planning and Placement**
  Career materials library
  Career interest assessments
  Career goal counseling
  Computerized guidance programs
  Assistance finding a major
  Full-time, part-time, co-op, internship, and campus job listings
  Opportunities for graduating students to interview with employers
  Help with resumes and job interview skills

- **Chaplains**
  Worship services and fellowship
  Personal counseling

- **Commuter and Off-Campus Services**
  Listings of nearby available housing
  Roommate listings

Orientation to the community
Maps, information on public transportation, babysitting lists, and so forth

- **Counseling Center**
  Confidential counseling on personal and interpersonal concerns ranging from roommate problems to prolonged states of depression
  Programs on managing stress

- **Financial Aid and Scholarship Office**
  Information about financial aid programs, scholarships, and grants

- **Health Center and Enrichment Services**
  Tips on personal nutrition, weight control, exercise, and sexuality
  Information on substance abuse programs, adult children of alcoholics, and general health care, often including a pharmacy

- **Housing Office**
  Assistance in locating on- or off-campus housing

- **Legal Services**
  Legal services for students (If your school is affiliated with a law school, check to see whether senior students in the law school are available for counseling.)

- **Math Center**
  Help with math courses

- **Physical Education Center**
  Free or inexpensive facilities for exercise
  Recreational sports facilities and equipment for swimming, racket sports, basketball, archery, weight training, dance, and so on

- **Services for Students with Disabilities**
  Support in overcoming physical barriers or learning disabilities

- **Writing Center**
  Help with writing papers and reports

PHOTO COURTESY OF BILL DENISON

Additional Keys for Returning Students

26. **Never doubt your abilities.** Studies have shown that learning ability does not decline with age. In fact, verbal ability increases.

27. **Expect instructors to be glad to see you.** Most will welcome you because your practical life experiences will enrich the class and provide material for written assignments. Instructors know that most re-entry students do well academically.

28. **If school seems stressful, enroll part-time.** Adjust the number of courses you're taking to control the amount of strain.

29. **Enlist the support of your spouse, partner, or family.** Adjust household routines and duties. Let others know when you need extra time to study. A supportive partner is a great ally, but a nonsupportive partner can threaten your success in college. If your partner feels threatened and tries to undermine what you are doing, sit down and talk it over or seek counseling.

30. **Find faculty and staff support on campus.** If you have young children, find out about child care. If your school has special advisors for adult students, they will know the most about weekend and evening courses. Seek adult advocates in student affairs or continuing education programs.

31. **Develop peer support.** Find out how to meet other adult learners. Or put an ad in the campus paper and form your own group. Find a classmate with whom you can meet for coffee, study, or to lend and borrow notes if one of you has to miss a class.

32. **Take additional courses in how to study.** After reviewing the study skills in this book, consider taking a comprehensive study skills course. You also may need to review basic math or writing skills. Fortunately, relearning something is much easier than learning new material.

33. **Embrace new technologies.** If you don't already know, ask how to use word processors, do a computerized library search, access journals online, and send and receive e-mail. The computer skills you develop in college will prove valuable in later employment.

SEE EXERCISE 1.7

Welcome to InfoTrac College Edition!

A POWERFUL LIBRARY RESEARCH DATABASE

InfoTrac College Edition is a large and powerful digital information database system. It includes numerous encyclopedias and other reference works as well as articles from many academic journals and periodicals. A comprehensive version of InfoTrac is most likely available for use at your college library as well as on other computer terminals on campus.

YOUR OWN DIRECT ACCESS TO INFOTRAC COLLEGE EDITION

If your instructor arranged for your purchase of this textbook to include a trial subscription, you can also use InfoTrac College Edition directly via the World Wide Web on your own computer. To set up your four-month InfoTrac College Edition account, go to web address *http://www.infotrac-college.com/wadsworth* and submit the account number that was issued on the InfoTrac College Edition insert that accompanied your shrink-wrapped book. InfoTrac College Edition will lead you through the enrollment process.

At the time this book was published the InfoTrac College Edition included more than 600 current magazines and journals. That number continues to grow. For a complete index of journal and reference titles, enter InfoTrac and click the PowerTrac option.

Like searching on the web, inside InfoTrac College Edition you can search for information by typing "key words." Unlike the web, you can also search by using InfoTrac College Edition's extensive Subject Guide.

Many entries include the complete text of an article, which you can download to your computer. Each entry starts with an abstract to give you an idea of whether the article is likely to meet your needs.

For each chapter in this book, we suggest search-word and subject-guide phrases to use in connection with the chapter. We also list specific articles you might want to read.

Make InfoTrac College Edition a regular part of your college success work this term. Also use it to find information for writing papers and broadening your learning in other courses.

■ SETTING GOALS FOR SUCCESS

Now that you've read the keys for success, what should you be doing to accomplish them? One method is to set specific goals for yourself, beginning now, that will help you maximize your potential in college.

We know from years of working with new college students that many hold a number of negative self-fulfilling prophecies. A self-fulfilling prophecy is something you predict is going to happen, and by thinking that's how things will turn out, you greatly increase the chances that they will. This book is designed to help you rid yourself of your negative prophecies, replace them with positive ones, and learn how to fulfill them. Look back at the list of comments and questions on page 2. If some of these sound familiar, take comfort: Most other entering students share the same fears. One way to overcome them is to begin setting positive—not negative—goals for yourself.

College is an ideal time to begin setting and fulfilling short- and long-term goals. A short-term goal might be to set aside three hours this week to study chemistry, whereas a long-term goal might be to devise a strategy for passing chemistry with an A. It's okay if you don't yet know what you want to do with the rest of your life. It's even okay if you don't know what to major in. Be patient. Using the keys to success as a starting point, practice the following process by setting some short-term goals now:*

1. **Select a goal.** State it in measurable terms. Be specific about what you want to achieve and when (for example, not "improve my study skills" but "master and use the recall column system of note-taking by the end of October").

2. **Be sure that the goal is achievable.** Have you allowed enough time to pursue it? Do you have the necessary skills, strengths, and resources? If not, modify the goal to make it achievable.

3. **Be certain you genuinely want to achieve the goal.** Don't set out to work toward something only because you feel you should or because others tell you it's the thing to do. Be sure your goal will not have a negative impact on yourself or others. Be sure it is consistent with your most important values.

4. **Know why the goal matters.** Be sure it has the potential to give you a sense of accomplishment.

5. **Identify and plan for difficulties you might encounter.** Find ways to overcome them.

6. **Devise strategies for achieving the goal.** How will you begin? What comes next? What should you avoid? Create steps for achieving your goal and set a timeline for the steps.

SEE EXERCISE 1.8

*Adapted from Human Potential Seminars by James D. McHolland and Roy W. Trueblood, Evanston, Illinois, 1972. Used by permission of the authors.

Search Online!

INFOTRAC COLLEGE EDITION

Try these phrases and others for Key Words and Subject Guide searches: "college success," "liberal arts," "goal setting," "college," "universities and colleges."

Also look up:

The job market offers good news for the class of 1998; an industry by industry analysis reveals a high demand for graduates across the board, especially those with technical and computer skills (includes predictions from top executives from leading industries). Patrick Scheetz, Rebecca Gratz. *The Black Collegian* Feb 1998 v28 n2 p42(7)

Among young adults, college students and graduates practiced more healthful habits and made more healthful food choices than did nonstudents. Constance C. Georgiou, Nancy M. Betts, Sharon L. Hoerr, Kathryn Keim, Paula K. Peters, Beth Stewart, Jane Voichick. *Journal of the American Dietetic Association* July 1997 v97 n7 p754(6)

First encounters of the bureaucratic kind: early freshman experiences with a campus bureaucracy. Glen J. Godwin, William T. Markham. *Journal of Higher Education* Nov-Dec 1996 v67 n6 p660(32)

■ YOUR FIRST-YEAR JOURNAL

At the end of each chapter in this book is a journal assignment to remind you to ask questions as you read the chapter and keep track of your thoughts in writing. Periodically, you should be jotting down responses to such questions as these:

1. What do I think of what I just read?
2. What did I learn? What is still unclear or unexplained?
3. What is my reaction to what I learned? What further questions would I ask?
4. How can I apply this learning to my own life or my general view of things?

Although each journal assignment is designed to help you focus your thoughts, you may wish to address other concerns. In your journal you may also wish to share events in your life with your instructor if you feel comfortable with that and need advice. Your instructor may ask you to write your journal entries strictly for your own reflection, or may collect and read them, make appropriate comments, and return them to you. This way, you can communicate privately with your instructor and develop a more meaningful relationship.

Be sure you save your returned journal entries with your instructor's comments so that you can periodically review them and check your progress.

■ EXERCISES

Many of the exercises in this book are marked by one or more of the following icons to help you and your instructor choose those best suited for your class.

 writing: a core skill in learning and one you will use practically every day

 collaborative learning: working in small groups and benefiting from one another's perspectives on a problem or idea

 critical thinking: learning to go beyond surface thinking and analyze data to arrive at new ideas, a skill that often sets college students apart from others

 self-assessment: the chance to think systematically about your abilities and concerns and arrive at solutions to help you succeed

 presentation: the chance to practice speaking skills in the classroom, a talent that will contribute to success in college and throughout life

 goal-setting: the chance to set specific goals, whether short-term or long-term and to have a clear picture of where you're going

 class discussion: the chance to engage the entire class in a discussion, a tactic that contributes to active learning, which is arguably the way we all learn best

 Internet and computer technology: a chance to use digital technology to enhance your college success.

EXERCISE 1.1
INTERNET
ACTIVITY

Using the *Digest of Education Statistics* Online

The Internet is particularly useful as a source of statistical information. The 1997 *Digest of Education Statistics* provides extensive data on postsecondary education. Figure 15 in Chapter 3 of the *Digest:*
http://nces.ed.gov/pubs/digest97/d970003.html
presents a graph "Enrollment in institutions of higher education, by age: Fall 1970 to fall 2000." (Note: Web addresses change. Go to *http://csuccess. wadsworth.com* for the most up-to-date URLs.) Visit the web site and answer the following questions:

Which age group has the highest percentage of individuals enrolled? _____

Which age group has the smallest percentage of individuals enrolled? _____

For the years 1970 to 1995, which age group increased the most? _____

For the years 1970 to 1995, which age group increased the least? _____

What do these trends say about how the profile of college students will change by the year 2000?

What explanation can you offer for these changes?

Note: A key-word search is not always the best way to find information on the web. When searching for statistical data, you may have better luck starting from a resource menu such as Statistical Resources on the web:
http://www.lib.umich.edu/libhome/Documents.center/stecon.html
or the Argus Clearinghouse, formerly known as the Clearinghouse for Subject-Oriented Internet Resource Guides:
http://www.clearinghouse.net

EXERCISE 1.2

Solving a Problem

What has been your biggest unresolved problem to date in college? What steps have you attempted to solve it? Write a letter or memo to your instructor about these two questions. Read your instructor's response and see if it's of any help to you. If you still have questions, ask to meet with your instructor.

EXERCISE 1.3

Focusing on Your Concerns

Browse the table of contents of this book. Find one or more chapters that address your most important concerns. Take a brief look at each chapter you have chosen. If a chapter appears to be helpful, read it before your instructor assigns it and try to follow its advice.

EXERCISE 1.4

Your Reasons for Attending College

List three reasons you chose to go to college:

1. _____

2. _____

3. _____

Which one of these was the most important? Why?

_____

_____

_____

_____

 **EXERCISE 1.5**

Why You Decided on College

A For homework, compare the reasons for attending college in this chapter to your own reasons. How are they the same? How are they different? In a small group discuss the reasons in this chapter for attending college. Share the ones that seem most relevant to you with the group. Compile a group list of the most important reasons and discuss them with your instructor. What did you learn about yourself and your classmates?

B Look back at the reasons for attending college you just listed. Did your list include any long-term goals—something you want to achieve five or ten years from now? Compare your goals to the benefits of higher education listed in this chapter. If you did not include a long-term goal, add one to your list. In small groups, compare these goals with the goals of others in the group. Do you share the same goals? How are they different? Compare your group's goals with those of other groups in the class.

EXERCISE 1.6

Learning About Campus Resources

Study the campus resources on page 9 ("Where to Go for Help"). Then make a list of campus support services or resources you might be interested in using. Include not only serious support needs but also things that will help you relax and enjoy campus life to the fullest.

Pool your list with the lists of others in your class. Use a campus map, student handbook, or other guide to find out which resources are available on your campus and how to find them.

EXERCISE 1.7

Assessing Your Basic Skills

Think about your strengths and weaknesses in such areas as reading, writing, and math. For each item below, rank yourself either 1 (very strong), 2 (okay), or 3 (not strong).

_____ taking notes in class

_____ learning facts and concepts from textbooks

_____ understanding what I read

_____ feeling comfortable with computers

_____ managing my time wisely

_____ speaking in front of a group

_____ studying for tests

_____ writing papers and exams

_____ understanding math and science

If you wrote some 3's, you'll want to seek help on campus. Keep this in mind as you do the next exercise.

EXERCISE 1.8   Set a Short-Term Goal

- Review your responses to the previous exercise.
- Pick one problem that you can resolve as a short-term goal—one you can complete this week or next.
- Start by discussing this goal with a small group in your class.
- Identify how this short-term goal relates to your long-term goal of success in college.
- In group discussion and writing, complete the six steps for achieving a short-term goal listed in this chapter.
- Establish a date (a week or month from now) when you will determine whether you have achieved the goal. At that time set at least one new goal. Be sure your goal is something you genuinely want to achieve, written down in measurable terms, and achievable.

Also be certain to

- Identify and explore potential problems.
- Create a specific set of steps for achieving the goal.
- Set a schedule for the steps as well as a date for completion.

SUGGESTIONS FOR FURTHER READING

Gordon, Virginia. *Foundations: A Reader for New College Students*. Belmont, CA: Wadsworth, 1995.

Newman, Richard. *The Complete Guide to College Success: What Every Student Needs to Know*. New York: New York University Press, 1995.

Pathways to Success. Washington, D.C.: Howard University Press, 1997.

Siebert, Al, & Bernadine Gilpin. *The Adult Student's Guide to Survival and Success*. Portland, OR: Practical Psychology Press, 1997.

Tufariello, Ann Hunt. *Up Your Grades: Proven Strategies for Academic Success*. Lincolnwood, IL: VGM Career Horizons, 1997.

RESOURCES

This book can be a continuing resource for you throughout your college career. Many of the activities and topics covered in this book will be important throughout your life (particularly the management of time, stress, and money). The resource pages at the end of each chapter are for you to fill with names, phone numbers, addresses, e-mail addresses, and other relevant information. Filling out these pages will help you create your own personal resource for college success.

YOUR PERSONAL INFORMATION

Your name

School name

Your local address

Permanent address (if different from above)

Social Security number   School ID number

Driver's license—state and number

(Marking or engraving your belongings with your Social Security and driver's license numbers can help you recover them if they are ever stolen.)

KEY PERSONAL RESOURCES

List several names, phone numbers, and addresses for the following categories. Choose people who are supportive of your college goals, good listeners when you need to talk, and fun people to hang out with.

Family	Friends	Extracurricular Groups	Faculty

JOURNAL

NAME _____

DATE _____

Which of the keys to success listed in this chapter have you already begun to incorporate into your college life?

....

....

....

....

....

Which others will you start working on soon? Why?

....

....

....

....

....

If you are a returning student, what advice would you give the younger students in your class?

....

....

....

....

....

If you are a younger student, what advice would you give returning students about studying effectively? Taking part in college life?

....

....

....

....

....

Consider sharing these thoughts in class.

CHAPTER

Becoming an Active Learner

2

KEYS TO SUCCESS

- *Show up for class.*
- *Assess and improve your study habits.*
- *Study with a group.*
- *Choose instructors who actively involve you in learning.*
- *Know how to find and work with information on your campus.*
- *Expect instructors to be glad to see you.*
- *Find faculty and staff support on campus.*

My college teachers aren't like my teachers in high school. They don't seem as easy to approach. They don't even seem to notice me very much. I wonder when they're going to come out and say exactly what they mean? What exactly am I supposed to be learning?

■ THE BIG DIFFERENCE BETWEEN HIGH SCHOOL AND COLLEGE

What is it that makes college such a totally different experience than high school for most new or returning students? For some students, you might say it's being away from home. Or the experience of meeting others from across the country and around the world. Or having time off from classes in the middle of the day. Or having class in the evenings after work. Or having some days with no classes at all.

SEE EXERCISE 2.1

Or maybe it's the amount of work and lack of time: three chapters of history by Wednesday, a lab experiment due in biology by Friday, a self-paced course in which you must set your own schedule to complete the requirements by the end of the term.

Any of these may be right answers, but what we believe makes college so different, so challenging, and so rewarding—once you become accustomed to it—is simply this: College offers you the chance to move from a pattern of *being taught passively* to one of *learning actively.*

■ WHAT ACTIVE LEARNING MEANS

Active learning involves participating in and out of class instead of passively recording notes and studying silently. Students who embrace active learning not only learn better but enjoy their learning experiences more. Granted, you may have an instructor who lectures for an entire period and leaves little or no time for questions. If the instructor is a good lecturer, you will still be learning but not as comprehensively as you would in a more interactive learning situation. One suggestion is to form a study group, so that you can benefit from what other students have learned. Or you might ask the teacher for an appointment to discuss unanswered questions from the lecture.

Active learners become involved in learning rather than simply being an audience. They create and produce as they learn. They try new ideas and learn by exploring the world around them instead of just memorizing facts. Here are some things you can do to promote active learning:

- Ask other students which teachers will actively engage you in learning.
- Even in a class of 200, never hesitate to raise your hand if you don't understand something. Chances are, the other 199 didn't understand it either.
- Put learning into your own words instead of just memorizing the book or the lecture.

SEE EXERCISE 2.2

- Study with other students. Talking about assignments and getting other points of view will help you learn the material faster and more thoroughly. More on this later.
- Follow the suggestions in Chapters 4 through 8 about managing your time, optimizing your learning style, taking class notes, reading texts, and studying for exams. There's a right way and a wrong way for each of these things.
- Politely question authority. When you don't agree, state your opinion. Good teachers will listen and may still disagree, but they may think more of you for showing you can think.
- Stay in touch with teachers, other students, and your academic advisor. One great way is through e-mail, or you can call and leave a voice mail if the person is out. You'll get a call back.

Why Active Learners Can Learn More than Passive Learners

Active learning puts students in charge of their own learning. It is also the philosophy on which this book is based. Although you may acquire knowledge listening to a lecture, you probably won't be motivated to think about that knowledge. Through active learning, you will learn not only content, but a number of processes to help you:

- work with others
- improve your critical thinking, listening, writing, and speaking skills
- be able to function independently and learn to teach yourself
- manage your time
- gain sensitivity to cultural differences

Asking a question in class has as much to do with developing assertiveness as with knowing the answer to a question. And keeping a journal will help you learn *how* you learn so that you can teach yourself.

Be aware that active learning requires preparation before class, not just before exams. It can also include browsing in the library, making appointments to talk to faculty members, making outlines from your class notes, going to concerts, working on a committee, asking someone to read something you've written to see if it's clear, or having a serious discussion with students whose personal values are different from yours.

With all its benefits, some students resist active learning out of fear of trying something new and challenging. One student described an active learning class as "scary" and a more traditional class as "safe." The traditional class was safe because the "teacher did not make students sit in a semicircle, and he used a textbook and lectures to support his cases. On the other hand, discussions were scary. The process, the uncertainty, and the openness were scary."*

The larger the class, the greater the risk to speak out. As one student explains, "If I give the wrong answer in a class of 150, 149 students will see me as a dunce." Yet when the instructor creates an atmosphere where such participation is comfortable and makes it clear that "wrong" answers are better than no answers at all, students participate more often and their learning increases.

*Adapted from Russell A. Warren, "Engaging Students in Active Learning," *About Campus*, March-April 1997.

Figure 2.1 Aspects of Student Development

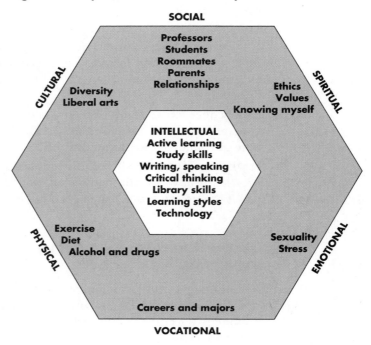

Active learning involves the whole self. According to student development theory, an active approach to learning and living has the potential to produce individuals who are well rounded in all aspects of life. The hexagon in Figure 2.1 depicts seven aspects of development, with intellectual development at its center. Optimal personal development depends on one area supporting every other area. For example, with good active learning skills, you will likely feel more comfortable socially, gain a greater appreciation for diversity and the liberal arts, and be better able to clarify your major and future career. Staying physically active can reduce stress and keep your mind alert while studying. Developing a sense of values (see Chapter 14) can help you choose your friends more carefully and decide how you choose to manage your time.

Many college teachers try new ideas in the classroom in hopes of discovering better, more exciting ways to help students learn. As a student, you can do the same. Instead of blending in with your peers—as many new students seem to do—ask the questions in class everyone else wants to ask but doesn't. Try to do something innovative with every paper and project. Sure, you'll make some mistakes, but your instructor probably will appreciate your inventiveness, reward you for it, and be more willing to help you improve your work.

The One-Minute Paper

One way to practice active learning and critical thinking daily is through a process called the one-minute paper. During a major study of teaching at Harvard University, one of many suggestions for improving learning through an activity was a simple feedback exercise. At the end of each class, students were asked to write what they felt was the main issue of that class and what their unanswered questions were for the next class.

Even if your instructors don't require it, try writing your one-minute paper each day at the end of class. Use it to think about the main issues discussed that day and save it so that you can ask good questions at the next class meeting.

■ THE VALUE OF COLLABORATION

Collaborative learning is any learning situation requiring input from more than one learner. In a sense, you might even say that if you have a conference with your instructor about a writing project in draft stage, you're engaged in collaborative learning. But usually, the term refers to groups of students working together for the good of all.

How does collaboration improve learning? Joseph Cuseo of Marymount College, an expert on collaborative learning, points to these factors:

- Learners learn from one another as well as from the instructor.
- Collaborative learning is by its very nature active learning, and so tends to increase learning by involving you more actively.
- "Two heads are better than one." Collaboration can lead to more ideas, alternative approaches, new perspectives, and better solutions.
- Learners who might not speak out in larger classes tend to be more comfortable speaking in smaller groups, resulting in better communication and better ideas.
- Students develop stronger bonds with other students in the class, which may increase their interest in attending.
- An environment of "positive competition" among groups is developed when several groups are asked to solve the same problem—as long as the instructor clarifies that the purpose is for the good of all.
- Students in groups tend to develop leadership skills.
- Students learn to work with others, a fact of life in the world of work.

College students learn as much, or more, from peers as they do from instructors and reading. When students work effectively in a supportive group, the experience can be a very powerful way to improve academic achievement and meaningful learning.

Interviews with college students at Harvard University revealed that nearly every senior who had been part of a study group considered this experience to be crucial to his or her academic progress and success.

Making Learning Teams Productive

SEE EXERCISE 2.3

You will be able to apply the teamwork skills you build in this course to your future courses, particularly those that you find most difficult. What's more, becoming an effective team learner should not only increase your success in college but should also enhance your career.

Search Online!

Try these phrases and others for Key Words and Subject Guide searches: **"active learning," "collaborative learning," and "college teachers."**
Also look up:
Innovation in large lectures—teaching for active learning. Diane Ebert-May, Carol Brewer, Sylvester Allred, *BioScience* Oct 1997 v47 n9 p601(7)

INFOTRAC COLLEGE EDITION

DOLLARHIDE/MONKMEYER PRESS PHOTO

A good study group shares a common goal of success for all its members. It also asks each member to contribute according to his or her own special perspective and style.

Not all learning groups are equally effective. Sometimes teamwork is unsuccessful or fails to reach its potential because no thought was given to how the group should be formed or how it should function. The following are strategies for developing high quality learning teams that maximize the power of peer collaboration:

1. **In forming teams, seek peers who will contribute quality and diversity to the group.** Resist the urge to include people just like you. Choose your teammates wisely. Look for fellow students who are motivated, attend class regularly, are attentive and participate actively while in class, and complete assignments. Include teammates from different ethnic, racial, or cultural backgrounds, different age groups, and different personality types and learning styles. Include males and females. Such variety will increase the team's quality and versatility. Choosing only your friends or classmates who have interests similar to yours can often result in a learning group that is more likely to get off track and not progress with the learning task.

2. **Keep the group small (three to six teammates).** Smaller groups allow for more face-to-face interaction and eye contact and less opportunity for any one individual to shirk responsibility to the team. Also, it's much easier for small groups to meet outside class. Consider choosing an even number of teammates (four or six), so you can work in pairs in case the team decides to divide its work into separate parts.

3. **Remember that learning teams are more than study groups.** Many students think that collaborative learning simply involves study groups that meet the night before major exams. However, effective student learning teams collaborate regularly for other academic tasks besides test review sessions. See the box on page 25 for other uses of learning teams.

4. **Hold individual team members personally accountable for their own learning and for contributing to the learning of their teammates.** Research on study groups at Harvard indicates that they are effective only if each member has done the required work in ad-

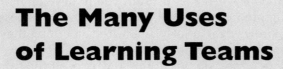

The Many Uses of Learning Teams

1. **Note-taking teams.** Team up with other students immediately after class to share and compare notes. One of your teammates may have picked up something you missed or vice versa. By meeting immediately after class, your group may still have the opportunity to consult with the instructor about any missing or confusing information before he or she leaves the room.

2. **Reading teams.** After completing reading assignments, team up with other students to compare your highlighting and margin notes. See if you all agree on what the author's major points were and what information in the chapter you should study for exams.

3. **Library research teams.** Studies show that many first-year students are unfamiliar with library research and sometimes experience library anxiety. Forming library research teams is an effective way to develop a social support group for reducing this fear and for locating and sharing sources of information. (*Note:* It is ethical for students to share the same information sources or references. This isn't cheating or plagiarizing as long as the final product you turn in represents your own written work.)

4. **Team/instructor conferences.** Having your learning team visit the course instructor during office hours to seek additional assistance in preparing for exams and completing assignments is an effective team learning strategy for several reasons. If you are shy, it may be easier to see an instructor in the company of other students. In addition, the feedback you receive from the instructor is also received by your teammates, and useful pieces of information are less likely to be missed, misinterpreted, or forgotten. Your team visit also sends a message to the instructor that you are serious about learning because you've taken the time and effort to work with your peers prior to the office visit.

5. **Team test results review.** After receiving test results, the members of a learning team can review their individual tests together to help one another identify the sources of their mistakes and to identify any model answers that received maximum credit. This way each team member can get a much clearer idea of what the instructor expects from students. You can use this information as feedback to fine-tune and improve your performance on subsequent tests or assignments.

vance of the group meeting (for example, completing required readings and other assignments). One way to ensure accountability is to have each member come to group meetings prepared with specific information or answers to share with teammates as well as questions or points of confusion for which he or she would like to receive help from the team. Another way to ensure that each teammate carries his or her load is to have individual members take on different roles or responsibilities. For example, each member may assume special responsibility for mastering a particular topic, section, or skill to be taught to others.

SEE EXERCISE 2.4

■CONNECTING WITH COLLEGE TEACHERS

Your college instructors want you to develop new ways of thinking about things, to realize there is often more than one possibility, to question existing knowledge, to take issue with something they say, to ask questions in class, and to offer possible solutions to problems. You may be surprised to find that most do not fit the stereotype of the ivory tower scholar. Though the present generation of college instructors still must spend some of their time doing scholarship and performing service for the institution, a majority of them admit they love teaching most of all, and for good reason: Motivating students like you to do their best in class can be a highly rewarding experience.

Yet they may also do things your high school teachers never did, such as:

- supplementing textbook assignments with other information
- giving exams covering both assigned readings and lectures
- questioning conclusions of other scholars
- accepting several different student opinions on a question
- never checking to see if you are taking notes
- demanding more reading in a shorter period of time
- giving fewer quizzes or many more quizzes

SEE EXERCISE 2.5

- expecting you to be familiar with topics related to their field
- being sympathetic to difficulties you may have while holding firm to high standards of grading. You may be on friendly terms with your instructor and find you have received a low grade because you missed too many classes, you did not complete all required work, or your work quality was low.

Making the Most of a Student–Teacher Relationship

1. **Make it a point to attend class regularly and on time.** And participate in the discussion; you'll learn more if you do. If you miss a class, you might get another student's notes, but that isn't the same thing as being present during class. Learning is easier when you're there every day. Save your cuts for emergencies. When you know you will be absent, let your instructor know in advance, even if the class is a large one. It could make a big difference in your teacher's attitude toward you, and if the class is really large, it's one way of introducing yourself.

2. **Sit near the front.** Studies indicate that students who do so tend to earn better grades.

3. **Speak up.** Ask questions when you don't understand or need clarification, and voice your opinion when you disagree. Your teacher will respond favorably as long as your comments or questions are relevant.

4. **See your instructor outside class when you need help.** Instructors are required to keep office hours for student appointments. Make an appointment by phone, e-mail, or at the end of class. You will likely be pleasantly surprised at how much your instructor is willing to work with you. Get your instructor's e-mail address and use it.

5. **Share one or more "one-minute papers," either in writing or through e-mail, with your instructor.** It could be the start of an interesting dialog.

Teachers and Active Learning

Here are the remarks of one teacher on the importance of active learning methods in his classroom:

> *My students learn best when they participate, so I make it my business to see that they do . . . through discussion, presentations, groupwork, and constant feedback. You know, we now have the ability to "teach" students anywhere on two-way closed circuit TV. We have computers in the classrooms, but we often fool ourselves into believing that the more we upgrade the software, the better a student will learn. Sometimes we get so wrapped up in technology that we tend to forget that good teaching consists of making a connection, building a relationship, inspiring a learner.*

Seek out teachers who encourage collaboration over competition. The teacher who urges students to collaborate on an assignment is aware that two or three heads may be far more creative than one. Each student turns in an original piece of work but is free to seek advice and criticism from another student. That's the way you most likely will be working after college, so it makes sense to begin collaborating now.

Good teachers also set deadlines for work and stick to them—not to be rigid for its own sake, but to instill in you the importance of effective time management, another skill you'll be using all your life. If you're not sure of a deadline, ask.

Good teachers keep the lines of communication open. They not only grade your work but also ask you for comments on how you're learning, what you're learning, and how well you believe they are teaching. Those comments may provoke open discussion in and out of the classroom. In fact, some of the best learning may take place not in the classroom but one on one in the instructor's office. So make use of this form of active learning when you need to confer with your instructor. Research shows students who do so have a greater chance of returning to college for their second year.

SEE EXERCISE 2.6

SEE EXERCISE 2.7
INTERNET ACTIVITY

SEE EXERCISE 2.8

From Certainty to Healthy Uncertainty

If you have just completed high school, you may be experiencing an awakening as you enter college. In high school, you may have been conditioned to believe that things are either right or wrong. If your high school teacher asked, "What are the three branches of the U.S. government?" you could answer, "legislative, judicial, and executive." A college instructor might ask instead, "What conflicts might arise among the three branches of government, and what does this reveal about the democratic process?"

Certainly, there is no simple—or single—answer. Most likely, your instructor is not attempting to embarrass you for a wrong answer but to engage you in a process of critical thinking, which you will read more about in the next chapter.

Academic Freedom in the Classroom

College instructors believe in the freedom to speak their thoughts, whether it be in a classroom discussion about economic policy or at a public rally on abortion or gay rights. What matters more than what instructors believe is their right to proclaim that belief to others without fear. Colleges and universities have promoted the advancement of knowledge by granting scholars virtually unlimited freedom of inquiry, as long as human lives, rights, and privacy are not violated.

Finding a Mentor

In his study of the aging process in men, the late Yale psychiatrist Daniel J. Levinson discovered several things about those who tended to be successful in life:

- They had developed a dream in adolescence, an idealized conception of what they wanted to become.

- They went on to find a mentor—an older successful individual—who personified that dream.

- They also enjoyed relationships with a few other people who encouraged, nurtured, and supported them in their pursuit of that dream.

A mentor is a person who, in some respect, is now what you hope to be in the future. What mentors have you had previously? What specific qualities have you tried to emulate? What are you seeking in a college mentor? If you have a mentor now, what might you do to make more use of this person? If you don't have a mentor, consider whether you might find one during your first year of college.

How do you go about finding a mentor? Look for the person who takes a special interest in you, who encourages you to challenge yourself, who willingly listens to you when you have questions or problems, who offers to meet with you to discuss your work in class. Mentors may be academic advisors, instructors, department chairs, older students, or anyone else who appears to offer interest, wisdom, and support. Most importantly, find a person you can trust, who will deal with you confidentially, and who is genuinely interested in your well-being but asks little or nothing in return.

PHOTO © DAVID WEINTRAUB/PHOTO RESEARCHERS, INC.

Source: D. J. Levinson et al., *The Seasons of a Man's Life.* New York: Ballantine, 1978.

Some teachers may insult or speak sarcastically about a politician you admire. Although you need not accept such ideas, you must learn to evaluate them for yourself, instead of basing your judgments on what others have always told you is right.

Academic freedom also extends to college students. This means you will have more freedom than in high school to select certain research topics or to pursue controversial issues. You will also have the right to disagree with the instructor if you feel differently about an issue, but be certain you can support your argument with reliable published or personal evidence. Above all, discuss—don't argue. Cite something you read or heard and ask what the instructor thinks about your approach to the issue. Done respectfully, such queries can be an enriching experience for the entire class.

When Things Go Wrong
Between You and a Teacher

What if you get a bad instructor? Arrange a meeting to try to work things out. Getting to know the teacher as a person may help you cope with the way he or she teaches the course. If that fails, check the "drop-add" date, which usually falls at the end of the first week of classes. You may have to drop the course altogether and pick up a different one. If it's too late to add classes, you may still wish to drop by the "drop date" later in the term and still avoid a penalty. See your academic advisor or counselor for help with this decision.

If you can't get satisfaction from the instructor and need to stay in the class, see the head of the department. If you are still dissatisfied, move up the administrative ladder until you get a definite answer. Never allow a bad instructor to sour you on college. Even the worst course will be over before long.

What if you're not satisfied with your grade? First, make an appointment to see the instructor and discuss the assignment. Your teacher may give you a second chance because you took the time to ask for help. If you get a low grade on an exam, you might ask the instructor to review certain answers with you. Never insist on a grade change, as this will most likely backfire. Keep in mind that a teacher's freedom to grade is sacrosanct.

What if you're dealing with sexual harassment and sexism? Sexual harassment is a serious offense and a cause for grievance. See your department chair if an instructor makes inappropriate or threatening remarks of a sexual nature to you. No instructor should ask to date his or her student or otherwise pressure students to become involved in personal relationships, because the implied threat is that, if you refuse, you may fail the course. Your campus has specific procedures to follow if you believe you are being harassed sexually; take advantage of them.

Sexism refers to statements or behaviors that demonstrate a belief in the greater general worth of one gender over the other. Comments such as "I don't know why girls take chemistry" are not only insulting but may cause women to lose confidence in their abilities. The same rules apply to defamatory remarks about one's ethnic group.

SEE EXERCISE 2.9

Dr. Eliot Engel of North Carolina State University offers the final word on teaching:

> *Great teachers know their subjects well. But they also know their students well. In fact, great teaching fundamentally consists of constructing a bridge from the subject taught to the student learning it. Both sides of that bridge must be surveyed with equal care if the subject matter of the teacher is to connect with the gray matter of the student. But great teachers transcend simply knowing their subjects and students well. They also admire both deeply.**

SEE EXERCISE 2.10
INTERNET ACTIVITY

And so, as a student, should you admire both your teacher and your subject deeply when you are engaged in active learning.

*From a column in the *Dickens Dispatch*, the newsletter of the North Carolina Dickens Club, January 1989.

EXERCISE 2.1

Differences Between High School and College

This chapter lists just a few of the differences between high school and college that you may encounter. With a small group of other students, brainstorm other differences. Appoint one person in the group to list which differences seem beneficial and which do not. Explain your choices to the rest of the class.

For returning students, you may wish to form your own group and discuss the differences in your life prior to college and now; or you may prefer to join a group of recent high school graduates to hear and provide a different point of view.

EXERCISE 2.2

Learning Actively

List the courses you are taking this term, and then make a list of the active learning techniques taking place in each course. Observe each course at least twice. What did you do to promote active learning? What did your instructor do? What did other students do? If no active learning took place in a class, how did you feel about that?

EXERCISE 2.3

Forming Your Ideal Learning Team

This chapter suggests that a good learning team comprises a clear goal, motivated students, diverse backgrounds, small size (three to six), and a method of accountability. If you were to form a group with two or three other students in this class, who would you choose and for what characteristics? Write a paper describing your group. Don't reveal their names. Instead, name your collaborators "A," "B," and so forth. If you had to choose one more person, who would that be and why? In what ways do members of this group complement one another's strengths and weaknesses, including yours?

EXERCISE 2.4

To Collaborate or Not?

Some people may prefer to work alone. This chapter has already listed many benefits of working together. What are some of the benefits of working by yourself? What might influence your decision to work alone as opposed to collaborating? What might influence you to prefer collaboration?

EXERCISE 2.5

What Do College Teachers Expect of Students?

Look back over the differences between high school and college teachers. Then list five to ten qualities and behaviors you believe college teachers want in their students. Compare your response with those of several classmates. Consider asking one of your teachers to comment as well.

EXERCISE 2.6

Giving and Getting Feedback

In writing, describe how your various college teachers are attempting to keep the lines of communication open to serve your best interests. Describe an occasion when you or a friend consulted a teacher for help. What happened? If some teachers send out signals that they do not wish to know you as a person, how does that affect your progress in their classes? If others make you feel that they care about your progress, how does this affect you?

**EXERCISE 2.7
INTERNET
ACTIVITY**

Your Teachers'—and Your Own— Responsibilities

Like everyone else, teachers must juggle many responsibilities. Indicate what percentage of their working time you think faculty spend in each of the following activities:

teaching _____

research/scholarship _____

administration _____

outside consulting _____

service/nonteaching activities _____

Check your answers against the data in the 1997 *Digest of Education:*
http://nces.ed.gov/pubs/digest97/d97t228.html
(Go to *http://csuccess.wadsworth.com* for the most up-to-date URLs.)

Remember that these percentages are averages for all faculty at all schools surveyed. The particular percentages at any school or for any particular faculty member may vary considerably.

Survey several of your professors to find out how they spend their working time. Compare the results to the Internet figures.

EXERCISE 2.8

Interviewing a Teacher

Choose a teacher to interview—perhaps your favorite instructor or one you'd like to know more about. You might even choose an instructor whose course is giving you problems, in hopes that you can find out how to resolve those problems in the course of the interview. Make an appointment for the interview and prepare your questions before you arrive, but also be ready to go with the flow of your conversation. Then write a paper about what you learned and what surprised you the most. *Note:* Arrive on time and dress comfortably but nicely to make the best impression; it may result in a better interview.

Suggested Questions

1. What was your first year of college like?
2. At what point in your life did you decide to teach? Why?
3. What steps did you take to become a teacher in your field?
4. What do you like most about teaching? Least? Why is that?
5. What are some of the things that keep you busiest outside the classroom?
6. What do you expect from students? What should they expect from you?
7. Where did you go to college? Why did you go there?
8. What advice can you offer to new college students?

EXERCISE 2.9

A Teaching Experience

Chapters 15 and 16 contain some useful information on relationships and diversity. Choose either topic (or another topic approved by your instructor) and read the chapter to prepare for a five- or ten-minute presentation to your class on some aspect of either topic. You might seek additional information on the Internet or in your campus library. Organize your presentation, prepare brief notes that also remind you to use at least one active learning method, and teach your topic to the class.

**EXERCISE 2.10
INTERNET
ACTIVITY**

Finding Faculty E-Mail Addresses

More and more, students communicate with their instructors using e-mail. Although e-mail is often a poor substitute for an office visit, it is useful for specific questions, to explain why you missed class, or other short messages. If you can't reach your teacher by phone, you might e-mail to request an appointment by including your phone number in your message.

To send e-mail, just as with regular mail, you must know someone's address. Find the e-mail addresses of your instructors on the campus network, or ask them for their e-mail addresses on the first day of class. You may also find their addresses in the course syllabus.

SUGGESTIONS FOR FURTHER READING

Bender, Eileen, Millard Dunn, Bonnie Kendall, Peggy Wilkes, & Catherine Larson. *Quick Hits: Successful Strategies for Award Winning Teachers.* Bloomington: Indiana University Press, 1994.

Brown, M. Neil, & Stuart M. Keeley. *Striving for Excellence in College: Tips for Active Learning.* Englewood Cliffs, NJ: Prentice-Hall, 1996.

Bruffee, Kenneth A. *Collaborative Learning: Higher Education, Interdependence, and the Authority of Knowledge.* Baltimore: Johns Hopkins University Press, 1995.

Halberstam, Joshua. *Acing College: A Professor Tells Students How to Beat the System.* Penguin USA, 1991.

Jalango, Mary R., Meghan Mahoney Twiest, & Gail J. Gerlach. *The College Learner: How to Survive and Thrive in an Academic Environment.* Englewood Cliffs, NJ: Prentice-Hall, 1996.

Mears, Peter. *Team Building: A Structured Learning Approach.* Delray Beach, FL: Saint Lucie, 1994.

Midura, Daniel W., & Donald R. Glover. *More Team Building Challenges.* Champaign, IL: Human Kinetics, 1995.

Silberman, Mel. *Active Learning: 101 Strategies to Teach Any Subject.* Boston: Allyn & Bacon, 1996.

Sykes, Charles J. *Profscam: Professors and the Demise of Higher Education.* New York: St. Martin's, 1990.

Watson, Richard A. *Good Teaching: A Guide for Students.* Carbondale: Southern Illinois University Press, 1997.

Woodhull, Angela. *Coping with Difficult Teachers.* Rochester, VT: Schenkman, 1996.

RESOURCES

Who are your instructors for this semester? You can learn a lot about your instructors both from the information they give you and from the information the school can give you. Connecting with your instructors inside and outside of class can make your college experience much more meaningful and successful. Fill in the following information about your instructors this semester. (Copy this page before you fill it out if you have more than five instructors.)

Instructor's name   Course name

Other courses he or she teaches

(You may want to take another class with him or her. Hint—look in your course catalog.)

Office hours   Office location   Phone

Home phone number   E-mail address

Is it okay to call this instructor at home?   To send e-mail?

Instructor's name   Course name

Other courses he or she teaches

Office hours   Office location   Phone

Home phone number   E-mail address

Is it okay to call this instructor at home?   To send e-mail?

Instructor's name   Course name

Other courses he or she teaches

Office hours   Office location   Phone

Home phone number   E-mail address

Is it okay to call this instructor at home?   To send e-mail?

Instructor's name   Course name

Other courses he or she teaches

Office hours   Office location   Phone

Home phone number   E-mail address

Is it okay to call this instructor at home?   To send e-mail?

Instructor's name   Course name

Other courses he or she teaches

Office hours   Office location   Phone

Home phone number   E-mail address

Is it okay to call this instructor at home?   To send e-mail?

JOURNAL

NAME _____

DATE _____

Obviously your college teachers are different from your high school teachers. What differences have you observed?

....

....

....

....

How are you reacting to those differences?

....

....

....

....

What are some of the advantages of collaborative learning for you?

....

....

....

....

What might be some of the disadvantages for you?

....

....

....

....

What have you learned about learning from this chapter?

....

....

....

....

Critical Thinking and Writing

3

KEYS TO SUCCESS

- *Improve your critical thinking skills.*
- *Know how to find and work with information on your campus.*
- *Be the best writer you can be.*
- *Learn from criticism.*
- *Try to have realistic expectations.*
- *Never doubt your abilities.*
- *Embrace new technologies.*

" On my history quiz my instructor asked us to analyze the causes of the American Civil War and to cite evidence showing which causes were the most important. I could've told him the dates of the war. I could've told him about most of the military decisions. But this! This really made me think! Maybe if I'd done some writing about the topic last night instead of just poring over my notes, I would've answered the question better. "

Employers hiring college graduates often say they want an individual who can find information, analyze it, organize it, draw conclusions from it, and present it convincingly to others. One executive said she looked for superior communication skills "because they are in such short supply these days." These skills are also the basic ingredients of critical thinking. In essence, critical thinking is the ability to manage and interpret information in a reliable way. It is the ability to examine existing ideas and to develop new ones. In college, the term argument refers not to an emotional confrontation but to reasons and information brought together in logical support of some idea. Critical thinking is the ability to recognize reliable evidence and form well-reasoned arguments.

When thinking about an argument, a good critical thinker considers questions like the following:

- Are the assumptions (the pieces of information given in support of the argument) true?
- Do the assumptions really support the conclusion?
- Do I need to withhold judgment until better evidence is available?
- Is the argument really based on good reasoning, or does it appeal mainly to my emotions?
- Based on the available evidence, are other conclusions equally likely (or even more likely)? Is there more than one right or possible answer?
- What more needs to be done to reach a good conclusion?

Good critical thinking also involves thinking creatively and imaginatively about what assumptions may be left out or what alternative conclusion may not have been considered. When communicating an argument or idea to others, a good critical thinker knows how to organize it in an understandable, convincing way in speech or in writing.

SEE EXERCISE 3.1

◼ HOW COLLEGE ENCOURAGES CRITICAL THINKING

Many college students believe at first that their teacher will have all the answers and that all they need to do is gather and remember information. Unfortunately, most important questions do not have simple answers, and there are always numerous ways to look at important issues. It is important to be willing to challenge assumptions and conclusions, even those presented by the experts.

Critical thinking depends on the ability to evaluate different perspectives and challenge assumptions made by you or others. A good college teacher will challenge the way you think and may insist that *how* you solve a problem is as important as the solution. Because critical thinking depends on discovering and testing connections between ideas, the instructor may ask open-ended questions that have no clear-cut answers, questions of "Why?" "How?" or "What if?" For example, an instructor might ask: "In these essays we have two conflicting ideas about whether bilingual education is effective at helping children learn English. What now?"

The instructor may ask you to break a larger question into smaller ones: "Let's take the first point. What evidence does the author offer for his idea that language immersion programs get better results?"

She or he may insist that there is more than one valid point of view: "So, for some types of students, you agree that bilingual education might be best? What different types of students should we consider?"

An instructor may require you to explain concretely the reason for any point you reject: "You think this essay is wrong. Well, what are your reasons?" Or an instructor may challenge the authority of experts: "Dr. Fleming's theory sounds impressive. But here are some facts he doesn't account for . . . "

He or she may reinforce the legitimacy of your personal views and experiences: "So something like this happened to you once, and you felt exactly the same way. Can you tell us why?" And, most likely, an instructor will let you know that you can change your mind: "When the discussion started, you thought the opposite. What happened in the last half hour to change your mind?"

The process may not be easy for you. It is natural for entering college students to find this mode of thinking difficult and to discover that answers are seldom entirely wrong or right but more often somewhere in between. Yet the questions that lack simple answers are the most worthy of study.

SEE EXERCISE 3.2

■ FOUR ASPECTS OF CRITICAL THINKING

Good critical thinking cannot be learned overnight nor always accomplished in a neat set of steps. Yet as interpreted by William T. Daly, professor of political science at The Richard Stockton College of New Jersey, the basic skills of critical thinking divide pretty well into four basic types. Because these four aspects are so important, we've woven them into discussions and exercises throughout this book. For example, wherever you see the critical thinking icon ⚠ by an exercise, we have incorporated one or more of the four following aspects of thinking into that exercise. Practicing these basic ideas can go a long way toward helping you become a more effective thinker.

I. Abstract Thinking: Discovering Larger Ideas from Details

From large amounts of facts, seek the bigger ideas or the abstractions behind the facts. What are the key ideas? Even fields like medicine, which involve countless facts, culminate in general ideas such as the principles of circulation or the basic pattern of cell biology.

A good class becomes a critical thinking experience. As you listen to the professor, try to predict where the lecture is heading and why. When other students raise issues, ask yourself whether they have enough information to justify what they have said. And when you raise your hand to participate, remember that asking a sensible question may be more important than trying to find the elusive "right" answer.

© 1992, CHUCK SAVAGE/PHOTO COURTESY OF BELOIT COLLEGE

Ask yourself what larger concepts the details suggest. Sometimes this process involves determining what broad ideas a writer is intending to convey. Other times it involves synthesizing information yourself in an effort to come up with a concept of your own.

For example, you read an article about the Internet that describes how many people are using the Internet now, how much consumer information it provides, what kinds of goods can be bought cheaply over the Internet, and also that many low-income homes are still without computers. Thinking carefully about these facts, you might arrive at several different important generalizations. One general idea might be that a problem is developing: As the Internet becomes more important for shopping, the lack of computers in low-income households will put poor families at an even greater disadvantage. Or your general idea might be a different hypothesis: Because the Internet is becoming important for selling things and companies want to make money, companies will probably find a way to put a computer in every home.

2. Creative Thinking: Finding New Possibilities

Use the general idea you have found to see what further ideas it suggests. This phase can lead in many directions. It might involve searching for ways to make the Internet more available to low-income households. Or it might involve searching out more detailed information on how much interest big companies really have in marketing various goods to low-income families. In essence, the creative thinking stage involves extending the general idea—finding new ways it might apply or further ideas it might suggest. The important thing at this stage is not to reject ideas out of hand, but to explore wherever your general idea may take you.

3. Systematic Thinking: Organizing the Possibilities

Systematic thinking involves looking at the outcome of the second phase in a more demanding, critical way. If you are looking for solutions to a problem, which ones really seem most promising? Do some conflict with others? Which ones can be achieved? If you have found new evidence to refine or further test your generalization, what does that new evidence show? Does your original generalization still hold up? Does it need to be modified? What further conclusions do good reasoning and evidence support? Which notions should be abandoned?

4. Precise Communication of Your Ideas to Others

SEE EXERCISE 3.3

SEE EXERCISE 3.4
INTERNET ACTIVITY

Great conclusions aren't very useful if you cannot communicate them to others. Consider what your audience will need to know to follow your reasoning and be persuaded. Because written communication is so important in school and in the workplace, we expand on writing in the following section. See also Chapter 11, "Speaking for Success."

■ WRITING TO THINK AND TO COMMUNICATE

William Zinsser, the author of several widely respected books on writing, reminds us that writing is not merely something that professional writers do but a basic skill for life. He claims that far too many Americans are held back and prevented from doing useful work because they never learned to express themselves. Writing is empowering because it enables you to share your ideas, not just with a roomful of people but with thousands or millions. Being able to show that you can write clearly and logically will also go a long way toward helping you land great jobs after college.

Explore First, Explain Later

Writing serves two general purposes. *Exploratory* writing helps you discover what you want to say. Carolyn Matalene, an award-winning teacher at the University of South Carolina, says that writing forces you to know what you don't know and enables you to see relationships. It also requires you to create structure for information so that you can remember it more easily. Writing, she adds, allows and inspires creativity. From an infinite number of

INFOTRAC COLLEGE EDITION

Search Online!

Try these phrases and others for Key Words and Subject Guide searches:
"critical thinking," "creative thinking," "composition," "writing,"
"grammar," "English language," "argument," "debate."
Also look up:
Critical thinking is totally inadequate. (Can you teach your people to think smarter?)(cover story) Edward de
   Bono. *Across the Board* March 1996 v33 n3 p25(2)
So you want to be a very good writer? First, lose the very (guidelines for effective communication) (column).
   Paula LaRocque. *The Quill* May 1994 v82 n4 p43(1)

SEE EXERCISE 3.5

SEE EXERCISE 3.6

sentences, we magically make meaning. Writing requires you to address an audience—first yourself, then your reader. Writing in response to a text helps you to understand that text. Writing smoothes the way to a higher level of literacy.

Explanatory writing transmits information or ideas to others. It is "published" writing in the sense that it is ready for others to read. It is important that most exploratory writing be private, to be read only by the author as a series of steps toward more public work.

■ THREE STEPS TO BETTER WRITING

Most writing teachers agree that the writing process consists of three steps:

- prewriting or rehearsing (including preparing to write by reading assigned work and doing other research)
- writing or drafting
- rewriting or revising

They also agree that the reason many students turn in poorly written papers is that they skip the first and last steps and make do with the middle one. When you build each step into your writing process, you will consistently write better.

Prewriting for Ideas

One way to start writing is simply to pick up a pen and begin to write your thoughts in response to some idea or topic. This is the basic idea of *freewriting*, an important prewriting technique. The goal is not to write something that anyone else can read, or even necessarily to stick with the topic, but simply to keep writing to explore your reactions to and ideas about some general area, to discover what interests you about it, what you know and don't know, where your thoughts are centered. In freewriting you don't worry about spelling, grammar, or punctuation. Even if you feel you have nothing to say, you keep writing about where your thoughts are going.

What happens in this type of writing is that, without forcing things, at some point a writer often begins to make connections between the initial topic or quote and the writer's own thoughts. The writing often turns into a series of questions, perhaps a challenge to the initial statement. The most important thing at this point is that you find you have something to say, and you capture those rough ideas in writing for later use.

Freewriting is a good starting point for many writing assignments. It is also one way to deal with writer's block—the feeling that you have something to say but just can't seem to get it down.

Many writing experts, such as Donald Murray, believe that, of all the steps, prewriting is the one that should take the longest. This is the stage where you explore what you want to say about something, write down all you think you need to know about a topic, and then go digging for the answers. Prewriting can involve freewriting, making lists or outlines of what you may decide to say, and doing enough research so that you have a clear idea of what your writing will be about.

Prewriting can also involve a lot of thinking time, whether or not any words appear on paper. It's a time to compare ideas and question things that seem illogical, to think about what others have said or written, and to ask yourself how your own views and information compare with theirs.

In many ways, the personal computer has revolutionized the act of writing. Above all, it has made the process of revising a number of drafts easier. Random thoughts can be easily grouped and related into a coherent discussion. When you make minor changes, you do not have to retype the complete manuscript; you simply insert the corrections and print. And you can disseminate your thoughts to a worldwide audience in seconds via an Internet discussion group.

PHOTO BY DAVID GONZALES

FINDING A TOPIC

Sometimes you are given a specific topic about which to write. If not, finding a specific topic can be the main task of prewriting. When is a topic appropriate? When is it neither too broad nor too narrow? The answers will depend on several things including the assignment length, how much you know or have time to find out, and how narrow or broad a topic the assignment requires. Think of the topic in terms of a question you will try to answer. Is the question big enough to reflect your learning? Is it narrow enough that you can answer with specific ideas, well-supported by evidence? Once you think you have a suitable topic, test it by completing the following sentence: "The purpose of this paper is to convince my instructor that . . ." If the completed sentence is clear and the task is doable, the topic is probably right.

In *Zen and the Art of Motorcycle Maintenance*, a classic of the 1970s, Robert Pirsig tells a story about teaching freshman composition. Each week the assignment was to turn in a 500-word essay. One week, a student failed to submit her paper about the town where the college was located, explaining that she had "thought and thought, but couldn't think of anything to write." Pirsig gave her an additional weekend to complete the assignment. As he did so, an idea flashed through his mind. "I want you to write a 500-word paper about Main Street, not the whole town," he said. She gaped at him and stared angrily. How was she to narrow her thinking to just one street when she couldn't think of anything to write about the entire town?

Monday she arrived in tears. "I thought and thought, and I think you're not being fair. I'll never learn to write." Pirsig's answer: "Write a paper about one building on Main Street. The opera house. And start with the first brick on the lower left side. I want it next class."

The student's eyes opened wide. Something was happening. Indeed, she walked into class the next time with a 5,000-word paper on the opera house.

"I don't know what happened," she exclaimed. "I sat across the street and wrote about the first brick, then the second, and all of a sudden I couldn't stop. Hope it's not too long."

What had happened? What had Pirsig done for this student? He had helped her find a focus, a place to begin. And getting started is what blocks most students from approaching writing properly. Had she continued to write about bricks? Of course not. She probably began to see, for the first time, the beauty of the opera house and went on to describe it, to find out more about it in the library, to ask others about it, and to comment on its setting among the other buildings on the block.

SEE EXERCISE 3.7

Writing for Organization

Once you have explored your information and ideas through prewriting, it's time to move to the writing stage. Now you begin to write in larger chunks, building your paper around the topic and, as much as possible, putting things in a suitable order. At this point you begin to pay attention to the flow of ideas from one sentence and from one paragraph to the next. For some kinds of papers you might add headings. When you have completed this stage, you will have the first draft of your paper in hand.

Put it away for a day or so and then read it. Does it say what you want to say? Are the ideas well organized? What changes may you need to make?

Rewriting to Polish

Are you finished? Not by a long shot. Now, in the third stage of writing you take a good piece of writing and make it great. The essence of good writing is rewriting. You read again. You correct. You add smoother transitions. You slash through wordy sentences or paragraphs that add nothing. You substitute strong words for weak ones. You double-check spelling and grammar. You continue to revise until you're satisfied. And then you "publish."

SEE EXERCISE 3.8

Allocating Your Time for Writing

When Murray was asked how long a writer should spend on each of the three stages, he offered this breakdown: prewriting, 85 percent (including research and rumination); writing, 1 percent (the first draft); rewriting, 14 percent (revising until it's right).

Do the figures surprise you? If they do, consider the writer who was assigned to create a brochure. He had other jobs to do and kept avoiding that one. But the other work he was doing had direct bearing on the brochure he was told to write. So as he was putting this assignment off, he was also researching material for it.

After nearly three months, he could stand it no longer. So he sat at his computer and dashed the words off in just under thirty minutes. He felt a rush of ideas, he used words and phrases he'd never used before, and he was afraid to stop until he finished. He did some revising, sent it around the office, took other suggestions, and eventually the brochure was published.

He had spent a long time prewriting (working with related information without trying to write the brochure). He went through the writing stage quickly because his mind was primed for the task. As a result, he had time to polish his work before deciding the job was done.

To become a better writer and thinker, start writing the day you get an assignment, even if it's only for ten or fifteen minutes. That way, you won't be confronting a blank paper later in the week.

Write something every day. The more you write, the better you write. Read good writing and begin to imitate the kinds of writing you admire. Above all, know that the hard work of becoming a better thinker and writer will pay off—in college and beyond.

SEE EXERCISE 3.9

■ SOME GOOD AND BAD HABITS IN THINKING AND WRITING

Practice the four aspects of critical thinking in writing, study, and discussion, especially when collaborating with classmates. You will find yourself better prepared, more willing to engage in logical discussions, and more likely to arrive at meaningful answers.

Certain errors often creep in when people try to construct or examine arguments. Several of these logical fallacies are mentioned in the following list, along with more positive advice for developing good habits.

- **Try to answer important questions.** Perhaps our greatest accomplishment as human beings is how very much we have managed to discover about the natural world, our history, and ourselves.

- **Expect the truth to be complicated and sometimes painful.** It is no small feat to understand the true cause of an important event. The obvious cause may not be the true one.

- **Be willing to say, "I don't know."** Suspend judgment or reconsider. Don't draw conclusions in haste. Good questions take time and patience to answer.

- **The fact that there is no evidence *against* an idea does not mean that the idea is true.** Until there is good evidence *for* the idea, it is still just an idea.

- **Don't substitute sincerity for real knowledge.** Sincere belief that aliens built the pyramids is no substitute for knowledge. Test your opinions in the light of the evidence and be willing to change your mind.

- **Get used to clarifying what you mean and asking others to do so.** Unproductive arguments are often the result of misunderstandings about definitions, especially of words like *freedom* or *fair*.

- **Question facts.** Do they come from a reliable source, from someone who is really an authority on the subject? Is there some way to check that they are really true?

- **Trust your own experience**. In the end, there is no higher authority for truth. At the same time, recognize its limits. There is nothing wrong with relying on experts when your own information is limited.

- **Judge an argument on its merits, not on the basis of who said it.** It is never appropriate to reject an argument simply because it comes from someone you dislike or disagree with on other matters.

- **Don't get trapped into thinking that you must win every argument.** That's just a way to make yourself lonely. The truth is more important.

SEE EXERCISE 3.10

A great way to better understand many of these principles is to take good courses in logic, writing, and critical thinking beyond what your school may require. Different departments offer such courses, but the best course for you in logic and thinking is probably taught by the philosophy department. Find out from other students who have taken the course how valuable it was.

SEE EXERCISE 3.11

EXERCISE 3.1

Reflecting on Arguments

Review the list of questions on page 36. Are they the kinds of questions that you tend to ask when you read, listen to, or take part in discussion? Each evening for the next week, revisit the list and think about whether you have asked such questions that day. Also ask yourself whether you have been noticing that day whether people are stating their assumptions or conclusions.

EXERCISE 3.2

The Challenge of Classroom Thinking

Think about your experiences in each of your classes up to now this term and the kinds of questions listed on page 37.

- Have your instructors pointed out any conflicts or contradictions in the ideas they have presented?
- Have they been asking questions for which they sometimes don't seem to have the answers?
- Have they challenged you or other members of the class to explain yourselves more fully?
- Have they challenged the arguments of other experts? Have they called on students in the class to question or challenge certain ideas?

How have you reacted and responded to their words? Do your responses reflect an attitude of active learning? Write down your thoughts for possible discussion in class. Consider sharing them with your instructors.

EXERCISE 3.3

Critical Thinking—"Unnatural Acts?"

William T. Daly, a professor at The Richard Stockton College of New Jersey, proposes that the four critical thinking skills he names are "unnatural acts"—not things that people do easily or without training. Do you agree? In what way has your previous education or other experiences prepared you to form abstractions? To generate new ideas or foresee new possibilities? To question the logic of what other people write and say? To examine the logic or evidence behind your own written or spoken arguments?

**EXERCISE 3.4
INTERNET
ACTIVITY**

Critical Thinking Resources on the Internet

The Center for Critical Thinking offers extensive resources and discussion of the fundamentals of critical thinking. Their web site includes discussion of "Three Categories of Questions: Crucial Distinctions," with examples. Look up this site at
http://www.sonoma.edu/cthink/university/univlibrary/3catquest.nclk
and compare the information on critical thinking it offers with what this chapter has discussed. (Go to *http://csuccess.wadsworth.com* for the most up-to-date URLs.) Using your critical thinking skills, write a paper comparing the similarities and differences. Share your ideas with other members of the class.

EXERCISE 3.5  ## Engage by Writing

A Sit down with a reading assignment you have recently completed in one of your courses. Write a summary of what you read. Write down any questions that the reading raised for you. Write about why you think you were asked to read the material and what reading it accomplished for you. Finally, write down any additional personal responses you may have had to the material. This is private writing so you don't have to share it with others, but your instructor may ask how going through this process has helped you with the material. Be prepared to answer.

B Look back over what you've written. In what ways does the thinking you did in the course of that writing reflect the first three phases of critical thinking?

EXERCISE 3.6 ## Freewriting

William Zinsser wrote: "The act of writing gives the teacher a window into the mind of the student." Write those words at the top of a piece of blank paper. Look at them for a few moments. Then, with a pen in hand, begin to write your thoughts about his statement. Don't worry about spelling, grammar, or punctuation. Just keep writing for at least five to seven minutes, even if what you are saying doesn't seem connected to the quote. Even if you feel you have nothing to say, keep writing for that length of time. Continue longer if you can.

What happened? Were you able to write anything? Was what you wrote very closely related to Zinsser's quote? Did it go off in some other direction? Did anything about it surprise you?

For the next week, try freewriting at least once a day in response to some topic of your own choosing. At the end of the week, assess the results. Does freewriting seem like a valuable practice for you?

EXERCISE 3.7 ## The Power of Focused Observation

Remember the student Pirsig wrote about, the one who began with the first brick of the opera house and went on to write a 5,000-word paper? Find a favorite spot of yours on campus where you can sit comfortably. Take a good look at the entire area. Now look again, this time noticing specific parts of the area. Choose something; it may be a statue, building, tree, fence, and so on. Now look carefully at just one portion of that part and start writing about it. See where the writing takes you and write about that experience.

EXERCISE 3.8   ## Polishing

Turn the freewriting you did in Exercise 3.7 into a first draft of a short paper (two to three pages) based on the same experience. Then revise for logic, organization, and grammar. Then reread to polish and fix any remaining errors, such as misspelled words. Find a partner in class and exchange papers. Read each other's paper and indicate where you find problems. You may notice that a second reader is likely to see more errors than you did, which is natural.

EXERCISE 3.9

Parallels

In what ways are the critical thinking and writing processes similar?

_____

_____

_____

_____

In what ways are they different?

_____

_____

_____

_____

EXERCISE 3.10

More and Less Productive Thinking

Think about some conversations you have overheard or taken part in recently. What happened in those conversations when behaviors occurred like those described in the list on page 43? What attitudes or behaviors enabled you or others to think more productively? What attitudes or behaviors made the discussion less productive?

EXERCISE 3.11

Building a Definition for Critical Thinking

Ask one or more of your instructors for their views of critical thinking and its importance to a college education. Ask what they do in their classes to stimulate critical thinking among students and how successful their methods are. What is their favorite or most successful method? Describe the interview in a paper and share it with your class.

SUGGESTIONS FOR FURTHER READING

Browne, M. Neil. *Asking the Right Questions: A Guide to Critical Thinking.* Englewood Cliffs, NJ: Prentice-Hall, 1997.

Daly, William. "Thinking as an Unnatural Act." *Journal of Developmental Education,* 18(2), Winter 1994.

Daly, William. *Teaching Independent Thinking.* Columbia, SC: National Resource Center for the First Year Experience and Students in Transition, 1995.

Elbow, Peter. *Writing Without Teachers.* New York: Oxford University Press, 1973.

Epstein, Richard L. *Critical Thinking.* Belmont, CA: Wadsworth, 1999.

Murray, Donald M. *Read to Write: A Writing Process Reader.* Fort Worth: Dryden Press/Harcourt Brace Jovanovich, 1993.

Smith, Donald E. P., Glenn M. Knudsvig, & Tim Walter. *Critical Thinking: Building the Basics.* Belmont, CA: Wadsworth, 1997.

Whitehead, Alfred North. *The Aims of Education.* New York: Mentor, 1949 (originally published 1929).

Zinsser, William. *On Writing Well.* New York: Harper Perennial, 1990.

RESOURCES

One way to improve your critical thinking and writing skills is to explore topics and issues you normally would not pay attention to. You might, for example, watch a PBS special on the Middle East instead of a major league baseball game. Or read a book about mood-triggering chemicals in the brain instead of reading the latest spy thriller. Or see a film based on a classic novel instead of the new sci-fi offering. Start making a list here.

	The Usual Choice	**The Unusual Choice**
Movies		
TV		
Books		
Magazines		

Compare lists with friends. You might even find a way to exchange preferences in order to complete this table.

Do a library or Internet search (or use the suggested readings in this chapter) to come up with a list of books or articles about critical thinking. List the ones that seem the most interesting here:

Now choose one or two, read them, and reflect on what you learned in writing.

JOURNAL

NAME _____

DATE _____

What did you think critical thinking meant before you read this chapter? How would you define it now?

....

....

....

....

....

If you find the writing process described in this chapter helpful, explain how it is. If you don't, describe the process you use and why it works better for you.

....

....

....

....

....

We believe it's important not to share your prewriting with anyone—even your instructor. Why do you think we are so adamant about this and what would you say if your instructor asked to read everything you have written?

....

....

....

....

....

How do you rate your writing on a scale of 1 through 5, with 5 being excellent? If you rate it high, explain why you believe it's high. If you rate it low, explain what you need to do to improve.

....

....

....

....

....

CHAPTER

Time Management: The Foundation of Academic Success

KEYS TO SUCCESS

- Show up for class.
- Set up a daily schedule and stick to it.
- If you are a full-time student, try not to work more than 20 hours a week.
- Get involved in campus activities.
- Take your health seriously.
- Try to have realistic expectations.
- Enlist the support of your spouse, partner, or family.

" Big test tomorrow! Gonna be a late night tonight. I was going to study with Jack, but then we started talking and the time just sort of disappeared. Now I have to pull it all together. Let's see, now. Did I read all those chapters? Did I read any of them? Do I remember what I read if I did? "

How do you approach time? Because people have different personalities and come from different cultures, they may also view time in different ways. Their perspectives on time can differ depending on age, gender, and culture.

As you will learn in the following chapter, some of these differences may have to do with your preferred style of learning. For example detail-oriented individuals (called "sensers") may spend an inordinate amount of time on those details, whereas conceptual thinkers ("intuitors") often have to redo tasks because they neglected important details or jumped to conclusions. Some learners ("judgers") tend to be natural time managers. They're the ones in class who enter on a calendar all due dates for assignments, exams, and quizzes as soon as they receive the syllabus. Their opposites, the "perceivers," can become so engaged with assignments that deadlines are of little importance to them. Because they enjoy what they're doing, they don't want to wrap things up until it's absolutely necessary, which too often is after the deadline has passed. Such a student may actually tell a teacher, "I need three more days because it isn't quite the way I want it yet."

■ SETTING PRIORITIES: ASSESSING YOUR USE OF TIME

Time management involves planning, judgment, anticipation, and commitment. First, you must know what your goals are and where you will need to be at some future time. Second, you must decide where your priorities lie and how to satisfy competing interests. Third, you must make plans that anticipate future needs as well as possible changes. Finally, you must commit yourself to placing yourself in control of your time and carrying out your plans.

To make optimum use of time, you'll need a schedule. But instead of simply dividing the day into blocks of time, it's important to prioritize. When you have your college degree and are working, you will attend to your professional responsibilities first, or risk losing your job! Usually work comes before pleasure. With that in mind, begin with the essentials: sleep, food, showering, and dressing, attending classes, studying. Leave time for fun things (socializing, watching TV, going out for the evening, and so forth); you deserve them. But finish what needs to be done before you move from work to pleasure. Exercises 4.1 and 4.2 will help you structure your time. Complete them and promise yourself you'll try to stick with the schedule you create for at least two weeks. See if it works. If it doesn't, make sensible adjustments.

SEE EXERCISE 4.1

SEE EXERCISE 4.2

■DEVELOPING A MASTER PLAN

As a college student, you will quickly learn that managing time is an important key not only to success but to survival. If it doesn't come naturally to you, how are you going to start thinking differently about time?

One way to put your goals in order is to make a term assignment preview (Figure 4.1) of your long-term assignments, a timetable of your weekly schedule (Figure 4.3), and a daily plan (Figure 4.4). Time management helps you control your time so that you can have more freedom to balance required and optional activities.

A good way to start the semester is to look at the big picture. Use the term assignment preview (Figure 4.1) on pages 52 and 53 to give yourself an idea of what's in store for you this term. You should complete your term assignment preview by the beginning of the second week of class so that you can continue to plan, anticipate, judge, and use your time effectively. Once you've done that, purchase a "week at a glance" organizer for the current year, copy the notes from your preview sheets, and continue to enter all due dates as soon as you know them. Write in meeting times, scheduled social events, study time for each class you're taking, and so forth. Carry your planner with you in a place where you can grab it quickly. Get into the habit of checking your notes daily for the current week and the coming week. Choose a specific time of day to do this, perhaps just before you begin studying in the evening or at a set time on weekends. But check it daily. It takes just a moment to be certain you aren't forgetting something important.

SEE EXERCISE 4.3

■GUIDELINES FOR SCHEDULING WEEK BY WEEK

- Examine your toughest weeks. If paper deadlines and test dates fall during the same week, find time to finish some assignments early to free up study time for tests. Go to your organizer and adjust your plans to accommodate the extra time you'll need.

SEE EXERCISE 4.4

- Break large assignments such as term papers into smaller steps (choosing a topic, doing research, writing an outline, writing a first draft, and so on). Add deadlines in your schedule for each of the smaller portions of the project.

- All assignments are not equal. Estimate how much time you'll need for each one and begin your work early. A good student time manager frequently finishes assignments before actual due dates to allow for emergencies.

- Set aside time for research and other preparatory tasks. Instructors may expect you to be computer literate, and they usually don't have time to explain how to use a word processor, spreadsheet, or statistical computer program. Seek out the academic support center on your campus for assistance. Most campuses offer tutoring, walk-in assistance, or workshops to assist students with computer programs, e-mail, or the World Wide Web/Internet. Your library may offer sessions on how to search for information using computer databases. Such services will save you time and usually are free to students.

**SEE EXERCISE 4.5
INTERNET ACTIVITY**

Using your term assignment preview, develop a weekly plan for one week of the semester, following the directions in Exercise 4.6. See Figure 4.2 as an example of a well-developed weekly timetable.

SEE EXERCISE 4.6

Figure 4.1 Term Assignment Preview

	Sunday	Monday	Tuesday	Wednesday	Thursday	Friday	Saturday
Week 1							
Week 2							
Week 3							
Week 4							

	Sunday	Monday	Tuesday	Wednesday	Thursday	Friday	Saturday
Week 5							
Week 6							
Week 7							
Week 8							

Figure 4.1 (continued)

	Sunday	Monday	Tuesday	Wednesday	Thursday	Friday	Saturday
Week 9							
Week 10							
Week 11							
Week 12							

	Sunday	Monday	Tuesday	Wednesday	Thursday	Friday	Saturday
Week 13							
Week 14							
Week 15							
Week 16							

Figure 4.2 Sample Timetable

	Sunday	Monday	Tuesday	Wednesday	Thursday	Friday	Saturday
6:00							
7:00							
8:00		History		History		History	
9:00		College 101	Read/ Study Psych.	College 101	Read/ Study Psych.	College 101	
10:00		Review Hist. & College 101	↓	Review Hist. & College 101	↓		
11:00		Geology	Psych.	Geology	Psych.		
12:00		LUNCH	↓ LUNCH	LUNCH	↓ LUNCH	LUNCH	
1:00		Study Geology		Study Geology, etc.		Read/ Study History,
2:00		Geology Lab	Work on Writing	↓		College 101, etc.	
3:00		↓				↓	
4:00			↓	Work on Writing			
5:00				↓			
6:00	Library Job		Expository Writing			Library Job	
7:00			Workshop				
8:00				Library Job			
9:00	↓		↓	↓		↓	
10:00							

Total class hours: 16
Total study hours needed: 16 x 2 = 32

Total study hours allotted: 17
Additional study hours needed: 15

PHOTO BY DAVID GONZALES

■ ORGANIZING YOUR DAY

Time management consultant Alan Lakein, comparing the efficient time manager to one who takes more time because of poor planning, advises you to "work smarter, not harder." Lakein's words ring true, particularly for college students who have to juggle many deadline pressures. Once you've set the framework of the term and weekly schedules, make a daily plan to set priorities. Stay flexible, and balance your work and leisure.

Being a good student does not necessarily mean grinding away at studies and doing little else. Keep the following points in mind as you write out your daily schedule:

SEE EXERCISE 4.7

- Set aside time to read and review notes to help prepare for class.
- Prevent forgetting by allowing time to review as soon as possible after class.
- It's hard to study on a full stomach. Schedule time right after lunch for other activities.
- Always build in a short break in the middle of a study session to keep yourself alert.
- Program an exercise session daily, if possible. Exercise helps you study better.
- Schedule free time. It keeps you balanced emotionally and refreshed for the next round of studies.
- Break extended study sessions into a variety of activities, each with a specific objective.
- Restrict repetitive tasks (such as checking your e-mail) to a certain time, not every hour.

■ MAKING YOUR TIME MANAGEMENT PLAN WORK

Many college students—with the best intentions of making their time management plans work—allow themselves to become overcommitted. Be realistic! Is there really enough time to carry your course load and meet your commitments? If not, be sure to drop any courses before the drop date so you won't have a low grade on your permanent record. Or learn to say no to commitments that you can afford to drop. If you are on financial aid, keep in mind that you must be registered for a certain number of hours (usually twelve per semester) to be considered a full-time student.

Some commuters prefer block scheduling, which runs classes together without breaks. Block scheduling allows students to cut down on travel time or to attend school one or two days a week. Although this may seem like an attractive alternative, it carries pitfalls. You'll have little time to process information between classes. If you become ill on a class day, you could fall behind in all of your classes. You may become fatigued sitting in class after class. Finally, you might become stressed when exams are held in several classes on the same day. Block scheduling may work better if you can attend lectures at an alternative time in case you are absent, if you alternate classes with free periods, and if you seek out instructors who allow you flexibility to complete assignments.

Reduce Distractions

Where should you study? Not at places associated with leisure, such as the kitchen table, the living room, or in front of the TV, because they lend themselves to interruptions by others. And your association with social activities in these locations can distract you even when others aren't there. The solution is to find quiet places, both on campus and at home, where you can concentrate and develop a study mindset each time you sit down to do your work.

Try to stick to a routine as you study. The more firmly you have established a specific time and a quiet place to study, the more effective you will be in keeping up with your schedule. Try to take advantage of large blocks of time that may be available on the weekend to review or catch up on major projects. If you break down large tasks and take one thing at a time, you'll make more progress toward your ultimate goal—high grades.

Beat Procrastination

Procrastination may be your single greatest enemy. Getting started when it's time to start takes self-discipline and self-control. Here are some ways to beat procrastination:

- Say to yourself, "A mature person is capable and responsible and is a self-starter. I'm that kind of person if I start now." Then start!
- On a 3 × 5 notecard write out a list of everything you need to do. Check off things as you get them done. Use the list to focus on the things that aren't getting done. Move them to the top of your next day's list and make up your mind to do them. Working from a list will give you a feeling of accomplishment and lead you to do more.
- Break down big jobs into smaller steps. Tackle short, easy-to-accomplish tasks first.

- Apply the goal-setting technique described in Chapter 1 to whatever you are putting off.

- Promise yourself a suitable reward (an apple, a phone call, a walk) whenever you finish something that was hard to undertake.

- Take control of your study environment. Eliminate distractions—including the ones you love! Say no to friends who want your attention at their convenience. Agree to meet them at a specific time later. Let them be your reward for doing what you must do now. Don't make or take phone calls during planned study sessions. Close your door.

SEE EXERCISE 4.8
INTERNET ACTIVITY

■ TIME AND CRITICAL THINKING

You may be tempted to think that most college assignments can and should be done quickly and that, once they are done, instructors simply have to mark them right or wrong. However, most questions worthy of study in college do not have clear and immediate yes or no answers; if they did, no one would be paying scholars to spend years doing research. Good critical thinkers have a high tolerance for uncertainty. Confronted by a difficult question, they begin by saying, "I don't know." They suspend judgment until they can gather information and take the time it requires to find and verify an answer.

Thus, effective time management doesn't always mean making decisions or finishing projects quickly. Effective critical thinkers resist finalizing their thoughts on important questions until they feel they have developed the best answers possible. This is not an argument in favor of ignoring deadlines, but it does suggest the value of beginning your research, reading, and even the writing phases of a project early, so that you will have time to change direction if necessary as you gather new insights.

Give your thoughts time to incubate. Allow time to visit the library more than once. Sometimes insights come unexpectedly, when you're not consciously thinking about a problem. So, begin reviewing as early as you can, take a break from your studies, and then return to the topic. If you're successful, you'll be well ahead of the game when it's time for class, quizzes, or that final exam.

Search Online!

INFOTRAC COLLEGE EDITION

Try these phrases and others for Key Words and Subject Guide searches: "time management," "procrastination," "goal setting."

Also look up:

Adult students in higher education: burden or boon? John T. E. Richardson, Estelle King. *Journal of Higher Education* Jan-Feb 1998 v69 n1 p65(24)

First things first: prioritizing and time management-keeping grades up, working at internships, & holding down a job. James A. Perry. *The Black Collegian* Oct 1997 v28 n1 p54(3)

Self-regulation and academic procrastination. Caroline Senecal, Richard Koestner, Robert J. Vallerand. *The Journal of Social Psychology* Oct 1995 v135 n5 p607(13)

EXERCISE 4.1

Self-Assessment: The First Step

 Take a few minutes to reflect on yourself and your past experience. Then write a few paragraphs on how you view time. Use these questions as guidelines:

- What are my personal views on time? How conscious am I of time passing? Do I wear a watch? How important is time in my life?

- How do I think my views on time have been influenced by my parents, my culture, my friends, my lifestyle, my gender, my age, or other factors?

- How do I behave in relation to time?

- Am I punctual or a procrastinator? Can I concentrate or am I easily distracted? Do I try to control time or does it seem to control me?

- Am I early, prompt, or late to class, appointments, or meetings? Do I often skip class or miss appointments?

- Do I complete my assignments and papers early, on time, or late?

- How much time do I generally spend on social activities, such as talking on the phone, watching TV, web browsing, or enjoying the company of friends? How important are each of these uses of time to me?

- How is my use of time affecting my level of stress? Am I good at estimating the amount of time it will take me to do a task? Do I tend to worry that I am not getting things done that need to be done? How does my anxiety level affect my performance?

- How is being in college affecting how I use my time?

- What are some specific things I do to manage my time? How do I balance work and social activities?

EXERCISE 4.2

Logging Your Time and Identifying Priorities

A Make a daily log of how you spend your time for one week. Copy the grid on page 59. Each evening jot down the amount of time you spent on different activities that day. At the end of the week, add up the time you spent and enter it in the different categories in the table below. Next, record the amount of time you would like to spend on each category. Remember, there are only 168 hours in a week! Your time management plan should reflect your personal philosophy and help you to reach both your personal and your professional goals.

B The following shows how typical residential first-year students allocate their time on a weekday.*

Activity	Hours per Day
Class time	3
Studying	3
Employment	$^1/_4$
Idle leisure	3
Social	$2^1/_4$
Travel (between classes)	1
Eating	$1^1/_2$
Grooming	1
Resting	$6^1/_2$
Recreation	$1^1/_2$
Other	1

*Data adapted from David W. Desmond and David S. Glenwick, "Time-Budgeting Practices of College Students: A Developmental Analysis of Activity Patterns," *Journal of College Student Personnel 28*, 4 (1987): 318–323.

Notice that new students who live on campus devote almost seven hours each day to socializing, recreation, and leisure pursuits. A commuter may spend much of this time on travel, work, and responsibilities.

Categories	Actual Hours per Day		Targeted Hours per Day
Class time	_____		_____
Studying	_____		_____
Work	_____		_____
Travel			
Home to college	_____		_____
Between classes	_____		_____
College to work	_____		_____
Work to home	_____		_____
Other	_____		_____
Total travel	_____	Total travel	_____
Home responsibilities			
Shopping	_____		_____
Meals	_____		_____
Housecleaning	_____		_____
Laundry	_____		_____
Other	_____		_____
Total home	_____	Total home	_____
Family responsibilities			
General time	_____		_____
Child care	_____		_____
Care for elderly or disabled	_____		_____
Other	_____		_____
Total family	_____	Total family	_____
Civic responsibilities			
Volunteer work	_____		_____
Other	_____		_____
Total civic	_____	Total civic	_____
Personal			
Grooming/dressing	_____		_____
Reading for pleasure	_____		_____
Hobbies, games, entertainment	_____		_____
Watching TV, listening to music	_____		_____
Talking, writing letters, or e-mail with friends	_____		_____
Exercising	_____		_____
Resting	_____		_____
Other	_____		_____
Total personal	_____	Total personal	_____
Other	_____		_____
Total time for all responsibilities	_____		_____

EXERCISE 4.3   ## Setting Goals and Priorities

Time management involves planning, judgment, anticipation, flexibility, and commitment. First, you must know what your goals are for college and for your future career. Look at the big picture and ask yourself some serious questions:

What were the reasons I chose to go to college?

_____

_____

_____

What are my immediate (short-term) goals for my first year of college?

_____

_____

_____

What are my long-term goals for successfully completing college?

_____

_____

_____

What are my longer-term goals at this point regarding where I want to be after college? (remember, these goals may change as you move closer to graduation)

_____

_____

_____

EXERCISE 4.4   ## Goal-Setting for Courses

A List each course you are taking this term. List the grade you hope to earn. Finally, estimate the time you think you will need each week to achieve your goal. When deciding how much time to study for a course, take into consideration this rule of thumb: one hour of study for every hour in class for a C, two hours of study for every hour in class for a B, and three hours for every hour in class for an A. Then consider the difficulty of the course as you complete the following chart.

Course	Grade	Estimated time per week
_____	____	_____
_____	____	_____
_____	____	_____
_____	____	_____
_____	____	_____

Total study time _____

B Now list additional steps you will need to take to achieve your goal. Some examples follow: attend tutoring sessions each week; join a study group or work with a study buddy; learn a computer program used for the course; learn to access a database for your paper in the library.

Limiting Your Time Online

Anyone who has surfed the World Wide Web has realized its addictive nature. The web can be a veritable black hole for your time. It is thus essential that you limit your online time.

As with any addiction, the first step is to realize that you have a problem. Make a log of how you spend your time at each of the following activities over a week's time. Then, create a target time for each area.

	Actual Time	Target Time
reading and writing academic e-mail	_____	_____
reading and writing personal e-mail	_____	_____
surfing casually for academic topics	_____	_____
surfing casually for personal interest	_____	_____
searching rigorously for academic materials	_____	_____
searching rigorously for personal information	_____	_____
How many times a day do you check your e-mail?	_____	_____

How might you limit the time you spend in each activity?

_____

_____

_____

Your Weekly Plan/Timetable

Using your term assignment preview, develop a weekly plan for one week of the semester. See Figure 4.2 as an example of a well-developed weekly plan.

A Using the timetable in Figure 4.3, block out your time commitments. Start by filling in all of your classes and any other regularly scheduled activities (refer to Exercise 4.2). Then look up that week on your term assignment preview and reread the syllabi for your courses. Most instructors use a syllabus to map out the entire semester. What are your tests, assignments, and readings for that week? What long-term assignments should you start this week? When should you plan your weekly reviews for each course?

B Fill in your total study time for the week in one-hour blocks at appropriate times. Remember that the best times to review course materials are directly before and after that class. It is best to schedule your hardest subjects earliest in the day when you feel fresh.

C Follow your timetable for a week. Keep a record of the major obstacles you encounter during the week. Brainstorm strategies to overcome these obstacles in a small group to share with the class.

Figure 4.3 Weekly Timetable

(1) List all class meeting times and other fixed obligations (work, scheduled family responsibilities, and so forth).
(2) Try to reserve about one hour of daytime study for each class hour. Reserve time for meals, exercise, and free time.
(3) Try to plan a minimum of one hour additional study in evenings or on weekends for each class.

	Sunday	Monday	Tuesday	Wednesday	Thursday	Friday	Saturday
6:00							
7:00							
8:00							
9:00							
10:00							
11:00							
12:00							
1:00							
2:00							
3:00							
4:00							
5:00							
6:00							
7:00							
8:00							
9:00							
10:00							
11:00							
12:00							

Your Daily Plan

Using one day from this week's schedule, make a daily plan by filling in the Daily Planner in Figure 4.4. Fill in the "To Do" list of the day's activities. Using a simple ABC priority system, label them with an A, B, or C, with A's deserving the most attention and so forth. By tackling the A's first, you may not complete your list but you will probably be more satisfied with your accomplishments.

Check out the different calendar and personal planner formats at your bookstore and get one that works for you. Make a commitment to use it. You may want to put your schedule on your computer using Personal Information Management (PIM) software or a spreadsheet program. Writing and revising the schedule, however, should not become a goal in itself. The important thing is that you make and keep a schedule that you can understand, not how you write it.

Figure 4.4

DAILY PLANNER

DATE ___ MON TUE WED THU FRI SAT SUN

APPOINTMENTS

TIME

8 ————————————
9 ————————————
10 ————————————
11 ————————————
12 ————————————
1 ————————————
2 ————————————
3 ————————————
4 ————————————
5 ————————————
6 ————————————
7 ————————————
8 ————————————
————————————

DAILY PLANNER

DATE ___ MON TUE WED THU FRI SAT SUN

☑ **TO DO**

PRIORITY   ESTIMATED TIME

☐ ————————————
☐ ————————————
☐ ————————————
☐ ————————————
☐ ————————————
☐ ————————————
☐ ————————————
☐ ————————————
☐ ————————————
☐ ————————————
☐ ————————————
☐ ————————————
☐ ————————————
☐ ————————————

**EXERCISE 4.8
INTERNET
ACTIVITY**

Procrastination Resources

The Internet offers access to a wide variety of academic, governmental, and association resources. For example, the Procrastination Research Group at Carleton University in Ottawa (*http://superior.carleton.ca/~tpychyl/*) offers access to information and research on procrastination from all over the world. (Go to *http://csuccess.wadsworth.com* for the most up-to-date URLs.)

What is the earliest reference they cite for the use of the term *procrastination*?

_____

What strategies do they offer for reducing procrastination?

_____

List three organizations for which links are offered for further study.

_____

SUGGESTIONS FOR FURTHER READING

Campbell, William E. *The Power to Learn: Helping Yourself to College Success*, "Managing Your Time" (Chapter 2). Belmont, CA: Wadsworth, 1997.

Carter, Carol, Joyce Bishop, & Sarah Lyman Krantz. *Keys to Effective Learning*, "Goal Setting and Time Management: Mapping Your Course" (Chapter 3). Upper Saddle River, NJ: Prentice-Hall, 1998.

Hunt, Diane, & Pam Hait. *The Tao of Time.* New York: Holt, 1989.

Smith, Laurence N., & Timothy L. Walter. *The Adult Learner's Guide to College Success*, rev. ed., "Five Strategies for Time Management" (Chapter 3). Belmont, CA: Wadsworth, 1995.

Sotiriou, Peter Elias. *Integrating College Study Skills: Reasoning in Reading, Listening, and Writing,* 4th ed., "Your Learning Inventory: Your Learning Style, Study Time, and Study Area" (Chapter 2). Belmont, CA: Wadsworth, 1996.

Wahlstrom, Carl, & Brian K. Williams. *Learning Success: Being Your Best at College and Life*, "Time," (Chapter 4). Belmont, CA: Wadsworth, 1996.

RESOURCES

One very helpful time-saver is your own personal phone directory of important numbers and addresses. Keeping it handy (tacked up near the phone) can save you the struggle of trying to find that scrap of paper with so-and-so's number on it. Continue the list you began in the Resources page for Chapter 1 by filling in the following:

FRIENDS Name	Phone number/address	e-mail

FAMILY Name	Phone number/address	e-mail

INSTRUCTORS Name	Phone number/address	e-mail

Academic advisor

Campus security/local police

Campus lost and found

Campus health center/hospital

Doctor/dentist

Campus counseling center

Dean of students

Campus legal services

Child-care centers

Emergency road service/mechanic

Landlord (home and work)

Employer (home and work)

Campus tutorial or learning center

Campus commuter student service center

Neighbors

Local taxi service

Campus and public libraries

Campus FAX numbers

JOURNAL

NAME _____

DATE _____

Look back to Exercise 4.1 when you first assessed your time management skills. How would you evaluate yourself as a time manager now?

....
....
....
....

How much did you have to change in your approach to time management?

....
....
....
....
....

How did you apply the term assignment plan, weekly plan, and daily plan? Which worked best for you? Why?

....
....
....
....
....

How can you modify the ideas in this chapter to fit your own biological clock?

....
....
....
....

What successes have you seen as a result of your work in this chapter?

....
....
....
....
....

Learning Styles: Discovering How You Learn Best

5

KEYS TO SUCCESS

- Study with a group.
- Choose instructors who actively involve you in learning.
- Improve your critical thinking skills.
- Assess and improve your study habits.

" Bill has a ball when he's around people. I like some time to myself. Janine can remember every date in a history lecture. I don't remember any, but I do pick up on the big ideas better than she does. Fred argues about issues based on how he feels, not on the facts themselves. I do just the opposite. What makes my friends so different and why is it that, despite those differences, I like them all? "

In high school, perhaps you found history easier than mathematics or biology easier than English. Part of the explanation for this has to do with what is called your learning style—that is, the way you acquire knowledge.

Learning style affects not only how you process material as you study but how you absorb it. Some students learn more effectively through visual means, others through listening to lectures, and still others through class discussion, hands-on experience, memorization, or various combinations of these. One may define a learning style in a number of ways. An auditory learner learns best by listening, a visual learner does best with visual aids, whereas a kinesthetic or hands-on learner acquires knowledge through some physical activity such as building a model, designing a project, or drawing a schematic. Some learn better by studying alone, and others prefer study groups.

Although no one learning style is inherently better than another, it is important to be able to work comfortably no matter what style is required in a given course. An awareness of your learning style can be helpful in emphasizing your strengths and helping you compensate for your weaknesses.

■ AN INFORMAL MEASURE OF LEARNING STYLE

Think about three or four of your favorite courses from high school or college. What do they have in common? Did they tend to be hands-on courses or more abstract? Did they focus more on mastering facts or on broader interpretations? Was there a lot of discussion or did the teacher mainly lecture? Then think about your least favorite courses. How did they tend to differ from the courses you liked?

If you prefer attending lectures, taking notes, and reading your notes aloud to yourself, you have a more auditory learning style. You might even read your notes into a tape recorder and play them back when you study for an exam. If you prefer instructors who outline their lectures on the blackboard or who make liberal use of the board by illustrating the important points they are making, you have a more visual learning style. You probably find that copying and recopying your notes helps you learn the material. If you learn best by a hands-on approach, you may prefer a kinesthetic or physical learning style.

One student's analytical style may thrive on the complexities of history. Another's satisfaction at mastering facts and understanding how they are related may lead her into science.

WALTER CALAHAN/EARLHAM COLLEGE

STATE UNIVERSITY OF WEST GEORGIA

**SEE EXERCISE 5.1
INTERNET ACTIVITY**

Being aware of learning style preferences can help you exploit your strengths in preparing for classes and exams. It can also help you understand why you're having difficulty with some of your courses and what you might do to improve.

CLASSROOM BEHAVIOR AND LEARNING STYLE

A number of instruments can help you determine what your preferred learning styles are. One approach is based on the ways in which students behave in the classroom. Psychologists Tony Grasha and Sheryl Riechmann have put together the Grasha-Riechmann instrument. This tool assesses six learning styles based on classroom behavior: (1) competitive, (2) collaborative, (3) participant, (4) avoidant, (5) dependent, and (6) independent.

To understand the classroom learning style with which you are most comfortable, you need to answer certain questions. For example, do you find study questions or review questions helpful? Do you enjoy and find helpful studying with and learning from other students in your class? Do you like it when the instructor engages the class in discussion? If so, then you probably have a more collaborative, participant, and dependent learning style and will work best with an instructor who has a corresponding teaching style. On the other hand, you may prefer an instructor who lectures in class with minimal class participation. You may feel that straightforward study of your lecture notes and textbook is the most effective means of study. If so, your learning style is more competitive, independent, and avoidant.

SEE EXERCISE 5.2

Search Online!

INFOTRAC COLLEGE EDITION

Try these phrases and others for Key Words and Subject Guide searches: "learning style," "Howard Gardner."

Also look up:

Integrating learning styles and multiple intelligences. (educational models and theories) (Teaching for Multiple Intelligences). Harvey Silver, Richard Strong, Matthew Perini. *Educational Leadership* Sep 1997 v55 n1 p22(6)

A survey of gender and learning styles. Marge Philbin, Elizabeth Meier, Sherri Huffman, Patricia Boverie. *Sex Roles: A Journal of Research* April 1995 v32 n7-8 p485(10)

■PERSONALITY PREFERENCES AND LEARNING STYLE

Another approach explores basic personality preferences that make people interested in different things and draw them to different fields and lifestyles. The Myers-Briggs Type Indicator, based on Carl Jung's theory of psychological types, uses four scales:

- **E/I (Extroversion/Introversion).** This scale describes two opposite preferences depending on whether you like to focus your attention on the outer or the inner world. Persons more introverted than extroverted tend to make decisions somewhat independently of culture, people, or things around them. They are quiet, diligent at working alone, and socially reserved. They may dislike being interrupted while working and may tend to forget names and faces.

  Extroverted persons are attuned to the culture, people, and things around them. The extrovert is outgoing, socially free, interested in variety and in working with people. The extrovert may become impatient with long, slow tasks and does not mind being interrupted by people.

- **S/N (Sensing/Intuitive).** This scale describes opposite ways you acquire information. Sensers tend to take facts as they are and remember the details, whereas intuitors are more likely to absorb a number of facts, look for relationships among them, and emerge with broad concepts. The intuitive person prefers possibilities, theories, invention, and the new and becomes bored with nitty-gritty details and facts unrelated to concepts. The intuitive person thinks and discusses in spontaneous leaps of intuition that may neglect details. Problem solving comes easily for this individual, although there may be a tendency to make errors of fact.

  The sensing type prefers the concrete, factual, tangible here and now, becoming impatient with theory and the abstract and mistrusting intuition. The sensing type thinks in detail, remembering real facts, but possibly missing a conception of the overall.

- **T/F (Thinking/Feeling).** This scale describes how you make decisions, whether by analyzing and weighing evidence or by analyzing and weighing feelings. The thinker makes judgments based on logic, analysis, and evidence, avoiding decisions based on feelings and values. As a result, the thinker is more interested in logic, analysis, and verifiable conclusions than in empathy, values, and personal warmth. The thinker may step on others' feelings and needs without realizing it, neglecting to take into consideration the values of others.

  The feeler makes judgments based on empathy, warmth, and personal values. As a consequence, feelers are more interested in people and feelings than in impersonal logic, analysis, and things, and in harmony more than in being on top or achieving impersonal goals. The feeler gets along well with people in general.

- **J/P (Judging/Perceiving).** This scale describes the way you relate to the outer world, whether in a planned, orderly way or in a flexible, spontaneous way. The perceiver is a gatherer, always wanting to know more before deciding, holding off decisions and judgments. As a consequence, the perceiver is open, flexible, adaptive, nonjudgmental, able to see and appreciate all sides of issues, always welcoming new perspectives. However, perceivers are also difficult to pin down and may become involved in many tasks that do not reach closure, so that they may become frustrated at times. Even when they finish tasks, perceivers will tend to look back at them and wonder whether they could have been done another way. The perceiver wishes to roll with life rather than change it.

The judger is decisive, firm, and sure, setting goals and sticking to them. The judger wants to make decisions and get on to the next project. When a project does not yet have closure, judgers will leave it behind and go on to new tasks.

You will often feel most comfortable around people who share your preferences, and you will probably be most comfortable in a classroom where the instructor's preferences for perceiving and processing information are most like yours. But the Myers-Briggs instrument also emphasizes our ability to cultivate in ourselves all processes on each scale.

Just as no person's fingerprints are right or wrong, so no one's personality shape is right or wrong. The purpose of this inventory is to give you a picture of the shape of your preferences. Keep in mind that the shape has nothing to do with intelligence.

The four pairs of dimensions are present to some degree in all people. It is the extremes that are described here. The strength of a dimension is indicated by the score for that dimension on an inventory such as the one in Exercise 5.3. The score determines how closely the strengths and weaknesses described fit an individual's learning preferences.

SEE EXERCISE 5.3

Strengths and Weaknesses of the Types

Each person has strengths and weaknesses as a result of these dimensions. Committees and organizations with a preponderance of one type will have the same strengths and weaknesses.

	Possible Strengths	Possible Weaknesses
Introvert	is independent	avoids others
	works alone	is secretive
	reflects	loses opportunities to act
	works with ideas	is misunderstood by others
	avoids generalizations	dislikes being interrupted
	is careful before acting	
Extrovert	interacts with others	does not work well without people
	is open	needs change, variety
	acts, does	is impulsive
	is well understood	is impatient with routine
Intuitor	sees possibilities	is inattentive to detail, precision
	works out new ideas	is inattentive to the actual and practical
	works with the complicated	is impatient with the tedious
	solves novel problems	loses sight of the here and now jumps to conclusions

Senser	attends to detail	does not see possibilities
	is practical	loses the overall in details
	has memory for detail, fact	mistrusts intuition
	is patient	is frustrated with the complicated
	is systematic	prefers not to imagine future
Feeler	considers others' feelings	is not guided by logic
	understands needs, values	is not objective
	is interested in conciliation	is less organized
	demonstrates feelings	is overly accepting
	persuades, arouses	
Thinker	is logical, analytical	may not notice people's feelings
	is objective	misunderstands others' values
	is organized	is uninterested in conciliation
	has critical ability	does not show feelings
	is just	shows less compassion
	stands firm	
Perceiver	compromises	is indecisive
	sees all sides of issues	does not plan
	is flexible	does not control circumstances
	decides based on all data	is easily distracted from tasks
	is not judgmental	does not finish projects
Judger	decides	is stubborn
	plans	is inflexible
	orders	decides with insufficient data
	makes quick decisions	is controlled by task or plans
	remains with a task	wishes not to interrupt work

As you reflect on the results of Exercise 5.3 at the end of this chapter, keep in mind that your score merely *suggests* your preferences; it does not stereotype or pigeonhole you. Remember, too, that no one learning style is inherently preferable to another and that everyone knows and uses a range of styles. The fact that many of us exhibit behaviors that seem to contradict our preferences shows that we each embrace a wide range of possibilities.

SEE EXERCISE 5.4
INTERNET ACTIVITY

Using Knowledge of Your Learning Style

Discovering your own strengths empowers you to recognize what you already do well. Discovering your weaknesses is also useful, because it is to your advantage to cultivate your less dominant learning styles. Although

Improving Your Less Dominant Learning Styles

The key ingredient in developing your less dominant style is awareness. Try to develop one process at a time.

RAISING YOUR SENSING (S) LEARNING STYLE

- Whenever you walk, try to notice and jot down specific details of the scenery—shapes of leaves; size, color, and types of rocks; and so on.

- Three or four times a day pay careful attention to, and then describe to a friend, what someone else is wearing.

- Do a jigsaw puzzle.

- Break down a physical activity into its component parts.

- Describe in detail something you just saw, such as a picture, a room, or the like.

RAISING YOUR INTUITIVE (N) LEARNING STYLE

- Imagine a given situation or circumstance in a new light by considering, What if? For example, what if the pilgrims had landed in California—how would their lifestyle have changed? What if you had gone to a bigger (smaller) school? What if X were your roommate instead of Y?

- Pretend you saw an article ten years from now about your hometown, your lifestyle, American values, or the like. What would it say?

- Read a novel and imagine yourself as one of the characters. What would happen to you following the novel's conclusion?

RAISING YOUR FEELING (F) LEARNING STYLE

- Write down a feeling statement about your class, your day, your job, or your emotions, and make sure you use a simile. For example, "I feel like a puppy that's just been scolded." Note that if you use think in a statement, it's not a feeling statement. Write down five feeling statements every day.

- Write down what matters most in your relationship with someone or something else.

RAISING YOUR THINKING (T) LEARNING STYLE

- Have someone write down a problem that's bothering him or her or a problem related to the college or your environment. Then answer questions that explain who, what, where, when, and why and provide the details that back up each response. Doing this every day for 15 or 20 minutes will teach you how to be objective.

certain disciplines and certain instructors may take approaches that favor certain styles, no course is going to be entirely sensing or entirely intuitive, entirely thinking or entirely feeling, just as you are not entirely one thing or another. You can also use your learning style data to determine how to study more effectively. Diagram? Study aloud? Annotate texts in margins? Focus on details or concepts?

STUDY GROUPS AND LEARNING STYLE

SEE EXERCISE 5.5

Knowing your own learning style preference can help you to study more effectively with other students (see Chapter 2). When you form a study group, seek out students with some opposite learning preferences, but be sure, too, that you have some preferences in common. The best teamwork seems to come from people who differ on one or two preferences. If you prefer intuitive fact gathering, you might benefit from the details brought forth by a sensing type.

DEALING WITH YOUR INSTRUCTORS' TEACHING STYLES

Just as your learning style affects how you study, perform, and react to various courses and disciplines, so your instructors' learning styles affect what and how they teach.

Clues to Instructors' Teaching Styles

The best clue to your instructor's teaching style is the language he or she uses. If your learning style is more visual, you can sense those clues more easily from printed material such as the syllabus or course handouts. If your learning style is more auditory, pay attention to the language your instructor uses when lecturing, asking discussion questions, or phrasing oral test questions.

For example, earlier we discussed two ways of receiving and processing information: (1) sensing (factual and informational) and (2) intuitive (analytical and conceptual). An instructor who uses words such as *define, diagram, label, list, outline,* and *summarize* will tend to have a more sensing teaching style. He or she will want you to be extremely specific and provide primarily factual information. Words such as these really ask for very restricted answers.

On the other hand, an instructor whose syllabus or lecture is sprinkled with words such as *concept, theme, idea, theory,* and *interpretation* will tend to have a much more intuitive and analytical learning style and expect similar kinds of responses from students. On exams or on assignments, he or she may use terms such as *describe, compare, contrast, criticize, discuss, evaluate, explain, interpret, justify,* or *relate.* You may notice that instead of asking you to provide factual data or information, these words ask you to act on that information—that is, to use it in relation to other pieces of information, to evaluate it, or to examine it in terms of your own experience. An instructor who uses these words has a much more intuitive teaching style and will expect more analytical, imaginative, and conceptual responses. He or she will expect you to see that information in a new context rather than simply restate the facts as they have been given to you or as they appear in the textbook.

Exam Preparation and Learning/Teaching Styles

Understanding learning styles can help you to perceive more clearly the expectations of an instructor whose teaching style is incompatible with your learning style and thus allow you to prepare more effectively for his or her exams.

When Steven Blume, the main contributor to this chapter, was learning about the Myers-Briggs Type Indicator, he attended a workshop for college instructors. Those attending the workshop were divided into two groups—sensing and intuitive. Each group was given a five-page essay about the effects of divorce on young children and asked to construct a short exam based on the reading. The sensing group was then asked to take the exam constructed by the intuitive group while the intuitive group was asked to take the exam constructed by the sensing group.

In dealing with the questions, they could not believe that both groups had read and discussed the same essay. Those in the intuitive group had been asked to construct lists of details and respond to much factual data that they had regarded as less essential than the more analytical and conceptual themes of the essay. And those in the sensing group were taken aback by the very broad thematic questions the intuitive group had asked about the implications of divorce on the children and the larger questions about the children's future.

It would have been much easier for those who favored sensing to respond to an exam constructed by other sensing people and vice versa. That same situation has probably been true for you in classes and will continue to be true: You will be most comfortable in a course taught by an instructor with a teaching style similar to your learning style.

If your instructor's teaching style is compatible with your learning style, then you should be able to perform well simply by keeping up with your work. If your instructor's style is incompatible with yours, you might consider either mastering more factual material or interpreting or analyzing that material in order to be better prepared for exams or papers. In any case a greater awareness of both your learning style and your instructor's teaching style can be of real benefit.

A variety of additional tests can help you learn more about your learning style. These are generally available through your career planning or learning center. A guidance counselor will both administer the test and help you interpret the results. Ask about the following:

SEE EXERCISE 5.6

- the Myers-Briggs Type Indicator
- the complete Hogan/Champagne Personal Style Inventory
- the Kolb Learning Style Inventory

And above all, remember: There are no good or bad learning styles, only different ones. And isn't that fortunate! What a dull and uncreative world this would be if each of us analyzed information in exactly the same manner!

Learning Style Inventory

Which of the following best describes your most efficient learning style?

Visual learner—rely on visual cues, on things you see

Auditory learner—rely on auditory stimuli, on things you hear

Tactile learner—rely on touch, on working with your hands

Your learning style: _____

Go to *http://www.hcc.hawaii.edu/intranet/committees/FacDevCom/guidebk/
teachtip/ernstyl.htm* and take the 24-question Learning Style Inventory. (Go
to *http://csuccess.wadsworth.com* for the most up-to-date URLs.) Which type
of learner are you?

Visual Preference Score _____

Auditory Preference Score _____

Tactile Preference Score _____

What do your scores suggest about how you might adjust your study habits
to optimize your learning?

_____

_____

Your Learning Style: A Quick Indication

A List three or four of your favorite courses from high school or college:

1. _____

2. _____

3. _____

4. _____

What did these courses have in common? Did they tend to be hands-on
courses? Lecture courses? Discussion courses? What were the exams like?
Do you see a pattern from one course to the next? For example, did your
favorite courses tend to use information-oriented tests such as multiple
choice or true-false? Or did they often include broader essay exams? Did
the tests cover small units of material or facts, or did they draw on larger
chunks of material?

Now list your least favorite courses from high school or college:

1. _____

2. _____

3. _____

4. _____

What did these courses and their exams have in common? How did they
tend to differ from the courses you liked?

B After doing part A, form a small group with two or three other members
of the class. Brainstorm about what courses you are taking that seem to
require factual learning styles, analytical learning styles, or a combination
of both. Prepare an oral group presentation to the class about your conclusions and the reasons for them. What is the best way to prepare for an
exam in these classes and why? (Read this entire chapter before you give
your presentation.)

Assessing Your Learning Style

 The following items are arranged in pairs (a and b), and each member of the pair represents a preference you may or may not hold. Rate your preference for each item by giving it a score of 0 to 5 (0 meaning you really feel negative about it or strongly about the other member of the pair, 5 meaning you strongly prefer it or do not prefer the other member of the pair). The scores for a and b must add up to 5 (0 and 5, 1 and 4, or 2 and 3). Do not use fractions such as $2\frac{1}{2}$.

I prefer:

_____ 1a. making decisions after finding out what others think

_____ 1b. making decisions without consulting others

_____ 2a. being called imaginative or intuitive

_____ 2b. being called factual and accurate

_____ 3a. making decisions about people in organizations based on available data and systematic analysis of situations

_____ 3b. making decisions about people in organizations based on empathy, feelings, and understanding of their needs and values

_____ 4a. allowing commitments to occur if others want to make them

_____ 4b. pushing for definite commitments to ensure that they are made

_____ 5a. quiet, thoughtful time alone

_____ 5b. active, energetic time with people

_____ 6a. using methods I know well that are effective to get the job done

_____ 6b. trying to think of new methods of doing tasks when confronted with them

_____ 7a. drawing conclusions based on logic and careful step-by-step analysis

_____ 7b. drawing conclusions based on what I feel and believe about life and people from past experiences

_____ 8a. avoiding making deadlines

_____ 8b. setting a schedule and sticking to it

_____ 9a. inner thoughts and feelings others cannot see

_____ 9b. activities and occurrences in which others join

_____ 10a. the abstract or theoretical

_____ 10b. the concrete or real

_____ 11a. helping others explore their feelings

_____ 11b. helping others make logical decisions

_____ 12a. communicating little of my inner thinking and feelings

_____ 12b. communicating freely my inner thinking and feelings

_____ 13a. planning ahead based on projections

_____ 13b. planning as necessities arise, just before carrying out the plans

_____ 14a. meeting new people

_____ 14b. being alone or with one person I know well

_____ 15a. ideas

_____ 15b. facts

_____ 16a. convictions

_____ 16b. verifiable conclusions

_____ 17a. keeping appointments and notes about commitments in notebooks or in appointment books as much as possible

_____ 17b. using appointment books and notebooks as minimally as possible (although I may use them)

_____ 18a. carrying out carefully laid, detailed plans with precision

_____ 18b. designing plans and structures without necessarily carrying them out

_____ 19a. being free to do things on the spur of the moment

_____ 19b. knowing well in advance what I am expected to do

_____ 20a. experiencing emotional situations, discussions, movies

_____ 20b. using my ability to analyze situations

PERSONAL STYLE INVENTORY SCORING

Instructions: Transfer your scores for each item of each pair to the appropriate blanks. Be careful to check the a and b letters to be sure you are recording scores in the proper spaces. Then total the scores for each dimension.

	Dimension			Dimension	
	I	**E**		**N**	**S**
	1b. _____	1a. _____		2a. _____	2b. _____
	5a. _____	5b. _____		6b. _____	6a. _____
	9a. _____	9b. _____		10a. _____	10b. _____
	12a. _____	12b. _____		15a. _____	15b. _____
	14b. _____	14a. _____		18b. _____	18a. _____
TOTALS:	I _____	E _____		N _____	S _____

	Dimension			Dimension	
	T	**F**		**P**	**I**
	3a. _____	3b. _____		4a. _____	4b. _____
	7a. _____	7b. _____		8a. _____	8b. _____
	11b. _____	11a. _____		13b. _____	13a. _____
	16b. _____	16a. _____		17b. _____	17a. _____
	20b. _____	20a. _____		19a. _____	19b. _____
TOTALS:	T _____	F _____		P _____	J _____

PERSONAL STYLE INVENTORY INTERPRETATION

Letters on the score sheet stand for:

I—*Introversion*	E—*Extroversion*
N—*iNtuition*	S—*Sensing*
T—*Thinking*	F—*Feeling*
P—*Perceiving*	J—*Judging*

If your score is:	*The likely interpretation is:*
12–13	balance in the strengths of the dimensions
14–15	some strength in the dimension; some weakness in the other member of the pair
16–19	definite strength in the dimension; definite weakness in the other member of the pair
20–25	considerable strength in the dimension; considerable weakness in the other member of the pair

Your typology is those four dimensions for which you had scores of 14 or more, although the relative strengths of all the dimensions actually constitute your typology. Scores of 12 or 13 show relative balance in a pair so that either member could be part of the typology.

Note: This exercise is an abridgment of the Personal Style Inventory by Dr. R. Craig Hogan and Dr. David W. Champagne, adapted and reproduced with permission from Organization Design and Development, Inc., 2002 Renaissance Blvd., Suite 100, King of Prussia, PA, 19406. For information on using the complete instrument, please write to the above address.

EXERCISE 5.4 INTERNET ACTIVITY

The Keirsey Temperament Sorter

Go to *http://www.keirsey.com* and take the Keirsey Temperament Sorter. (Go to *http://csuccess.wadsworth.com* for the most up-to-date URLs.) Read through the type descriptions linked to the site. How well do they reflect what you know about yourself? In what ways is this instrument like the inventory you took in this chapter? How similar were the results? If they were not similar, how might you explain this?

EXERCISE 5.5

Working with Other Learning Styles

A Form a group with one or two other students whose learning style preferences are different from yours in one or two dimensions. Review the chart on pages 71–72 on strengths and weaknesses and make some notes about yours so that you can find the best match with other study group members:

My strengths: _____

_____

_____

_____

My weaknesses: _____

_____

_____

_____

How will your strengths help others? What strengths will you look for in others that will help you?

How I can help others: _____

_____

_____

How others can help me: _____

_____

_____

In your next session, ask that each person share his or her strengths and weaknesses and talk about how the group might work for everyone's benefit.

B Try working on an assignment with someone who has a preference that is the opposite of yours on either the sensing/intuiting or the thinking/feeling scale. Discuss how this worked. Did you get more out of the assignment? Did you consider more issues than you might have alone? Did you learn something about how to study? What did you discover about the other person's learning style?

EXERCISE 5.6

Assessing Your Courses and Instructors

Take some time over the next few days to think about the courses you are taking now. How well does your preferred learning style fit the style reflected in the syllabus, handouts, lectures, and study questions in at least two of your courses? Ask several of your instructors how they teach and learn best.

Do any of the key sensing words mentioned previously (*define, diagram,* and so on) or some close approximation of them appear? If so, list them and place a check mark next to them each time the word appears. Do any of the key intuition words (*describe, compare,* and so on) or similar words appear? List them also and note their frequency. Listen carefully in class. What key words do you hear? Write these down also. Which type of word do you hear most frequently? That will begin to give you some idea of each instructor's learning/teaching style.

INSTRUCTOR/COURSE _____

Sensing Words	**Intuition Words**
_____	_____
_____	_____
_____	_____
_____	_____
_____	_____
_____	_____
_____	_____

Instructor's preferred style: Sensing _____ Intuitive _____

Other teaching style observations: _____

_____

_____

_____

How does your learning style as measured in Exercise 5.3 fit with the learning/teaching style of each instructor? Which courses will require some adjustment on your part? Discuss these problems with other students in class. Are there things your instructors do to help you take advantage of your strengths and learn more efficiently? In class discuss what these ideas are and how you might convey them to the appropriate instructor.

SUGGESTIONS FOR FURTHER READING

Lawrence, Gordon. *People Types and Tiger Stripes*. Gainesville, FL: Center for the Application of Psychological Types, 1982.

Malone, John C., Jr. *Theories of Learning: A Historical Approach*. Belmont, CA: Wadsworth, 1991.

Perry, William. *Forms of Intellectual and Ethical Development in the College Years: A Scheme*. New York: Holt, Rinehart & Winston, 1970.

RESOURCES

Read the following descriptions of the sixteen different Myers-Briggs types. Put your name in the box that best describes your type. Where do the other significant people in your life fit? Put their names in the boxes that best describe their type preferences.

	SENSING TYPES		INTUITIVES	
	WITH THINKING	WITH FEELING	WITH FEELING	WITH THINKING

INTROVERTS

JUDGING

ISTJ
Serious, quiet, earn success by concentration and thoroughness. Practical, orderly, matter-of-fact, logical, realistic and dependable. See to it that everything is well organized. Take responsibility. Make up their own minds as to what should be accomplished and work toward it steadily, regardless of protests or distractions.

_____

_____

ISFJ
Quiet, friendly, responsible and conscientious. Work devotedly to meet their obligations and serve their friends and school. Thorough, painstaking, accurate. May need time to master technical subjects, as their interests are not often technical. Patient with detail and routine. Loyal, considerate, concerned with how other people feel.

_____

_____

INFJ
Succeed by perseverance, originality and desire to do whatever is needed or wanted. Put their best efforts into the work. Quietly forceful, conscientious, concerned foe others. Respected for their firm principles. Likely to be honored and followed for their clear convictions as to how best to serve the common good.

_____

_____

INTJ
Have original minds and great drive which they use only for their own purposes. In fields that appeal to them they have a fine power to organize a job and carry it through with or without help. Skeptical, critical, independent, determined, often stubborn. Must learn to yield less important points in order to win the most important.

_____

_____

JUDGING

INTROVERTS

PERCEPTIVE

ISTP
Cool onlookers, quiet, reserved, observing and analyzing life with detached curiosity and unexpected flashes of original humor. Usually interested in impersonal principles, cause and effect, or how and why mechanical things work. Exert themselves no more than they think necessary, because any waste of energy would be inefficient.

_____

_____

ISFP
Retiring, quietly friendly, sensitive, modest about their abilities. Shun disagreements, do not force their opinions or values on others. Usually do not care to lead but are often loyal followers. May be rather relaxed about assignments or getting things done, because they enjoy the present moment and do not want to spoil it by undue haste or exertion.

_____

_____

INFP
Full of enthusiasms and loyalties, but seldom talk of these until they know you well. Care about learning ideas, language, and independent projects of their own. Apt to be on yearbook staff, perhaps as editor. Tend to undertake too much, then somehow get it done. Friendly, but often too absorbed in what they are doing to be sociable or notice much.

_____

_____

INTP
Quiet, reserved, brilliant in exams, especially in theoretical or scientific subjects. Logical to the point of hair-splitting. Interested mainly in ideas, with little liking for parties or small talk. Tend to have very sharply defined interests. Need to choose careers where some strong interest of theirs can be used and useful.

_____

_____

PERCEPTIVE

EXTRAVERTS

PERCEPTIVE

ESTP
Matter-of-fact, do not worry or hurry, enjoy whatever comes along. Tend to like mechanical things and sports, with friends on the side. May be a bit blunt or insensitive. Can do math or science when they see the need. Dislike long explanations. Are best with real things that can be worked, handled, taken apart or put back together.

_____

_____

ESFP
Outgoing, easygoing, acceptive, friendly, fond of a good time. Like sports and making things. Know what's going on and join in eagerly. Find remembering facts easier than mastering theories. Are best in situations that need sound common sense and practical ability with people as well as with things.

_____

_____

ENFP
Warmly enthusiastic, high-spirited, ingenious, imaginative. Able to do almost anything that interests them. Quick with a solution for any difficulty and ready to help anyone with a problem. Often rely on their ability to improvise instead of preparing in advance. Can always find compelling reasons for whatever they want.

_____

_____

ENTP
Quick, ingenious, good at many things. Stimulating company, alert and outspoken, argue for fun on either side of a question. Resourceful in solving new and challenging problems, but may neglect routine assignments. Turn to one new interest after another. Can always find logical reasons for whatever they want.

_____

_____

PERCEPTIVE

EXTRAVERTS

JUDGING

ESTJ
Practical realists, matter-of-fact, with a natural head for business or mechanics. Not interested in subjects they see no use for, but can apply themselves when necessary. Like to organize and run activities. Tend to run things well, especially if they remember to consider other people's feelings and points of view when making their decisions.

_____

_____

ESFJ
Warm-hearted, talkative, popular, conscientious, born cooperators, active committee members. Always doing something nice for someone. Work best with plenty of encouragement and praise. Little interest in abstract thinking or technical subjects. Main interest is in things that directly and visibly affect people's lives.

_____

_____

ENFJ
Responsive and responsible. Feel real concern for what others think and want, and try to handle things with due regard for other people's feelings. Can present a proposal or lead a group discussion with ease and tact. Sociable, popular, active in school affairs, but put time enough on their studies to do good work.

_____

_____

ENTJ
Hearty, frank, able in studies, leaders in activities. Usually good in anything that requires reasoning and intelligent talk, such as public speaking. Are well-informed and keep adding to their fund of knowledge. May sometimes be more positive and confident than their experience in an area warrants.

_____

_____

JUDGING

"Effects of the Combinations of All Four Preferences in Young People," pp. A-7, A-8, *People Types and Tiger Stripes: A Practical Guide to Learning Styles* by Gordon Lawrence, published by Center for the Application of Psychological Type, Inc. Gainesville, Florida, 1982.

JOURNAL

NAME _____

DATE _____

**What are your learning styles? (Auditory, visual, or kinesthetic? Introvert/
Extrovert, Sensing/Intuitive, Thinking/Feeling, Judging/Perceiving?)**

....

....

....

....

**What methods are you employing to adapt your style to the communication styles of some of your
instructors and academic advisors?**

....

....

....

....

**Do you tend to associate outside of class with people whose learning styles are different from yours?
What types do they tend to be? (You can use the Resources page in this chapter to chart the types of
your friends and instructors.) This process may help you uncover some clues about compatibility
between you and some of the significant people in your life, both in short-term and long-term
relationships.**

....

....

....

....

**How can you use your understanding of types to deal with differences and tensions you encounter
with teachers, friends, or other students? Think of a specific situation, and consider how you might
use an understanding of learning styles to resolve a problem.**

....

....

....

....

CHAPTER

6

Listening and Learning in the Classroom

KEYS TO SUCCESS

- *Show up for class.*
- *Assess and improve your study habits.*
- *Choose instructors who actively involve you in learning.*
- *Get to know at least one person on campus who cares about your survival.*
- *Never doubt your abilities.*
- *Expect instructors to be glad to see you.*
- *Take additional courses in how to study.*

Bummer. Bad grade on my first history test, and I thought I took good notes every day. I read all the assigned chapters in the text, too, and underlined the important points. Maybe I just wasn't listening hard enough in class. Guess I'll have to write faster and take down everything the instructor says or I'll never pass this course.

In virtually every college class you take, you'll need to master two skills to earn high grades: listening and note-taking. Taking an active role in your classes—asking questions, contributing to discussions, or providing answers—will help you listen better and take more meaningful notes, and that in turn will enhance your ability to abstract ideas, find new possibilities, organize those ideas, and recall the material once the class is over.

◼ YOUR NOTE-TAKING IQ

Mark each of the following statements either T (true) or F (false).

_____ 1. If you can't tell what is really important in a lecture, you should write down everything the instructor says.

_____ 2. If an instructor moves through the material very fast, it is better to tape-record the lecture and not worry so much about listening in class.

_____ 3. If the instructor puts an outline on the board or on an overhead projector, you should copy it down immediately.

_____ 4. In a class that is mainly discussion, it is best just to listen and talk rather than to take notes.

_____ 5. The best way to take notes is to use a formal outlining system with Roman numerals, letters, and numbers.

Check the answers on page 94 before you go on reading.
Listening and note-taking are critical to your academic success because your college instructors are likely to introduce new material in class that your texts don't cover, and chances are that much of this material will resurface on quizzes and exams. So, pay attention to the suggestions in this chapter, practice them regularly, and watch your grades improve.

◼ LISTENING AND FORGETTING

Ever notice how easy it is to learn the words of a song? Yet you may read a few pages of a book several times or hear a lecture and find it difficult to retain the important ideas and concepts after a few hours. We remember songs and poetry more easily in part because they follow a rhythm and a beat. We

Psychologists have studied human forgetting in many laboratory experiments. Here are the forgetting curves for three kinds of material: poetry, prose, and nonsense syllables. The shallower curves for prose and poetry indicate that meaningful material is forgotten more slowly than nonmeaningful information. Because poetry contains internal cues such as rhyme and rhythm, it is forgotten less quickly than prose.

Figure 6.1 Learning and Forgetting

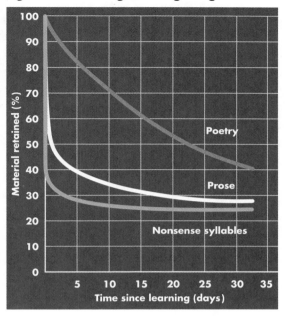

Source: Used with permission from Wayne Weiten, *Psychology: Themes and Variations* (Pacific Grove, CA: Brooks/Cole, 1989, p. 254. Based on data from D. van Guilford, Van Nostrand, 1939).

SEE EXERCISE 6.1 INTERNET ACTIVITY

remember prose less easily, and, because it is the most unstructured form of communication, we can hardly remember gibberish or nonsense words at all (see Figure 6.1).

You may sometimes labor over class notes, trying to figure out exactly what they mean and what the central idea is. That's because most forgetting takes place within the first 24 hours after you see or hear something. In two weeks, you will have forgotten up to 70 percent of the material!

Forgetting can be a serious problem when you are expected to learn and remember a mass of different facts, figures, concepts, and relationships. Once you understand how to improve your ability to remember, you will retain information more easily and completely.

Many instructors draw the bulk of their test items from their lectures; remembering what is presented in class is crucial to doing well on exams. The following system will help you remember and understand material better and relate certain information to other things you already know. It consists of three major parts: preparing to listen before class, listening and taking notes during class, and reviewing and recalling information after class.

■ BEFORE CLASS: PREPARE TO REMEMBER

Even if lectures don't allow for active participation, you can take a number of active learning steps to make your listening and note-taking more efficient. Remember that your goals are improved learning in the classroom, a longer attention span, improved retention of information, and clear, well-organized notes to use when it's time to study for exams.

Because many lectures constitute demanding intellectual encounters, you need to be intellectually prepared before class begins. You would never walk in cold to give a speech, interview for a job, plead a case in court, or compete

PHOTO BY DAVID GONZALES

You'll get more out of a lecture if you prepare ahead of time. Stay abreast of the readings. Get your own ideas flowing by reviewing notes from the previous lecture. What questions were left unanswered? Where should today's session begin?

in sports. For each of these situations, you would prepare in some way. For the same reasons, you should begin active listening, learning, and remembering before the lecture.

1. **Do the assigned reading.** A student may blame lecturers for seeming disorganized and confusing when in fact the student has not done the assigned reading. Some instructors refer to assigned readings for each class session; others may hand out a syllabus and assume you are keeping up with the assigned readings. Completing the assigned readings on time will help you listen better, and active listening promotes good reading.

2. **Warm up for class.** Read well and take good notes. Then warm up by referring to the underlined sections in your text and your classroom notes. This prepares you to pay attention, understand, and remember.

3. **Keep an open mind.** Don't assume that you already know this topic and what is going to be said. Every situation holds the promise of discovering new information and uncovering different perspectives.

◼ DURING CLASS: LISTEN CRITICALLY, TAKE NOTES

Listening in class is not like listening to a TV program, listening to a friend, or even listening to a speaker at a meeting. Knowing how to listen in class can help you get more out of what you hear, understand better what you have heard, and save you time.

Listen for Information

1. **Be ready for the message.** Prepare yourself to hear, to listen, and to receive the message.

2. **Listen to the main concepts and central ideas, not just to fragmented facts and figures.** Although facts are important, they will be easier to remember and make more sense when you can place them in a context of concepts, themes, and ideas.

3. **Listen for new ideas.** Even if you are an expert on the topic, you can still learn something new. Assuming you have already heard all this before means that your mind will be closed to any new information.

4. **Really hear what is said.** Hearing sounds is not the same as hearing the intended message. Listening involves hearing what the speaker wants you to understand. Don't give in to distractions, such as daydreaming or looking at other students. And try not to pass quick judgment on what is being said as you listen because this will distract you, too. As a true critical thinker would, note questions that arise in your mind as you listen but save the judgments for later.

5. **Repeat mentally.** Words can go in one ear and out the other unless you make an effort to retain them. Think about what you hear and make an active effort to retain it by repeating it silently to yourself.

6. **Decide whether what you have heard is not important, somewhat important, or very important.** If it's really not important, let it go. If it's very important, make it a major point in your notes by underscoring it or using it as a major topic in your outline. If it's somewhat important, try to relate it to a very important topic by writing it down as a subset of that topic. Or keep a separate page of minor topics and check them later to see whether to use them in your notes.

7. **Ask questions.** If you did not hear or understand what was said, raise your hand. Now is the time to clarify things. If you can't hear another student's question, ask that the question be repeated.

8. **Listen to the entire message.** Try to avoid agreeing or disagreeing with the speaker based only on the opening of the lecture.

9. **Respect your ideas.** You already know a lot of things. Your own thoughts and ideas are valuable, and you need not throw them out just because someone else's views conflict with your own. At the same time, you should not reject the ideas of others too casually.

10. **Sort, organize, and categorize.** When you listen, try to match what you are hearing with what you already know. Take an active role in deciding how best to recall what you are learning.

Take Effective Notes

You can make class time more productive by using your listening skills to take effective notes. Here's how:

1. **Identify the main ideas.** Good lectures always contain certain key points. The first principle of effective note-taking is to identify and write down the most important ideas (usually four or five) around which the lecture is built. Although supporting details are important as well, focus your note-taking on the main ideas. These main ideas may be buried in details, statistics, anecdotes, or problems, but you need to locate and record them for further study.

   Instructors sometimes announce the purpose of a lecture or offer an outline, thus providing you with the skeleton of main ideas, followed by the details. Some lecturers change their tone of voice or repeat themselves at each key idea. Some ask questions or promote discussion. These are all clues to what is important. If a lecturer says something three times, it is probably essential information. Ask yourself, What does my instructor want me to know at the end of today's session?

Listening: The Neglected Liberal Art

Some time ago, as I was trying to list the fundamental skills we try to teach in a liberal arts education, I found myself drawing on the usual litany: reading, writing, speaking, argument, analysis. Almost as an afterthought, I added the skill of listening.

If one looks around, one could argue that listening is the least-developed skill in American culture. Jennifer Bloxam, associate professor of music, observed that we may well be suffering from a kind of "numbness" from the excess of noise around us. I do not think that numbness is unique to our relationship to music. We are barraged from all sides by sounds, words, and images in our daily lives. Everyone seems to be talking; nobody seems to be listening. (There is an old joke that in America the opposite of talking is not listening but waiting to talk.) And yet there is hardly anything we value more in other people than a sense that they are good listeners.

We do not think of sight, smell, taste, or touch leading to moral perfection. But at some point someone who is good at hearing can become a good listener, possessing a moral skill worthy of admiration, requiring empathy, patience, and courtesy. A simple exercise requires each person in a conversation to use one word from the last sentence uttered by the other. As one does not know exactly when the other person is going to finish, one must take each sentence seriously and listen with care, rather than anticipating responses to display one's own knowledge.

Good listening requires one not to impress one's categories too rapidly on what the other is saying. A physician alumnus with whom I spoke told me how he used to interrogate patients with a series of preestablished questions, thinking that this method was rigorous and efficient. Yet he found that he still missed important information. Now he simply seeks to get the patient to talk in a comfortable and open-ended way; he finds that he discovers more essential information in less time.

Although we can teach listening as a calculatedly practical skill—my favorite in this genre is a book called *Listen to Win*—it is hard to avoid moral categories. As Peter deLisser, who works in the field of communications, emphasized to me, good listening relies on all sides taking responsibility for gaining clarity and understanding.

If all this is so, why is listening so rarely mentioned as a practical and moral skill we teach? Partially this comes from the value we place on appearing active and taking charge. Listening seems, at first blush, passive, as it involves silence. But this image of passivity is an illusion. It requires a strong person to be a good listener—able to be patient and confident enough to suspend judgment and yet not sacrifice one's capacity to analyze and reply. Not without reason people often indicate listening as a crucial skill for leadership, thereby linking listening with strength of character and judgment.

We can assume that learning to listen happens naturally in classes and in our residential life, but I am not at all sure that is the case. We should not shy away from teaching listening in the same way we teach writing, argument, quantitative skills, and the like. As we talk with one another about approaches and methods to teaching, we might want to talk about how well we listen to students and how we might improve our teaching through improving our own listening.

Might we not think about how better to value and reward good listening in our classes? Students generally equate participation with "speaking in class." Have any of us ever told a class that they will be evaluated on their listening, on how well their participation reflects wise, empathetic, vigorous attention to others?

There may, however, be an even larger project. We tend to conceive of our goals in liberal education as creating leaders, and we still tend to visualize leadership as a question of forceful imposition of vision. What if listening were viewed as a higher skill and prior to all the others, and we tried to nurture that value in our civic life and in our classrooms?

—Harry C. Payne, President, Williams College
Abridged and reprinted by permission of the author from the *Williams Alumni Review*, Winter 1998, Williams College, Williamstown, MA.

SEE EXERCISE 6.2

Don't try to write down everything. Because of insecurity or inexperience, some first-year students try to do just that. They stop being thinkers and become stenographers. Learn to avoid that trap. If you're an active listener, you will ultimately have shorter but more useful notes.

As you take notes, leave spaces so that you can fill in additional details later that you might have missed during class. But remember to do it as soon after class as possible; remember the forgetting curve!

2. **Don't be thrown by a disorganized lecturer.** When a lecture is disorganized, you need to try to organize what is said into general and specific frameworks. When this order is not apparent, you'll need to take notes on where the gaps lie in the lecturer's structure. After the lecture, you may need to consult your reading material or classmates to fill in these gaps.

   You might also consult your instructor. Most instructors have regular office hours for student appointments, yet it is amazing how few students use these opportunities for one-on-one instruction. You can also raise questions in class. Asking such questions may help your instructor discover which parts of his or her presentation need more attention and clarification.

3. **Leave space for a recall column.** This is a critical part of effective note-taking. In addition to helping you listen well, your notes become an important study device for tests and examinations. In anticipation of using your notes later, treat each page of your notes as part of an exam-preparation system.

   Here's how to create a recall column. Using one side of the paper only, draw a vertical line to divide the page into two columns. The column on the left, about 2 to 3 inches wide, is the recall column and remains blank while you are taking notes during class in the wider column on the right. The recall column is essentially the place where you highlight the main ideas and important details for tests and examinations as you sift through your notes after class.

   Completing the blank recall column as soon after class as possible (and perhaps with a small group of your classmates) is a powerful study device that reduces forgetting, helps you warm up for class, and promotes understanding in class.

Note-Taking in Nonlecture Courses

Always be ready to adapt your note-taking methods to match the situation. In fact, group discussion is becoming a popular way to teach in college because it involves active learning. How do you keep a record of what's happening in such classes?

Assume you are taking notes in a problem-solving group assignment. You would begin your notes by asking yourself, What is the problem? and writing down the answer. As the discussion progresses, you would list the solutions offered. These would be your main ideas. The important details might include the positive and negative aspects of each view or solution.

The important thing to remember when taking notes in nonlecture courses is that you need to record the information presented by your classmates as well as from the instructor and to consider all reasonable ideas, even though they may differ from your own.

When a course has separate lecture and discussion sessions, you will need to understand how the discussion sessions augment and correlate with the

Other Kinds of Notes

- **Outline notes are widely used.** If you use this approach, try to determine the instructor's outline and recreate it in your notes. Add details, definitions, examples, applications, and explanations. Be careful not to confuse the supporting information with the main points. The main points are the major divisions of the course, of the day's lecture, or of the overall topic. The next level should represent the logical divisions of the main topics. Then you can add the more detailed explanatory material at successive levels.

- **Definitional notes work in some courses.** Using this method, you would enter the major terms on the left edge of the page, then place all material for that term—definitions, explanations, examples, and supporting evidence—beside it.

- **Paragraph notes work for some people and in some situations.** Write comprehensive paragraphs containing a summary of an entire topic. This may work better for summarizing what you have read rather than for class notes, because it may be difficult to summarize the topic until your teacher has covered it completely, by which time it may be too late to recall critical information.

- **Fact notes include only the more critical facts from the lecture or discussion.** The major problem with this method is trying to organize the facts into meaningful groups. Too often they wind up as a collection of terms with little organization, reason, or rationale.

Keep in mind that you can also take notes on your notes. It can help to go back through your course notes, reorganize your thoughts, highlight the essential items, and write new notes. Besides adding one more engagement with the material, your revised notes may be easier to follow.

lectures. If different material is covered in lecture than is covered in discussion, you may need to ask for guidance in organizing your notes. If similar topics are covered, be sure to combine your notes so that you have comprehensive, unified coverage of each topic.

How to organize the notes you take in a class discussion depends on the purpose or form of the discussion. But it usually makes good sense to begin with a list of issues or topics that the discussion leader announces. Another approach is to list the questions that the participants raise for discussion. If the discussion is exploring reasons for and against a particular argument, it makes sense to divide your notes into columns or sections for pros and cons. Even if you do not agree with others, you need to understand their views and rationales, and your teacher may ask you to defend your own opinions in light of the others.

Comparing Notes

You may be able to improve your notes by comparing notes with another student. When you know that you are going to compare notes, you will tend to take better notes. Knowing that your notes will be seen by someone else will prompt you to make your notes well organized, clear, and accurate. See whether your notes are as clear and concise as the other person's and

SEE EXERCISE 6.3

whether you agree on the important points. Share how you take and organize your notes with each other. If you used the recall column in your notes, share notes after class and take turns reciting to each other what you have learned.

Incidentally, comparing notes is not the same as copying somebody else's notes. You simply cannot get the course material from someone else's notes, no matter how good they are, if you have not attended class.

Class Notes and Homework Problems

Good class notes can help you complete homework assignments. Follow these steps:

1. **Take 10 minutes to review your notes.** Skim the notes and put a question mark next to anything you do not understand at first reading. Draw stars next to topics that warrant special emphasis. Try to place the material in context: What has been going on in the course for the last few weeks? How does today's class fit in?

2. **Do a warm-up for your homework.** Before doing the assignment, look through your notes again. Use a separate sheet of paper to rework examples, problems, or exercises. If there is related assigned material in the textbook, review it. Go back to the examples. Cover the solution and attempt to answer each question or complete each problem. Look at the author's work only after you have made a serious personal effort.

3. **Do any assigned problems and answer any assigned questions.** Now you are actually starting your homework. As you read each question or problem, ask: What am I supposed to find or find out? What is essential and what is extraneous? Read the problem several times and state it in your own words. The last sentence may be where you will find the essential question or answer.

4. **Persevere.** Don't give up too soon. When you encounter a problem or question that you cannot readily handle, move on only after a reasonable effort. After you have completed the entire assignment, come back to those items that stumped you. Try once more, then take a break. You may need to mull over a particularly difficult problem for several days. Let your unconscious mind have a chance. Inspiration may come when you are waiting for a stoplight or just before you fall asleep.

5. **Complete your work.** When you finish an assignment, talk to yourself about what you learned from this particular assignment. Generalize about how the problems and questions were different from one another, which strategies were successful, and what form the answers took.

You may be thinking, That all sounds good, but who has the time to do all that extra work? In reality, this approach does work and actually can save you time. Try it for a few weeks. You will find that you can diminish the frustration that comes when you tackle your homework cold.

Computer Notes in Class?

Laptops are often poor tools for taking notes. Computer screens are not conducive to making marginal notes, circling important items, or copying diagrams. And, although most students can scribble coherently without watching their hands, few are really good keyboarders. Finally, notes on a computer are often harder to access or scan when it's time to review.

Entering notes on a computer after class for review purposes may be helpful. On the other hand, if you enter everything the lecturer says during class, you may be wasting time that could be spent more productively.

■AFTER CLASS: RESPOND, RECITE, REVIEW

Remember and Respond

Relate new information to other things you already know. Organize similar kinds of information. Fit new facts into your total system of knowledge. Make a conscious effort to remember. One way is to repeat important data to yourself every few minutes. Another approach is to tie one idea to another idea, concept, or name, so that thinking of one will prompt recall of the other.

Often, the best way to learn something is to teach it to someone else. You will understand something better and remember it longer if you try to explain it. This helps you discover your own reactions and uncover gaps in your comprehension of the material. (Asking and answering questions in class also provides you with the feedback you need to make certain your understanding is accurate.)

Listening is an ongoing activity. Before the next class, get ready to listen again. You have already learned how to prepare yourself to listen well. Maintain that readiness so that you are prepared to listen daily.

SEE EXERCISE 6.4

Fill in the Recall Column, Recite, and Review

Don't let the forgetting curve take its toll on you! As soon after class as possible, review your notes and fill in the details you still remember, but missed writing down, in those spaces you left in the right-hand column. Then go through these three important steps for remembering the key points in the lecture:

1. **Write the main ideas in the recall column.** For five or ten minutes, quickly review your notes and select key words or phrases that will act as labels or tags for main ideas and key information in the notes. Highlight the main ideas and write them in the recall column next to the material they represent.

2. **Use the recall column to recite your ideas.** Cover the notes on the right and use the prompts from the recall column to help you recite *out loud* a brief version of what you understand from the class in which you have just participated. If you don't have a few minutes after class to review your notes, find some other time during that same day to review what you have written. You might also want to ask your teacher to glance at your recall column to determine whether you have noted the proper major ideas.

3. **Review the previous day's notes just before the next class session.** As you sit in class the next day waiting for the lecture to begin, use the time to quickly review the notes from the previous day. This will put you in tune with the lecture that is about to begin and also prompt you to ask questions about material from the previous lecture that may not have been clear to you.

These three engagements with the material will pay off later, when you begin to study for your examinations.

SEE EXERCISE 6.5

Figure 6.2 Sample Lecture Notes

Sept. 21 <u>How to take notes</u>	
Problems with lectures	Lecture <u>not</u> best way to teach. Problems: Short attention span (may be only 15 minutes!). Teacher dominates. Most info is forgotten. "Stenographer" role interferes with thinking, understanding, learning.
Forgetting curves	Forgetting curves critical period: over ½ of lecture forgotten in 24 hours.
Solution: Active listening	Answer: Active listening, really understanding during lecture. Aims— (1) immediate understanding (2) longer attention (3) better retention (4) notes for study later
Before: Read Warm up	BEFORE: Always prepare. Read: Readings parallel lectures & make them meaningful. Warm up: Review last lecture notes & readings right before class.
During: main ideas	DURING: Write main ideas & some detail. No stens. What clues does prof. give about what's most important? Ask. Ask other questions. Leave blank column about 2½" on left of page. Use only front side of paper.
After: Review Recall Recite	AFTER: Left column for key recall words, "tags." Cover right side & recite what tags mean. Review/Recall/Recite

Why This Process Is So Powerful

The key to this system is that you are encountering the same material through four different approaches: active listening, writing effective notes, reviewing and summarizing in the recall column, and reciting aloud what you understand from class. All of these promote active learning and retention.

Recitation is a particularly effective way to avoid forgetting. The very act of speaking and hearing concepts gives your memory sufficient time to grasp

SEE EXERCISE 6.6

them. You move material from short-term memory to long-term memory, where you can call upon it when you need it.

What if you have three classes in a row and no time for recall columns or recitations between them? Recall and recite as soon after class as possible. Review the most recent class first. Never delay recall and recitation longer than one day: It will then take you longer to review, make a recall column, and recite. With practice, you can complete your recall column quickly, perhaps between classes or while eating lunch or riding a bus.

Answers to "Your Note-Taking IQ" on page 84

1. *False.* Writing down everything the instructor says won't help you find the main points. Instead, raise your hand and ask questions that will help you capture the main points, get help from your study skills center, or compare your notes with a friend's to see if you both agree on the main points.

2. *False.* Tape-recording a lecture means you must sit through it at least twice in order to understand it. Instead, (a) ask the instructor to speak more slowly because you are having trouble following him or her (chances are others are having the same problem) or (b) ask the instructor to repeat points that you missed.

   Note: Commuters may wish to record a lecture so they can listen to it traveling to and from school. Yet they, too, should listen carefully and take detailed notes in class.

3. *False.* Copying an outline immediately may not allow enough room for filling in the finer details. A good instructor will cover each point in sequence. Write down the first point and listen. Take notes. When the next point is covered, do the same, and so forth.

4. *False.* Discussion can be deceiving. Your instructor may be taking notes on what is said and could use them on exams. You should be taking notes as well, in addition to participating in the discussion.

5. *False.* A single system isn't going to work for everyone. If a formal outline works for you, fine. If it doesn't, find some other way to organize your notes so you can come back to them later and understand them.

Take special note of any statement that you marked as true. Watch for explanations in this chapter about why the answer is false or what other strategy is likely to be more effective. You may not agree completely. Be prepared to discuss your responses in class.

Search Online!

Try these phrases and others for Key Words and Subject Guide searches: "study skills," "note-taking."
Also look up:
Visual notetaking: drawing on my doodling past. Andrew John Katz. *School Arts* Sep 1997 v97 n1 p33(3)

INFOTRAC COLLEGE EDITION

Study Skills Guides on the Internet

The Internet can be a major source of study-skills and self-help materials. Handouts prepared by many college learning centers are available online. Check out the following:

- The CalREN Project, a series of tips and exercises to help develop better study strategies and habits: *http://128.32.89.153/CalRENHP.html*
- College of Saint Benedict and Saint John's University Study Skills Guides: *http://www.csbsju.edu/advising/helplist.html*
- Dartmouth Study Skills Guide Menu: *http://www.dartmouth.edu/admin/acskills/index.html*
- Study Tips—a collection of some of the handouts used in the University of Texas at Austin, Learning Skills Center: *http://www.utexas.edu/student/lsc/handouts/stutips.html*
- Virginia Polytechnic Institute Study Skills Self-Help Information: *http://www.ucc.vt.edu/stdysk/stdyhlp.html*
- University of Minnesota Duluth Study Strategies home page: *http://www.d.umn.edu/student/loon/acad/strat/study_strat_enr.html*

What information did you find that you will be able to use? (Go to *http://csuccess.wadsworth.com* for the most up-to-date URLs.)

Listening

Form groups of five and chat about the importance of listening, how well students listen in class, what they should do to improve their listening. Each student who speaks after the first speaker must use at least one word from the *last* sentence spoken by the last speaker. The first speaker should do the same after the last student has spoken. How did this affect the quality of your listening? How can you apply it to the classroom?

Comparing Notes

Pair up with another student and compare your class notes for this course. Are your notes clear? Do you agree on what is important? Take a few minutes to explain to each other your note-taking systems. Agree to use a recall column during the next class meeting. Afterward, share your notes again and check on how each of you used the recall column. Again, compare your notes and what each of you deemed important.

Using Critical Thinking to Determine Main Ideas and Major Details

Divide a piece of looseleaf paper as shown in Figure 6.2. In one of your classes other than your first-year seminar, take notes on the right side of the paper, leaving the recall column and the last few lines on the page blank. As soon after class as possible, use the critical thinking process to abstract the main ideas and write them in the recall column. Use the blank lines at the bottom to write a summary sentence or two for that page of notes. Use the recall column to jot down any thoughts or possibilities that occur to you. For example, your possibilities may include, "I wonder what I can attach this information to so I can recall it later?" or, "Maybe if I break my American lit notes into small chunks, I'll recall them easier."

EXERCISE 6.5

Using a Recall Column

Suppose the information in this chapter had been presented to you as a lecture rather than a reading. Using the system described previously, your lecture notes might look like those in Figure 6.2. Cover the right-hand column. Using the recall column, try reciting in your own words the main ideas from this chapter. Uncover the right-hand column when you need to refer to it. If you can phrase the main ideas from the recall column in your own words, you are well on your way to mastering this note-taking system for dealing with lectures. Does this system seem to work? If not, why not?

EXERCISE 6.6

Applying an Active Listening and Learning System

Examine the study schedule on page 54 in Chapter 4, and then answer the following questions:

1. Where do you see evidence of plans to use the recall column?

_____

_____

_____

2. What problems might you have in performing review/recall/recite as soon after class as possible?

_____

_____

_____

3. How might these problems be addressed and solved?

_____

_____

_____

Share your answers with other students in a small group.

SUGGESTIONS FOR FURTHER READING

Pauk, Walter. *How to Study in College*, 6th ed. "Listening to Take Good Notes" (Chapter 9), "Taking Good Notes" (Chapter 10). Boston: Houghton Mifflin, 1997.

Schumm, Jeanne S., & Shawn A. Post. *Executive Learning: Successful Strategies for College Reading and Studying*. Upper Saddle River, NJ: Prentice-Hall, 1997.

Wolff, Florence I., & Nadine C. Marsnik. *Perceptive Listening*, 2nd ed. Orlando, FL: Harcourt Brace Jovanovich, 1992.

RESOURCES

Throughout this book, we mention the helpfulness of study groups for your success in college. Use this Resources page to list names, numbers, and meeting times for the study groups you are in. Keep the list handy, especially close to test time. If you are not in a study group, list potential study-group members and contact them.

Study Group _____ meets _____

Name	Phone number	e-mail

Study Group _____ meets _____

Name	Phone number	e-mail

Study Group _____ meets _____

Name	Phone number	e-mail

Library Hours

Library	Regular hours	Hours during finals	Phone number

JOURNAL

NAME _____

DATE _____

Try at least three approaches to taking notes, either from approaches discussed in this chapter or that you develop on your own. Which methods seem to work best with which subjects? (Remember the different learning styles from Chapter 5.)

....

....

....

....

How does your learning style affect your listening (that is, what you listen for)? How can you use this information to listen more actively and effectively?

....

....

....

....

How might your note-taking be altered to match the needs of a particular course? How might it be fine-tuned to match the presentation approaches of a particular instructor?

....

....

....

....

How might you improve your note-taking and study habits by working with a study group?

....

....

....

What would it take to form such a group, and how would you begin working together?

....

....

....

CHAPTER ➤ 7

Learning from Textbooks

KEYS TO SUCCESS

- *Assess and improve your study habits.*
- *Study with a group.*
- *Improve your critical thinking skills.*

“I've read this paragraph five times and I still don't understand it. How am I supposed to be ready to discuss this tomorrow when I can't even get through the first page? There's gotta be a better way. Can't someone just drill a hole in my head and pour it in?”

■ PREPARING TO READ

Reading college textbooks is a more challenging activity than reading high school texts or general interest books. College texts are loaded with concepts, terms, and complex information that you are expected to learn on your own in a short period of time. These demands on your time and your reading skills require that you use a study-reading method such as the one presented in this chapter.

Evaluating Your Reading Strengths and Weaknesses

Before you read further, it's a good idea to consider your study-reading strengths and weaknesses. Answer the following questions to assess your college reading skills:

1. Do you overview a chapter before you begin to read?
   yes _____   no _____
2. Do you often lose concentration while reading a text?
   yes _____   no _____
3. Do you highlight or mark the text after you read?
   yes _____   no _____
4. Do you take notes after you read?
   yes _____   no _____
5. Do you pause at the end of each section or page to note what you have read?
   yes _____   no _____
6. Do you use different reading strategies depending on your purpose for reading?
   yes _____   no _____
7. After reading do you recount key ideas to yourself or with a partner?
   yes _____   no _____
8. Do you review what you have read at least once a week?
   yes _____   no _____

A "yes" to any question, except 2, indicates a strength. A "no" indicates an area of weakness. Look for strategies that will improve your concentration and your comprehension as you study this chapter.

The following plan for study reading will increase your focus and concentration, promote greater understanding of what you read, and thereby prepare you to study for tests and exams. This system is based on four steps: overviewing, reading, marking, and reviewing.

OVERVIEWING

Begin by reading the title of the chapter. Ask yourself, What do I already know about this subject? Next, quickly read through the introductory paragraphs, then turn to the end of the chapter and read the summary (if one is there). Then take a few minutes to page through the chapter headings and subheadings.

Note any study exercises at the end of the chapter. As part of your overview, note how many pages the chapter contains. It's a good idea to decide how many pages you will try to cover in your first 50-minute study period before you begin to actively read. This can help build your concentration as you work toward your goal of reading a specific number of pages.

Mapping

Mapping the chapter as you overview it provides a visual guide of how different chapter ideas fit together. Because about 75 percent of students identify themselves as visual learners, visual mapping is an excellent learning tool that will be useful for test preparation as well as active reading.

How do you map a chapter? While you are overviewing, use either a wheel or branching mapping structure (Figure 7.1). In the wheel structure, place the central idea of the chapter in the circle, place secondary ideas on the spokes emanating from the circle, and place offshoots of those ideas on the lines attached to the spokes. In the branching map, the main idea goes at the top, followed by supporting ideas on the second tier, and so forth. Fill in the title first. Then as you skim through the rest of the chapter, use the headings and subheadings to fill in the key ideas on the type of map you have chosen.

This active learning step may require more time up front, but it will save you time later because you have created an excellent review tool for quizzes and tests. You will be using your visual learning mode as well as creating "advance organizers" to help you associate details of the chapter with the larger ideas. Such associations will be essential for later recall.

As you overview the text material, look for connections between the text and the related lecture material. Call to mind the related terms and concepts that you recorded in lecture. Use these strategies to warm up and create a plan for reading. Ask yourself, Why am I reading this? and What do I want to know?

SEE EXERCISE 7.1

READING YOUR TEXTBOOK

After completing your overview, you are ready to read the text actively. Having created a skeleton cognitive map or outline, you now will be able to read more quickly and with greater comprehension. Read the first section, up to the next heading or subheading, and stop. To avoid overmarking or marking the wrong information, read first without using your pencil or highlighter. When you have reached the end of a section, ask yourself, What are the key ideas in this section? and What do I think I'll see on the test? Then, and only then, decide what to mark.

Figure 7.1 Wheel and Branching Maps

Wheel Map

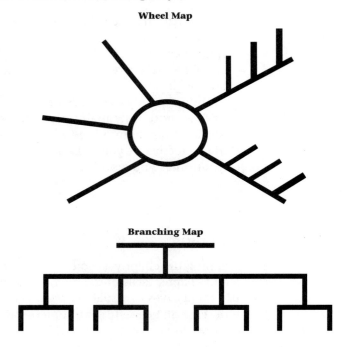

Branching Map

Building Concentration and Understanding

Two common problems are lack of concentration and inability to understand the reading. Many factors may affect one's ability to concentrate and understand texts: the time of day, your energy level, your interest in the material, and your study location.

Consider these suggestions for promoting optimal concentration or flow and decide which would work to increase your reading focus:

- Find a study location, preferably in the library if you are on campus, that is removed from traffic and distracting noises.
- Read in 50-minute blocks of time, with short breaks between. By reading for 50 minutes more frequently during the day instead of cramming all your reading in at the end of the day, you should be able to process material more easily.
- Set goals for your study period, such as, "I will read 20 pages of my psychology text in the next 50 minutes." Reward yourself with a 10-minute break after each 50-minute study period.
- If you are having trouble concentrating or staying awake, take a quick walk around the library or down the hall. Take some deep breaths and talk positively about your study goals.
- To keep your focus, jot study questions in the margin, take notes, or recite the key ideas. Reread confusing parts of the text and make a note to ask your instructor for clarification.
- Experiment with your reading rate. Try to move your eyes more quickly over the material by focusing on a phrase, not a word, at a time.
- Focus on the high-yield portions of the text: Pay attention to the first and last sentences of paragraphs and to words in italics or bold print.
- Use the glossary in the text to define unfamiliar terms.

■ MARKING YOUR TEXTBOOK

Think a moment about your goals for marking in your texts. Some students report that marking is an active reading strategy that helps them focus and concentrate on the material as they read. In addition, most students expect to use their text notations when studying for tests. To meet these goals, some students like to underline, some prefer to highlight, and others use margin notes. Look at Figure 7.2 for examples of different methods of marking. You can also combine methods.

No matter what method you prefer for collecting the key ideas in a section, remember these two important guidelines:

1. **Read before you mark.** Finish reading a section before you mark it. Then decide which are the most important ideas and concepts. Mark only those ideas, using your preferred methods (highlighting, underlining, circling key terms, making margin notes).

2. **Think before you mark.** Use selective marking. When you read a text for the first time, everything may seem important. Only after you have completed a section and reflected on it will you be ready to identify the key ideas. Ask yourself, What are the most important ideas? and What will I see on the test? This can help you avoid marking too much material. An overzealous use of highlighting can convert a text to pages of Day-Glo yellow or pink, in which nothing stands out as important.

One caution about only marking in your textbooks without also creating an outline, a concept map, or taking notes in your notebook: If you just mark pages, you are committing yourself to at least one more viewing of all the pages that you have already read—all 400 pages of your anatomy or art history textbook! Better to use margin notes or create a visual map or outline as you read.

Although these study-reading methods will take more time initially, they can save you time in the long run because the active reading you will do not only promotes concentration as you read but also facilitates regular review. So you probably won't have to pull an all-nighter before an exam.

Monitoring

An important step in a study-reading method is to monitor your comprehension. As you read ask yourself, Do I understand this? If not, stop and reread the material. Look up words that are not clear. Try to clarify the main points and how they relate to one another.

Another way to check your comprehension is to try to recite the material aloud to yourself or your study partner. Using a study group to monitor your comprehension gives you immediate feedback and is very motivating. One way that group members can work together is to divide up a chapter for pre-reading and studying and get together later to teach the material to one another.

Recycle Your Reading

After you have read and marked key ideas from the first section of the text, proceed to each subsequent section until you have finished the chapter. After you have completed each section, again ask, What are the key ideas? or What will I see on the test? before you move on to the next section. At

Figure 7.2 Sample Marked Pages

7. Some students who read a chapter slowly get very good grades; others get poor grades. Why?

8. Most actors and public speakers who have to memorize lengthy passages spend little time simply repeating the words and more time thinking about them. Why? (Check your answers on page 288.)

People need to monitor their understanding of a text to decide whether to keep studying or whether they already understand it well enough. Most readers have trouble making that judgment correctly.

SELF-MONITORING OF UNDERSTANDING

Whenever you are studying a text, you periodically have to decide, "Should I keep on studying this section, or do I already understand it well enough?" Most students have trouble monitoring their own understanding. In one study, psychology instructors asked their students before each test to guess whether they would do better or worse on that test than they usually do. Students also guessed after each test whether they had done better or worse than usual. Most students' guesses were no more accurate than chance (Sjostrom & Marks, 1994). Such inaccuracy represents a problem: Students who *~~why~~* do not know how well they understand the material will make bad judgments about when to keep on studying and when to quit.

Even when you are reading a single sentence, you have to decide whether you understand the sentence or whether you should stop and reread it. Here is a sentence once published in the student newspaper at North Carolina State University:

> He said Harris told him she and Brothers told French that grades had been changed.

How

Ordinarily, when good readers come to such a confusing sentence, they notice their own confusion and reread the sentence or, if necessary, the whole paragraph. Poor readers tend to read at their same speed for both easy and difficult materials; they are less likely than good readers to slow down when they come to difficult sentences.

Although monitoring one's own understanding is difficult and often inaccurate, it is not impossible. For example, suppose I tell you that you are to read three chapters dealing with, say, thermodynamics, the history of volleyball, and the Japanese stock market.

Later you will take tests on each chapter. Before you start reading, predict your approximate scores on the three tests. Most people make a guess based on how much they already know about the three topics. If we let them read the three chapters and again make a guess about their test performances, they do in fact make more accurate predictions than they did before reading (Maki & Serra, 1992). That improvement indicates some ability to monitor one's own understanding of a text.

A systematic way to monitor your own understanding of a text is the SPAR method: Survey, Process meaningfully, Ask questions, and Review and test yourself. Start with an overview of what a passage is about, read it carefully, and then see whether you can answer questions about the passage or explain it to others. If not, go back and reread.

SPAR
Survey
Process
Ask
Review

Also decide about larger units?

THE TIMING OF STUDY

Other things being equal, people tend to remember recent experiences better than earlier experiences. For example, suppose someone reads you a list of 20 words and asks you to recall as many of them as possible. The list is far too long for you to recite from your phonological loop; however, you should be able to remember at least a few. Typically, people remember items at the beginning and end of the list better than they remember those in the middle.

That tendency, known as the **serial-order effect,** includes two aspects: The *primacy effect* is the tendency to remember the first items; the *recency effect* refers to the tendency to remember the last items. One explanation for the primacy effect is that the listener gets to rehearse the first few items for a few moments alone with no interference from the others. One explanation for the recency effect is that the last items are still in

Cause of primacy effect

Figure 7.2 (continued)

Cause of recency effect

the listener's phonological loop at the time of the test.

The phonological loop cannot be the whole explanation for the recency effect, however. In one study, British rugby players were asked to name the teams they had played against in the current season. Players were most likely to remember the last couple of teams they had played against, thus showing a clear recency effect even though they were recalling events that occurred weeks apart (Baddeley & Hitch, 1977). (The phonological loop holds information only for a matter of seconds.)

So, studying material—or, rather, *reviewing* material—shortly before a test is likely to improve recall. Now let's consider the opposite: Suppose you studied something years ago and have not reviewed it since then. For example, suppose you studied a foreign language in high school several years ago. Now you are considering taking a college course in the language, but you are hesitant because you are sure you have forgotten it all. Have you?

Harry Bahrick (1984) tested people who had studied Spanish in school 1 to 50 years previously. Nearly all agreed that they had rarely used Spanish and had not refreshed their memories at all since their school days. (That is a disturbing comment, but beside the point.) Their retention of Spanish dropped noticeably in the first 3 to 6 years, but remained fairly stable from then on (Fig-

ure 7.18). In other words, we do not completely forget even very old memories that we seldom use.

In a later study, Bahrick and members of his family studied foreign-language vocabulary either on a moderately frequent basis (practicing once every 2 weeks) or on a less frequent basis (as seldom as once every 8 weeks), and tested their knowledge years later. The result: More frequent study led to faster learning; however, less frequent study led to better long-term retention, measured years later (Bahrick, Bahrick, Bahrick, & Bahrick, 1993).

The principle here is far more general than just the study of foreign languages. *If you want to remember something well for a test,* your best strategy is to study it as close as possible to the time of the test, in order to take advantage of the recency effect and decrease the effects of retroactive interference. Obviously, I do not mean that you should wait until the night before the test to start studying, but you might rely on an extensive review at that time. You should also, ideally, study under conditions similar to the conditions of the test. For example, you might study in the same room where the test will be given, or at the same time of day.

However, *if you want to remember something long after the test is over,* then the advice I have just given you is all wrong. To be able to remember something whenever you want, wherever you are, and whatever you are doing, you should study it under as varied circumstances as possible. Study and review at various times and places with long, irregular intervals between study sessions. Studying under such inconsistent conditions will slow down your original learning, but it will improve your ability to recall it long afterwards (Schmidt & Bjork, 1992).

Studying for Test vs. Studying for long term

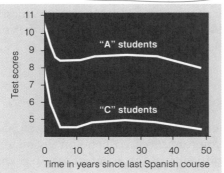

FIGURE 7.18
(Left) Spanish vocabulary as measured by a recognition test shows a rapid decline in the first few years but then long-term stability. (From Bahrick, 1984.) (Right) Within a few years after taking your last foreign-language course, you may think you have forgotten it all. You have not, and even the part you have forgotten will come back (through relearning) if you visit a country where you can practice the language.

Source: Pages adapted with permission from James W. Kalat, *Introduction to Psychology,* 4th ed. Pacific Grove, CA: Brooks/Cole, 1996.

Write as you read. Taking notes on your reading helps you focus on the key ideas and summarize as you go. You take in and digest the material rather than skim it.

TOM JORGENSON/PHOTO COURTESY OF THE UNIVERSITY OF IOWA

**SEE EXERCISE 7.2
INTERNET ACTIVITY**

the end of each section try to guess what information the author will present in the next section. Good writing should lead you from one section to the next, with each new section adding to your understanding.

■ REVIEWING

The final step in a study-reading method is reviewing. Many students expect the improbable—that they will read through their text material one time and be able to remember the ideas four, six, or even twelve weeks later at test time. Rather, you will need to include regular reviews in your study process. Here is where your margin notes, study questions, and visual maps or outlines will be most useful. Your study goal is to review the material from each chapter every week.

SEE EXERCISE 7.3

■ MAINTAINING FLEXIBILITY

With effort, you can improve your reading dramatically, but remember to be flexible. How you read should depend on the material. Assess the relative importance and difficulty of the assigned readings and adjust your reading style accordingly. Connect one important idea to another by asking yourself, Why am I reading this? and Where does this fit in? When the textbook material is virtually identical to the lecture material, you can save time by concentrating mainly on one or the other. It takes a planned approach to read textbook materials and other assigned readings with good understanding and recall. So always keep in mind the following rules:

1. Plan to read in your prime study time.
2. Use warm-up time to prepare to read and to set a purpose for reading.
3. Set a specific number of pages to read within a specific amount of time.

Analyzing and Thinking Critically About Texts

When we analyze an argument we have read, we first must understand its parts and then see how they combine. Is the argument a good one? Suppose someone alleges that the rise in the number of violent crimes is caused by the increase in violence on television. Although it may at first appear easy to agree or disagree with this idea, the following analysis makes us think more carefully about it:

1. **Define the terms.** Which crimes are considered violent? Is destruction of property a violent crime, or do people have to be physically harmed? Under one definition, graffiti might be a violent crime but not armed robbery. What does violence consist of on television? Are the NBA playoffs an example of violence on TV? Is a horror movie that terrifies viewers but contains no physical violence okay?

2. **Examine the premises (the assumptions).** Has the number of violent crimes actually risen or are they simply reported more frequently? Has there actually been an increase in violence on television (as you defined it), or are viewers now simply more sensitive to violence on television?

3. **Examine the logic.** If those who commit violent acts also watch violence on television, can we conclude without seeking further evidence that watching TV violence causes their violent acts? More data will be needed to rule out the possibility that people who are already violent simply tend to watch violent television. Certainly there are those who watch violent programs who do not become violent. Perhaps we need to find evidence showing that the more violence an individual watches, the more likely he or she is to become violent.

Try applying these critical thinking strategies when you read.

4. Organize your work into short tasks for high concentration.

5. Take notes, recite, and review for each section of the reading.

6. Reward yourself.

ANOTHER STUDY METHOD: SQ3R

Developed in 1941, SQ3R has proven its worth as a study method many times over. If other methods don't seem to be working, try this one:

S = SURVEY   Survey the material you are going to read. Get a good idea of what you'll be learning by reading the introductory paragraphs, the summary at the beginning or end, and the major and minor headings.

Q = QUESTION   As you survey, write some questions to ask yourself later. For example, if you saw the heading above—"Another Study Method: SQ3R"—you might write down, "What is SQ3R and how does it help you study?"

R = READ   Now you're ready to read in earnest. Read a paragraph and think about what it says. Pay attention to the picture and tables. Look up words you don't know. Continue until you have finished the reading.

R = RECITE   Ask yourself the questions you jotted down. Answer them in your own words instead of trying to memorize the author's exact words. If you can't answer a question, look for the answer and write it down. Look for connections between this material and what you already know about this subject.

R = REVIEW   Now go back and review the entire reading, perhaps with your study group. Be certain you understand the major points. Keep reviewing until the material becomes familiar. Do another review just before the exam, using your questions and answers as a guide.

■ DEVELOPING VOCABULARY

Textbooks are full of new terminology. In fact, one could argue that learning chemistry is largely a matter of learning the language of chemists and that mastering philosophy or history or sociology requires a mastery of the terminology of each particular discipline. Because words are such a basic and essential component of our knowledge, what is the best way to learn them? Follow these basic vocabulary strategies.

- During your overview of the chapter, notice unfamiliar terms.
- When you encounter these terms in your reading, review their definitions and devote a section in your notebook to collecting and defining them. Or create flash cards for these terms.
- For other challenging words that you encounter in your texts, consider the context. See if you can predict the meaning of the unfamiliar term using the surrounding words.
- If context by itself is not enough, try analyzing the term to discover the root or other meaningful parts of the word. For example, *emissary* has the root "to emit" or "to send forth," so we can guess that an emissary is someone sent forth with a message.
- Use the glossary of the text or a dictionary to locate the definition. Note any multiple definitions and search for the meaning that fits this usage.
- Take every opportunity to use these new terms in your writing and speaking. If you are able to use a new term, then you'll know it! In addition, studying new terminology on flash cards or study sheets is a very effective way to prepare for exams.

Search Online!

INFOTRAC COLLEGE EDITION

Try these phrases and others for Key Words and Subject Guide searches: "reading," "college reading."

Also look up:

Effects of advance questions on reading comprehension. David S. Kreiner. *The Journal of General Psychology* Oct 1996 v123 n4 p352(13)

The living dead: what the dickens are college students reading? Renee Swanson. *Policy Review* Wntr 1994 n67 p72(2)

Valuing fiction. (reading fiction is sometimes seen as a passive, non-creative activity) (Writers & Readers). Duncan Smith. *Booklist*, March 1, 1998 v94 n13 p1094(2)

EXERCISE 7.1

Overviewing and Creating a Visual Map

Overview this chapter and create a visual map, noting the following information: title, key points from the introduction, any graphics (maps, charts, tables, diagrams), study questions or exercises built into or at the end of the chapter, introduction and summary paragraphs. Create either a wheel or a branching map as shown in Figure 7.1. Add spokes or tiers as necessary. In a small group, compare your work.

EXERCISE 7.2
INTERNET
ACTIVITY

Reading Web Pages Critically

Since anyone can publish on the Internet, you should read material on the Internet with a critical eye.

Examine the "Checklist for an Informational Web Page" offered by the Widener University Wolfgram Memorial Library, *http://www.science.widener.edu/~withers/inform.htm*. This page offers questions to ask about an informational web page. (Go to *http://csuccess.wadsworth.com* for the most up-to-date URLs.)

Evaluate that web page using its own five criteria:

1. What evidence is there to indicate how authoritative the site is? _____

   _____

   _____

   _____

2. What confirms that the information is accurate? _____

   _____

   _____

   _____

3. What leads you to believe the site is objective? Biased? _____

   _____

   _____

   _____

4. How current is the information on the site? _____

   _____

   _____

   _____

5. How complete is the coverage of the topic as cited in the page title? _____

   _____

   _____

   _____

See also "Evaluating World Wide Web Information" presented by the Libraries of Purdue University: *http://thorplus.lib.purdue.edu/library_info/instruction/gs175/3gs175/evaluation.html*, which includes an Internet evaluator checklist, and "Thinking Critically about World Wide Web Resources" at *http://www.library.ucla.edu/libraries/college/instruct/critical.htm*. See also Chapter 9, pages 136–138, in this text.

EXERCISE 7.3

How to Read Fifteen Pages of a Textbook in an Hour or Less

It takes practice—but it can be done! Find a chapter in one of your textbooks that is at least fifteen pages long. Plan to read the first fifteen pages only. Then, with a watch or clock nearby, complete the following process:

Chapter overview		4 minutes
pages 1–3:	Read and mark	10 minutes
	Review and recite	2 minutes
pages 4–7:	Read and mark	10 minutes
	Review and recite	2 minutes
pages 8–12:	Read and mark	10 minutes
	Review and recite	2 minutes
pages 13–15:	Read and mark	10 minutes
	Review and recite	2 minutes

Review and recite for all fifteen pages. Answer aloud the questions: What did I learn? How does it relate to the course? 8 minutes

Total	60 minutes

Done. Take a break—you've earned it!

SUGGESTIONS FOR FURTHER READING

Allen, Sheila. *Making Connections.* "The Student's Role as Learner," Unit 4. Fort Worth, TX: Harcourt Brace College Publishers, 1998.

Chaffee, John. *The Thinker's Guide to College Success,* "Reading Critically" (Chapter 6). Boston: Houghton Mifflin, 1995.

Laskey, Marcia L., & Paula W. Gibson. *College Study Strategies: Thinking and Learning,* "Questioning Strategies that Lead to Critical Thinking" (Chapter 11). Boston: Allyn & Bacon, 1997.

Pauk, Walter. *How to Study in College,* 6th ed., "Learning from Your Textbook" (Chapter 11), "Noting What Is Important" (Chapter 12), "Thinking Visually" (Chapter 13). Boston: Houghton Mifflin, 1997.

Seyler, Dorothy U. *Steps to College Reading,* "Developing a Reading Strategy" (Chapter 2). Needham Heights, MA: Allyn & Bacon, 1998.

Van Blerkom, Dianna L. *College Study Skills: Becoming a Strategic Learner,* 2nd ed., "Reading Your Textbook" (Chapter 6), "Marking Your Textbook" (Chapter 7). Belmont, CA: Wadsworth, 1997.

RESOURCES

The only way to improve your study reading is to read more. The more reading you do on your own, for pleasure, unrelated to school or study, the more you will begin to absorb information about writing, presentation, and vocabulary, in addition to whatever the material is about. Reading anything (almost) can contribute to your success in college—as long as you keep up with your study reading as well. Use this Resources page to brainstorm a list of extracurricular reading materials. Use the second half of the page to list 10-minute rewards that you can give yourself when you finish a 50-minute study-reading session.

Things I would enjoy reading for pleasure. Need ideas? Wander through the library or a good bookstore. (*Try spending at least one hour a week reading something just for you.*)

Fiction books	Nonfiction books	Magazines	Newspapers	Internet pages

Make a list of 10-minute rewards that you can give yourself after a 50-minute study reading session. Include a few bigger rewards for a week of successful studying.

10-minute rewards:

End-of-the-week rewards:

JOURNAL

NAME _____

DATE _____

Compare the planned approach to textbook reading presented in this chapter with ways that you have previously read textbooks (in high school or previously in college).

....

....

....

....

....

....

Which aspect of this study-reading approach is most appealing to you? Why?

....

....

....

....

....

....

Which aspect is least appealing? Why?

....

....

....

....

....

What problems do you foresee in using the entire study-reading plan? How might you overcome these problems?

....

....

....

....

....

....

CHAPTER

Making the Grade

CHAPTER OUTLINE

Exams: The Long View

Planning Your Approach

How to Study for Exams

Taking the Test

KEYS TO SUCCESS

- Show up for class.
- Assess and improve your study habits.
- Study with a group.
- See your instructors outside class.
- Improve your critical thinking skills.
- Be the best writer you can be.
- Learn what helping resources your campus offers and where they are.
- Try to have realistic expectations.

Three tests in the next two days! I am never going to live through this week. I mean, I did everything they said about how to read and how to take notes. Now here I am walking into class and my mind is a total blank. Help!

Now that you've learned how to listen and take notes in class and how to read and review your notes and assigned readings, you're ready to put those skills to use so that you'll do your best on exams. Just as there are a number of right and wrong ways to take notes and read texts, there also are certain study methods that work better than others.

EXAMS: THE LONG VIEW

Your preparation for a test began on the first day of the term. All of your lecture notes, assigned text pages, and homework problems were part of that preparation. As the test day nears, it is important to know how much additional time you will need to review, what material the test will cover, and what format the test will take.

Three things will help you study well: good communication with your instructor, effective time management, and organization of your materials. Audit your study practices to see if you are strong in each of these areas.

SEE EXERCISE 8.1

- Have you learned everything you need to know from your instructor about the purpose, conditions, and content of the exam? Have you talked with your instructor to clarify any misunderstandings you may have about the content of the course?
- Have you laid out a schedule that will give you the time you need to review effectively for the exam, without waiting until the night before?
- Have your study patterns created a body of material from which you can effectively review the material that is likely to be on the exam? Have you collaborated with other students in a study group or as study partners who can work with you now on final preparations?

PLANNING YOUR APPROACH

Physical Preparation

1. **Maintain your regular sleep routine.** Don't cut back on your sleep in order to cram in additional study hours. Remember that most tests will require you to apply the concepts that you have studied, and in order to do that effectively, you must have all your brain power available.
2. **Maintain your regular exercise program.** Walking, jogging, swimming, or other aerobic activities are effective stress reducers and provide positive—and needed— breaks from studying.
3. **Eat right.** Avoid drinking more than one or two caffeinated drinks a day or eating foods that are high in sugar. Eat fruits, vegetables, and foods that are high in complex carbohydrates so that you won't experience highs and lows in your energy level.

Emotional Preparation

1. **Know your material.** If you have given yourself adequate time to review terms, concepts, and formulas, you will find that you can enter the classroom confident that you are in control.

2. **Practice relaxing.** Some students have taught themselves to feel anxious about taking a test. They often experience an upset stomach, sweaty palms, a racing heart, or other unpleasant physical symptoms. A relaxation technique like the one in Chapter 17 can help. Your counseling center probably offers relaxation training sessions, especially near exam time.

3. **Use positive self-talk or affirmation.** You can choose to pay attention to the negative statements you are saying to yourself, such as "I never do well on math tests," or "I'll never be able to learn all the information for my history essay exam," and replace them with positive statements, such as "I have attended all the lectures, done my homework, and passed the quizzes. Now I'm ready to pass the test!"

Find Out About the Test

It is at best inefficient and could be disastrous to prepare for the wrong type of exam. Ask whether it will be essay, multiple choice, true-false, or another kind of test. Ask your instructor how long the test will last and how it will be graded. Some instructors may let you see copies of old exams. By finding out and practicing the same types of questions, you will be more confident. Never miss the last class before an exam, because your instructor may summarize valuable information that you will need to know.

Design an Exam Plan

SEE EXERCISE 8.2

Use the information about the test as you design a plan for preparing. Build that preparation into the master plan and schedule you created in Chapter 4. Develop a to-do list of the major steps you need to take in order to be ready, ideally including a study group or other resources listed below. For the week before the exam, be sure to lay out a schedule of one-hour blocks of time for review along with notes on what you specifically plan to accomplish during each block.

**SEE EXERCISE 8.3
INTERNET ACTIVITY**

Search Online!

**Try these phrases and others for Key Words and Subject Guide searches:
"mnemonics," "memory," "examinations."**

Also look up:

Improve your memory. (includes memory quizzes and related articles on remembering names and humor) Kalia Doner, Ralph Schoenstein. *American Health* March 1994 v13 n2 p56(6)

Testing for truth: Joseph Conrad and the ideology of the examination. *CLIO* Spring 1994 v23 n3 p271(14)

INFOTRAC COLLEGE EDITION

Personal Emergency? Your Instructor Needs to Know

Emergencies happen. Even if your instructor has warned you that there is no excuse for missing a quiz or turning in a late paper, he or she may bend the rules in a true emergency. Here are some things you can do to soften the consequences of missing class or an exam:

1. **Let your instructor know about a recurring medical condition that may occasionally keep you home unexpectedly.** Make it clear you are not asking for relief from required work but for some allowance for turning in work late if necessary.

2. **Get phone numbers and/or e-mail addresses in advance.** If possible, leave word. Many faculty have answering machines and will get your message even if they're not in the office when you call. Leave a number where you can be reached. If you don't know where you'll be, leave the number of a friend or relative who could relay the message to you. At some colleges your academic advisor or counselor or the student services office can distribute a memo to all of your instructors to inform them of your emergency, especially if you will be missing classes for a week or more.

3. **When you know in advance you can't make a class, tell the instructor as soon as possible.** There's a possibility that you can turn in work early or make up work when you return.

Even if you missed an important quiz or deadline for dubious reasons, let your instructor know anyway. It's better to admit you overslept or even forgot a paper was due or left the essay at home than to get a zero. You may be surprised how willing your instructor is to help you in your dilemma.

Join a Study Group

As we noted in Chapter 2, joining a study group or finding a study partner is critical to success. Ask your instructor, advisor, or tutoring center to help you identify interested students and decide on guidelines for the group. Study groups help students develop better study techniques. In addition, students benefit from different views of instructors' goals, objectives, and emphasis; have partners to quiz on facts and concepts; and gain the enthusiasm and friendship of others to help sustain their motivation.

Study groups can meet all semester, or they can form to review for midterms or final exams. Group members should complete their homework or assignments before the group meets and prepare study questions or points of discussion ahead of time. If your study group decides to meet just before exams, allow enough time to share notes and ideas. Together, devise a list of potential questions for review. Then each of you should spend time studying alone to develop answers, outlines, and mind maps. The group should then reconvene shortly before the test to share answers and review.

SEE EXERCISE 8.4

Tutoring and Other Support

If you think tutoring is just for failing students, you're wrong! Often excellent students seek tutorial assistance to insure their A's. Struggling students can benefit greatly by modeling their studying techniques after tutors. Large lecture classes are often the norm for first-year general education requirements. Students have limited opportunity to question instructors. Tutors know the highlights and pitfalls of the course. Many tutoring services are free. Ask your academic advisor/counselor or campus learning center.

Most academic support centers or learning centers have computer labs that can provide assistance for course work. Some offer walk-in assistance for help in using word processing, spreadsheet, or statistical computer programs. Often computer tutorials are available to help students refresh basic skills. Math and English grammar programs may also be available, as well as access to the Internet.

■ HOW TO STUDY FOR EXAMS

If you have been using the note-taking and study-reading methods prescribed in these chapters, you will be able to make the best use of the critical days before a test. This assumes that you have recorded the key ideas from the text using a map or an outline and have created a recall column with study questions in your notebook or margins of your text.

Through the steady use of recall columns and recite-and-review techniques, you already will have processed and learned most of what you need to know. As you prepare for the test, you can focus your study efforts on the most challenging concepts, practice recalling information, and familiarize yourself with details.

Recall Sheets and Mind Maps

In preparing for an exam covering large amounts of material, you need to condense the volume of notes and text pages into manageable study units. Review your materials with these questions in mind: Is this one of the key ideas in the chapter or unit? Will I see this on the test? Some students like to highlight the most important ideas; others like to create recall sheets and mind maps containing only the key ideas.

Recall sheets summarizing main ideas can be organized chapter by chapter or according to the major themes in the course. Look for relationships between ideas. Try to condense your recall sheets to just one page of essential information. Key words on this page can call up blocks of information previously studied.

A mind map is essentially a recall sheet with a visual element. Its word and visual patterns provide you with highly charged clues to jog your memory. Because they are visual, mind maps help many students recall information more easily.

Figure 8.1 shows what a mind map might look like for Chapter 6, "Listening and Learning in the Classroom." Take time to study and recite from the map to put the information in your long-term memory. Visualizing the mind map during the test will help recall the information you need.

Figure 8.1 Sample Mind Map on Listening and Learning in the Classroom

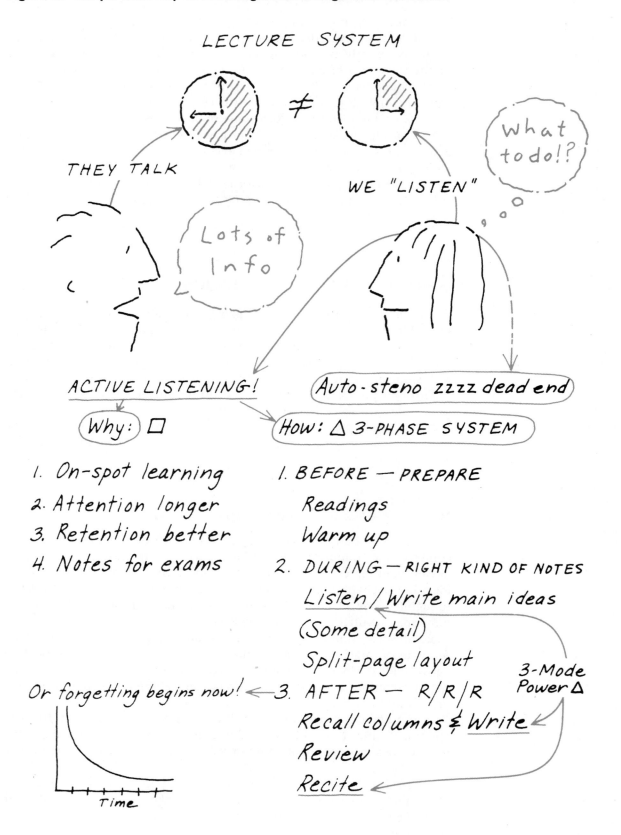

Summaries

SEE EXERCISE 8.5

A written summary is one of the best techniques for improving memory and recall. This technique is especially helpful when preparing for essay and short-answer exams. By condensing the main ideas of a longer document, or from several sources, into a concise written summary in your own words, you store this information in your long-term memory so it can be retrieved to answer an essay question. Here is the process:

1. **Predict a test question from your lecture notes or other resources.**

2. **Read the chapter, article, notes, or other resources.** Use a combination of materials, if needed. Underline or mark main ideas as you go or make notations on a separate sheet.

3. **Analyze and abstract.** What is the purpose of the material? Does it compare, define a concept, or prove an idea? What are the main ideas?

4. **Make connections between main points and key supporting details.** Reread to identify each main point and supporting evidence. Analyze the author's argument for bias or insufficient details.

5. **Select, condense, order.** Review underlined material and begin putting the ideas into your own words. Number what you underlined in a logical order.

6. **Write your ideas precisely in a draft.** In the first sentence, state the purpose of your summary. Follow with each main point and its supporting ideas.

7. **Rewrite.** Read it over, adding missing transitions or insufficient information. Check the logic of your summary. Annotate with the material you used for later reference.

8. **Make a brief outline of key ideas of your summary.** Start with your posed question or purpose statement. Number each main point. Associate supporting evidence with each main idea. Use flash cards for your outline. Memorize your outline to help you recall the information.

Aids to Memory

Thirty days hath September, April, June, and November. . .
Doe a deer, a female deer. Ray, a drop of golden sun.
A pint's a pound, the world around.

The human mind has discovered ingenious ways to remember information. Here are some methods that may be useful to you when you're nailing down the causes of the Civil War, trying to remember the steps in a physics problem, or absorbing a mathematical formula.

1. **Overlearn.** Even after you know the material, go over it again to make sure you'll retain it for a long time.

2. **Categorize.** If the information seems to lack an inherent organization, impose one. Most information can be organized in some way, even if only by the look or sound of the words.

3. **Draw a mind map** (see the previous discussion in this chapter). Arrange the main topics on a single sheet of paper and connect the points in logical fashion by arrows, dots, and so forth. Large points are

written in large boxes or circles, smaller points in smaller ones. Sub-groups are placed under major headings. Drawing relationships on paper—even faces, objects, or stick figures—can help you visualize them later.

To remember limited amounts of specific details, try one or more of these methods, reminding yourself that they are more likely to help you remember lists of facts rather than relationships between facts:

4. **Use mnemonics.** Create rhymes, jingles, sayings, or nonsense phrases that repeat or codify information. "Homes" is a mnemonic for remembering the five Great Lakes: Huron, Ontario, Michigan, Erie, and Superior. "Spring forward, fall back" tells many Americans how to set their clocks. Setting a rhyme to music is one of the most powerful ways to make words memorable.

5. **Associate.** Relate the idea to something you already know. Make the association as personal as possible. If you're reading a chapter on laws regarding free speech, pretend that your right to speak out on a subject that's important to you may be affected by those laws. In remembering the spelling difference between *through* and *threw,* think of walking through something "rough," and that "threw" comes from "throw."

6. **Peg.** Visualize in order a number of locations or objects in your home. To remember a list of things, associate each item in the list with one of the locations or objects. For example, let's memorize three classic appeals of advertising (appetite, fear, and sexual attraction):

   - *Appetite:* The first peg is the kitchen countertop. Visualize some creature devouring your favorite chocolate cake.
   - *Fear:* The second peg is the coat rack. Visualize a menacing coat rack running after you.
   - *Sexual attraction:* The third peg is a sofa. Think about it.

7. **Visualize.** Make yourself see the things that you've associated with important concepts. Concentrate on the images so they'll become firmly planted in your memory.

8. **Use flash cards.** Write the word or information to be learned on one side and the definition or explanation on the other. Review the cards often. Prepare them early and spend more time on the hard ones.

SEE EXERCISE 8.6
INTERNET ACTIVITY

▌TAKING THE TEST

1. **Focus on the test.**
   - Read all the directions so that you understand what to do.
   - Ask for clarification if you don't understand something.
   - Be confident.
   - Don't panic! Answer one question at a time.

2. **Make the best use of your time.** Quickly survey the entire test and decide how much time you will spend on each section.

3. **Answer the easy questions first.** Expect that you'll be puzzled by some questions. Make a note to come back to them later.

4. **If you finish early, don't leave.** Stay and check your work for errors.

© SETH RESNICK/STOCK, BOSTON/PNI

Essay Exams

Although you will take objective (multiple choice, matching, and true-false) exams in college, the editors of this book have a strong preference for the essay exam for a simple reason: It promotes higher-order critical thinking, whereas other types of exams tend to be exercises in memorization. Why do some instructors use objective tests, then? It may have to do with the size of the class. Grading over 100 essay exams might take days, whereas objective exams can be machine scored and returned quickly. Generally, the closer you are to graduation, the more essay exams you'll take.

1. **Budget your exam time.** Quickly survey the entire exam and note the questions that are the easiest for you, along with their point values. Take a moment to weigh their values, estimate the approximate time you should allot to each question, and write the time beside each number. No rule says you must answer the questions in chronological order. To build confidence, start with the questions that are easiest for you. It can be a costly error to write profusely on easy questions of low value that take up precious time you may need on more important questions. Be sure to wear a watch so you can monitor your time for each question. Allow time at the end for a quick review of your writing.

2. **Write focused, organized answers.** The summary writing process should help you stay organized during an essay exam. In your quick survey of the test, did you find questions that you were prepared to answer? If so, quickly jot down your memorized outline for such questions. This action both relieves pressure to remember and also saves time; the answer is now waiting for your full attention. Many well-prepared students write fine answers to questions that may not have been asked. This problem stems from not reading a question carefully. Others hastily write down everything they know on a topic. Answers that are vague and tend to ramble will be downgraded by instructors. Avoid these pitfalls by learning to write focused, organized answers.

3. **Know the key task words in essay questions.** Being familiar with the key word in an essay question will help you answer it more specifically. The following key task words are most frequently asked on essay

tests. Take time to learn them, so that you can answer essay questions more accurately and precisely.

Analyze: to divide something into its parts in order to understand it better. Show how the parts work together to produce the overall pattern.

Compare: to look at the characteristics or qualities of several things and identify their similarities. "Compare" is often intended to imply that you may also contrast them.

Contrast: to identify the differences between things.

Criticize/Critique: to analyze and judge something. Criticism can be either positive or negative. A criticism should generally contain your own judgments (supported by evidence) and those of other authorities who can support your point.

Define: to give the meaning of a word or expression. Giving an example of something sometimes helps to clarify a definition, but giving an example is not in itself a definition.

Describe: to give a general verbal sketch of something, in narrative or other form.

Discuss: to examine or analyze something in a broad and detailed way. Discussion often includes identifying the important questions related to an issue and attempting to answer these questions. A good discussion explores all relevant evidence and information.

Evaluate: to discuss the strengths and weaknesses of something. Evaluation is similar to criticism, but the word *evaluate* places more stress on the idea of how well something meets a certain standard or fulfills some specific purpose.

Explain: to clarify or interpret something. Explanations generally focus on why or how something has come about.

Illustrate: to give one or more examples of something, either in words or in diagrams.

Interpret: to explain the meaning of something. In science you might explain what an experiment shows and what conclusions can be drawn from it. In a literature course you might explain—or interpret—what a poem means beyond the literal meaning of the words.

Justify: to argue in support of some decision or conclusion by showing sufficient evidence or reason in its favor. Whenever possible, try to support your argument with both logic and concrete examples.

Narrate: to relate a series of events in the order in which they occurred. Generally, you will also be asked to explain something about the events you are narrating.

Outline: to present a series of main points in appropriate order, omitting lesser details. An outline shows the order and grouping of ideas.

Prove: to give a convincing logical argument and evidence in support of the truth of some statement.

Review: to summarize and comment on the main parts of a problem or a series of statements. A review question usually also asks you to evaluate or criticize.

Summarize: to give information in brief form, omitting examples and details. A summary is short yet covers all of the most important points.

SEE EXERCISE 8.7

Trace: to narrate a course of events. Where possible, you should show connections from one event to the next.

If you've set realistic goals and used good study techniques, chances are you'll make high marks.

PHOTO BY LYNN HOWLETT PHOTOGRAPHY

Multiple-Choice Exams

Preparing for multiple-choice tests requires you to actively review all of the material covered in the course. Reciting from flash cards, summary sheets, or mind maps is a good way to review large amounts of material.

Take advantage of the many cues that multiple-choice questions contain. Careful reading of each item may uncover the correct answer. Always question choices that use absolute words such as *always, never,* and *only.* These choices are often incorrect. Also, read carefully for terms such as *not, except,* and *but* that are introduced before the choices. Be sure to choose the answer that is the most inclusive of the choices after carefully reading them all.

True-False Exams

Here are some hints that may help you on true-false questions. For the question to be true, every detail of the question must be true. Questions containing words such as *always, never,* and *only* are usually false, whereas less definite terms such as *often* and *frequently* suggest the statement may be true. As with multiple-choice questions, read through the entire exam to see if information in one question will help you answer a question of which you are unsure.

Matching Exams

The matching question is the hardest to answer by guessing. In one column you will find the term, in the other the description of it. Before answering any question, review all of the terms or descriptions. Match those terms you are sure of first. As you do so, cross out both the term and its description.

In summary, good listening, good note-taking, and good study habits add up to good grades. You need not study every waking hour of the day or night; that can be disastrous. At the same time, we hope you won't be tempted to party on the evening when studying matters most. The time to celebrate is after you know you've aced the exam. You've earned it.

EXERCISE 8.1 **Test-Taking Inventory**

Place a check mark in front of the sentence in each pair that best describes you.

_____ 1a. I always study for essay tests by developing questions and outlines.

_____ 1b. I rarely study for essay tests by developing questions and outlines.

_____ 2a. I always begin studying for an exam at least a week in advance.

_____ 2b. I rarely begin studying for an exam a week in advance.

_____ 3a. I usually study for an exam with at least one other person.

_____ 3b. I rarely study for an exam with another person.

_____ 4a. I usually know what to expect on a test before I go into the exam.

_____ 4b. I rarely know what to expect on a test before I go into the exam.

_____ 5a. I usually finish an exam early or on time.

_____ 5b. I sometimes do not have enough time to finish an exam.

_____ 6a. I usually know that I have done well on an exam when I finish.

_____ 6b. I rarely know whether I have done well on an exam when I finish.

_____ 7a. I usually perform better on essay tests than on objective tests.

_____ 7b. I usually perform better on objective tests than on essay tests.

Write a paragraph about yourself as a test-taker based on your answers to this inventory and your general feelings about taking tests.

EXERCISE 8.2 **Designing an Exam Plan**

Consult the master plan you created in Chapter 4. Use the following guidelines to design an exam plan for one of your courses:

1. What are the characteristics of the exam?

_____

What material will be covered?

_____

What type of questions will it contain?

_____

How many questions will there be?

_____

What is the grading system?

_____

2. Identify the approach you intend to use to study for this exam.

_____

3. How much time and how many study sessions will you need?

_____

4. Using your to-do list format, list all material to be covered.

_____

What still needs to be read?

_____

5. Using the timetable you created in Chapter 4, create a study schedule for the week prior to the exam, allowing as many one-hour blocks for review as you need and specifically stating what you need to do.

EXERCISE 8.3
INTERNET
ACTIVITY

Online Exam Schedules

Find out whether your college publishes examination schedules online as a World Wide Web page or in some other electronic form. If it does, get access to the schedule for the next examination period. Record the information for your exams on your calendar.

EXERCISE 8.4

Forming a Study Group

Use the goal-setting process from Chapter 1 to form a study group for at least one of your courses this term. As you do this, think about your strengths and weaknesses in a learning or studying situation. For instance, do you excel at memorizing facts but find it difficult to comprehend theories? Do you learn best by repeatedly reading the information or by applying the knowledge to a real situation? Do you prefer to learn by processing information in your head or by participating in a hands-on demonstration? Make some notes about your learning and studying strengths and weaknesses here.

Strengths: _____

_____

Weaknesses: _____

_____

In a study group how will your strengths help others? What strengths will you look for in others that will help you?

How you can help others: _____

_____

How others can help you: _____

_____

In your first study group session, suggest that each person share his or her strengths and weaknesses and talk about how abilities might be shared for everyone's maximum benefit.

EXERCISE 8.5

Writing a Summary

Using underlining, highlighting, and margin notes for reference, write a summary of this chapter (or some other material) following the directions for summary writing. Exchange your summary with another student to discuss how well you summarized the material.

EXERCISE 8.6
INTERNET
ACTIVITY

Memory

Use the internet to learn more about using mnemonic devices as memory aids. Answer the following questions after checking this web site:
http://home.att.net/~barrett.evolution/Super.Learning/Memory.html

1. Name an effective way to make associations.
2. Name an effective way to remember names of people.
3. Describe methods of pegging as a memory device.
4. Describe a method for remembering numbers.
(Go to *http://csuccess.wadsworth.com* for the most up-to-date URLs.)

EXERCISE 8.7 Key on Task Words

Essay questions may require quite different responses, depending on their key task words. Discuss the following in class. In your discussion, include what each task word is asking you to do and how it differs from the other two listed here.

1. How would you define the purposes of this chapter?

_____

_____

_____

_____

2. How would you evaluate the purposes of this chapter?

_____

_____

_____

_____

3. How would you justify the purposes of this chapter?

_____

_____

_____

_____

SUGGESTIONS FOR FURTHER READING

Campbell, William E. *The Power to Learn: Helping Yourself to College Success,* "Remembering and Reproducing What You Learn" (Chapter 6). Belmont, CA: Wadsworth, 1997.

Galica, Gregory S. *The Blue Book: A Student's Guide to Essay Exams.* Troy, MO: Harcourt Brace Jovanovich, 1991.

Longman, Debbie Guice, & Rhonda Holt Atkinson. *College Learning and Study Skills,* 3rd ed., "Tests: Preparing for and Taking Them" (Chapter 7). Minneapolis/St. Paul: West, 1993.

McKowen, Clark. *Get Your A Out of College: Mastering the Hidden Rules of the Game,* rev. ed., "The Art of Remembering" (Chapter 2) and "Raising Test Scores" (Chapter 3). Menlo Park, CA: Crisp Publications, 1996.

Pauk, Walter. *How to Study in College,* 8th ed., "Mastering Objective Tests" (Chapter 15). Boston: Houghton Mifflin, 1997.

RESOURCES

Motivation and confidence are key to success on exams. Building on the reward idea from the Resources page in Chapter 7, think of some really nice ways to congratulate yourself for exams well done.

Write a list of celebrations and rewards for finishing quizzes, exams, and papers.

....

....

....

....

....

....

Make a list of your exams, quizzes, and papers here. For each one, add one of the celebration ideas.

....

....

....

....

....

....

....

....

....

Go to the calendars you made in Chapter 4, "Time Management." Put your celebrations into your calendars. Make sure that you actually do them, too. Sometimes, highly motivated students put off rewarding themselves for a job well done for so long that they burn themselves out, or forget why they want to be in college, or lose touch with their successes. Even if it's only a mental affirmation, right after the test or speech, pat yourself on the back; it's important.

Visit your academic skills center and study their resources. Write what you learned.

....

....

....

....

....

....

....

JOURNAL

NAME _____

DATE _____

If you have already taken at least one exam, reflect on how it went. If you haven't, complete this page after you take an exam.

What strategies did you use to prepare? How well did they work?

....

....

....

....

Did you get the results you were aiming for? If not, why not?

....

....

....

....

What specific strategies from this chapter might you want to apply on your next exam?

....

....

....

....

Think about yourself as a student. How do you prepare for an exam or quiz?

....

....

....

....

How well does your method work? What comments have instructors made to you about your grades?

....

....

....

....

CHAPTER

The Information Environment I: Your Campus Library

CHAPTER OUTLINE

Get a Grip on the Library

Finding Your Way

World Wide Web Information Resources

KEYS TO SUCCESS

- Assess and improve your study habits.
- "See" your instructors outside class (using e-mail).
- Improve your critical thinking skills.
- Know how to find and work with information on your campus.
- Learn what helping resources your campus offers and where they are.

" I've heard about people who've been lost for years in the New York City Public Library. They just go in and never come out. They fall asleep and die, or else they get slimed like those guys did in Ghostbusters. *Actually, I kind of like the long, tall rows of books. They seem to absorb all human sound, like snow. I even like the CD-ROMs and computers, except they don't have any games on them. I don't mind libraries. I just never seem to know what I'm looking for or how to find it. "*

What makes the information age exciting and potentially empowering for millions of people is not that information has just been invented or that people are just beginning to look for it. Rather, it's the amount and diversity of information that is available through innumerable sources, the ease and speed with which you can obtain this information, and the incredible possibilities for applying it to everyday situations.

The growth of computer technology has had a tremendous impact on libraries. Most campus libraries now use computerized library catalogs or networks rather than the traditional card catalog. Many libraries also provide access to resources like the Internet, online computer databases, and CD-ROMs, in addition to the library's typical printed sources.

The growth of your critical thinking skills in college will depend a great deal on how much and how well you learn to use your campus library. Abundant and valid information is the starting point for thinking effectively in any academic field. The power of your arguments will depend on how well you can support them with facts and data. Hearing or reading numerous competing arguments about a question is a great way to begin creating sound arguments of your own.

If you have any concerns about using the library, you should certainly address them. A lack of good information-gathering skills may adversely affect you not only in the classroom but in other areas, including your career beyond college.

■ GET A GRIP ON THE LIBRARY

Familiarize yourself with your library system before you have to use it. Is there more than one library on campus? If so, is one geared toward helping undergraduates? Does your library offer tours? Your class may be able to schedule one to discover what some of the services and various departments offer you. Maybe your library offers an orientation via a computer system.

Does your library have handouts describing various services and different library departments and their hours? Get these handouts. Note the different library departments that might interest you—for example, government documents, reserve, interlibrary loan, or a special collection devoted to one subject area.

Selecting and Surveying a Topic

Whether or not your instructor has assigned a topic, it's best to visit the library with one in mind. Finding a topic is not always easy. If this is difficult for you, focus on selecting something in which you are genuinely interested. Go through your course materials for ideas. You can also use the process for finding a topic described in Chapter 3. Browse through recent newspapers and newsmagazines. Also, talk to your instructor or your peers. Some libraries have books listing possible research topics, or you may ask a librarian.

Remember that defining and refining your topic is one of the objectives of research. When you visit the library, your goal should be to survey the topic and obtain ideas on how you might want to develop it. When you don't have a clear sense of what you are looking for, give yourself time to reflect before trying to find information.

While surveying the topic, ask "Does there seem to be enough information? Is there too much?" If there is not enough information, consider a broader approach. If there is too much, try zeroing in on one aspect of a more general topic. Instead of looking for information on crime, you might want to focus on a particular crime—relationship violence, for example—and examine how the police are responding to it.

Defining Your Need for Information

Begin to gather information by asking yourself several questions before you begin your information search. Carefully thinking through your topic will not only help you focus but also help you communicate your needs to a librarian. Sometimes the following questions may be difficult to answer when you are starting out. Don't worry. Try talking through your topic with a friend or consulting a librarian or your instructor.

1. **What do you already know about your topic?** Consider names, events, dates, places, terms, and relationships to other topics.

2. **Who would be writing about your topic?** For example, what scholars, researchers, professionals in specific fields, or other groups of people might be interested?

3. **What do you want to know about this topic?** Asking this question further focuses your research or your assignment. Sometimes your first question may be too general and not easily answered.

4. **What is the vocabulary of your topic?** What words describe it? Are there specialized terms for which you could search?

5. **What do you want to do with this information?** Are you writing a research paper, giving a speech, or preparing for a debate or an interview? Knowing how you plan to use the information will help you determine how much information you need and where to look.

6. **What are the characteristics of the information you need to find?** Characteristics or qualities of information don't necessarily fall into discrete categories but can occur in combinations or along a continuum:

   - **Introductory:** general information on a topic, written for an audience without prior knowledge of the topic
   - **In-depth:** specialized and detailed information on a topic, written for those with prior or special knowledge of the topic

PHOTO BY ANGELA MANN

Libraries everywhere have been computerizing their catalogs. In many cases, however, not all resources are listed yet in the computer. Ask a librarian about sources that may not show up on the screen.

- **Biographical:** about someone but by another person
- **Autobiographical:** about someone and by that same person
- **Current:** about an event or idea that just occurred
- **Contemporary:** a perspective written at the time an event occurred
- **Retrospective:** a reflection written about an event from the past
- **Summative:** summarizing or giving an overview of a topic
- **Argumentative or Persuasive:** expressing a strong point of view
- **Analytical:** breaking an idea into its components

Tips on Talking to Librarians

1. **Recognize that librarians are usually more than willing to help you.** Know that they can save you time and effort.

2. **Don't feel you have to know everything about a topic.** You also don't have to know every aspect of using the library or any specialized language or jargon. When a librarian uses a term you do not know, ask for clarification.

3. **Accept responsibility for your work.** Librarians will expect you to know what your assignment is; to bring relevant assignment sheets, class notes, textbooks, and so on; to make decisions about the usefulness of sources; to ask questions; and to discuss what steps you have already taken.

SEE EXERCISE 9.1

4. **Not all librarians are alike.** Different librarians have different communication styles and areas of expertise. If you are not satisfied after talking to one librarian, seek another.

5. **Ask as many questions as you need to.** Librarians do not have a quota for the number of questions you may ask.

6. **Word your requests carefully.** Ask for what you want and be descriptive. In most cases the librarian will interview you to determine how to meet your needs.

7. **Don't worry if your topic is controversial or personal.** Librarians have a professional responsibility to treat your request confidentially.

Research Tips

1. **Come to the library prepared with the necessary supplies:** paper, notecards, pen or pencil, computer disks for downloading, your college ID, and cash for photocopying.

2. **Be clear in your notes if you are taking down information verbatim (direct quotes) or if you are paraphrasing.** Be wary of plagiarizing, which is using someone else's ideas or specific words without giving that person credit.

3. **Write down all appropriate information about sources.** This avoids unnecessary and frustrating backtracking when it comes time to write up your bibliography or cite your sources.

4. **If the necessary sources are not on the shelf, ask for help.** They may be misshelved, checked out, or available in another library through interlibrary loan, a service that finds the material in another library and then borrows it for you.

5. **Start early.** Allow yourself the time it will take to gather sources before you have to write the paper.

■ FINDING YOUR WAY

General Encyclopedias

Although general encyclopedias, such as *Encyclopaedia Brittanica,* are useful tools for getting you started, instructors will not want you to rely on them as the major source for the papers you submit. Using an encyclopedia as a starting point, you should seek information in other sources. Good encyclopedias have bibliographies that can be useful. Your campus may have an electronic encyclopedia available on compact disc or via the World Wide Web.

Subject Encyclopedias

Subject encyclopedias are constructed the same way as general encyclopedias, but they are more specialized. They concentrate on a narrower field of knowledge and cover it in greater depth. Although more focused than general encyclopedias, the information they contain within their fields is still fairly general, and you should not stop your research here.

The subject encyclopedias listed here are grouped by general areas. This is not a comprehensive list. If you cannot find a title that fits your area of interest, ask a librarian to suggest one. You can also search the library catalog. Try a key-word search using your subject and the word "encyclopedias":

Arts

The New Grove Dictionary of Music and Musicians
The Dictionary of Art
McGraw-Hill Encyclopedia of World Drama

Current Events and Social Issues

CQ Researcher

Humanities

Dictionary of Literary Biography
Encyclopedia of Philosophy
Encyclopedia of Bioethics
Encyclopedia of Religion
Handbook of American Popular Culture

History

Encyclopedia of American Social History
Encyclopedia of African American Culture and History
Dictionary of American History

Social Sciences

International Encyclopedia of the Social Sciences
Encyclopedia of Educational Research
International Encyclopedia of Communications
Encyclopedia of American Economic History
Encyclopedia of American Foreign Policy
Encyclopedia of Psychology
Encyclopedia of Sociology
Guide to American Law
Encyclopedia of Human Behavior

Natural Sciences

McGraw-Hill Encyclopedia of Science and Technology
Encyclopedia of Computer Sciences

Catalogs

A catalog lists what a library owns. If you want to know what books, magazines, videos, and so on, a library has, check the catalog. Your library's catalog may be a traditional card catalog; it may be computerized; it could be a combination of cards and computers; or it could even be available on microform (microfiche or microfilm) or in another format. You also may be able to gain electronic access or log on to your catalog without even going to the library.

Search Online!

INFOTRAC COLLEGE EDITION

Try these phrases and others for Key Words and Subject Guide searches: "library," "liberal arts," "college library." Use PowerTrac to see the index of encyclopedias available on InfoTrac College Edition.

Also look up:

A "disconnect" between academic librarians and students. (includes related article on online searching) Maribeth Ward. *Computers in Libraries* Nov-Dec 1996 v16 n10 p22(2)

You never told us what to do when the roof leaks: a professor and student take a tongue-in-cheek look at some holes in library education. Charles Curran, Laura Kelley. *American Libraries* Sep 1996 v27 n8 p62(2)

In its quiet way, having explored the "stacks" of the library may become one of your fondest memories of college. But you'll get the most out of your exploration if you've prepared well beforehand by exploring catalogs and indexes.

PHOTO COURTESY OF UNIVERSITY OF CONNECTICUT

Indexes

Indexes identify articles in periodicals. The most common periodicals you will use are newspapers, magazines, and journals. Because articles are published more frequently and more quickly than books, they often contain more current information. When you look in an index, you do not actually find the article itself: You find a citation listing the author(s), title of the article, title of the magazine or journal, date of the issue, and volume and page numbers. Some indexes, called abstracts, also provide a short summary of the article's content, which can tell you if the article is relevant.

Your library may also have a computerized version of a particular index, and some of these indexes may contain the full text of the articles.

MAGAZINE AND NEWSPAPER INDEXES

If you want to find articles written for the general public or a popular audience, use an index for magazines or newspapers. Some computerized indexes may cover a wide range of articles from magazines, newspapers, and journals. Depending on the time period, your index might not be available on the computer. The index for *The New York Times* begins in 1851 and *Readers' Guide to Periodical Literature* goes back to 1900.

LIBRARY OF CONGRESS SUBJECT HEADINGS

If you have trouble finding the right subject headings, you may want to consult an official list, such as that found in the set of volumes entitled the *Library of Congress Subject Heading,* or LCSH. If your term is not a preferred subject heading, LCSH will refer you to appropriate terms. For instance, if you look up the term "College life," LCSH will tell you to use the term "College students." LCSH will also offer related terms and even subheadings or subject divisions once you have located the preferred subject heading. Ask a librarian for help using the LCHS.

SUBJECT OR SPECIALIZED INDEXES

Your instructors probably expect you to use scholarly sources for most of your library assignments. They may not be explicit about this expectation, so if it isn't clear be sure to ask. To find articles written by researchers or scholars in journals, you need only use a source that indexes these types of materials. If you aren't certain which subject index to use, ask a librarian to recommend one. The librarian will also show you how to use it to find the information you need.

Information Databases

Library catalogs and indexes are examples of databases. A database is a collection of records that is organized so that people can search it to find information. A cookbook could be called a database of recipes. When using a computer to find information, two little words are crucial in constructing key-word searches:

and   searches for both terms
       love and interpersonal
or   searches for either term
       love or intimacy

Remember your high school math? *And* is similar to the concept of intersection. Because both terms must be present, *and* narrows a search. Use *and* to target your search when your initial search finds too much. *Or* is like union and it is useful when you aren't finding much on your topic or when there are synonyms for your topic that you want to search at the same time.

If you use both *and* and *or* when entering a search, there is a tip you should know:—Enclose the terms you are joining with *or* in parentheses. For example, *(love or intimacy) and interpersonal*. This is called nesting, and it ensures that the computer does what you intend it to do. By using the parentheses, you are commanding the computer to look for either the word *love* or *intimacy* and to combine either word with the term *interpersonal*. In some computer systems, if you didn't nest the terms, the computer would find items that had both terms *intimacy* and *interpersonal* but would retrieve all occurrences of the word *love* whether *interpersonal* was included or not.

SEE EXERCISE 9.2

Periodicals

The most frequently asked questions in an academic library are about finding periodicals. Some libraries list their periodicals in the library catalog, whereas others keep a separate list. Even if you discover that your library owns a particular periodical, it isn't always obvious where it will be. For a variety of reasons some libraries shelve periodicals with books. Other libraries have a separate section for periodicals. Magazines and journals might be shelved by their call number or by title. Perhaps some years are available on microfilm whereas current issues are shelved in a different place.

SEE EXERCISE 9.3

■ WORLD WIDE WEB INFORMATION RESOURCES

The World Wide Web is rapidly becoming a resource of choice for students doing class papers. The web is an exciting and powerful way to communicate information through pictures, sounds, and text. What makes the web so engrossing is hypertext or hot links, which usually appear as buttons or words underlined in color. When you click on a link, the World Wide Web does the work of taking you to that section of a home page or connecting you to a different web site altogether.

Right now, the World Wide Web is a little like a library with all of the books piled all over the place in no order. The information may be there, but it can be difficult to sort through. No one is in charge of the World Wide Web, which is both an advantage and a disadvantage. The web is changing all the time, and you can't be sure that what you find today will be in the same place or even on the web tomorrow. Also, there is a great deal of previously published print information that is not yet available on the web.

To be an effective web searcher, you need to know strategies for efficient searching and evaluation of the information, and sometimes misinformation, you will find. Here are several key strategies for finding information on the web. Which one works best will depend upon your situation—what you are looking for and what you already know.

Going Directly to a Web Site

If you already know the address, called a URL (uniform resource locator), you can enter it into the location box of your browser. You must type in the exact URL, and capitalization matters. A URL has three main parts:

protocol domain name directory path
http://www.yahoo.com/Entertainment

Common endings for domain names include:

.com   for commercial sites
.edu   for sites made available by educational institutions
.gov   for government sites
.org   for sites created by organizations

Using a Subject Directory

A web directory leads you to web resources by organizing sites into various categories. Yahoo was one of the first web subject directories, and it is still a good way to browse the Internet. Use a directory when:

- You aren't really certain what might be on the web.
- Your topic is broad, or you can't be specific because you don't know much about the subject.
- The words you would use in your search are very general.

You can browse using the links provided by the directory or search for a word or phrase within the directory or section of the directory.

Using a Search Engine

A search engine is basically a large database of web sites previously found by a computer search. The problem with search engines is that you can easily be overwhelmed by the sheer amount of the search results.

No single search engine can find everything on the web, and they all work a little differently. It's a good idea to become proficient at first with one or two search engines. Some search engines will allow you to use *and* and *or* in constructing a search. The following additional searching conventions are also used by a variety of search engines.

- **You will change the results of your search if you enter capital letters.** Capital letters force an exact match, so usually it is a good idea to avoid using them.
- **To search for a phrase, you should enter your words in quotation marks.** Search *"census bureau"* instead of *census bureau*.
- **You can require that a term be present by typing a plus sign before the word.** To quickly find Lincoln's Gettysburg Address, a good search would be to enter *+ lincoln + gettysburg*.
- **You can also exclude words in the results by typing a minus sign before the word.** You want to find information on the country New Guinea, but your initial search finds lots of items of interest to guinea pig owners. Try the search *new guinea − pigs*.

To become a good searcher, it is wise to read the Help screens for a search engine. You'll also find some good advice at these two sites:

"Tips on Popular Search Engines"
http://www.hamline.edu/library/bush/handouts/slahandout.html
"Internet Searching Strategies"
http://riceinfo.rice.edu/Fondren/Netguides/strategies.html

**SEE EXERCISE 9.4
INTERNET ACTIVITY**

Some of the widely used search engines are:

Alta Vista   *http://www.altavista.digital.com/*
Infoseek   *http://www.infoseek.com/*
HotBot   *http://www.hotbot.com/*

(Go to *http://csuccess.wadsworth.com* for the most up-to-date URLs.)

Critical Thinking About Sources

Successfully gathering information involves more than just locating enough sources. It also involves critically evaluating articles, books, and other materials once you have found them. As the volume of available information increases daily, you should not settle for the first available sources, for they may not be as relevant as others; they may be dated; or they may be inaccurate. To evaluate a source you might ask:

- **Is the source relevant to my information needs?** Begin by looking at the title of the book or article, its length, the type of source you need, and the type that is available or that you have at hand.
- **Is the information in the source accurate?** If your topic is controversial, if you are relying on just a few sources, or if you are using a questionable fact, you might want to find some reviews or additional commentary to check on the accuracy of the information.
- **Does the author or the source show bias?** Consider why material was written or for whom it was written. When might you need to seek a different opinion?
- **Is the author credible and reliable?** What are the author's credentials? If you can't answer this question, see a reference librarian.
- **Is the information timely?** Using up-to-date information and statistics is important, especially in a field constantly undergoing change (for example, computer science, medicine, economics).

See Chapter 7 Exercise 7.2, for information on evaluating web sites.

EXERCISE 9.1

Some Possible Misconceptions

Look over the following list of common concerns and misconceptions about libraries and librarians:

- I should automatically know how to use the library.
- The library is too big, and I never find what I need.
- Librarians speak a language that only they understand.
- Librarians look too busy to help me.
- I don't know how to use the library's materials; its computers just make it more complicated.
- Librarians in the past haven't helped me.
- I hate doing research and writing papers.
- Doing research usually requires having to talk to someone and ask for help, which can be tough.

Think about your own experiences using libraries—both the rewarding ones and the challenging or frustrating ones. What are some of your concerns or feelings? Discuss them with others in a group. Of the items listed above, are there any that you would not consider misconceptions?

EXERCISE 9.2

Key-Word and Subject Searching

If your library has an online or computer catalog, see if you can search by key word and by subject.

A Using the word *love*, enter a key-word search.

How many hits or items did you retrieve?_____

Look at the information given about some of the items. Did you ever find "love" as an author?_____

How about as a subject, but not the emotion of love? _____

Where else did you find the word?

_____

_____

B Now using the same word, *love,* enter a subject search.

What were your results? How many items did the search find?

_____

_____

Did the catalog organize the results differently than it did for the key-word search? How?

_____

_____

EXERCISE 9.3

Getting Oriented to Periodicals

Find out how your library arranges the periodicals. It probably isn't obvious so don't be afraid to ask. Why do you think the periodicals are organized this way?

_____

**EXERCISE 9.4
INTERNET
ACTIVITY**

Finding Information on the World Wide Web

1. If you know the basics of how URLs are typically constructed, sometimes you can guess what they will be. What do you think is the URL for the Public Broadcasting Service—the network of public television stations? Check to see if this is correct.

   _____

   Try finding it by directly entering a URL into your web browser's location box.

2. Using the subject directory Yahoo (*http://www.yahoo.com/*), find the current exchange rate for foreign currencies. Describe the steps you took:

   _____

   _____

3. Still using Yahoo, find newspapers that have web sites from your local area or within your state. How did you go about trying to find this information? (There isn't necessarily just one route.)

   _____

   _____

   What is the URL for at least one local newspaper?

   _____

4. Using a search engine like Alta Vista (*http://www.altavista.digital.com/*) find statistics on violence in public schools. (Go to *http://csuccess. wadsworth.com* for the most up-to-date URLs.) Either try to put in words directly related to that topic or to think about who—what organizations or agencies—might make such information available and search for them. What searches did you try?

   _____

   _____

   Compare your experience with others in your class. What searches worked the best?

   _____

5. Now search for guidelines on how to cite web resources in a bibliography. List the URL for one good web site.

   _____

SUGGESTIONS FOR FURTHER READING

Kurland, Daniel J. *The Net, the Web, and You: All You Really Need to Know About the Internet and a Little Bit More.* Belmont, CA: Wadsworth, 1996.

Lubar, Steven D. *InfoCulture: The Smithsonian Book of Information Age Inventions.* Boston: Houghton Mifflin, 1993.

Roszak, Theodore. *The Cult of Information: The Folklore of Computers and the True Art of Thinking.* New York: Pantheon, 1986.

Wurman, Richard Saul. *Information Anxiety Is Produced by the Ever-Widening Gap.* New York: Doubleday, 1989.

RESOURCES

LIBRARY DATABASES

At your campus library or at a computer that is linked to the library, find out what databases are available on-line or on CD-ROM at the library. Fill out the following for ten different databases.

Name of database:	How to reach it:	Material it includes:	Nature of output (citations only, abstracts, on-screen text, downloadable computer files, etc.):

SEARCHING A TOPIC

Select a topic to research. If you are working on a paper in one of your classes, use that topic. Briefly answer the following questions as you go through your search:

1. What did I find on my topic in a general encyclopedia? How useful was it?

2. What subject encyclopedias pertain to my topic?

3. What did I find in them and how useful was it?

4. What did I find in the online library catalog that pertained to my topic?

5. How easy was it to find pertinent information in those sources?

6. What information did I find searching article databases' CD-ROMs? How useful was it?

7. How helpful were subject indexes in my search? What did I find there?

8. How helpful was a search on the World Wide Web? How did I judge the accuracy of the material I found there?

JOURNAL

NAME _____

DATE _____

What has been your biggest concern about finding information?

....

....

....

....

....

What steps have you taken to reduce that concern? If you haven't taken any steps, what should you be doing?

....

....

....

....

....

....

Who can you turn to for help in improving your information retrieval skills? If you're not certain, stop by at the reference desk of the campus library and tell the reference librarian what kind of help you need. Afterward, write how this helped (or didn't help) you.

....

....

....

....

Aside from getting a better grade on your papers, why do you think it is important to know how to do a proper information search—not only while you're in school, but later in life?

....

....

....

CHAPTER

The Information Environment II: Computing for Personal Success

KEYS TO SUCCESS

- Assess and improve your study habits.
- Choose instructors who actively involve you in learning (using e-mail to communicate with them).
- Improve your critical thinking skills.
- Know how to find and work with information on your campus.
- Learn what helping resources your campus offers and where they are.

*" Spreadsheets, databases, the World Wide Web, e-mail . . .
I never realized how many things you could do with computers. Still, my instructors keep warning me that a computer is only as good as the person using it. Wonder what
they mean by that? "*

Not too many years ago, students planning nontechnical majors
could, with some effort, avoid computers and information technology. No more! Regardless of your major or career plans, computers and information technology will be important tools and resources during your
college years—and beyond.

By the time you graduate from college, there will be new ways to use information technology that are difficult to imagine today. The World Wide
Web already provides electronic access to books, newspapers, and magazines, scientific and commercial data, pictures, audio and video recordings,
and other text and graphics. Soon, movies, interactive entertainment, and
more will enter our homes, schools, and offices through this medium. This
could provide tremendous benefits (or distractions!) for students.

Here we offer an introduction to some of the most obvious and accessible
applications of information technology at this time. As you become more
knowledgeable about the tools available today, you will also be better prepared to take advantage of future options and new technologies.

■ WHAT YOU NEED TO KNOW ABOUT COMPUTERS

If you had a computing class in high school, you probably learned something about bits, bytes, RAM, ROM, and other technical terms that help explain how a computer works. The traditional way of learning about
computers emphasizes the technical aspects rather than the applications
(how it works rather than what you can do with it). For most people, however, using a computer has become like driving a car: You don't really need
to know what's under the hood. Rather, you need a general sense of how
the car works—and how to make it work well for you. You also must know
what to do if the computer won't do what you need it to do.

One reassurance and a caution: In normal use, it is almost impossible for
you to damage a computer—unless, of course, you spill a drink on the key-
board or hit the machine angrily because it ate or destroyed some of your
work. Although you cannot break a computer through normal use, you
should understand that a computer can do major damage to your work: For
example, it can quickly (and completely) erase the term paper you labored
on late at night and through several weekends unless you get into the habit
of saving a file frequently.

When you need help, ask. Good helpers show you how rather than doing
it themselves. They also know how to explain things to you in a way that
you can understand. If they don't, ask questions. If they start messing with
your computer in an attempt to save you trouble, look for a different helper.

Ask for help. Good helpers will show you how rather than doing it themselves. They will also know how to explain things to you in a way that you can understand.

PHOTO BY ANGELA MANN

■ A COMPUTING STRATEGY

What Are Your Options?

Consider the following three choices to see which strategy will work best for you.

- **Option 1: The extended avoidance strategy.** Try to avoid computers completely. Eventually, however, you will encounter some situation in which it will be nearly impossible to proceed without computing skills. For most students, a term paper provides that occasion. Writing instructors will tell you that good writing is really good rewriting; word processing makes it easier to change, correct, modify, and amend your work. Additionally, once you become comfortable with word processing software, you'll probably find it easier to learn other computer applications.

  Extended avoidance involves major risks. Most faculty are using computers and information technology resources in their classes: sending students to computer labs to use various kinds of simulation software, assigning students to find resources on World Wide Web sites as part of the reading materials for a class, or using electronic mail to communicate with students outside class sessions. Technology today involves much more than word processing. If you consciously choose to avoid technology, you may lose out on some important aspects of your college learning.

- **Option 2: The "everybody's doing it" strategy.** Pay attention to what your peers are doing with computers and information technology. Look at other students who have career goals similar to yours and are majoring in the same field. Are 20 percent (or more) of them using computers for term papers and other class work? If so, perhaps you should begin to do the same. Having the same computer tools as many of your peers means that you are likely to have several people you can ask for help when you're having trouble.

- **Option 3: The leader of the pack strategy.** Become a technology expert. Your career goals or your personal interest in technology may prompt you to be among the first of your friends and peers to exploit the power of information technology. You might decide that you definitely need great information technology skills as you compete for jobs or academic opportunities. Find out if your institution has a formal program for training and managing student assistants who can help their peers and even faculty learn to use information technology.

Each strategy clearly leads to different decisions and activities. Each approach depends both on you (your skills, talents, and interests in computers) and on your campus computing resources.

SEE EXERCISE 10.1

What If You Really Hate Computers?

Face the facts: Technology skills will play a significant role in the job market of the twenty-first century. So meet this issue head on. You might begin with a book or workshop geared toward beginners. Or make a pact with a friend who shares your attitudes about computers. Help each other by attending the same training session and reviewing class assignments that require you to use computers. Push (and pull) each other along.

Your college may incorporate computer instruction into some first-year courses to help you learn the basics. Many residence halls, libraries, or computer labs are staffed with troubleshooters who can help you learn.

■ COMPUTER BASICS

Keyboarding

Keyboarding remains the core skill for using a computer. If you can type, you're in good shape for working with a computer. If you can't type, you need to learn. Find a keyboarding course that fits into your schedule or learn on your own with an inexpensive "typing tutor" software package. (To find the right one, look at ads in a computer magazine or ask someone in a computer store or your campus bookstore for suggestions.)

Accessing Computers

Does your college sell computers through the bookstore? Will you have to pay a lab fee for computer time and access for some of your classes? Will you be charged printing fees? The answers to these questions may depend on your major or your courses.

A small number of schools require (or strongly encourage) all students to own computers. These institutions have committed themselves to bringing information technology into nearly every aspect of academic life—from wiring residence halls into a campus network to including the cost of a computer as part of total college costs.

SEE EXERCISE 10.2

Campuses encourage computer use in many ways: selling computers in the bookstore, providing campus labs for student use, offering e-mail accounts to students, establishing a campus home page on the World Wide Web, allowing students to set up their own home pages, and offering various support services such as training classes and computer consultants to help solve specific problems.

Finding the Right Kind of Help

SEE EXERCISE 10.3

As you learn routine computing tasks, you'll have occasional problems or questions. Most often, you'll ask questions such as "Now that I'm doing X, how can I get the computer to do Y?" Some questions may concern the kinds of information sources and services available through your computer and telecommunications options. Here are some sources of help:

- **FAQs.** When you're getting started using computers, most of the help you will need is what insiders call "frequently asked questions," or FAQs. Your campus may have a source of FAQs and answers "online." ("Online" means that you can locate answers via the computer itself.)

- **Support for academic computing.** Many campuses have a center or department responsible for academic computing—the use of computing and information technology for instruction and research. This unit often includes a user support service that can help you. Ask.

- **A few good souls.** Find a few people with whom you feel comfortable asking questions about computing. Also, try to find at least one librarian to answer questions about computer-related information resources in the library and through your campus network (if you have one) and the Internet and World Wide Web.

- **A few good notes.** Don't assume that you will automatically be able to remember the magic words and motions next time. Write down the steps. Keep handouts or notes where the information will be handy when you need it again.

- **A few good books.** Most bookstores will have dozens of books about computing, information technology, and computer software.

Preventing Disaster

Whether you're using your own computer or another one, take precautions to avoid the most serious catastrophes.

1. **Don't do anything silly to a computer.** Don't spill things on it. Don't drop it. Don't hit it.

2. **Learn how to start, stop, and restart the computer you are using.** Two common problems are (a) a computer gets hung up so that no matter what you do, absolutely nothing changes on the screen, and (b) you get lost in an application program and suddenly don't know what you're doing and can't figure out how to move back to doing something that was making sense. When these things happen, ask for help. In both cases, the last (and very desperate) option is to turn the computer off and then restart ("reboot") it. Usually, you will lose whatever work you had done since the last time you saved or filed your work. But at least you will be back in operation.

3. **Learn how to make backups.** Be sure you understand the different ways to make backup copies and know where you can save and store copies of your computer work (your computer files). Learn what diskettes, hard disks, internal memory, portable drives, and network server shared storage are and which are available. Learn how to use them. For most projects, you should probably:

    a. *Save the document at least every five or ten minutes while you work on it.* Give the file or document a name that you can easily recognize and remember. Use numbers to help identify the version number of the document. (Is it your first draft or your fourth rewrite?)

b. *Virtually all computers allow you to copy documents (files) from the computer to a diskette (and vice versa).* Be sure you save your work on the document frequently and also at the end of a work session. If what you're working on is extremely important, keep the diskette in a different room or building than the computer, or purchase a portable drive and connect it to your computer.

SEE EXERCISE 10.4

c. *Print a hard (paper) copy of the most up-to-date version at the end of each work session and keep it in a safe place.* Use it to make corrections for future revisions.

SEE EXERCISE 10.5

■ COMPUTER APPLICATIONS

Word Processing

For most students, word processing is by far the most important application of information technology. Learning to use word processing with a spelling checker is essential. It is equally important to learn the limitations of most word processing software: It cannot help you pick the right word, cannot supply the ideas, and cannot do the research for you. But if you learn to use a reasonably powerful word processor, your papers will look better and require less effort to write and revise. Some word processing packages can even automatically place and number footnotes for you.

Word processing involves some risks and costs. If you are careless, you can lose the results of your work just at the wrong time. It may be addictive: You can find yourself getting too fancy with choosing type fonts (sizes and styles) instead of working on the content. Access to a good word processing program also may increase your tendency to procrastinate. If you can produce a nice-looking paper in a few hours and can make changes right up until you are ready to print, you may be inclined to put off starting, forgetting that what a paper says is more important than how good it looks.

When you use a spelling checker, keep in mind that such programs don't end the need for your own intelligent proofreading. For example, spelling checkers won't pick up errors such as typing "there" for "their" or "too" for "to." Thus you will need to continue to proof your own work.

SEE EXERCISE 10.6

The main advantage of word processing over other forms of writing is that you can revise with much less effort, and revision is the key to successful writing. With practice, you can find your own most effective techniques and rhythm of writing—but this will work only if you also learn how to plan your time to let yourself do more than one draft before the final version. "Sleeping on it" is one of the best things you can do between drafts.

Spreadsheets

A spreadsheet program divides the computer screen into cells arranged in rows and columns. In each cell, you can type a number, a short bit of text, or a formula that performs some calculation on the content of other cells. Spreadsheets are most widely used for budgeting and financial analysis. They are also useful wherever you need to experiment and calculate with numerical data. A good spreadsheet program can also calculate statistics. One great advantage of a spreadsheet over old-fashioned pencil-and-paper methods is that, once you have typed in the data, the computer does all the calculations, such as finding the total of a column of numbers. Spreadsheets are better than calculators in that the spreadsheet stores the data so that it never has to be retyped. One way to learn about spreadsheets is to use one to work out your personal budget.

Databases

A database can manage, sort, summarize, and print out large amounts of systematic alphabetic or numerical data. Businesses use databases to keep records of things such as inventory, customers, and transactions. The electronic catalog in your campus library is a database. Researchers use databases to record and manipulate research data, such as survey results. One way to get started with a database is to use it in place of an old-fashioned personal address book.

Graphics and Presentation Software

Graphics and presentation software let you capture, create, and display words and visual images, maps, and other graphic data on the computer monitor, on projection screens, and in printed form. Computer graphics are everywhere you look today in art and advertising. They also have many uses on campus. For example, medical schools are now creating and using graphics software to teach human anatomy and medical diagnosis.

Personal Productivity Software

Personal productivity software includes personal information managers (PIMs) such as electronic phone books, calendars, and other tools that help you manage information about your activities and contacts. Sometimes these come as bonus products when you buy computers.

■ COMMUNICATION OVER THE INTERNET

In the mid-1990s, there was an explosion of public awareness of and interest in the Internet. Newspapers and magazines started covering the Internet, and bookstores began to sell new titles intended to help people make sense of this phenomenon.

What is the Internet? At its simplest level, the Internet is many thousands of computers connected by telephone lines used to exchange messages and to find or offer other forms of information. It has no recognized governing

INFOTRAC COLLEGE EDITION

Search Online!

Try these phrases and others for Key Words and Subject Guide searches: "computer," "microcomputers."

Also look up:

Who's the boss: you or your computer? (avoiding misuse of computer technology) (book excerpt from "What Will Be: How the New World of Information Will Change Our Lives") (Technology Information) (Transcript). Michael L. Dertouzos. *Home Office Computing* Oct 1997 v15 n10 p90(3)

The new resume for the new millennium: how to write an electronic resume. Ronald L. Krannich. *The Black Collegian* Oct 1996 v27 n1 p48(6)

Computer graphics aren't only for art and video commercials. They are also revolutionizing how computers help us see, share, and analyze complex information.

PHOTO COURTESY OF UNIVERSITY OF UTAH

body—just widespread agreement among users on some standard ways of packaging and sending information.

Most colleges and universities have computer networks of their own that are connected to the Internet. The personal computer that you now own or may soon own can be hooked to the Internet through a direct connection to your campus network or through a modem, a small device that lets your computer communicate with other computers via telephone lines. If your institution has a web site or other online information system, you may find information on a computer about course offerings, campus policies and regulations governing students and faculty (perhaps including an "acceptable use" policy or guidelines suggesting appropriate online behavior), phone numbers, faculty ratings, course schedules, other institutional publications, and the campus events calendar.

Electronic Mail—Some Basics

Like many business networks, your campus network may have a system of electronic mail (e-mail) that lets you send and receive messages via computer. These messages may be local—on your campus to other students and to faculty—or they may be sent to people at other campuses and to off-campus addresses via the Internet.

Perhaps the main advantage of e-mail is that it is asynchronous—you and the other person do not have to be using it at the same time. You can send a message that will travel almost instantly to someone else and wait until he or she sits down, reads it, and sends an answer back.

Faculty members often use e-mail to communicate with students. It may be easier for you to get a faculty member to answer a question via e-mail than to wait in line after class to try to set up an appointment.

SEE EXERCISE 10.7
INTERNET ACTIVITY

COMPUTER ETIQUETTE: REPLYING, PAUSING, AND FLAMING

One nice feature of most e-mail systems is that you don't have to look up someone's e-mail address every time. Usually, there is an easy way to reply to an incoming message. Unfortunately, people often use the "reply" feature too quickly or without thinking carefully.

One common mistake occurs when you reply to a message that came from a listserv—a kind of online information service that relays messages provided by one person to all others on the service. When you respond to a message forwarded from a listserv, it is easy to think you are replying to the original author. However, the local e-mail system may send your message to the address that sent it to you—which may be someone other than the author and may even be a list of hundreds of people. It's usually easy to find out how your reply feature works and to check that your outgoing reply is going where you intend.

Flaming refers to sending highly emotional, highly critical messages via e-mail. Sometimes this is exactly what you want and need to do, but most "flames" result from someone having an immediate strong emotional reaction to a message just received, writing an almost stream-of-consciousness response, and sending it without thinking about the consequences. Once you have sent a message you cannot unsend it, and an apology offered afterward rarely undoes the harm or takes away the hurt.

And if you type anything in all caps, IT HAS THE EFFECT OF MAKING IT SEEM LIKE YOU ARE YELLING AT THE RECIPIENT!

It is usually easy to forward e-mail—to send a copy of a message you receive to someone else or to a list of e-mail addresses. Technically, this process usually can be done without permission from the original author. The ease and speed with which a message or document can spread through the Internet is truly amazing. This has two consequences for you.

- The possibility exists that an e-mail message you send to one person will be seen by others. Pause and think about that before you send it.
- It reflects common courtesy and may be a legal requirement to get permission from the author (or copyright holder) before forwarding a message or document.

Be careful to avoid publicizing what was intended as a private message. If you have any doubt about the author's wishes, check with the author before sending a copy to someone else.

ETHICAL AND LEGAL ISSUES

Your campus may have materials or courses explaining local policy and relevant law. You are responsible for knowing enough to avoid breaking the law. With so many new technologies, the environment in which you work has become much more complex. Old laws don't quite address all the new situations. You may be tempted to do things with computers that would seem clearly wrong in other situations.

SEE EXERCISE 10.8

The best advice is to maintain your ethical principles and to learn enough of the relevant law and to whom to go for advice about what is and is not permitted. The library and the computing center are good places to start.

EXERCISE 10.1 **Rating Your Computer Skills**

A Rate your current computer skills from 1 (low) to 5 (high) for each of the following:

_____ 1. keyboarding or typing

_____ 2. word processing

_____ 3. electronic mail

_____ 4. searching the World Wide Web

_____ 5. creating web pages

_____ 6. using computer graphics programs

_____ 7. computer programming

_____ 8. computerized library resources

_____ 9. spreadsheets/budgeting software

Where do your answers cluster? Mostly 3's, 4's, or 5's suggest you have some advanced skills. Mostly 1's or 2's suggest you're just getting started and should think carefully about ways to acquire skills that will help you during and after college.

B Next, check the technology skills that are important for students in your major. Which skills are important for people in the career field you intend to pursue? If you don't know, find out. Ask an academic advisor, a faculty member, or a career counselor about the key technology skills for your major and intended career. Match their answers about key skills against your self-assessment of your skills. Taken together, this will help you set priorities and map a strategy for developing and enhancing your technology skills.

My Current Skills	My Planned Major	My Intended Career	
_____	_____	_____	keyboarding or typing
_____	_____	_____	word processing
_____	_____	_____	electronic mail
_____	_____	_____	the Internet and the World Wide Web
_____	_____	_____	computerized library resources
_____	_____	_____	spreadsheets/budgeting software
_____	_____	_____	presentation graphics
_____	_____	_____	computer programming
_____	_____	_____	database management
_____	_____	_____	statistical analysis
_____	_____	_____	other: _____
_____	_____	_____	other: _____

C Use the goal-setting process from Chapter 1 to address any needs suggested by this exercise.

EXERCISE 10.2

Campus Strategies and Access

A As a class find out what steps your school has taken to make information technology available to students and faculty. What seems to be its overall plan, if any? Be sure to check for any booklets and guides intended for students and faculty that describe services and resources.

B Place a check mark next to each of the following that is available on your campus.

_____ 1. "Intro to Computers" classes

_____ 2. training seminars/workshops on specific computer applications such as word processing, graphics, e-mail, and Internet/World Wide Web

_____ 3. a computer support center for assistance

_____ 4. a call-in phone number for computer assistance

_____ 5. computers for sale in the bookstore

_____ 6. dial-up access to the campus network from a computer in campus living quarters or at off-campus locations such as your home or place of work

_____ 7. resources to help you construct your own home page on the campus World Wide Web site

_____ 8. networked library resources available outside of the library

_____ 9. something else: _____

EXERCISE 10.3

Help at Hand

1. Locate the user support services part of the academic computing office (it may have some other name). Fill in the following:

   Office name: _____

   Location: _____

   User support phone: _____

   User support hours: _____

2. Ask academic computing or others whether there is a list of FAQs and answers and how to get it.

3. Names, addresses, phone numbers, and hours of availability of people who are good for basic questions: _____

   _____

   _____

   _____

   _____

4. Names, addresses, phone numbers, and hours of availability of people who are good for advanced questions: _____

   _____

   _____

   _____

   _____

EXERCISE 10.4 ■ ## Preventing Disaster

For any of the following information that you don't already know, ask someone and record enough notes on a sheet of paper to remind yourself what to do.

1. To start your computer.

2. To turn off and restart your computer (be sure that this procedure is considered safe by your expert).

3. To file or save a document on the computer. While you're at it, check to see if there's a way to set the computer to file or save automatically every fifteen minutes; if so, do so.

4. To file or save a document from the computer onto a diskette and to format or initialize a diskette (only format or initialize a diskette if you must and if you are ready to have any existing data on the disk erased—forever).

5. To print a document from the computer onto paper.

EXERCISE 10.5 ■ ## Knowing What Can Be Done

Review the software descriptions in this chapter. If you're already familiar enough with an application to know how it might be useful to you, place a check mark by it. For the rest, consult someone else or a magazine or other source for some fairly simple explanations and write them down. Exchange your explanations with others in your class until each of you understands these terms. Add more of your favorite new applications, if any (or ones you are curious about), and do the same thing.

EXERCISE 10.6 ■ ## Word Processing—Beginning and Advanced

A *For those not already using word processing:* Learn by doing a real task. Pick an assignment in one of your courses in which you must produce a paper, preferably not too long and due somewhere between one and five weeks from now.

If your campus offers some sort of noncredit or nominal credit workshops to introduce word processing, sign up and go. If you can find a tutorial disk or video, try it.

Use the computer to write, save, revise, and print your paper. Remember that famous computer advice: If all else fails, try reading the manual. If the manual is impenetrable, buy another easier book about your particular software package. Learn the basics of how to make your report look nice, but don't try to get too fancy this time. Keep your design simple.

B *For those already using word processing:* Mark each of the following either T (true) or F (false).

1. When I use the computer to prepare a paper, I routinely use a spell-checking program.

2. I check spelling before I turn in my work.

3. I know advanced features of my word processing program such as headers, footers, and footnotes, and I use them often.

4. I always save my work regularly and never lose long or important pieces of my work.

5. From session to session, I back up my work on disk.

6. I rarely waste much time getting fancy with fonts, paragraph formats, and other superficial stuff.

7. When I write a paper, I always go through a stage in which I focus hard on deciding what I want to say and how I plan to organize my thoughts (perhaps more than once).

8. When possible, I start writing a paper early and leave time to think about it between drafts. I always plan time to revise.

9. I always proofread work before I turn it in or share it with others.

Do your answers suggest any need for improvement? Discuss this in a group.

**EXERCISE 10.7
INTERNET
ACTIVITY**

Learning to Use E-Mail

A Is e-mail available to students on your campus? If so, learn how to use it. Find out if and how you will be charged for using e-mail. If possible, get an account and an e-mail address. Write your e-mail address here:

_____

Write your password, if any, somewhere else where you won't lose it.

B Exchange e-mail addresses with another student enrolled in this course and also with the faculty member teaching this course. Write in the e-mail addresses below:

Teacher name _____

E-mail address _____

Student name _____

E-mail address _____

Student name _____

E-mail address _____

Send some messages to each other. Learn how to use the reply and forward features and practice them together.

1. Learn how to use your e-mail system in conjunction with your word processing package. (If the process is too difficult, save it for special occasions that involve very long messages.)

2. Try exchanging messages with someone else on your campus and with someone at another campus who also has an e-mail account.

C Many faculty members on your campus are using e-mail. Find out if any of your own teachers are using e-mail, and make a point of asking an intelligent question via e-mail and making use of the answer.

D Send an e-mail message to the publishers of this book. Tell them how you like the book and how you think it could be improved for future first-year students. Address your message over the Internet to the editor: *karen_allanson@wadsworth.com*

E Use e-mail to speak out on an issue that is important to you. Send a letter, via e-mail, to any of the following:

NBC's "Dateline" news program, in response to a story: *dateline@nbc.news.com*

The White House: *president@whitehouse.gov*

Newsweek magazine in response to a recent article: *letters@Newsweek.com*

F Subscribe to a listserv. Consult your library for advice about finding a listserv that discusses some topic of interest or use to you. Find out whether it is "open" (permits anyone to subscribe himself or herself) or "closed" (requires the permission and intervention of the list owner to subscribe).

Find out whether it is "unmoderated" (anyone can send a message that will be automatically and immediately distributed to everyone who has already subscribed) or "moderated" (messages submitted are reviewed and edited by a human moderator before they are distributed). Once you have the name and e-mail address of the listserv, make sure you understand how to "unsubscribe" before you subscribe! To subscribe, the usual arrangement is simply to send an e-mail message to an address associated with the listserv. This message should usually have the subject or header section blank. The body of the message should say "SUBSCRIBE nameoflistserv yourfirstname yourlastname" and nothing more. For example, to subscribe to the list that discusses issues of teaching, learning, and technology, for higher education, send a message to *LISTPROC@LIST.CREN.NET* saying "SUBSCRIBE AAHEGIT JOHN DOE" and wait for the messages you will be receiving. (Go to *http://csuccess.wadsworth.com* for the most up-to-date URLs.)

EXERCISE 10.8   Computer Ethics

Find out if your college or university has adopted a policy or guidelines for ethical and legal use of computers and telecommunications. (This may be called an "acceptable use" policy. Ask people in the academic computing office, the computer science department, or the library.) If it has, get a copy. Be sure you understand the policy. Are there any aspects of the policy that seem unclear or difficult to follow? Be prepared to discuss your thoughts in class.

SUGGESTIONS FOR FURTHER READING

Things change so fast in this field that it is almost impossible to recommend books that won't be outdated by the time you read this. In addition to the following recommendations, try skimming some computer magazines, especially if you're trying to make a decision about buying a computer. If your campus computing center has pamphlets or training materials such as videocassettes those may be very useful to you. Consider taking (even noncredit) workshops offered by your campus computing organization or your library.

Gaffin, Adam. Preface to *The Big Dummy's Guide to the Internet*. Cambridge, MA: MIT Press, 1984. (This source is also available on the Internet; ask for help.)

Kurland, Daniel J. *The Net, the Web, and You: All You Really Need to Know About the Internet and a Little Bit More*. Belmont, CA: Wadsworth, 1996.

Lubar, Steven D. *InfoCulture: The Smithsonian Book of Information Age Inventions*. Boston: Houghton Mifflin, 1993.

Roszak, Theodore. *The Cult of Information: The Folklore of Computers and the True Art of Thinking*. New York: Pantheon, 1986.

Tehranian, Majid. *Technologies of Power: Information Machines and Democratic Prospects* (p.155). Norwood, NJ: Ablex, 1990.

Wriston, Walter B. *The Twilight of Sovereignty: How the Information Revolution Is Transforming Our World* (p. 21). New York: Scribner, 1992.

Wurman, Richard Saul. *Information Anxiety Is Produced by the Ever-Widening Gap . . .* New York: Doubleday, 1989.

RESOURCES

USER SUPPORT

Locate the user-support services of the academic computing office (it may have another name). Fill in the following information:

Office name

Location

User support hours

User support phone number

Ask the academic computing office if there is a list of FAQs and their answers, and, if so, how to get it. Fill in the following information about people who can answer basic and advanced computer questions:

Name	Phone number	Hours available	Beginning/advanced?

BOOKMARKING USEFUL SOURCES ON THE WORLD WIDE WEB

If you have a computer of your own and are using it frequently to search the web, you'll find it handy to use bookmarks that call the page up without your having to type in the correct address. Below is a suggested list of bookmarks for you. What others should you add? If you do not have your own computer, do a search anyway, and jot down the http addresses here for future reference.

Some Bookmarks to Begin With

Favorite search engine (Yahoo, Infoseek, Lycos, Hotbot, and so on). These are indexes you can search, using key words to find information. Find out how they work and how enclosing words in quotes, or inserting a + or − mark between words can change the results of your search.

Preferred search engine

Second choice

Home page for my college or university

Home page for my academic major

Airlines I frequently use to fly home

Pages I read for entertainment

Newspaper (*The New York Times* and *The Atlanta Constitution* are but two of the many papers with web editions)

Magazine or journal in my academic field

Other

Other

Other

JOURNAL

NAME _____

DATE _____

What do you need to do now to improve your computer skills?

....

....

....

....

....

....

Can you make a commitment to take at least one computer course this year? Why? Why not?

....

....

....

....

....

....

....

How many computer applications are you already comfortable with? Which ones are they?

....

....

....

....

....

....

Which other applications should you be using to help you become more productive? What steps should you take to become more comfortable with them?

....

....

....

....

....

....

CHAPTER

Speaking for Success

KEYS TO SUCCESS

- *Improve your critical thinking skills.*
- *Learn from criticism.*
- *Try to have realistic expectations.*
- *Never doubt your abilities.*

" Get up and speak in front of the class? No way! It's bad enough when I have to say something while I'm sitting in my chair, but when we have to stand up in front of the class, I get so nervous my hands start shaking and my stomach does flip flops. This is one part of active learning I don't think I'm going to like. "

The *Book of Lists* reports that speaking in front of others is the number one fear of Americans. It's more frightening for most of us than death, sickness, deep water, financial problems, insects, or high places. It's really a shame that what humans fear most is one another.

PUBLIC SPEAKING NEED NOT BE SCARY

Speaking in front of others may be one of our most prevalent fears, but it doesn't have to be. For example:

- **Once you begin speaking, your anxiety is likely to decrease.** Anxiety is highest right before or during the first two minutes of a presentation.

- **Your listeners generally will be unaware of your anxiety.** Although your heart sounds as if it were pounding audibly or your knees feel as if they were knocking visibly, rarely is this the case.

- **Some anxiety is beneficial.** Anxiety indicates that your presentation is important to you. Channel your nervousness into energy and harness it to propel you enthusiastically through your talk.

- **Practice is the best preventive.** The best way to reduce your fears is to prepare and rehearse thoroughly. World-famous violinist Isaac Stern is rumored to have once said, "I practice eight hours a day for forty years, and they call me a genius?!"

SEE EXERCISE 11.1

SIX STEPS TO SUCCESS

If you're assigned a speaking task in class, how should you proceed? Successful speaking involves six fundamental steps:

- **Step 1:** Clarify your **objective.**
- **Step 2:** Analyze your **audience.**
- **Step 3:** Collect and organize your **information.**
- **Step 4:** Choose your **visual aids.**
- **Step 5:** Prepare your **notes.**
- **Step 6:** Practice your **delivery.**

When it comes to holding forth in public, a few of us seem blessed with a wonderful sense of freedom. Most are more hesitant. Fortunately, your anxiety can help release the energy it takes to speak well to a group.

© 1992 CHUCK SAVAGE/PHOTO COURTESY OF BELOIT COLLEGE

Step 1: Clarify Your Objective

Begin by identifying what you want to accomplish. To persuade your listeners that your campus needs additional student parking? To inform your listeners about student government's accomplishments? What do you want your listeners to know, believe, or do when you are finished?

Step 2: Analyze Your Audience

You need to understand the people you'll be talking to. Ask yourself:

1. **What do they already know about my topic?** During your preliminary analysis, discover how much your audience knows about your topic. If you're going to give a presentation on the health risks of fast food, you'll want to know how much your listeners already know about fast food so you don't risk boring them or wasting their time.

2. **What do they want or need to know?** How much interest do your classmates have in nutrition? Would they be more interested in some other aspect of college life?

3. **What are their attitudes toward me, my ideas, and my topic?** How are they likely to feel about the ideas you are presenting? What attitudes have they cultivated about fast food?

Step 3: Collect and Organize Your Information

Now comes the critical part of the process: building your presentation by selecting and arranging blocks of information. One useful analogy is to think of yourself as guiding your listeners through the ideas they already have to the new knowledge, attitudes, and beliefs you would like them to have.

Imagine you've been selected as a guide for next year's prospective first-year students and their parents visiting campus. Picture yourself in front of the administration building with a group of people assembled around you. You want to get their attention and keep it in order to achieve your objective: raising their interest in your school. Let's be more specific by discussing the GUIDE checklist in Figure 11.1.

[G] GET YOUR AUDIENCE'S ATTENTION

To help your audience understand the purpose of your talk, you must get their attention right away. You can relate the topic to your listeners:

"Let me tell you what to expect during your college years here—at the best school in the state."

Or you can state the significance of the topic:

"Deciding on which college to attend is one of the most important decisions you'll ever make."

Or you can arouse their curiosity:

"Do you know the three most important factors students and their families consider when choosing a college?"

Or you can begin with a compelling quotation or paraphrase:

"Alexander Pope once said, 'A little learning is a dangerous thing; Drink deep or taste not the Pierian spring.' That's what a college education is all about."

You can also tell a joke, startle the audience, question them, tell a story, or ask a rhetorical question. Regardless of which method you select, remember that a well-designed introduction must not only gain the attention of the audience but also develop rapport with them, motivate them to continue listening, and preview what you are going to say during the rest of your speech.

SEE EXERCISE 11.2

[U] "YOU"—DON'T FORGET YOURSELF

In preparing any speech, don't exclude the most important source of your presentation—*you*. Even in a formal presentation, you will be most successful if you develop a comfortable style that's easy to listen to. Don't play a role. Let *your* wit and personality shine through.

[I] IDEAS, IDEAS, IDEAS!

Create a list of all the possible points you might want to make. Then write them out as conclusions you want your listeners to accept. For example, imagine that in your campus tour for prospective new students and their parents you want to make the following points:

- Tuition is reasonable.
- The faculty is composed of good teachers.
- The school is committed to student success.

Figure 11.1 The GUIDE Checklist

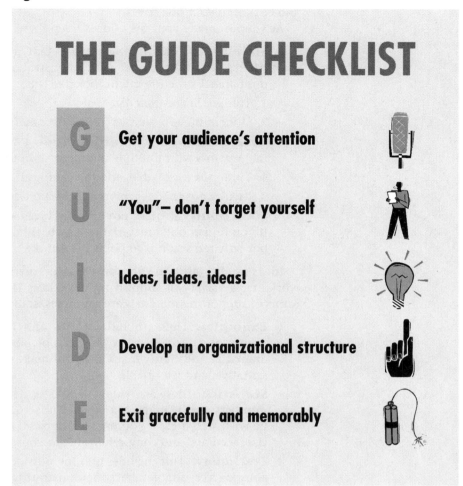

THE GUIDE CHECKLIST

G Get your audience's attention

U "You"– don't forget yourself

I Ideas, ideas, ideas!

D Develop an organizational structure

E Exit gracefully and memorably

- College can prepare you to get a good job.
- Student life is a blast.
- The library has adequate resources.
- The campus is attractive.
- The campus is safe.
- Faculty members conduct prestigious research.
- Our college is the best choice.

For the typical presentation, about five main points are the most that listeners can process. After considering your list for some time, you decide that the following five points are critical:

- Tuition is reasonable.
- The faculty is composed of good teachers.
- The school is committed to student success.
- The campus is attractive.
- The campus is safe.

Try to generate more ideas than you think you'll need so that you can select the best ones. Don't judge them at first (use your critical thinking).

Then, from the many ideas you come up with, decide which are relevant and critical to your objectives.

As you formulate your main ideas, keep these guidelines in mind:

- **Main points should be parallel, if possible.** Each main point should be a full sentence with a construction similar to the others. A nonparallel structure might look like this:

  1. Tuition. *(a one-word main point)*

  2. Student life is a blast. *(a full-sentence main point)*

- **Each main point should include a single idea.** Don't crowd main points with multiple messages, as in the following:

  1. Tuition is reasonable, and the campus is safe.

  2. Faculty are good teachers and researchers.

- **Main points should cover relatively equal amounts of time.** If you find enough material to devote three minutes to point 1 above, but only ten seconds to point 2, rethink your approach.

Ideas rarely stand on their own merit. To ensure that your main ideas work, use a variety of supporting materials. The three most widely used forms of supporting materials are examples, statistics, and testimony.

- **Examples.** These include stories and illustrations, hypothetical events, and specific cases. They can be powerful, compelling ways to dramatize and clarify main ideas but make sure they're relevant, representative, and reasonable.

- **Statistics.** These are widely used as evidence in speeches. Of course, numbers can be manipulated, and unscrupulous speakers sometimes lie with statistics. If you use statistics, make sure they are clear, concise, accurate, and comprehensible to your listeners.

- **Testimony.** This includes quoting outside experts, paraphrasing reliable sources, and generally demonstrating the quality of individuals who agree with your main points. When you use testimony, make sure that it is accurate, qualified, and unbiased.

Finally, because each person in your audience is unique, you are most likely to add interest, clarity, and credibility to your presentation by varying the types of support you provide.

[D] DEVELOP AN ORGANIZATIONAL STRUCTURE

Now that you've decided on the main points, you must decide how to arrange your ideas. You'll be able to choose from a variety of structural formats, depending on the nature and objectives of your presentation. For example, you may decide to use a chronological narrative approach by discussing the history of the college from its early years to the present. Or you might wish to use a problem–solution format in which you describe a problem (such as choosing a school), present the pros and cons of several solutions (or other schools), and finally identify your school as the best solution.

Begin with your most important ideas. Writing an outline might be one of the most useful ways to begin organizing. List each main point and subpoint separately on a 3 × 5 or 4 × 6 notecard. Spread the cards out on a large surface (such as the floor), and arrange, rearrange, add, and delete cards until you find the most effective arrangement. Then simply number the cards, pick them up, and use them to prepare your final outline.

As you organize your presentation, remember that your overall purpose is to *guide* your listeners. That means you must not neglect connectors between your main points. For example:

Now that we've looked at the library . . .

The first half of my presentation has identified our recreational facilities. Now let's look at the academic hubs on campus.

So much for the academic buildings on campus. What about the campus social scene?

In speaking as in writing, transitions make the difference between keeping your audience with you and losing them at an important juncture.

[E] EXIT GRACEFULLY AND MEMORABLY

Someone once commented that a speech is like a love affair: Any fool can start it, but to end it requires considerable skill. Most of the suggestions for introductions also apply to conclusions.

Whatever else you do, go out with style, impact, and dignity. Don't leave your listeners asking, "So that's it?" Subtly signal that the end is in sight (without the overused "So in conclusion"), summarize your major points, and then conclude.

Step 4: Choose Your Visual Aids

When visual aids are added to presentations, listeners can absorb 35 percent more information—and over time they can recall 55 percent more. Should you prepare a chart? Show a videotape clip? Write on the blackboard? Distribute handouts? You can also make excellent overhead transparencies on the computer using large and legible typefaces. As you select and use your visual aids, consider these rules of thumb:

- Make visuals clear and easy to follow—use readable lettering and don't crowd information.
- Introduce each visual before displaying and explaining it.
- Allow your listeners enough time to process visuals.
- Proofread carefully—misspelled words hurt your credibility as a speaker.
- Maintain eye contact with your listeners while you discuss visuals.

Rehearse your talk with a friend. Ask for feedback about your words, your posture, your gestures, and anything else that contributes to the total effect of your presentation. Practicing erect and out loud will help you much more than memorizing with your head bowed.

© MARK BURNETT/STOCK, BOSTON INC./PNI

Step 5: Prepare Your Notes

If you are like most speakers, having an entire text before you may be an irresistible temptation to read much of your presentation. A second temptation to avoid is speaking from memory. Your memory may fail you. And even if it doesn't, your presentation could sound canned. A better strategy is to memorize only the introduction and conclusion so that you can maintain eye contact and therefore build rapport with your listeners.

The best notes are a minimal outline from which you can speak extemporaneously. You will rehearse thoroughly in advance, but because you are speaking from brief notes, each time you give your presentation, your choice of words will be slightly different, causing you to sound prepared but natural. You may wish to use notecards, because they are unobtrusive. (Make sure you number them just in case you accidentally drop the stack on your way to the front of the room.)

After you become more experienced, you may want to let your visuals serve as notes. A handout listing key points may also serve as your basic outline. Eventually you may find you no longer need notes.

Step 6: Practice Your Delivery

As you rehearse, form an image of success rather than failure. Practice your presentation aloud several times beforehand to harness that energy-producing anxiety we've been talking about.

Begin a few days before your target date, and continue until you're about to go on stage. Make sure you rehearse aloud; thinking through your speech and talking through your speech have very different results. Practice before an audience—your roommate, a friend, your dog, even the mirror. Talking to something or someone helps simulate the distraction listeners cause. Consider audiotaping or videotaping yourself to pinpoint your own mistakes and to reinforce your strengths. If you ask your audience to critique you, you'll have some idea of what those changes should be.

USING YOUR VOICE AND BODY LANGUAGE

Let your hands hang comfortably at your sides, reserving them for natural, spontaneous gestures.

Don't lean over the lectern. Plan to move comfortably about the room, without pacing nervously. Some experts suggest changing positions between major points in order to punctuate your presentation. The unconscious message is "I've finished with that point; let's shift topics." Face your audience and don't be afraid to move toward them while you're speaking.

Make eye contact with as many listeners as you can. This also helps you read their reactions and establish command.

A smile helps to warm up your listeners, although you should avoid smiling excessively or inappropriately. Smiling through a presentation on world hunger would send your listeners a mixed message.

As you practice, also pay attention to the pitch of your voice, your rate of speech, and your volume. Project confidence and enthusiasm by varying your pitch. Speak at a rate that mirrors normal conversation—not too fast and not too slow. Consider varying your volume for the same reasons you vary pitch and rate—to engage your listeners and to emphasize important points.

Pronunciation and word choice are important, too. A poorly articulated word (such as "gonna" for "going to"), a mispronounced word (such as "nucular" for "nuclear"), or a misused word can quickly erode credibility. Check meanings and pronunciations in the dictionary if you're not sure, and use a thesaurus for word variety. Fillers such as "uhm," "uh," "like," and "you know" are distracting, too. If your practice audience hears you overusing these fillers, then, uh, like, cut them out, you know?

Finally, consider your appearance. Convey a look of competence, preparedness, and success. As Lawrence J. Peter, author of *The Peter Principle*, says, "Competence, like truth, beauty, and a contact lens, is in the eye of the beholder."

SEE EXERCISE 11.3

SPEAKING ON THE SPOT

Most of the speaking you will do in college and after will be given on the spot with little or no preparation. When your instructor asks your opinion on last night's reading, when a classmate stops you in the hall to find out your position on an issue, or when your best friend asks you to defend your views, you give impromptu speeches.

SEE EXERCISE 11.4

When you must speak on the spot, it helps to use a framework that allows you to sound organized and competent. Suppose your instructor asks, "Do you think the world's governments are working together effectively to ensure a healthy environment?" One of the most popular ways to arrange your thoughts is through the PREP formula (Wydro, 1981). Short for *preparation*, this plan requires the following:

[P] Point of view. Provide an overview—a clear direct statement or generalization: *"After listening to yesterday's lecture, yes, I do."*

[R] Reasons. Broadly state why you hold this point of view: *"I was surprised at the efforts the United Nations General Assembly has focused on the environment."*

[E] Evidence or examples. Present specific facts or data supporting your point of view: *"For example, the industrialized nations have set stringent goals on air pollution and greenhouse gases for the year 2010."*

[P] Point of view restated. To make sure you are understood clearly, end with a restatement of your position: *"So, yes, the world's governments seem to be concerned and working to improve the situation."*

SEE EXERCISE 11.5

▉WHAT IF ALL ELSE FAILS?

What if you plan, organize, prepare, and rehearse, but calamity strikes anyway? What if your mind goes completely blank, you drop your notecards, or say something totally embarrassing?

For the most part, we're sure you'll find that things will go smoothly and your preparation will pay off. If you make a mistake, the most important factor is not that the mistake occurred, but rather that you as the speaker handled and minimized the problem. Don't forget that your audience has been in your position and probably empathizes with you. Accentuate the positive; rely on your wit; use the opportunity to emphasize that you're not perfect. Your recovery is what they are most likely to recognize; your success is what they are most likely to remember.

SEE EXERCISE 11.6
INTERNET ACTIVITY

EXERCISE 11.1 **Introduce Yourself**

To try your hand at speaking in front of the class, prepare a three-minute presentation introducing yourself to your classmates. Bring or wear a prop that characterizes or caricatures you. For example, if you like to ski, wear your goggles; if you flip burgers on the weekends, wear your apron and carry a spatula. You can talk about your hometown, your high school days, your family, your reasons for going to college, or some other topic your instructor suggests.

EXERCISE 11.2 **Writing an Opening**

Assume you've been assigned to give a speech at another college or university on the value of your first-year seminar class. Write an introductory paragraph using one of the methods outlined.

_____

_____

_____

_____

_____

_____

EXERCISE 11.3 **Thoughts on Delivery**

Think about your teachers this term or in the past; your rabbi, pastor or priest, television speakers, and so on. What aspects of their deliveries impressed or bothered you?

EXERCISE 11.4 **Speaking on the Spot**

A To practice becoming a dynamic speaker, come to class prepared to give a one-minute speech on your worst pet peeve—something that really annoys you. Your instructor will give you a rolled newspaper. Use it to accentuate your main points and emphasize your feelings by hitting the lectern or desk with the newspaper.
Or:

B For this exercise your instructor will bring a shopping bag filled with common objects to class. Each class member will have an opportunity to draw out an item and give the class a one-minute sales pitch. The catch, however, is that you must find a new use for the item. (For example, if you draw an egg slicer, you could sell it as a pocket guitar.)
Or:

C Select two students to go to the front of the classroom for a "speakdown." Your instructor will assign a controversial impromptu topic (for example, "the worst thing about the opposite sex"), and both students will begin speaking on the subject at the same time, each trying to capture the audience's attention and steal attention from the other speaker. After two minutes the instructor will call time and class members will vote on which speaker they listened to most and discuss why.

EXERCISE 11.5

Using PREP

Bring five notecards to class with each one listing a question on which your classmates would have an opinion (for example, "Should the first-year seminar be a required course at all campuses?" or "Should students have a say in the hiring and firing of college faculty?"). Your instructor will collect the cards and place one card face down on each student's desk. One at a time, each student will turn over his or her card and answer whatever question is written there, using the PREP formula. You may not turn your card over until the person before you begins to speak.

EXERCISE 11.6 INTERNET ACTIVITY

Online Tutorial in Speaking

The Communication Studies Department at the University of Kansas has created The Virtual Presentation Assistant *(http://www.ukans.edu/cwis/units/ coms2/ vpa/vpa.htm)*, an online tutorial for improving your public speaking skills, with links to additional sites on public speaking. Compare the steps outlined in The Virtual Presentation Assistant to the steps outlined in this chapter. (Go to *http://csuccess.wadsworth. com* for the most up-to-date URLs.)

SUGGESTIONS FOR FURTHER READING

Bartlett's Quotations online: *http://www.cc.columbia.edu/acis/bartleby/bartlett/*

Deshug, Peter. *No More Butterflies: Overcoming Stage Fright, Shyness, Interview Anxiety, and Fear of Public Speaking.* Oakland, CA: New Harbinger, 1996.

Downloadable software to help prepare speeches: *http://www.lm.com/~chipp/spkrcmpn.htm*

Dwyer, Karen Kangus. *Conquer Your Speech Fright: Learn How to Overcome the Nervousness of Public Speaking.* Fort Worth: Harcourt Brace College Publishers, 1998.

Image and graphic resource web sites: *http://www.presentersuniversity.com/library/*

Kushner, Malcolm L. *Successful Presentations for Dummies.* Foster City, CA: IDG Books Worldwide, 1996.

Online tutorial for improving your public speaking skills. *http://www.ukans.edu/cwis/units/coms2/vpa/vpa.htm*

Proper Public Speaking Postures: example of a student project. *http://www.cis.upenn.edu/~nicholso/CSE400/pres.html*

Summary: Elements of Public Speaking from Toastmasters International. *http://www.phys.ufl.edu/~selman/service/tm/onepage.html*

Walters, Lillet. *Secrets of Successful Speakers: How You Can Motivate, Captivate, and Persuade.* New York: McGraw-Hill,1993.

(Go to *http://csuccess.wadsworth.com* for the most up-to-date URLs.)

RESOURCES

Although speaking to a group is difficult the first time for most of us, it gradually becomes natural if we consistently practice. With that in mind, keep a record here of your "public" speeches and how you felt after speaking up in class.

I. ASKING A QUESTION

What question did you ask? ....

How thoroughly was it answered? ....

Was there a follow-up question? .... If so, what was it? ....

....

....

How did you feel afterwards? ....

Are you motivated to ask another question in class? .... Why/why not? ....

....

....

2. MAKING A SPEECH OR PRESENTATION TO THE CLASS

What was your topic? ....

Approximately how long did you speak? ....

....

How did you feel while you were speaking? ....

....

How did you feel afterward? ....

Are you motivated to give a speech again? .... Why/why not? ....

....

....

3. PERSUADING OTHER STUDENTS TO AGREE WITH YOU IN A SMALL GROUP

What was your idea? ....

What resistance did you encounter? ....

How successful were you at convincing others to agree with you? ....

What did you do that made them agree/dissuaded them from agreeing? ....

....

....

Watch a video, hear a recording, or see live a speaker you admire before you make a presentation in class. Imagine yourself speaking with ease and confidence, connecting with your audience, and inspiring them, as your admired speaker has inspired you. And when giving your speech, remember to breathe, not to lock your knees, and to enjoy yourself.

JOURNAL

NAME _____

DATE _____

If you already have given a speech in college, reflect on how it went.

....

....

....

....

What strategies did you use to prepare? How well did they work?

....

....

....

....

Did you get the results you were aiming for? If not, why not?

....

....

....

....

What specific strategies from this chapter might you want to apply to your next speech?

....

....

....

....

What suggestions have instructors made to you about your speaking?

....

....

....

....

Why Math and Science Are Important for Everyone

12

KEYS TO SUCCESS

- Set up a daily schedule and stick to it.
- Assess and improve your study habits.
- Study with a group.
- See your instructors outside class.
- Improve your critical thinking skills.
- Know how to find and work with information on your campus.
- Learn what helping resources your campus offers and where they are.
- Develop peer support.
- Embrace new technologies.

66 Solving word problems? Ouch! I never could figure those things. Don't even mention math or science to me. I never could understand why everybody had to take those courses. I mean, if you're going to be a doctor or an engineer, it makes sense. But what about the rest of us? What are we going to learn that's of any use? 99

Mathematics and science are informing an ever-greater portion of your world. Over three-fourths of the jobs in this country require algebra and geometry, at least for licensure or entrance to training programs. At the professional level, calculus has become the gateway (some would say, the barrier) to a growing number of fields. Even when calculus is optional for a bachelor's degree, it is often required for graduate work. You know the importance of mathematics and science in engineering and in medical research. But consider environmental law, product liability, and patents. Even the traditionally verbal professions such as law require scientific and technical expertise. Psychology, business, social science, journalism—in these and many other fields quantitative and scientific concepts and skills have become essential.

Students often question math requirements: "I'm a verbal person, not a quantitative type" or "There is no algebra in my future." But times have changed; very few non-math jobs are left. It's not a matter of words or numbers anymore. Most employers require skills involving words *and* numbers, and more and more jobs demand knowledge of one or more areas of science.

It is almost a certainty that mathematics or science—or both—will be a part of your undergraduate program. This chapter will show you how to adapt strategies from previous chapters to the particular demands of mathematics and science.

■ TO GET IT, DO IT YOURSELF

Jump ahead a few years. Imagine you are working for a Fortune 500 company and that you and a co-worker are sent to a distant city for a three-day meeting. Your hotel is located several miles from the convention center, and your colleague rents a car to get around the city. By the end of the conference, you have made the trip several times, and the streets and landmarks look familiar to both of you. But your friend has been the driver and you have been the passenger. Think about it. Who has really learned the route that you've traveled each day—you or your co-worker who has been in the driver's seat?

There is a moral to this story for students in problem-solving courses such as mathematics, physics, and chemistry. Richard Feynman, a scientist who won the coveted Nobel prize in physics, once said, "You do not know anything until you have practiced." You have probably seen cartoons of mathematicians out for a social evening, writing equations all over the napkins. Mathematics and science are subjects that you think about by doing.

Think of the many times you sat in class and watched as your instructor presented a concept and worked a set of problems. You followed every step. And you were convinced that you understood the procedure perfectly. Then came the quiz—and you were completely stumped. You discovered once again that watching as someone else works problems is never enough. Mastering a new concept and its applications requires determination and perseverance, along with a good supply of pencils and paper.

■ GIVE YOURSELF PLENTY OF TIME

Mathematics and science require more time than many other subjects. With laboratories and workshops, your weekly hours in class probably will exceed the credit hours you will earn. Outside class you'll need to learn a huge volume of material, and the problem sets will require extra time and effort.

Time management is especially critical for math and science courses. In the 1980s Uri Treisman studied students who were doing well in calculus and found they often spent three or four hours completing the homework and learning the material for subjects like calculus and chemistry, more than the "average" two hours for other courses.

Use your schedule planner to determine how much time you need for each course. Keep a careful record by subject, to help you evaluate your preparation for major tests. Once you receive a graded exam, look back over the previous days and weeks. Add up the hours you spent preparing for the test and reflect on how you reviewed the material. This will give you a good sense of effort versus results. If you hit the mark, you'll say something like "Now I know what it takes to get an A in physics!" If you need to do better, you can refer to Chapters 6 through 8 for a refresher on study skills.

■ TAKING NOTES IN MATH AND SCIENCE COURSES

Although you should not record everything said in class, in a math or science course you will need to remember much more than the main ideas. Your class notes will be more useful if you understand their connection to the textbook. To see this, try to determine how your instructor uses class time. Does he or she teach the material from the ground up or, rather, assume you have a basic knowledge from the textbook and devote class time to extensions and applications of the concepts and to working sample problems? In the first case, your class notes and text notes will overlap a great deal. In the second case, you will get your introduction to a topic from the text and build on that foundation in your class notes.

In either case, you will get more out of class if you observe two simple rules:

1. **Do the reading on the topic ahead of the lecture.** This makes it much easier to decide what to write down during the lecture. It also prepares you regarding the relative importance of various topics and how they fit together.
2. **In the few minutes before class begins, look over your notes from the previous class.** This puts your mind in the proper context for the class and reminds you of questions you wanted to ask.

Although these are excellent and simple strategies, only the most dedicated students seem to follow them. Try them both for a few weeks.

Build Your Book

Think of your notes as a book that you write over the term. Math and science courses come in sequences. You will refer to your Calculus I notes while you are taking Calculus II, so take care to create a book of lasting value by following these guidelines.

- Do homework problems and exams in pencil, but take notes in ink, preferably on looseleaf paper, written on only one side.
- Keep your notes and materials for each math or science course in a separate three-ring binder.
- Place handouts alongside the notes of the class in which they were discussed.
- Organize your notebooks chronologically or by topic.
- Intersperse returned homework assignments, text notes, tests and quizzes, or keep them in a separate section of the binder.
- Buy a portable three-hole punch to add materials as you go along. Some classes have so many handouts and worksheets that staying organized is half the battle!

This book will be a priceless resource during the course, and on into the future, as a reference in a subsequent course or as a study aid for standardized tests like the MCAT (Medical College Admission Test) or the GRE (Graduate Record Exam).

Tips for Class

It is always a good idea to sit near the front of a classroom, but it is especially important in mathematics and science courses because of the significance and complexity of the visual content. You need to be able to see and decipher all that is written on the board or the overhead. Observe the following suggestions to improve your learning in the classroom:

- **Record everything your instructor writes:** scientific terms and the systems that connect them, special symbols and notations, formulas, derivations, diagrams and charts, definitions, theorems, equations, and other computations.
- **Be sure to write down all worked examples, step by step, as these are often the basis of test questions.** Many students only record what is written. Include a lot of what is said—clarifying comments, questions that students ask along with the answers, and especially any closing summaries at the end of class.
- **Use the two-column note-taking approach.** In the blank column next to your notes write your own comments or enter question marks indicating topics to ask your instructor or your study group. Put a star next to topics that your instructor emphasized. Take notes in outline form. Use the instructor's words as much as possible. Technical terms often have exact meanings and cannot be easily paraphrased. Use standard symbols and abbreviations (Cl for chlorine, Σ for sum, $\uparrow$ for increasing) but be sure you'll know what they mean months from now.

Typing or rewriting notes is not very common in math courses, but it is often done in the sciences. You will have to determine if it is necessary and a good use of your time. If you decide to rewrite, do it while the material is fresh in your mind.

■UNDERSTANDING MATH AND SCIENCE TEXTS

The typical textbook in a beginning course in mathematics or science is a thousand-page compilation of densely packed technical material. The best way to use the book depends on the instructor's emphasis and on the particular discipline. You can't approach a math book the way you would a biology book, for example.

Reading Math Texts

Traditional textbooks in mathematics tend to have lots of symbols and very few words. Each statement, every line in the solution of a problem, needs to be considered and digested slowly. The material is often presented through definitions, theorems, and sample problems. Derivations of formulas and proofs of theorems are usually included to maintain mathematical rigor, but you are not likely to be responsible for them. If you get lost in the proof of a theorem, go on to the next item in the section. When you come to an example, pick up a pencil and paper and work through the problem with the author. The heart of a math text lies in the problem sets. To appreciate the scope of a particular topic, skim through all the problems, not just the ones you have been assigned to work.

Reading Science Texts

You will take a different approach to your science texts. Become acquainted with the overall format of the book. Review the table of contents and the glossary and check the material in the appendices. You will need to know how to find lists of physical constants, unit conversions, and various charts and tables. Many physics and chemistry books also include a minireview of the math you will need in the course. Notice the organization of each chapter and pay special attention to graphs, charts, and boxes. If the back of the book contains answers to odd-numbered problems and each chapter ends with a summary, you can use these to test yourself on your mastery of the chapter.

As you begin an assigned section in a science text, survey the material with a cursory reading. Spend time absorbing the new vocabulary and technical symbols. Then read the problems so that you will know what to look for. At this point you're ready to begin a careful reading.

Should you underline/highlight or should you outline the material in your science textbooks? It is probably best to underline or highlight in a subject such as anatomy, which involves a lot of memorization. Remember that a highlighter should help pull your eye to important terms and facts. Use it sparingly and seriously.

In most other sciences, it is best to outline. You can usually identify main topics, subtopics, and specific items under each subtopic in your text by the size of the print. Save time by not using full sentences, but be sure to write clear explanations of new technical terms and symbols. If you aren't sure whether your outlines contain too much or too little detail, compare and discuss chapter outlines with members of your study group. Before a test, you may want to condense your outlines and merge them with your lecture notes.

■ PREPARING FOR MATH AND SCIENCE EXAMS

More so than in other disciplines, your grades in math and science will be determined by your scores on major exams. Quizzes, homework, and occasional group projects and writing assignments may play a minor role, but to pass the course, you must perform well on timed tests.

- **Ask about the test.** Begin preparing two or three weeks before an exam. Ask your instructor for a list of topics or text sections if the material to be tested is not clear from the syllabus. Ask about the format (multiple choice, short answer, essay, or quantitative problems requiring complete solutions) and the rules of the test. Are calculators allowed? All types of calculators? Are formula sheets permitted? If not, will any formulas be provided? Will you be asked to state definitions, derive formulas, state and/or prove theorems? If the test is objective, will there be a penalty for guessing?

    The format of a science test will have a major effect on your preparation. If you have organized the material to be tested in a classic outline form, an essay test will deal with the big Roman numeral topics, a short-answer test more with the midrange capital letter topics, and an objective test with the specific facts and items that have arabic numerals in your outline. Flash cards and mnemonic devices can help you to memorize the specific bits of information you will need for an objective test in science.

- **Work as many problems as you can before the test.** Prepare for a problem-solving test by working as many problems as possible. Move systematically through a list of topics to be tested, working the problems in the textbook for which answers are provided or other practice exercises, gaining confidence that you can handle each type of problem before you move to the next one. After you've tackled the topics one at a time, do some shuffling to avoid a common test-taking mistake: failure to recognize problems out of context. Be sure that you can work the problems when they are presented in random order.

**SEE EXERCISE 12.1
INTERNET ACTIVITY**

- **Study from your condensed outline.** In a subject like anatomy, which requires memorization of technical terms and an understanding of how systems are related, your preparation will focus on your study outline. Pay special attention to material on handouts. To prepare for a major test, many students create an initial study outline and then reduce it one or more times.

- **Take charge on test day.** On test day, arrive early with sharp pencils, erasers, a ruler, and fresh batteries in your calculator. Skim the test. Gain confidence by first working the problems you know best, then the ones you know second best. After that, divide your time according to the point value of the questions. Do not be distracted by an "impossible" problem if it is worth only a few points. Before you turn in your exam, recheck the reasonableness of each answer. Check the format and overall legibility of your work. Diagrams should be large enough and clearly labeled, notations should be complete and accurate, units must be correct and should "check," and the final answer to each problem should be clearly indicated—either "boxed in" or given in a complete sentence that restates the question.

- **Aim for a perfect score.** Students often ask "What do I need to make on this test to keep a passing average?" This is no way to set a goal for an exam. How do you decide which 70% of the material to learn? When you aim for a B or a C on a test, you are giving yourself permission to settle for a partial understanding of some topics, or to omit a few difficult topics from your preparation. Then those topics show up on the exam, and your confidence is immediately shaken. The best way to alleviate math anxiety or to prevent a mental block during a science test is to prepare until you are ready to score 100%.

■ STUDY GROUPS IN MATH AND SCIENCE

Good students always have known that working together leads to better results for all—especially in courses focused on problem solving. In many math and science courses, a well-functioning study group is almost a requirement for success. Challenging problems and all the possible strategies for tackling them almost demand that you consider, discuss, and work through the material with others. The larger the class and the more complex the material, the more valuable the study group.

What can a study group do for you? Go back to Chapter 2 to refresh your knowledge of how study groups function best. Then read these suggestions regarding study groups in math and the sciences:

- **Lecture notes.** Discuss your question marks: places where you got lost in an example problem, technical terms or symbols you didn't understand or couldn't decipher on the board, questions asked by other students that you couldn't quite hear. In some groups, members bring copies of their lecture notes for everyone.

- **Assignments.** Math and science students spend a lot of time working problems together. They work independently for a while and stop to discuss problems that are causing them trouble. Other groups do the assignments ahead of time and work together on the toughest problems.

- **Test preparation.** Group members can split up the job of making a study outline. Each person brings his or her section, the members discuss and modify the outlines, and a final version is created for all. Group members can quiz one another, focusing on facts and specific pieces of information for an objective test and on systems and relationships for an essay exam. A study group can create a sample exam, and take it under timed conditions.

- **Make-up notes.** Aim for perfect attendance. When you miss a math or science class, it is important to get the notes and the assignment and to do the homework before the next class. Otherwise, you effec-

Search Online!

INFOTRAC COLLEGE EDITION

Try these phrases and others for Key Words and Subject Guide searches: **"mathematics," "science," "logical thinking," "logic," "thinking," "problem solving."**

Also look up:

First- and second-grade students communicate mathematics. Aika Spungin. *Teaching Children Mathematics* Dec 1996 v3 n4 p174

The science of thought. Mike Powers. *Human Ecology Forum* Spring 1997 v25 n2 p12

Almost any problem can be solved more quickly and more pleasingly when people work together. Start by talking about ways that the problem could be defined. Listen for different perspectives that suggest different ways of resolving it.

tively have missed two classes. Because of the way each class builds on previous work, you will get very little out of the class following your absence unless you catch up on the work you missed. With a study group, you have somewhere to turn.

- **Moral support.** It is important that each member feels included and comfortable in the study group. No question should be ridiculed and no suggestion ignored. In a well-functioning group the role of "explainer" will rotate, and the strengths and weaknesses of the group members will tend to balance out. Things won't always go smoothly, of course. Don't give up. A good study group is well worth the effort it will take to resolve difficulties and get back to work.

■ MATH AND SCIENCE RESOURCES

Services are available to help you meet the challenges of mathematics and science. Check out the particular resources of your course and your campus.

- **Placement services.** The entry-level mathematics course that is best for you probably has been determined by the placement policy of your school and the requirements of your academic program. Generally, these time-tested placement policies have served the best interests of students. Those who decide to dig in and give their best effort to pre-calculus will be ready to succeed in calculus and will have stronger algebra and trigonometry skills to apply in a variety of courses. You may also receive placement advice in science as well as in foreign language, English, and other disciplines. Of course, if you feel your placement is clearly inappropriate, you should appeal to the department involved.

- **Office hours.** Your chemistry lectures may be in a large auditorium with 200 other students. In your biology class, the syllabus may be so full and the pace so fast that questions are subtly discouraged. Your mathematics instructor may not be a native English speaker, and sometimes you may not understand what is said in class.

Your first recourse in situations like these is to complete the assigned reading and make a serious attempt to do the homework before you go to the instructor. Arrive armed with specific questions, such as, "I followed you through line three, but I don't understand how you got line four." Visit your instructor on a regular basis. Never let a question go unanswered. Even an instructor who is difficult to understand in class may be clear and helpful in a one-on-one setting.

- **Instructional team.** Besides your primary instructor, you may have teaching assistants, a recitation instructor, a laboratory instructor and/or a lab assistant to whom you can turn. In addition, the course may offer supplemental instruction (SI) or another type of workshop. You may feel more comfortable working with a TA, an SI leader, or a recitation instructor. If you have international teaching assistants, visit them during office hours to help your ear adjust to an unfamiliar accent.

- **Learning centers or math labs.** Here's where you can get some free tutoring, do your homework, ask for help if you get stuck, work together in small groups, and consult with a staff member. If your campus offers such a facility, find it, note the hours, and become a regular.

- **Review sessions.** Many instructors offer optional sessions to help students prepare for exams, especially in courses such as chemistry, physics, and mathematics. Typically, the instructor will take requests and work problems. Such sessions are quite valuable if students have reviewed well ahead of time and come prepared with good questions.

- **Supplemental materials.** Your textbook may offer a study guide, a student solution manual, a set of calculator programs, or other materials. Check in your bookstore to see what is available. When you cannot understand a topic in your text, it's helpful to read the explanation of another author. Ask your instructor if you may borrow an alternative text. Your bookstore also carries outline series such as Schaum's and Barron's that provide a wealth of worked examples.

  One final example of useful supplemental materials (one that has stood the test of time!) is a bank of old tests. Some instructors place old exams on the Internet or on reserve in the library. You also may locate some old exams in your learning center or math lab or in the academic center of your residence hall.

- **Technology.** Your physics instructor may offer online tutoring. You may watch chemistry review sessions from your room via closed-circuit television. All types of computer-aided instruction are being developed in math and the sciences. Your instructor may post assignments and other information about the course on the Internet. Web sites from other campuses and national laboratories offer virtual lab experiences and breaking news from scientific research.

Among more personally useful resources, you may encounter calculators that not only graph functions but incorporate symbolic algebra programs; word processing packages with built-in equation editors; student versions of mathematics software such as Maple, Mathematica, and Mathcad; and spreadsheet applications tailored to the needs of science.

How to Do Your Math— or Chemistry, Biology, Electromagnetics, or Statistics—Homework

No matter what the science or math course, the following five-step process can help ensure that you successfully complete homework assignments.

1. **Take ten minutes to review.** Don't let your notes get cold. As soon as possible after class, skim through them. Put a question mark next to anything you don't understand at first reading. Put stars next to topics that warrant special emphasis. Try to place the material in context. What has been going on in the course for the last few weeks? How does today's class fit in?

2. **Warm up.** When you are ready to sit down and do the assignment, look through your notes again. But this time, use pencil and paper to *rework all the example problems.* Compare your solutions to the ones in your notes. Now read through the related material in the text. Go back to the examples, one at a time. Cover the solution, and *attempt to do each problem on your own.* Look at the author's work only after a serious personal effort.

3. **Do the assigned problems.** Now you can start on the homework itself. As you read each problem, ask, What is the given? What needs to be found? Of the given information, what is essential and what is extraneous? Read the problem several times and state it in your own words. The last sentence may provide a starting point; it usually spells out what you are trying to find.

4. **Persevere.** When you hit a problem you cannot readily solve, move on after a reasonable effort. After you've worked on the entire assignment, come back to those that stumped you. Try once more, and then take a break or work on another subject. You may have to mull over a particularly difficult problem for several days. Think about the problem at odd moments. Inspiration may come when you are waiting for a stoplight or just before you fall asleep.

5. **Wrap up.** When you complete an assignment, look back and reflect on the experience. Talk to yourself about what you learned from this particular problem set. Generalize about how the problems differed, which strategies were successful, and what form the answers took. Think about variations and extensions of the problems where appropriate.

You may be thinking, "The ten-minute review and the warm up are well and good, but who has time to do all that extra work? I'm lucky to get the assigned problem done." In reality, the approach does work and it actually saves time. Try it for a few weeks. The frustration that comes when you tackle your homework problems cold will disappear. The hours you devote to assignments will be more productive, and you will become more comfortable and confident in the subject area.

▮ PROBLEM SOLVING

G. Polya's book on problem solving, *How to Solve It,* first appeared in 1945 and most students have been exposed to his classic four-step approach. The universality of Polya's method extends far beyond quantitative problem solving. His steps have been rephrased and adapted for design problems in engineering, marketing decisions in business, research projects in biology, and life's challenges in general. Problem-solvers who follow Polya's methods rarely move through the steps consciously and intentionally. Rather, each of the essential components is a habit of mind they have cultivated. According to Polya, to successfully solve any problem you must:

1. **Understand the problem.**
2. **Devise a plan.**
3. **Carry out the plan.**
4. **Look back.**

In simplest terms, you should *think, plan, do,* and *check.* At each stage, you must ask yourself the right questions, and Polya's book offers many possibilities. Textbooks frequently include a list of strategies for solving problems, often set off in a highlighted box. These lists are expansions on Polya's method, with special emphasis on Step 2—offering the approaches that work best for problems in that particular subject.

Understand the Problem

To understand a problem you must read it carefully. Skim the problem to get the general context; then read it slowly a second time—phrase by phrase.

Draw a large diagram so that you can label all the parts clearly. A diagram is an important aid to understanding the problem. Next write down all the given information, converted from English to mathematical or scientific notations. If you are unsure, read the problem once again. Key words pointing to the givens should begin flashing off the page at you, as if in neon. Units of "cubic feet per minute," for example, indicate a rate of change: volume with respect to time, commonly written as dV/dt.

Read the last sentence of the problem one more time. The last sentence is often a question that reveals the unknown. When asked "How long . . ." you write "Let t = the time (in seconds) to . . ." A word on variables: In a subject like physics, the variables and the attached units are fairly standard. In mathematics, you may have a choice. Give an explicit description, indicate units, and specify a domain (the interval of values that make sense for the variable) for each variable you introduce.

To be sure you understand the problem: Can you estimate the answer and specify the units before you begin?

Devise a Plan

Now you've arrived at the real challenge. Here the possibilities are endless— trial and error, charts and tables, manipulatives, formulas that involve the quantities on the "knowns and unknowns" list, techniques from algebra or calculus. Think about similar problems you have worked in the past. Look through the text and your class notes for examples. Be persistent. Let the problem simmer for a while. Write about the problem: "I've always had trouble with this type of problem, but I am determined to figure it out. Do I have enough information? I know this . . . and if I only knew this . . . then I could . . ." And, as always in problem solving, work with your study group. Debate and discussion, along with different perspectives, will eventually lead to a plan that works.

SEE EXERCISE 12.2

Carry Out the Plan

Your work should be neat and accurate, and all quantities correctly labeled. Be sure your steps follow logically. Check for algebra and arithmetic errors.

Look Back

Don't overlook this final step. Is your answer reasonable? If you've found the height of a tree to be 10,000 meters, or the volume of a tank to be a negative number, you need to check the computations you did in the previous step. Is your answer clearly stated, preferably in a complete sentence that expresses the original question? Review the problem and the strategy you used. Will you recognize a similar problem and know how to solve it? Do you see where this problem fits into the big picture of the course? Can you think of a different way to solve this problem? Can the results of this problem be extended or generalized? If your solution worked for a circle of radius 5, will it work for a circle of radius R?

You will do various forms of problem solving in all courses—not just in science and mathematics. The goal is to develop your analytical and reasoning powers—one of the fundamental objectives of education. Your problem-solving abilities will be assessed by prospective employers and on the admissions tests required by graduate and professional schools. Develop an appreciation for logic games and recreational problems. You'll find them in books by Martin Gardner, among others, and in magazines and newspapers.

■ MAJORING IN MATH OR SCIENCE

Biotechnology researcher, environmental manager, computer software engineer—these are the kind of jobs that top the lists of today's hot careers. From traditional number cruncher and laboratory-based positions, through the ever-expanding list of health careers, to cutting-edge business and industrial opportunities, there is a world of interesting, well-paying jobs waiting for those with scientific and technical backgrounds.

SEE EXERCISE 12.3

If you have always asked "why" and "what if," chances are you may be considering a major in mathematics or one of the sciences. As you explore the possibilities and plan your undergraduate program, find out what your major has to offer. Get to know the undergraduate director and some of the office staff members. Inquire about handouts that describe the major, list the requirements, and provide a sample four-year plan. Ask if there is an organization for students in your major. Find out if the department has ongoing research in which undergraduates can participate.

SEE EXERCISE 12.4

Once you've made a decision, explore all avenues of relevant experience. An ideal program would include a summer of research in an academic setting, a summer of related work experience in industry, and perhaps a summer at another campus or at a national laboratory. Your advisor or a favorite instructor may help you locate opportunities, or even involve you in his or her own research. Is there a special person at your career center assigned to science and mathematics majors? This person can help you find co-op and internship positions. These are plentiful in technical fields and highly recommended. Volunteer work and community service also offer excellent opportunities, especially for those aiming for medicine or another health career.

SEE EXERCISES 12.5 TO 12.12. THEN CHECK YOUR ANSWERS ON PAGE 188.

When you choose a major in science or mathematics, you become a member of the scientific community. Even during your undergraduate years, there are opportunities for you on the frontiers of science and learning experiences available beyond the coursework required for your degree. You should follow the news reports of exciting scientific breakthroughs, and you should attend talks by faculty or visitors describing the cutting-edge work they are doing in the field. As one of the newest members of the community, this is your world and your future.

Equip Yourself for Success in Math

Do you feel

- that being lost in mathematics is the natural state of things?

- that mathematics is just a collection of formulas and theorems that one somehow has to cram into one's head?

- that math courses are just hurdles one has to cross as an undergraduate student? That mathematics is irrelevant?

- that you are taking mathematics only because it's required?

Understanding Mathematics, a multiple-page study guide by Peter Alfeld of the University of Utah *(http://www.math.utah.edu/~alfeld/ math.html)* discusses questions about attitudes and study practices involving math. It also gives examples of ways to learn math concepts and problem-solving techniques.

A Visit and explore the site to see what resources it contains that may be useful to you in your math courses. Also read Professor Alfeld's summary of G. Polya's problem-solving method *(http://www.math.utah.edu/~alfeld/math/ polya.html)* and compare it with the summary in this text. What further suggestions does it give? (You may want to download Alfeld's summary for your notes.) (Go to *http://csuccess.wadsworth.com* for the most up-to-date URLs.)

B Find at least two useful strategies described at Alfeld's site that you can apply to your study of math. Use your goal-setting process from Chapter 1 to put the strategies into practice.

EXERCISE 12.2

Planning for Success

Choose part A or part B.

A *If you are currently taking math or science courses:* List each science and/or each math course that you are taking. For each course, write a statement of your goals for the class including what you expect/hope to learn and your plan for achieving those goals.

From the courses you have listed, choose the one that you expect to find most challenging. Then review Chapter 2 on forming study groups. Write out a plan for organizing a study group in that course. Are there people in that class that you already know? Are there people you know who are in the same course but in other sections? Can you ask the instructor for help in setting up a group? Plan how you can best handle the logistics: time, place, and commitments to meet regularly.

B *If you are not taking math or science courses now but plan to do so in the future:* Consult your course catalog. List a science and/or math course that you plan to take. Write a statement of your goals for the course including what you expect or hope to learn and your plan for achieving those goals.

Ask at least three people who have taught or taken the course what the course is like. Find out more about the purpose and requirements of the course. Find out which instructors are most likely to be right for you. Plan to do your best to take the course with one of them.

EXERCISE 12.3 Exploring Your Options

Consider the major you are in or are planning to pursue. Explore your college catalog. Find at least two mathematical or science-related majors that you might consider. What makes your current major better for you than the others? Discuss your choice with a group of students in other majors. Explain why your present choice is number one and why the other possibilities also make sense. Plan to explore (and possibly enroll in) at least one course related to each of those majors.

EXERCISE 12.4 Creating a Major Plan

If you are considering a major in a math- or science-related discipline, write out a plan of courses that could carry you to graduation. Study your school's catalog and consult with your advisor to be sure that your list meets all requirements. If your class will also be reading Chapter 13 on choosing a major, talk with your instructor about how to coordinate this exercise with your work in that chapter.

EXERCISE 12.5 Einstein's Students

Albert Einstein was once asked how many students he had. He replied "One-half of them study only arithmetic, one-third of them study only geometry, one-seventh of them study only chemistry and twenty study nothing at all!" How many students did he have?

EXERCISE 12.6 Nuts

A store has received a shipment of nuts. One box has almonds, another has cashews, and a third has both almonds and cashews. The labels on the boxes are mixed up and none is correct. How can the store manager correctly label the boxes by taking only one nut from one box? (No looking at or feeling the other nuts is involved.)

EXERCISE 12.7 From Area to Volume

A rectangular box has sides with areas 24 in^2, 32 in^2, and 48 in^2. What is the volume of the box?

EXERCISE 12.8 The Missing Dollar

A hotel clerk charged Smith $15 for a room for the night. When the clerk discovered that he had overcharged Smith by $5, he sent a bellboy to Smith's room with five $1 bills. The dishonest bellboy gave only three to Smith, keeping the other two for himself. Smith has now paid $12 for his room. The bellboy has acquired $2. This accounts for $14. Where is the missing dollar?

EXERCISE 12.9 Which Is Whose?

Ina, Jill, Louis, and Miguel each have a different favorite color among red, blue, green, and orange. No person's name contains the same number of letters as his or her favorite color. Louis and the boy who likes blue live in different parts of town. Red is the favorite color of one of the girls. What is each person's favorite color?

EXERCISE 12.10

Logs or Money?

A cottage heated by wood was shared for the night by three people: Larry, Moe, and Curly. Larry brought five logs for the fire, Moe brought three logs for the fire, and Curly did not bring any logs. Instead, Curly brought $8 to pay for his share. All the logs were burned that night, so how should Larry and Moe split up the $8?

EXERCISE 12.11

The Shopper

You enter a store and spend half your money and then $20 more. Then you enter a second store and spend half your remaining money and then $20 more. Now you have no money left. How much money did you have when you went into the first store?

EXERCISE 12.12

Coffee or Tea?

Two 1-liter containers are half full of coffee and tea/ respectively. Take a spoonful of coffee and put it in the container of tea and stir. Then take a spoonful of this mixture and put it into the coffee. Which of the two containers holds the more adulterated mixture? That is, is there more coffee in the tea container or more tea in the coffee container?

Answers are on page 188.

SUGGESTIONS FOR FURTHER READING

Drewes, Fred. *How to Study Science.* New York: McGraw-Hill, 1997.

Polya, G. *How to Solve It: A New Aspect of Mathematical Method,* 2nd ed. Princeton, NJ: Princeton University Press, 1955.

Smith, Richard Manning. *Mastering Mathematics: How to Be a Great Math Student,* 2nd ed. Belmont, CA: Wadsworth, 1994.

Tobias, Sheila. *Succeed with Math: Every Student's Guide to Conquering Math Anxiety.* New York: College Entrance Examination Board, 1987.

Answers to Exercises 12.5 through 12.12

Exercise 12.5: 840 students

$$\frac{N}{2} + \frac{N}{3} + \frac{N}{7} + 20 = N$$

Exercise 12.6: Remember that each label is wrong. Every label will have to move to another box. He should choose one nut from the box marked "mixed nuts." (As he does this he should peel off the "mixed nut" label.) He will see what is really in that box (either cashews or almonds) and can label it correctly and set it aside. He will correctly label the two remaining boxes if he does a switch so that no box retains its original label.

Exercise 12.7: The dimensions of the box must be 4″ × 6″ × 8″. Thus the volume of the box (length × width × height) is 192 cubic inches.

Exercise 12.8: There is no missing dollar. At the end of the transactions, the $15 can all be accounted for: Smith has $3, the bellboy has $2, and $10 is in the till of the hotel.

Exercise 12.9: Read each statement separately to eliminate possibilities. This will allow you to select exactly one box in each row and column, which leads to the indicated favorite colors.

	Ina	Jill	Louis	Miguel
Red	no	yes	no	no
Blue	no	no	no	yes
Green	yes	no	no	no
Orange	no	no	yes	no

Exercise 12.10: In terms of logs, the fire required eight logs. In terms of money, the group accepted $8 as one-third share, so the total value of the fire was $24. Thus, eight logs are equivalent to $24. Each log is worth $3. Larry brought $15 worth of logs, so he gets $7 back. Moe brought $9 worth of logs, so he gets $1 back. At that point, each person has contributed an equal $8 share.

Exercise 12.11: Equations and algebra tend to make this shopper problem much more awkward than it needs to be. Simple logic and thinking backwards will lead to the answer: We want to know the shopper's original amount. Let $$$ be the amount of money the shopper has coming out of the first store. We are told that spending half of $$$ + $20 leaves nothing, so $$$ must be $40. Working backwards, we know that $$$ + $20 is half the original amount. Because $$$ equals $40, $60 is half the original amount. So the original amount was $120. Drawing a chart of what happened from step to step can also be a help.

Exercise 12.12: They are the same. The size of the spoonful doesn't matter, nor does the exact quantity of liquid you start with, as long as the original amount of coffee equals the original amount of tea, and the spoonfuls are exactly the same. To make the fractions easier, suppose you start with 10 ounces of coffee and 10 ounces of tea, and that a spoonful is 1 ounce. After a little arithmetic you will see that the coffee container ends up with a mixture that contains 100/11 ounces of coffee and 10/11 of an ounce of tea, whereas the tea container ends up with a mixture that contains 100/11 ounces of tea and 10/11 of an ounce of coffee.

RESOURCES

The more you practice scientific and mathematical logic, the more you will realize why everyone can benefit from these problem-solving skills. To discover more about the benefits of problem solving, complete the items below.

Using library sources, find a science hero, living or dead, who changed the world for the better. After reading about this person, explain why he or she might be an inspiration to you and others.

Make a list of the number of things you do in one week that require mathematical or scientific thinking. Here's a start:

1. *Balancing my checkbook*
2. *Dividing the day into blocks for studying and other activities.*
3.
4.
5.
6.

Follow the advice in this chapter for reading a science textbook. After reading one chapter in the book, describe how the method worked for you and how it compares to the reading method you previously used. If you're not taking a science course this term, ask a friend if you can borrow his or her book.

JOURNAL

NAME _____

DATE _____

If you enjoy math and science, tell what you enjoy about them. If you dislike math and science, explain why these fields are difficult for you.

....

....

....

....

....

Think back to the math and science teachers you had in school. Was there something about the way they presented these subjects that made you feel they were easy or difficult? What were those things? Why did they make you feel that way?

....

....

....

....

....

....

....

....

State your academic major and then describe how important mathematics and science are for the career you are considering. Defend your answer thoroughly.

....

....

....

....

....

....

....

....

Choosing Courses and Careers

13

CHAPTER OUTLINE

Learning from Your Academic Advisor/Counselor

Your College Catalog

Planning for Your Career

Time for Action

KEYS TO SUCCESS

- Choose instructors who actively involve you in learning.

- See your instructors outside class.

- Find a great academic advisor or counselor.

- Visit your career center.

- Learn what helping resources your campus offers and where they are.

- Get to know at least one person on campus who cares about your survival.

- Try to have realistic expectations.

66 Got the results of my career inventory today. It said I might want to go into the funeral business! And I thought I was interested in computers. Think I'd better see my advisor and see what it all means. Better check the catalog, too, to see if there are any courses in mortuary science. I just got here and I'm already confused! 99

*O*ne of the most important individuals you will meet in college is your academic advisor or counselor. This person can guide you through the complexities of choosing courses that follow your interests and meet the requirements of your major. If you have doubts about the major you have chosen, your advisor/counselor may suggest that you visit the career center, where you can examine your interests and explore careers and majors through career inventories, career data, and guidance from a career counselor.

■ LEARNING FROM YOUR ACADEMIC ADVISOR/COUNSELOR

One of the keys to success is that when a student has one person on campus who cares about his or her survival, that student stands a better chance of succeeding. A mounting body of evidence suggests that poor academic advising is a major reason students leave college in the first year.

SEE EXERCISE 13.1

At most colleges, you will have to visit your advisor or counselor at least once a term to obtain approval for courses that you will take the following term. The advising period is usually widely publicized on campus. It is very important that you schedule a conference during this period.

Beyond that, your advisor or counselor is available when you need help—when you're having trouble in a course, when a medical emergency forces you to miss classes beyond the drop date, when you're doubtful about the major you have chosen, or for a myriad of other reasons, academic and personal, that affect your success in college.

At many colleges, academic advisors and counselors are full-time faculty. At some campuses they may include professional educators. In many community colleges, academic advising is done by counselors in the counseling/advising center. These counselors are trained in and responsible for assisting students with both academic and personal issues. If you haven't declared a major, you may be assigned to an advisor who specializes in undeclared students. Your institution may not assign you to an advisor in your intended major until you are formally admitted to a program. In any event, your advisor should be familiar with the requirements of your program.

SEE EXERCISE 13.2

What Are You Looking for in Your Academic Advisor?

This graph from a study of students at Harvard shows that men and women tend to seek different qualities in advisors. When asked about advising, men want an advisor who "knows the facts." Or "if he doesn't know the data, he knows where to get it or to send me to get it." Or one who "makes concrete and directive suggestions, which I'm then free to accept or reject."

Women more often want an advisor who "will take the time to get to know me personally." Or who "is a good listener and can read between the lines if I am hesitant to express a concern." Or who "shares my interests so that we will have something in common." The women's responses focus far more on a personal relationship.*

What do you plan to look for in your advisor? What can you do to ensure that you get the advisor who is best for you?

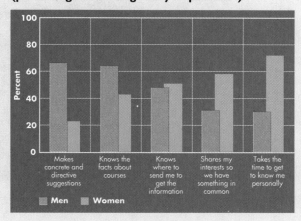

What Students Want from Academic Advisors (percentage indicating "very important")

*Richard J. Light. *The Harvard Assessment Seminars, First Report.* Cambridge, MA: Harvard University Graduate School of Education and Kennedy School of Government, 1990.

Preparing for Your Meeting

Your advising sessions will be more productive if you are already familiar with your college catalog. Make up a list of questions before your appointment and also arrive with a tentative schedule of courses and alternate choices for the coming term.

Discuss any major decisions—adding or dropping a course, changing your major, or transferring or withdrawing from school—before making them. You may also wish to discuss personal problems with your advisor. If he or she can't help you with a certain problem, ask for referral to a professional on campus who can. Be sure to clarify whether your advisor will respect your request for confidentiality on such matters.

Is Your Advisor/Counselor Right for You?

Do you feel comfortable with your advisor/counselor? Does this individual seem to take a personal interest in you, listen actively, provide enough time for you to accomplish what needs to be done, and either make an effort to get you the information you request or tell you where you can find it yourself?

If things don't go well, find someone else. Ask one of your favorite instructors or check with your department. Never stay in an advising/counseling relationship that isn't working for you.

SEE EXERCISE 13.3

The best academic advisor is someone who really wants to get to know you and welcomes your questions and concerns. If these qualities seem to be missing, think about whether there is something you can do to improve communication. Or consider looking for an advisor with whom you feel more at home.

© BRIAN SMITH/STOCK BOSTON

SEE EXERCISE 13.4

■ YOUR COLLEGE CATALOG

College is complex and expensive, and the college catalog is a user's manual for your institution. Learn what's in your catalog—it can be a valuable resource throughout your college years.

Much of the information once found only in college catalogs is also available online. Campus computer bulletin boards and Internet home pages are especially useful for information that is in constant flux or that has changed recently. In addition to lists of classes and prerequisites, office hours, and student services, you can often search listings of job opportunities, scholarships, schedules, and departmental telephone numbers and e-mail addresses.

What's in the Catalog?

PUBLICATION DATE AND GENERAL INFORMATION

SEE EXERCISE 13.5

Colleges and universities are constantly changing admissions standards, degree requirements, academic calendars, and so on. But the catalog in use at the time of your matriculation (the day you enrolled for the first time) will generally stand as your individual contract with the institution.

Most college catalogs include a current academic calendar, which states the beginning and ending dates of academic terms as well as dates of holidays and other events within each term. If you are not doing well in a particular class, you may want to drop the course rather than receive a failing grade, but you must do so before the deadline for withdrawal.

GENERAL ACADEMIC REGULATIONS

To be fully and accurately informed, don't rely on secondhand grapevine information. Become familiar with general academic regulations directly from the catalog. If you don't understand something in the catalog, seek clarification from an official source, such as your academic advisor.

The financial section may have detailed information on financial aid, scholarships, loans, and work opportunities.

ACADEMIC PROGRAMS

By far the lengthiest part of most catalogs is the section on academic programs. It summarizes the various degrees offered, the majors within each department, and the requirements for studying in each discipline. The academic program section also describes all courses offered at your institution: course number, course title, units of credit, prerequisites for taking the course, and a brief statement of the course content.

SEE EXERCISE 13.6

The catalog, however, is only a summary. Individual departments frequently offer more detailed academic information.

■ PLANNING FOR YOUR CAREER

Majors = Careers? Not Always

For a number of new students, choosing a major can be a difficult decision. Most students entering college straight out of high school (and even some who've worked a while) don't know which major to select or which career they may be best suited for. What's more, many students change their majors at least once before earning their degree.

There are many reasons for this: a broader selection of fields of study than in high school; pressure from parents or others; or the lure of majoring in one of the high-paying fields even when you have no interest in it, knowledge about it, or aptitude for it.

The most common question college students ask is, What can I do with my major? Career planning helps you focus on a more important question: What do I *want* to do?

First, consider several truths about majors and their effect on careers. Obviously, if you want to be a nurse, you must major in nursing. Engineers major in engineering. Pharmacists major in pharmacy. There's no other way to be certified as a nurse, engineer, or pharmacist.

However, most career fields don't require a specific major, and people with specific majors don't have to use them in usual ways. For example, if you major in nursing, history, engineering, or English, you might still choose to become a bank manager, sales representative, career counselor, production manager, or any number of other things.

What's more, if you're not certain about a major, it's perfectly okay—and normal—to enter as an undeclared major. From 60 to 85 percent of entering students will change majors at least once, and it may be better to shop around during your first year before you make that important decision.

In most cases a college major alone may not be enough to land you a job. With the tremendous competition for good jobs, you'll need experience and skills related to your chosen field. Internships, part-time jobs, and co-curricular activities provide opportunities to gain experience and develop these competencies.

Table 13.1 Career Planning Time Line

First Year: Check out career possibilities.

Meet with a career counselor to discuss your career goals.

Complete a career assessment or use computer resources at your career center.

Familiarize yourself with the career library. Note occupations of interest to you.

Second Year: Find ways to get career-related experience.

Start building your resume.

Seek a part-time or summer job related to your career goals.

Ask your academic advisor or career counselor about an internship in your field.

Shadow a professional on the job in your field of interest.

Third Year: Keep gaining experience and learn how to market it.

Attend resume-writing workshops at your career center.

Complete an internship or co-op position in your field. An internship usually lasts one term and may offer academic credit. It may be paid or unpaid. A co-op is a two- to three-term commitment to an employer and almost always is paid. Or find a part-time job in your field for added experience.

Research graduate programs.

Practice interviewing through mock interviews at the career center.

Fourth Year: Decide where and how to market yourself.

Apply to graduate schools and take the appropriate qualifying exams.

Work with a career counselor to fine-tune your resume.

Attend job search and interviewing workshops.

Decide where you want to search and what you want to search for.

Use on-campus recruiting and placement services in addition to conducting your own job search.

Table 13.1 is a college time line for exploring career ideas as you develop your qualifications. In the context of such a plan, your choice of an academic major takes on new meaning. Instead of being concerned with what the prescribed route of certain majors allows you to do, you'll use your career goals as a basis for academic decisions about your major, your minor, elective courses, internships, and co-curricular activities.

Consider these goals when you select part-time and summer jobs, too. Don't confine yourself to a short list of jobs directly related to your major; think more broadly.

Your choice of an academic major takes on new meaning. Instead of being concerned with what the prescribed route of certain majors allows you to do, you'll use your career goals as a basis for academic decisions about your major, your minor, elective courses, internships, and co-curricular activities.

Factors in Your Career Planning

Some people have a very definite self-image when they enter college, but most of us are still in the process of defining (or redefining) ourselves when we enter college and long after. There are several useful ways to look at ourselves in relation to possible careers:

Biology . . . evolution . . . history . . . literature . . . ? Start your search for your major with some wide-ranging thought about your interests.

© ROGERS/MONKMEYER PRESS PHOTO

- **Interests.** Interests develop from your experiences and beliefs and can continue to develop and change throughout life. You may be interested in writing for the college newspaper because you wrote for your high school paper. It's not unusual to enter Psych 101 with a great interest in psychology and realize halfway through the course that psychology is not what you imagined.
- **Skills.** Skills are measured by past performance and usually can be improved with practice.
- **Aptitudes.** Aptitudes are inherent strengths, often part of your biological heritage or the result of early training. They are the foundation for skills. We each have aptitudes we can build on. Build on your strengths.
- **Personality.** The personality you've developed over the years makes you *you* and can't be ignored when you make career decisions. The quiet, orderly, calm, detail-oriented person probably will make a different work choice than the aggressive, outgoing, argumentative person.
- **Life goals and work values.** Each of us defines success and satisfaction in our own way. The process is complex and very personal. Two factors influence our conclusions about success and happiness: (1) knowing that we are achieving the life goals we've set for ourselves and (2) finding that we gain satisfaction from what we're receiving from our work.

SEE EXERCISE 13.7

Dr. John Holland, a psychologist at Johns Hopkins University, has developed a number of tools and concepts that can help you organize these various dimensions of yourself so that you can identify potential career choices.

Holland separates people into six general categories based on differences in their interests, skills, values, and personality characteristics—in short, their preferred approaches to life:*

R • **Realistic.** These people describe themselves as concrete, down to earth, and practical—as doers. They exhibit competitive/assertive

*Adapted from John L. Holland, *Self-Directed Search Manual* (Psychological Assessment Resources: 1985). Copyright © 1985 by PAR, Inc. Reprinted with permission.

behavior and show interest in activities that require motor coordination, skill, and physical strength. They prefer situations involving action solutions rather than tasks involving verbal or interpersonal skills, and they like to take a concrete approach to problem solving rather than rely on abstract theory. They tend to be interested in scientific or mechanical areas rather than cultural and aesthetic fields.

I ● **Investigative.** These people describe themselves as analytical, rational, and logical—as problem solvers. They value intellectual stimulation and intellectual achievement and prefer to think rather than to act, to organize and understand rather than to persuade. They usually have a strong interest in physical, biological, or social sciences. They are less apt to be people oriented.

A ● **Artistic.** These people describe themselves as creative, innovative, and independent. They value self-expression and relations with others through artistic expression and are also emotionally expressive. They dislike structure, preferring tasks involving personal or physical skills. They resemble investigative people but are more interested in the cultural-aesthetic than the scientific.

S ● **Social.** These people describe themselves as kind, caring, helpful, and understanding of others. They value helping and making a contribution. They satisfy their needs in one-to-one or small group interaction using strong verbal skills to teach, counsel, or advise. They are drawn to close interpersonal relationships and are less apt to engage in intellectual or extensive physical activity.

E ● **Enterprising.** These people describe themselves as assertive, risk-taking, and persuasive. They value prestige, power, and status and are more inclined than other types to pursue it. They use verbal skills to supervise, lead, direct, and persuade rather than to support or guide. They are interested in people and in achieving organizational goals.

C ● **Conventional.** These people describe themselves as neat, orderly, detail oriented, and persistent. They value order, structure, prestige, and status and possess a high degree of self-control. They are not opposed to rules and regulations. They are skilled in organizing, planning, and scheduling and are interested in data and people.

SEE EXERCISE 13.8

Holland's system organizes career fields into the same six categories. Career fields are grouped according to what a particular career field requires of a person (skills and personality characteristics most commonly associated with success in those fields) and what rewards those fields provide for people (interests and values most commonly associated with satisfaction). Here are a few examples:

R ● **Realistic.** Agricultural engineer, electrical contractor, industrial arts teacher, navy officer, fitness director, package engineer, electronics technician, computer graphics technician

I ● **Investigative.** Urban planner, chemical engineer, bacteriologist, flight engineer, genealogist, laboratory technician, marine scientist, nuclear medical technologist, obstetrician, quality control technician, computer programmer, environmentalist, physician, college professor

A ● **Artistic.** Architect, film editor/director, actor, cartoonist, interior decorator, fashion model, graphic communications specialist, journalist, editor, orchestra leader, public relations specialist, sculptor, media specialist, librarian, reporter

S • **Social.** Nurse, teacher, social worker, genetic counselor, marriage counselor, rehabilitation counselor, school superintendent, geriatric specialist, insurance claims specialist, minister, travel agent, guidance counselor, convention planner

E • **Enterprising.** Banker, city manager, FBI agent, health administrator, judge, labor arbitrator, salary and wage administrator, insurance salesperson, sales engineer, lawyer, sales representative, marketing specialist

C • **Conventional.** Accountant, statistician, census enumerator, data processor, hospital administrator, insurance administrator, office manager, underwriter, auditor, personnel specialist, database manager, abstractor/indexer

Your career choices ultimately will involve a complex assessment of the factors that are most important to you. To display the relationship between career fields and the potential conflicts people face as they consider them, Holland's model is commonly presented in a hexagonal shape (Figure 13.1). The closer the types, the closer the relationships among the career fields; the farther apart the types, the more conflict between the career fields.

SEE EXERCISE 13.9

Holland's model can help you address the problem of career choice in two ways. First, you can begin to identify many career fields that are consistent with what you know about yourself. Once you've identified potential fields, you can use the career library at your college to get more information about those fields, such as daily activities for specific jobs, interests and abilities required, preparation required for entry, working conditions, salary and benefits, and employment outlook.

Second, you can begin to identify the harmony or conflicts in your career choices. This will help you analyze the reasons for your career decisions and be more confident as you make choices.

College students often view the choice of a career as a monumental and irreversible decision. But, in its broadest sense, a career is the sum of the decisions you make over a lifetime. There is no "right occupation" just waiting to be discovered. Rather, there are many career choices you may find fulfilling and satisfying. The question to consider is, What is the best choice for me now?

Figure 13.1 Holland's Hexagonal Model of Career Fields

SEE EXERCISE 13.10

SEE EXERCISE 13.11
INTERNET ACTIVITY

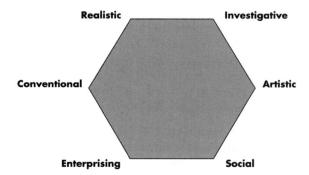

■ TIME FOR ACTION

Building a Resume

Before you finish college, you'll need a resume—whether it's for a part-time job, for an internship or co-op position, or for a teacher who agrees to write a letter of recommendation for you. Note the two resumes in Figure 13.2. One is written in chronological format, and the other is organized by skills. Generally, choose the chronological resume if you have related job experience and choose the skills resume if you can group skills from a number of jobs or projects under several meaningful categories. Try for one page, but if you have a number of outstanding things to say and they run over, add a second page. Other suggestions for good resumes:

- **Always put a contact block at the top.** This includes name, address, permanent address if applicable, e-mail address, telephone number.

- **State an objective if appropriate.** If you're seeking a specific position, absolutely state an objective. But be realistic. You're probably seeking an entry-level position at this stage. If you're applying for several different types of jobs, change your objective to fit each mailing.

- **List education to date.** As a first-year student, you can list under "Education" something like the following: "Enrolled in Bachelor of Arts, Psychology, University of Nebraska." When you're nearer to graduation and seeking full-time employment, state the degree and when you expect to receive it.

- **Give grade point average only if it's impressive.** What's important is that you demonstrate a balance between good grades and involvement in other areas of campus life.

- **Use action verbs in stating accomplishments.** "*Developed* bookkeeping system for company." "*Organized* special event that raised $5,000 for charity." "*Supervised* editorial staff of twelve."

- **Separate the work experience related to your academic major from other work experience.** If you have no related work experience, simply list jobs under "Work Experience." Even though the job may not be related, it indicates someone thought enough of you to hire you and pay you.

- **Explain honors and awards thoroughly.** People will probably know what Phi Beta Kappa is, but how many will understand "Golden Dagger Award from Order of Service Supporters"?

- **Include interests.** These tell employers that you have interests in life beyond your work. Few prospective employers seek workaholics.

- **Be sure you have references if you state "references available upon request."** Be sure you have obtained them in writing before sending out your resume. Let references know that a prospective employer may call. Nothing is more awkward—or harmful—than a reference getting a call and thinking, "Who in the heck is that?" when your name is mentioned.

- **Ask someone to review your resume.** Ask your academic advisor, counselor, or someone else whose judgment you trust to look at your resume before you put it into final form.

SEE EXERCISE 13.12

The Cover Letter

Sending a resume without a cover letter is somewhat like forgetting to put on your clothes over your underwear: You can do it, but people will notice something important is missing. In writing a cover letter, heed the following suggestions:

- **Find out who to write to.** It's not the same in all fields. If you were seeking a marketing position at an advertising agency, you would write to the director of account services. If you were writing General Motors regarding a position in their engineering department, you might either write the director of human resources for the entire company or a special one in charge of engineering. Your academic advisor or career counselor can help you here.

- **Get the most recent name and address.** Advisors or counselors can guide you to references in your campus or career library. Never write "To whom it may concern."

- **Use proper format for date, address, and salutation,** as shown in Figure 13.2.

More Things You Can Do

In this chapter, you have done exercises aimed at gathering information about yourself and about the world of work and clarifying the most important issues involved in your choice of career and academic major. Here are a few other activities that may help:

- **Career exploration.** Once you've selected possible career fields, talk with people working in those fields and try to spend a day observing them at work. Read what people in this field read. Visit local professional association meetings. Visit your campus career center and speak with a career counselor. Ask about the resources available there. For example, many career centers have extensive libraries focusing on occupations, employers, and graduate programs. A counselor can direct you to web links containing appropriate and current information about the job market. You may even find programs that allow you to preview positions and working environments and others that make it possible for you to conduct a "virtual interview" on a computer.

- **Choice of major.** Talk with faculty members about the skills and areas of expertise you'll develop in studying the disciplines they're teaching. Ask if they're aware of careers or jobs in which the skills and knowledge they teach can be used.

Search Online!

INFOTRAC COLLEGE EDITION

Try these phrases and others for Key Words and Subject Guide searches: "academic advisor," "career planning," "careers," "college majors."
Also look up:
Consultants see action. But travel and pressure mean the job isn't for everyone. Ilan Greenberg. *InfoWorld* April 27, 1998 v20 n17 p115
The future: two views. (interviews with authors Chin-Ning Chu and Edith Weiner on career planning)(Interview) Haidee E. Allerton. *Training & Development* April 1998 v52 n4 p41(3)
Information technology: big major on campus. Leslie Goff. *Computerworld* June 16, 1997 v31 n24 p100

Figure 13.2
Cover Letter and
Sample Resumes

Janet R. Mars
3130 Appian Way
Columbia, SC 29229

January 10, 2003

Mark B. Stoneridge
VP, Sales and Marketing
Ainsley Pharmaceuticals
3000 Appalachian Way
Pittsburgh, PA 49877

Dear Mr. Stoneridge:

(In your opening paragraph, tell why you are writing) When I receive my B.A. degree this spring, I would very much like to begin a career as a pharmaceutical salesperson.

(In the ensuing paragraphs, tell what makes you the right person for the job) I had no idea I would be interested in this field when I majored in speech. Then I chose a minor in marketing and discovered they fit together beautifully. The third part of the equation was knowing a friend of my mother who works for a pharmaceutical company in sales. I spent a good deal of time with her, shadowed her on calls, and decided this was the career I was meant for.

(In the last paragraph, tell what you will do next) I plan to visit Pittsburgh sometime around June 15 and would greatly appreciate a few moments of your time. If you have no openings at your company, perhaps you might refer me to other organizations. I will call you at least a week before I make my trip to see if you have time to visit with me.

(End with a proper closing)
Sincerely,

(signature) *Janet R. Mars*

Janet R. Mars

- **Connection between major and career.** Ask employers if they look for graduates with certain majors or academic backgrounds for their entry-level positions.
- **Skill development.** Get involved in work experiences or campus activities that will allow you to develop skills and areas of expertise useful to your career plans. Find a summer job in that area or volunteer as an intern. Keep a record of skills you have demonstrated.
- **Understanding the marketplace.** What's popular today may not be so popular in four or five years. Never choose a major based on the "in" thing to do when you're a new student. For one thing, it may be all wrong for your skills, aptitudes, personality, and so forth. For another, by the time you graduate, it may be unimportant or even nonexistent.

Career planning isn't a quick and easy way to find out what you want to do with your life, but it can point you to potentially satisfying jobs and help you find your place in the world of work.

CHRONOLOGICAL RESUME

Rita Resume
3130 Appian Way
Columbia, SC 29229
(803) 989-000, rway@infi.com

OBJECTIVE
Seeking entry-level position in finance utilizing analytical, supervisory, and organizational skills.

EDUCATION
Bachelor of Science in Business Administration, May 2003
University of South Carolina, Columbia, SC
- Major: Finance
- GPA in major: 3.2/4.0
- Financed 60% of educational expenses

RELATED EXPERIENCE
Intern, Bank of Carolina, Summer 1998, Columbia, SC
- Developed procedures manual for tellers
- Performed financial analyses for loan packages
- Supervised summer student staff

OTHER EXPERIENCE
Assistant Manager, Pop's Deli, September 1998–present, Columbia, SC
- Supervised wait staff of ten
- Ordered $1,000 in supplies weekly
- Trained twelve new employees
- Increased sales by 10%

Manager's Assistant, Aiken Pool, Summer 1997, Aiken, SC
- Assisted with supervision of aquatic facility used daily by 300 people
- Organized concession stand with $300 daily sales

ACTIVITIES
President, Zeta, Zeta, Zeta Sorority
USC, Columbia, SC
- Organized and supervised work of ten committees
- Allocated annual budget of $15,000
- Interacted with university, city, and state officials
- Membership increased 10% during presidency

Chairman, Panhellenic Council
USC, Columbia, SC
- Convened and led weekly meetings
- Supervised work of all committees
- Organized fund-raising that raised $25,000
Delta Sigma Pi Business Fraternity
Water skiing Club
Equestrian Club

INTERESTS
Golf, tennis, English literature

REFERENCES
Available upon request

SKILLS RESUME

Sammie S. Skillful
Sskillful@infi.com

Present Address
2424 Main Street
Columbia, SC 29211
(803) 999-9999

Permanent Address
39 Sherman Avenue
Lake George, SC 29999
(803) 267-8989

OBJECTIVE
Seeking hospitality related managerial position utilizing sales, organizational, and supervisory experience.

EDUCATION
Bachelor of Arts in English, December 2003
University of South Carolina, Columbia, SC
- GPA: 3.87/4.0
- Financed 100% of educational expenses

SKILLS

Initiative
- Developed and promoted summer pool parties
- Established and managed in-home dining service
- Developed marketing strategy and arranged promotions

Organization
- Organized parties for up to 500 area residents
- Hired and trained staff of six
- Ordered supplies on a monthly basis

Supervision
- Supervised staff of ten hired for New Year's Eve party
- Hired and trained staff of four for own dining business

Computer
- Designed promotional materials using desktop publishing
- Created and maintained customer database

EXPERIENCE
Self-Employed, June 1996–August 1998
Diner's Delight, Columbia, SC

Self-Employed, August 1994–May 1996
Parties Plus, Columbia, SC

Bagger, May–August 1993
Wee Pig Food Store, Charleston, SC
- Received six monthly awards for most courteous service

HONORS
Sigma Tau Delta English Honor Society, Golden Key National Honor Society, Dean's List, Phi Beta Kappa

INTERESTS
Jogging, skiing, reading

REFERENCES
Available upon request

Figure 13.2 (continued)

Who's Your Academic Advisor?

Find out and record the name of your academic advisor or counselor, along with his or her office location, phone number, and normal advising hours. If you have not already done so, arrange to meet this person.

Name: _____

Office location: _____

Phone(s): _____

_____

Hours: _____

EXERCISE 13.2

Advising Process and Schedules

To prepare for your basic academic advising sessions, do the following:

1. Find out when the course selection and scheduling process for next term begins, and record the date here: _____

2. Record what you need to do to prepare for this process (include any important dates):

_____

_____

_____

_____

_____

Don't forget to transfer the important dates to your calendar so you'll be prepared!

EXERCISE 13.3

Preparing to Meet with Your Advisor

Think ahead to your next appointment with your advisor. What questions do you have in each of the following areas? Record those questions here. (You may be able to answer some of these questions yourself by consulting your catalog.)

1. Your major and potential career:

_____

_____

2. Alternate majors and potential careers:

_____

_____

3. Classes you need next term:

_____

_____

4. Proper sequencing of classes you need to take:

_____

_____

5. Difficulty level of classes you may be taking next term:

_____

_____

6. Good balance in the combination of class work loads and types of classes you have chosen:

_____

_____

7. Electives you might be interested in:

_____

_____

8. Schedule problems:

_____

_____

9. Teaching styles of specific instructors:

_____

_____

10. General campus information:

_____

_____

11. Information about scholarships, internships, cooperative education, or other opportunities:

_____

_____

12. Other questions or issues including change of major:

_____

_____

Throughout the rest of this term, use this worksheet to record other questions for your advisor as you think of them. To make good use of your appointment time, take this list and your catalog with you. If you're considering transferring, also bring the catalog from the school to which you may want to transfer.

EXERCISE 13.4 ## Finding Your Catalog and Starting a File

A If you haven't already received your catalog, check with your advisor or counselor. Make sure you have the catalog that is dated the year you matriculated, or entered a program of study, at your institution, not the year you applied for admission and were accepted.

B Start a file for your catalog and other documents such as your grade reports, advisement forms, fee payment receipts, schedule change forms, and other proof of financial and academic dealings with your institution. Plan to keep all these things until your diploma is in your hands.

C If it is likely that you may transfer to another college to complete an associate or bachelor's degree, also obtain a copy of the catalog for that school. It will be useful when you meet with your advisor to plan your courses.

EXERCISE 13.5 Finding Some Key Dates

Look through your college catalog. Find and record the following important dates:

Publication date of the catalog: _____

	This Term	Next Term
First day of classes	_____	_____
Last day to add a class	_____	_____
Last day (if any) to drop a class without penalty	_____	_____
Midpoint in the term	_____	_____
Last day of classes	_____	_____
Final exam period (first day)	_____	_____
Final exam period (last day)	_____	_____
Official last day of term	_____	_____
Holidays (no classes held):		
_____	_____	_____
_____	_____	_____
_____	_____	_____
_____	_____	_____
_____	_____	_____

Add these dates to your calendar. If your campus has a web site or other online information system, see how many of the items are available online.

Note: If not in your catalog, this information should be available in the master schedule of classes for the current term.

EXERCISE 13.6 Scoping Out the Catalog

Bring your catalog to class. Form a small group with several other students who plan to follow a program or enroll in a major similar to your own. Do the following as a group.

1. From information in the catalog, answer the following questions about the program or major:
   a. What are the core requirements of the program?
   b. What prerequisites (if any) are there for the program?
   c. Is there a sequence that must be followed when taking specific courses? (For example, are there some courses that must be taken in order but are taught only in certain terms?)
   d. What courses will each person in the group need or plan to take next term? If your campus has a web site or other online information system, use it as a resource to look for this information.
2. Find at least one specific piece of information that might be useful or surprising to other members of the class. Prepare to report on that information.

EXERCISE 13.7 What Are Your Life Goals?

The following list includes life goals some people set for themselves. This list can help you begin to think about the kinds of goals you may want to set. Place a check mark next to the goals you would like to achieve in your life. Next, review the goals you have checked and circle the five you want most. Finally, review your list of five goals and rank them by priority (1 for most important, 5 for least important).

_____ the love and admiration of friends

_____ good health

_____ lifetime financial security

_____ a lovely home

_____ international fame

_____ freedom within my work setting

_____ a good love relationship

_____ a satisfying religious faith

_____ recognition as the most attractive person in the world

_____ an understanding of the meaning of life

_____ success in my profession

_____ a personal contribution to the elimination of poverty and sickness

_____ a chance to direct the destiny of a nation

_____ freedom to do what I want

_____ a satisfying and fulfilling marriage

_____ a happy family relationship

_____ complete self-confidence

_____ other:_____

Note: Adapted from *Human Potential Seminar* by James D. McHolland, Evanston, IL, 1975. Used by permission of the author.

EXERCISE 13.8 **Personality Mosaic**

Circle the numbers of the statements that clearly feel like something you might say or do or think. When you have finished, circle the same numbers on the answer grid on page 209.

1. It's important for me to have a strong, agile body.

2. I need to understand things thoroughly.

3. Music, color, beauty of any kind can really affect my moods.

4. People enrich my life and give it meaning.

5. I have confidence in myself that I can make things happen.

6. I appreciate clear directions so I know exactly what I can do.

7. I can usually carry/build/fix things myself.

8. I can get absorbed for hours in thinking something out.

9. I appreciate beautiful surroundings; color and design mean a lot to me.

10. I love company.

11. I enjoy competing.

12. I need to get my surroundings in order before I start a project.

13. I enjoy making things with my hands.

14. It's satisfying to explore new ideas.

15. I always seem to be looking for new ways to express my creativity.

16. I value being able to share personal concerns with people.

17. Being a key person in a group is very satisfying to me.

18. I take pride in being careful about all the details of my work.

19. I don't mind getting my hands dirty.

20. I see education as a lifelong process of developing and sharpening my mind.

21. I love to dress in unusual ways, to try new colors and styles.

22. I can often sense when a person needs to talk to someone.

23. I enjoy getting people organized and on the move.

24. A good routine helps me get the job done.

25. I like to buy sensible things that I can make or work on myself.

26. Sometimes I can sit for hours and work on puzzles or read or just think about life.

27. I have a great imagination.

28. It makes me feel good to take care of people.

29. I like to have people rely on me to get the job done.

30. I'm satisfied knowing that I've done an assignment carefully and completely.

31. I'd rather be on my own doing practical, hands-on activities.

32. I'm eager to read about any subject that arouses my curiosity.

33. I love to try creative new ideas.

34. If I have a problem with someone, I prefer to talk it out and resolve it.

35. To be successful, it's important to aim high.

36. I prefer being in a position where I don't have to take responsibility for decisions.

37. I don't enjoy spending a lot of time discussing things. What's right is right.

38. I need to analyze a problem pretty thoroughly before I act on it.

39. I like to rearrange my surroundings to make them unique and different.

40. When I feel down, I find a friend to talk to.

41. After I suggest a plan, I prefer to let others take care of the details.

42. I'm usually content where I am.

43. It's invigorating to do things outdoors.

44. I keep asking "why."

45. I like my work to be an expression of my moods and feelings.

46. I like to find ways to help people care more for each other.

47. It's exciting to take part in important decisions.

48. I'm always glad to have someone else take charge.

49. I like my surroundings to be plain and practical.

50. I need to stay with a problem until I figure out an answer.

51. The beauty of nature touches something deep inside me.

52. Close relationships are important to me.

53. Promotion and advancement are important to me.

54. Efficiency, for me, means doing a set amount carefully each day.

55. A strong system of law and order is important to prevent chaos.

56. Thought-provoking books always broaden my perspective.

57. I look forward to seeing art shows, plays, and good films.

58. I haven't seen you for so long. I'd love to know what you're doing.

59. It's exciting to be able to influence people.

60. Good, hard physical work never hurt anyone.

61. When I say I'll do it, I follow through on every detail.

62. I'd like to learn all there is to know about subjects that interest me.

63. I don't want to be like everyone else. I like to do things differently.

64. Tell me how I can help you.

65. I'm willing to take some risks to get ahead.

66. I like exact directions and clear rules when I start something new.

67. The first thing I look for in a car is a well-built engine.

68. Those people are intellectually stimulating.

69. When I'm creating, I tend to let everything else go.

70. I feel concerned that so many people in our society need help.

71. It's fun to get ideas across to people.

72. I hate it when they keep changing the system just when I get it down.

73. I usually know how to take care of things in an emergency.

74. Just reading about new discoveries is exciting.

75. I like to create happenings.

76. I often go out of my way to pay attention to people who seem lonely and friendless.

77. I love to bargain.

78. I don't like to do things unless I'm sure they're approved.

79. Sports are important in building strong bodies.

80. I've always been curious about the way nature works.

81. It's fun to be in a mood to try to do something unusual.

82. I believe that people are basically good.

83. If I don't make it the first time, I usually bounce back with energy and enthusiasm.

84. I appreciate knowing exactly what people expect of me.

85. I like to take things apart to see if I can fix them.

86. Don't get excited. We can think it out and plan the right move logically.

87. It would be hard to imagine my life without beauty around me.

88. People often seem to tell me their problems.

89. I can usually connect with people who get me in touch with a network of resources.

90. I don't need much to be happy.

Now circle the same numbers below that you circled above.

R	I	A	S	E	C
1	2	3	4	5	6
7	8	9	10	11	12
13	14	15	16	17	18
19	20	21	22	23	24
25	26	27	28	29	30
31	32	33	34	35	36
37	38	39	40	41	42
43	44	45	46	47	48
49	50	51	52	53	54
55	56	57	58	59	60
61	62	63	64	65	66
67	68	69	70	71	72
73	74	75	76	77	78
79	80	81	82	83	84
85	86	87	88	89	90

Now add up the number of circles in each column.

R _____ I _____ A _____ S _____ E _____ C _____

Which are your three highest scores?

1st _____ 2nd _____ 3rd _____

Now go back and reread the descriptions of these three types and see how accurately they describe you.

Note: From Betty Neville Michelozzi, *Coming Alive from Nine to Five*, 4th ed. Mountain View, CA: Mayfield, © 1980, 1984, 1988, 1992. Used by permission of the publisher.

EXERCISE 13.9 **The Holland Hexagon**

A Go back to Exercise 13.8 and look at your three categories. Based on the list of careers listed above, how well do the three categories match your career interests?

_____

_____

_____

_____

B Now look at the Holland hexagon in Figure 13.1. See where your first, second, and third choices in Exercise 13.8 are located on the hexagon. Are they close together or far apart? If far apart, do you feel they reflect a conflict in your goals or interests? Write a brief statement about how the conflict has affected you so far.

_____

_____

_____

_____

EXERCISE 13.10 **Exploring New Fields**

If you are a returning student who's chosen college as a path to a new career, the following exercise may be especially helpful in sorting out your options.

1. What interests have you developed from life and work that might be part of your future career planning?

_____

_____

2. What skills do you bring from life and work that might be assets in other careers?

_____

_____

_____

3. What things do you most enjoy about your present or most recent work?

_____

_____

_____

4. What things do you least enjoy about your present or most recent work?

_____

_____

_____

5. Go through your college catalog and list any majors that interest you. At this point, don't worry too much about whether the subject seems unfamiliar or too difficult. List the majors below, along with the reasons they appeal to you. As much as possible, try to link the reasons to your comments in the first four items of this exercise.

Major: _____   Reasons: _____

Major: _____   Reasons: _____

Major: _____   Reasons: _____

Major: _____   Reasons: _____

6. Discuss your responses in class, with your academic advisor, or with a career counselor. Rethink your choices in light of these discussions.

EXERCISE 13.11
INTERNET
ACTIVITY

Internet Career Resources

The Internet offers a variety of resources for choosing a career. These resources include Oakland University's "Definitive Guide to Internet Career Resources" *(http://phoenix.placement.oakland.edu/career/guide.htm)*, an extensive listing of career sites; "The Catapult on Job Web" *(http://www.jobweb. org/catapult/catapult.htm)*, a major guide with links to career and job-related sites; "The Riley Guide to Employment Opportunities and Job Resources on the Internet" *(http://www.dbm.com/jobguide/)*; and "Find Your Career Guide from U.S. News Online" *(http://www4.usnews.com/usnews/edu/beyond/ bccguide.htm)*. Other Internet career resources include:

American Career InfoNet Career Resources Library: *http://www.acinet.org/ resource/misc/#diverse*

Yahoo Business/Employment menu: *http://www.yahoo.com/Business/ Employment/*

E-Span Association Library: *http://www.espan.com/library/asso.html*

Career Resources Center: *http://www.careers.org/*

Advancing Women Career Center: *http://www.advancingwomen.com/awcareer. html*

Peterson's web site: *http://www.petersons.com/*

What Color Is Your Parachute: The Net Guide: *http://www.washingtonpost. com/parachute*

(Go to *http://csuccess.wadsworth.com* for the most up-to-date URLs.)

Describe the resources available at four or more sites.

_____

_____

_____

_____

Of the sites you visited, which is better for gathering information about a future job? Which is better for finding a job immediately?

_____

_____

Writing a Resume and Cover Letter

A Following the models on page 203 of this chapter, write two resumes of your accomplishments to date, using the chronological model for one and the skills model for the other. Then write a second resume that projects what you would like your resume to contain five years from now, using one model or the other.

B Next, use your career or campus library to find the name and address of someone in a field in which you think you would like to work. Write a cover letter to go with your resume using this name and address and turn it in to your instructor.

SUGGESTIONS FOR FURTHER READING

Berg, A. *Finding the Work You Love: A Woman's Career Guide.* San Jose, CA: Resource Publications, 1993.

Birsner, E. P. *Mid-Career Job Hunting: Official Handbook of the Forty Plus Club.* New York: Prentice-Hall, 1991.

Bolles, Richard N. *What Color Is Your Parachute? A Practical Manual for Job Hunters and Career Changers.* Berkeley, CA: Ten Speed Press, 1996.

Criscito, P. *Resumes in Cyberspace: Your complete guide to a computerized job search.* Hauppauge, NY: Barron's Educational Services, Inc., 1997.

Dictionary of Occupational Titles (DOT). Washington, DC: Bureau of Labor Statistics.

Directory of Directories. Detroit: Gale Research. Published annually.

Encyclopedia of Associations. Detroit: Gale Research. Published annually.

Field, S. *100 Best Careers for the 21st Century.* New York: Macmillan, 1996.

Gelberg, S., & Chojnacki. *Career and Life Planning with Gay, Lesbian, and Bisexual Persons.* Alexandria, VA: American Counseling Association, 1996.

Harbin, Carey E. *Your Transfer Planner: Strategic Goals and Guerrilla Tactics.* Belmont, CA: Wadsworth, 1995.

Holland, John. *The Self-Directed Search Professional Manual.* Gainesville, FL: Psychological Assessment Resources, 1985.

Jackson, Tom, & E. Jackson. *The New Perfect Resume.* New York: Doubleday, 1996.

Kennedy, J. L. *Hook Up, Get Hired! The Internet Job Search Revolution.* New York: John Wiley, 1995.

Kissane, S. F. *Career Success for People with Physical Disabilities.* Lincolnwood, IL: MTC Publishing Group, 1997.

Kocher, E. *International Jobs: Where They Are and How to Get Them.* Reading, PA: Addison-Wesley, 1993.

Lauber, D. *Professional's Job Finder.* River Forest, IL: Planning/Communications, 1997.

Michelozzi, B. N. *Coming Alive from Nine to Five.* Mountain View, CA: Mayfield, 1996.

Occupational Outlook Handbook. Washington, DC: U.S. Government Publication Staff. Published annually.

Riley, M., F. Roehm, & S. Oserman. *The Guide to Internet Job Searching.* Lincolnwood, IL: NTC Publishing Group, 1996.

Rivera, M. *The Minority Career.* Holbrook, MA: Bob Adams, 1991.

Salzman, Marian, & Nancy Marx Better. *Wanted: Liberal Arts Graduates.* New York: Doubleday, 1987.

Smith, Devon Coltrell, ed. *Great Careers: The Fourth of July Guide to Careers, Internships, and Volunteer Opportunities in the Non-Profit Sector.* Garrett Park, MD: Garrett Park, 1990.

RESOURCES

Thinking about what you want for a career may feel overwhelming, or you may have a clear idea even now, or you may fall somewhere in between. Career interest information, academic program information, and major and course descriptions can sometimes seem abstract. One thing that can help you find the best fit for your talents and strengths is to talk to people who are taking the courses, following the majors, and pursuing the careers that you are interested in. Use this Resources page to list people whom you could interview for information about courses, majors, and careers. Be creative. Over the years, this list could grow into a major networking tool.

STUDENTS WHO COULD BE RESOURCES FOR MAJORS AND COURSES

Name:	Major:	Course(s):	Phone number:

PEOPLE WHO COULD BE RESOURCES FOR CAREER AREAS

Don't forget your advisor, instructors, relatives, family, and friends. Also include people you may have met volunteering (see the Resources exercise in Chapter 14).

Name:	Career/Job title:	Phone number:

JOURNAL

NAME _____

DATE _____

Academic advising and career planning are closely linked in terms of the preparations you should be making for the balance of your college years and beyond.

What steps have you already considered or taken that relate to these topics?

....

....

....

....

....

....

....

....

Now that you've read this chapter, what steps are you thinking about taking?

....

....

....

....

....

....

....

....

....

What steps can you take at this stage in your college career to help reach your goals?

....

....

....

....

....

....

....

....

Values: Setting Standards for Academic and Personal Integrity

CHAPTER OUTLINE

Defining Values

Discovering Values

Challenges to Personal Values in College

Changing Intellectual Values

Academic Honesty

Choosing Values

KEYS TO SUCCESS

- *Improve your critical thinking skills.*
- *Understand why you are in college.*
- *Get to know at least one person on campus who cares about your survival.*
- *Get involved in campus activities.*
- *Try to have realistic expectations.*

> **"** *It amazes me to hear people talk about what's important to them. Two of my friends think nothing of spending the night together. Someone else I know admits to cheating on an exam to raise his grade. Another friend feels guilty if he misses church, and someone else says she's plagiarized material for her term paper. I thought people here were going to feel more like I do.* **"**

Discussions about values often generate more heat than light because the word *values* means different things to different people. For some the word refers to specific positions a person holds on controversial moral issues such as capital punishment. For others it refers to whatever might be most important to a person, such as a good job, a fancy car, or the welfare of the family. For still others it refers to abstractions such as truth, justice, or success. In this chapter, we offer a definition of values and explore ways to discover your values and apply them to the college experience.

■ DEFINING VALUES

Perhaps we can best define a value as an important attitude or belief that commits us *to take action, to do something*. We may not necessarily act in response to others' feelings, but when we truly hold a value we act on it.

For instance, we might watch a television program showing starving people and feel sympathy or regret but take no action whatsoever. If our feelings of sympathy cause us to take action to help those who are suffering, those feelings qualify as values. Actions do not have to be overtly physical. They may involve thinking and talking continually about a problem, trying to interest others in it, reading about it, or sending letters to officials regarding it. The basic point is that when we truly hold a value, it leads us to do something.

We can also define values as beliefs that we accept *by choice*, with a sense of responsibility and ownership. Much of what we think is simply what others have taught us. Many things we have learned from our parents and others close to us will count as our values, but only once we fully embrace them ourselves, for *we must personally accept or reject something before it can become a value*.

Finally, we should be proud of our values and the choices to which they lead and want others to know it. We should also find ourselves ready to sacrifice for them and to establish our priorities around them. Our values govern our loyalties and commitments.

In summary, then, our values are those important attitudes or beliefs that we

- accept by choice
- affirm with pride
- express in action

SEE EXERCISE 14.1

SEE EXERCISE 14.2

SEE EXERCISE 14.3

As you clarify your values in college, you can choose activities that affirm several of them at the same time. What different values can you guess are important to this student volunteer? (Two seem obvious; what others do you see?)

PHOTO BY ANGELA MANN

■ DISCOVERING VALUES

You should already have at least a fair sense of what your values are. Yet one of your key tasks in college is to more consciously define your own approach to life and articulate, or clarify, those values. College presents an opportunity to locate and test those values by analyzing their full implications, comparing them with the values of others, and giving voice to your beliefs.

Identifying your values is at once simple and complex. One way to start is by asking yourself directly what your most important values are.

Another way to begin discovering your values is by looking at some choices you have already made in response to life's demands and opportunities. Many students will say that they chose a certain college because of its academic reputation. How much do you value your school's reputation? And more precisely, what does the word *reputation* mean to you? Are you interested in the prestige that comes from enrolling in the college? Does this signify an interest in high achievement and in meeting demanding standards? Obviously, a value such as prestige can run in several directions—one being social, another intellectual. To find the values that stand behind your choices, you must continually explore the reasons behind those choices.

Many students say they have chosen a college because it offers the best opportunity for a good job in the future. Is this true for you? The choice to seek education in terms of your future career suggests any number of possible values. Does this mean that economic security is one of your top values, or does it suggest that you are defining personal success or power in terms of wealth? And once again, what are the implications of your choice? How much are you willing to sacrifice to achieve the goals connected with this economic value? How well will your obligations to family and to society correlate with this value?

Conflict in values is a frequent and sometimes difficult problem. How far are you willing to go to uphold this value? What sacrifices do you accept in its name? How do the values you have chosen provide you with a meaning for your future?

Identifying your values is not a one-time task—strongly held values may change with time and experience. Thus you should not only develop a sense of your present values but also gain some sense of how they are evolving in a variety of areas: personal, moral, political, economic, social, religious, and intellectual, just as you are gaining some sense of the many ways you are developing as an individual (see "Aspects of Student Development," Figure 2.1 on page 22).

SEE EXERCISE 14.4

■ CHALLENGES TO PERSONAL VALUES IN COLLEGE

Most students find that college life challenges their existing personal and moral values. First-year students are often startled at the diversity of personal moralities found on campus. For instance, some students have been taught that it is wrong to drink alcohol, yet they find that friends whom they respect and care about see nothing wrong with drinking. Students from more liberal backgrounds may be astonished to discover themselves forming friendships with classmates whose personal values are very conservative.

When you don't approve of some aspects of a friend's way of life, do you try to change his or her behavior, pass judgment on the person, or withdraw from the relationship? Often, part of the problem is that the friend demonstrates countless good qualities and values that make the troublesome conduct seem less significant. In the process, your own values may begin to change under the influence of a new kind of relativism: I don't choose to do that, but I'm not going to make any judgments against those who do.

SEE EXERCISE 14.5

In cases where a friendship is affected by differing values, tolerance is generally a good goal. Tolerance for others is a central value in our society and one that often grows during college. Even so, it is easy to think of cases in which tolerance gradually becomes an indulgence of another's destructive tendencies. It is one thing to accept a friend's responsible use of alcohol at a party and quite another to fail to challenge a drunk who plans to drive you home. Sexual intimacy in an enduring relationship may be one thing; a never-ending series of one-night stands is quite another. Remember, the failure to challenge destructive conduct is no sign of friendship.

At the same time, it is appropriate to talk about values with those whose values seem to be in conflict with our own. What are the other person's true values (consciously identified, freely chosen, and actively expressed)? Do his or her current behaviors correspond to those values? Both of you can learn a great deal from talking about why you value what you do.

Many people make the mistake of fleeing from diversity and failing to confront conflicting value systems. The problem is that such people soon will find themselves unable to cope with the next set of challenges facing them. They will find it difficult to grow as persons because they do not prize their own values enough to speak for them, and their behaviors are not consistent with what they say they value. Although it's only a first step, you must work through challenges to your own personal values by finding answers that truly make sense to you and help you move ahead with your life.

■ CHANGING INTELLECTUAL VALUES

Intellectual values such as clarity, accuracy, rigor, and excellence cluster around the central value of truth. One of the most striking transitions that occurs during college has to do with the way in which a person's notion of truth changes.

Many students enter college assuming the process of education is one in which unquestioned authorities pour truth into students' open ears. They may believe every problem has a single right answer and the instructor or the textbook is always a source of truth. Yet most college instructors don't believe this, and their views on truth may initially shock these students.

It's not that the teacher is cynical about the possibility of truth, but rather that he or she is seeking as many valid interpretations of the information as can be found. College instructors continually ask for reasons, for arguments, for the assumptions on which a given position is based, and for the evidence that confirms or discounts it.

Just as with personal and moral values, college-level education assumes that as a student you will become a maker of your own meaning, with the ultimate responsibility for judging truth and falseness resting in your hands.

SEE EXERCISE 14.6

■ ACADEMIC HONESTY

Honesty and integrity are values crucial to the search for truth and academic freedom. Imagine where our society would be if researchers reported fraudulent results that were then used to develop new machines or medical treatments. Integrity is a cornerstone of higher education, and activities that compromise that integrity damage everyone.

Colleges and universities have academic integrity policies or honor codes that clearly define cheating, lying, plagiarism, and other forms of dishonest conduct, but it is often difficult to know how those rules apply to specific situations. Is it really lying to tell an instructor you missed class because you were "not feeling well" (whatever "well" means) or because you were experiencing vague "car trouble" (some people think car trouble includes anything from a flat tire to difficulty finding a parking spot!)?

Types of Misconduct

Institutions vary widely in how specifically they define broad terms such as *lying* or *cheating*. For instance, one university's code of student academic integrity defines cheating as "intentionally using or attempting to use unauthorized materials, information, notes, study aids or other devices . . . [including] unauthorized communication of information during an academic exercise." This would apply to looking over a classmate's shoulder for an answer, using a calculator when it is not authorized, procuring or discussing an exam without permission, copying lab notes, and duplicating computer files.

Plagiarism is especially intolerable in the academic culture. *Plagiarism* means taking another person's ideas or work and presenting them as your own. Just as taking someone else's property constitutes physical theft, taking credit for someone else's ideas constitutes intellectual theft.

Rules for referencing (or citing) another's ideas apply more strictly to the papers you write than to your responses on a test. On tests you do not have to credit specific individuals for their ideas. On written reports and papers, however, you must give credit any time you use (1) another person's actual words, (2) another person's ideas or theories—even if you don't quote them directly, and (3) any other information not considered common knowledge. Check with your instructors about how to cite material they've covered in classroom lectures. Usually you do not need to provide a reference for this, but it is always better to ask first.

Many schools prohibit other activities besides lying, cheating, and plagiarism. For instance, the University of Delaware prohibits fabrication

The Right to Vote

No matter what their political preferences, college students have a poor record of showing up to vote. The 18- to 21-year-old group has the lowest turnout of any age group and its participation has been falling—with one exception—since 1972, when 18-year-olds voted in their first presidential election. Participation fell every presidential election after 1972, bottoming out in the 1988 contest between George Bush and Michael Dukakis. That year just 39 percent of 18- to 21-year-olds said they voted, and that number may be high, because many people are reluctant to admit that they didn't vote. The exception? The Clinton–Bush presidential battle of 1992, when more young people voted for the first time in twenty years.

How would you explain the apparent lack of interest in voting? Why do you think more young people voted in the Clinton–Bush election year?

Source: Knight–Ridder/Tribune News Service, June 30, 1996.

(intentionally inventing information or results); the University of North Carolina outlaws multiple submission (earning credit more than once for the same piece of academic work without permission); Eastern Illinois University rules out tendering of information (giving your work or exam answer to another student to copy during the actual exam or before the exam is given to another section); and the University of South Carolina prohibits bribery (trading something of value in exchange for any kind of academic advantage). Most schools also outlaw helping or attempting to help another student commit a dishonest act.

Some outlawed behaviors do not seem to fall within any clear category. Understanding the mission and values of higher education will help you make better decisions about those behaviors that fall through the cracks.

Reducing the Likelihood of Problems

In order to avoid becoming intentionally or unintentionally involved in academic misconduct, consider the reasons it could happen.

Ignorance is one reason. In a survey at the University of South Carolina, 20 percent of students incorrectly thought that buying a term paper wasn't cheating. Forty percent thought using a test file (a collection of actual tests from previous terms, usually kept by an organization such as a fraternity or sorority) was fair behavior. Sixty percent thought it was all right to get answers from someone who had taken an exam earlier in the same or in a prior semester. What do you think?

In other countries and on some U.S. campuses, students are encouraged to review past exams as practice exercises. It is also acceptable on some cam-

Does Cheating Hurt Anyone?

WHAT ABOUT THE INDIVIDUAL?

- **Cheating sabotages academic growth.** Cheating confuses and weakens the process by which students demonstrate understanding of course content. Because the grade and the instructor's comments apply to someone else's work, cheating prevents accurate feedback.

- **Cheating sabotages personal growth.** Educational accomplishments inspire pride and confidence. What confidence in their ability will individuals have whose work is not their own?

- **Cheating may have long-term effects.** Taking the easy way in college may become a habit that can spill over into graduate school, jobs, and relationships. And consider this: Would you want a doctor, lawyer, or accountant who had cheated on exams handling your affairs?

WHAT ABOUT THE COMMUNITY?

- **Cheating jeopardizes the basic fairness of the grading process.** Widespread cheating causes honest students to become cynical and resentful, especially when grades are curved and the cheating directly affects other students.

- **Widespread cheating devalues a college degree.** Alumni, potential students, graduate schools, and employers learn to distrust degrees from schools where cheating is widespread.

SEE EXERCISE 14.7 INTERNET ACTIVITY

puses to share answers and information for homework and other assignments with friends. These behaviors are considered acts of generosity.

Instructors also may vary in their acceptance of such behaviors. Because there is no universal code that dictates such behaviors, you should ask your instructors for clarification. When a student is caught violating the academic code of a particular school or teacher, pleading ignorance of the rules is a weak defense.

A second reason some people cheat is that they overestimate the importance of grades, apart from actual learning, and fall into thinking they must succeed at any cost. This may reflect our society's competitive atmosphere. It also may be the result of pressure from parents, peers, or teachers. The desire for success at any cost is often accompanied by a strong fear of failure that is hard to confront and deal with.

A third common cause of cheating is a student's own lack of preparation or inability to manage time and activities. The problem is made worse if he or she is unwilling to ask an instructor to extend a deadline so that a project can be done well. Here are some steps you can take to reduce the likelihood of problems:

1. **Know the rules.** Learn the academic code for your school. If a teacher does not clarify his or her standards and expectations, ask exactly what the rules are.

2. **Set clear boundaries.** Work with a partner or study group to prepare for a test, but refrain from discussing past exams with others unless it is specifically permitted. Tell friends exactly what is acceptable or

unacceptable if you lend them a term paper. Refuse to "help" others who ask you to help them cheat. In test settings, keep your answers covered and your eyes down, and put all extraneous materials away. Help friends resist temptation. Make sure your typist understands that he or she may not make any changes in your work.

3. **Improve self-management.** Be well prepared for all quizzes, exams, projects, and papers. This may mean unlearning some bad habits (such as procrastination) and building better time management and study skills. Keep your own long-term goals in mind.

4. **Seek help.** Find out where you can obtain assistance with study skills, time management, and test-taking. If your methods are in good shape but the content of the course is too difficult, consult with your instructor.

5. **Withdraw from the course.** Consider cutting your losses before it's too late. Your school has a policy about dropping courses and a last day to drop without penalty (drop date). You may choose this route and plan to retake the course later. Some students may choose to withdraw from all their classes and take some time off before returning to school. This may be an option if you find yourself in over your head or if some unplanned event (a long illness, a family crisis) has caused you to fall too far behind. Check with your advisor or counselor.

6. **Reexamine goals.** You need to stick to your own realistic goals instead of giving in to pressure from family or friends to achieve impossibly high standards. What grades do you need, and what grades do you have the potential to earn? You may also feel pressure to enter a particular career or profession. If this isn't what you want, your frustration is likely to appear in your lack of preparation and your grades. If so, sit down with others—perhaps professionals in your career and counseling centers or your academic advisor and counselor—and explore alternatives.

■CHOOSING VALUES

We have stressed that the essential steps in developing a value system are to choose your own beliefs, affirm them to others with pride, and express them through your actions. But these are merely first steps. You must choose carefully so that your value system can lead to a coherent and fulfilling life. As crucial as it is to develop your own values, it is equally important that you

Search Online!

INFOTRAC COLLEGE EDITION

Try these phrases and others for Key Words and Subject Guide searches: "values," "academic integrity," "cheating in college."

Also look up:

The quest for shared values. (Wells College Pres. Robert A. Plane speech) (Transcript). *Vital Speeches* Feb 1, 1995 v61 n8 p250

Undergraduate cultures: whatever happened to Dink Stover? (review essay) Helen Lefkowitz Horowitz. *Change* Sept-Oct 1993 v25 n5 p62

What we know about cheating in college. (includes resources for maintaining academic integrity) Donald L. McCabe, Linda KlebeTrevino. *Change* Jan-Feb 1996 v28 n1 p28

Tales out of school: cheating has long been a great temptation, and the Internet makes it easier than ever. (Universities 97: the Seventh Annual Ranking) Joe Chidley. *Maclean's* Nov 24, 1997 p76

"The Only A"

As a student at a large, predominantly White university, I enrolled in an advanced composition course. The class of twenty-five or so was all White with the exception of me and another Black student. As part of the writing process, the instructor required the class to read each other's papers. After the first peer critiquing session, the other Black student and I compared notes and thought we saw a pattern.

Not only did our student critics seem to be critical of our writing, but their comments carried what we perceived as racial overtones. Needless to say we were both bothered by this, but decided to dismiss it as oversensitivity on our part—until we encountered the same sort of comments on our drafts the next week. The other student decided that our classmates were racially biased and dropped the class. I searched for a different approach, especially since I needed the course to complete my degree requirements in time.

I carefully considered the comments my classmates were making and decided that some of them were unfounded and probably motivated by personal bias. Many of their comments, however, were based upon instructions from the professor and appeared to be valid. I then sifted through their comments, discarding the obvious personal ones and paying attention to those that seemed justified. And each time the peer critique session was held, I wrote and rewrote my papers, basing many of my changes on the comments of my peer critics.

When grades were posted that semester, I made the traditional trek to the professor's office door, where he had promised to post the final grades. When I arrived, four or five of my classmates were perusing the grade roster, and I could tell that they were trying to decipher who had made what grade. Since only Social Security numbers appeared on the sheet, figuring out who was who was a little difficult. I approached the grade roster and looked for my grade. When I saw what it was, I placed my finger at the top of the list and ever so gently let it slide down the page, where, residing beside my Social Security number, was the only A in the class. The other students at the professor's door congratulated me, and I thanked them—both for their kind comments and for their help in netting me that A.

So what was an unbearable situation for one student became a success story for another, all because the two of us chose to react to a negative situation differently. Yes, I still think that some of the comments my classmates made on my papers were unnecessarily personal and harsh, but I also recognized the worthwhile comments. This approach allowed me to glean from a negative situation the positive elements that I used to my advantage.

—John Slade, Humanities Division of Arts and Sciences, Forsyth Technical Community College, Winston-Salem, North Carolina.

What values are evident in this story? Slade had many options but chose the one that led to success. What lesson does this example provide for you?

find ethical values. Little is accomplished if you develop a genuine system of values that leads to egocentric, dishonest, cruel, or irresponsible conduct.

There's no simple answer to the question of what constitutes ethical values. There are no automatic criteria (though perhaps the Golden Rule will serve as well as any). Yet all of us who have accepted life in a democratic society and membership in an academic community such as a college or university are committed to many significant values. To participate in democratic institutions is to honor values such as respect for others, tolerance, equality, liberty, and fairness. Members of an academic community are usually passionate in their defense of academic freedom, the open search for truth, honesty, collegiality, civility, and tolerance for dissenting views.

EXERCISE 14.1   Prioritizing Your Values

A Rank-order the following list of twenty-five values. (1 for the most important value, 2 for the second-most important value, and so on).

_____ companionship

_____ family life

_____ security

_____ being financially and materially successful

_____ enjoying leisure time

_____ work

_____ learning and getting an education

_____ appreciating nature

_____ competing and winning

_____ loving others and being loved

_____ a relationship with God/spirituality

_____ self-respect and pride

_____ being productive and achieving

_____ enjoying an intimate relationship

_____ having solitude and private time to reflect

_____ having a good time and being with others

_____ laughter and a sense of humor

_____ intelligence and a sense of curiosity

_____ opening up to new experiences

_____ risk-taking and personal growth

_____ being approved of and liked by others

_____ being challenged and meeting challenges well

_____ courage

_____ compassion

_____ being of service to others

B Look at your top three choices. What was the source for each of these values? We usually learn values from important people, peak events, or societal trends. List each value and try to indicate where you learned it.

C Review the values and their sources. Do you see an overall pattern? If so, what does the pattern tell you about yourself? Were there any surprises?

Note: List used with permission from Gerald Corey and Marianne Schneider Corey, *I Never Knew I Had a Choice*, 5th ed. Pacific Grove, CA: Brooks/Cole, 1993.

EXERCISE 14.2   Evidence of Values

Another way to start discovering your values is by defining them in relation to some immediate evidence or circumstances. First list fifteen items in your room (or apartment or house) that are important or that symbolize something important to you.

Now cross out the five items that are least important—the ones you could most easily live without. Of the remaining ten, cross out the three that are least important. Of the remaining seven, cross out two more. Of the remaining five, cross out two more. Rank-order the final three items from most to least important. What has this exercise told you about what you value?

Shared Values?

A List all the reasons you chose to attend college. (Look back at your responses to Chapter 1, Exercises 1.4 and 1.5, regarding your reasons for attending college.) Share your reasons in a small group. Attempt to arrive at a consensus about the five most important reasons people choose to attend college. Then rank the top five, from most important to least important.

B Share your final rankings with other groups in the class. How similar were the results of the groups? How different? How easy or hard was it to reach a consensus in your group? In other groups? What does the exercise tell you about the consistency of values among members of the class?

EXERCISE 14.4   Your Values and Your Family's Values

The process by which we assimilate values into our own value systems involves three steps:

1. choosing (selecting freely from alternatives after thoughtful consideration of the consequences)
2. prizing (cherishing the value and affirming it publicly)
3. acting (consistently displaying this value in behavior and decisions).

A List three values your family has taught you are important. Document how you have completed the three-step process above to make each of their values yours.

B If you haven't completed the three steps, does it mean you have not chosen this value as your own? Explain your thoughts about this.

Friends and Values

A Consider several friends and think about their values. Pick one who really differs from you in some important value. Write about the differences.

B In a small group, discuss this difference in values. Explore how it's possible to be friends with someone so different.

EXERCISE 14.6   Applying Your Values in College

Recall Chapter 4 on time management, which discussed prioritizing activities by their importance to you. This is a way of expressing your values through actions. For the following two values, list a variety of actions that would express your values for (a) achieving excellence in college and (b) maintaining a great social life.

Although achieving excellence and maintaining a social life may not seem like conflicting values, the actions that express the values may cause conflict. In other words, acting on one value may prevent you from staying true to the other. Which of the actions you've listed might conflict with one another? If you held these two values, how would you reconcile each of these conflicts?

Institutional Values

Many colleges and universities post campus rules and regulations on their Internet sites. One such college is Southern Methodist University, whose student code of conduct is found at *http://www.smu.edu/~stulife/res_halls. html.*

A What policies and/or infractions does SMU provide for the following cases?

- keeping bicycles in dormitory rooms
- drinking alcohol in public
- (any other area of interest to you)

B Are these policies more or less strict than those at your institution? How so?

C Would you prefer to live under the code of conduct at Southern Methodist? Give your reasons.

D Compare SMU's regulations with the listing of "Student Rights and College Regulations of Brooklyn College of the City University of New York" (*http://www.brooklyn.cuny.edu/bc/info/right.htm*). How do they differ and with which do you feel more comfortable?

E Now compare both codes of conduct with those on your campus. How do your rules differ, and with which of them do you feel more comfortable? (Go to *http://csuccess.wadsworth.com* for the most up-to-date URLs.)

SUGGESTIONS FOR FURTHER READING

Bok, Sissela. *Lying.* New York: Vintage, 1989.

Broadus, Loren. *Ethics for Real People: A Guide for the Morally Perplexed.* St. Louis: Chalice Press, 1996.

Kolak, Daniel, & Raymond Martin. *Wisdom Without Answers: A Guide to the Experience of Philosophy,* 3rd ed. Belmont, CA: Wadsworth, 1996.

Pojman, Louis P. *Ethics: Discovering Right and Wrong,* 2nd ed. Belmont, CA: Wadsworth, 1995.

Spinello, Richard A. *Case Studies in Information and Computer Ethics.* Englewood Cliffs, NJ: Prentice-Hall, 1997.

Stein, Harry. *Ethics and Other Liabilities.* New York: St. Martin's, 1983.

Strike, Kenneth A., & Pamela A. Moss. *Ethics and College Student Life.* Allyn & Bacon, 1997.

RESOURCES

In keeping with this chapter's emphasis on values as chosen, affirmed, and acted upon, think about how you have acted, and can act in the future, on the values that you hold. Use this Resources page to make a list of activities and organizations that you can work with to express the values that you hold.

Look in the phone book, on the Internet, on bulletin boards, and so on, and make a list of organizations whose work you agree with and support.

Name of organization: Phone number:

Call several organizations that you are most interested in working with. Ask about volunteer opportunities. (Remember that volunteering can take many different forms: a daily or weekly commitment, helping out once a month or whenever needed, bringing in donations, working on newsletters, and so on. There are probably more possibilities than you realize.) Make a list of the opportunities or kinds of support that you could give at each organization.

Organization: Support I can give:

JOURNAL

NAME _____

DATE _____

Describe your current system of true values (chosen, affirmed, and acted upon).

....

....

....

....

In what ways has college already tested or changed these values?

....

....

....

....

....

Are you facing any issues related to academic honesty? What are they? What are you doing about them?

....

....

....

....

....

How are your actions serving your own best interests? The interests of other students? Your institution?

....

....

....

....

....

CHAPTER

Relationships and Campus Involvement

KEYS TO SUCCESS

- *Study with a group.*

- *See your instructors outside class.*

- *Get to know at least one person on campus who cares about your survival.*

- *Get involved in campus activities.*

- *Maintain connections with your home base, but be aware of the changes you may be going through and the impact of those changes on family and friends.*

- *Immerse yourself in your culture as you learn to interact with people of other cultures.*

❝ *So many different kinds of people here. It's not like my high school class. Should I stick with people who are more like me, or should I try to make friends with a bunch of different kinds of people? Might learn something from them. Then again, what I learn might not be so great, either.* **❞**

Once in a while, a class is so good or so bad that you may spontaneously write about it in your journal. Much of the time, however, you'll write about relationships: with dates, lovers, or lifelong partners; with friends and enemies; with parents and family; with roommates and classmates; and with new people and new groups.

Relationships are more than just aspects of your social life; they can also strongly influence your survival and success in college. Distracted by bad relationships, you can find it difficult to concentrate on your studies. Supported by good relationships, you will be better able to get through the rough times, reach your full potential, remain in college—and enjoy it.

■ DATING AND MATING

Loving an Idealized Image

Carl Gustav Jung, the Swiss psychiatrist, identified a key aspect of love: the idealized image we have of the perfect partner, which we project onto potential partners we meet.

The first task of any romantic relationship, then, is to see that the person you are in love with really exists. Specifically, you need to see beyond attraction to the person who is really there. Face it: Sex drives can be very powerful. Anything that can make your knees go weak and your mouth go dry at a single glance can affect your perceptions as well as your body. Are you in love or are you in lust? People in lust often sincerely believe they are in love, and more than a few will say almost anything to get what they want. But would you still want that person if sex were out of the question? Would that person still want you? A "no" answer bodes poorly for a relationship.

Folklore says love is blind. Believe it. Check out your perceptions with trusted friends; if they see a lot of problems that you do not, at least listen to them. Another good reality check is to observe a person's friends. Exceptional people rarely surround themselves with jerks and losers. If the person of your dreams tends to collect friends from your nightmares, watch out!

You should think carefully and repeatedly about what kind of person you really want in a relationship. If a prospective partner does not have the qualities you desire, don't pursue it. Also, pay attention to where you are looking. You won't catch mountain trout if you fish in a sewer.

Sexual Orientation

Although many people build intimate relationships with someone of the opposite sex, some people are attracted to, fall in love with, and make long-term commitments to a person of the same sex. Your sexuality, and who you choose to form intimate relationships with, is an important part of who you are.

An important component of understanding your own sexuality is listening closely to your own feelings, beliefs, and values. Your sexuality is your own; it isn't dictated by your family, by society, or by what the media present as normal. Although listening to your feelings is important, you will also find many resources if you are struggling with questions about your own sexuality. Talk about your feelings with someone you trust. Read some of the many books on the subject of sexuality and sexual orientation (some are listed in the "Suggestions for Further Reading" at the end of the chapter). Wherever you are in terms of your sexuality, it is important to remember that relationships that involve communication, trust, respect, and love are crucial to all people.

Developing a Relationship

Usually, relationships develop in stages. Early in a relationship, you may be wildly "in love." You may find yourself preoccupied—if not obsessed—with the other person, with feelings of intense longing when you are apart. When you are together, you may feel thrilled, blissful, yet also insecure and demanding. You are likely to idealize the other person, yet you may overreact to faults or disappointments. If the relationship sours, your misery is likely to be intense, and the only apparent relief from your pain lies in the hands of the very person who rejected you. Social psychologist Elaine Walster calls this the stage of *passionate love*.

Most psychologists see the first stage as being unsustainable—and that may be a blessing! A successful relationship will move on to a calmer, more stable stage. At this next stage, your picture of your partner is much more realistic. You feel comfortable and secure with each other. Your mutual love and respect stem from predictably satisfying companionship. Walster calls this more comfortable, long-lasting stage *companionate love*.

If a relationship is to last, it is vital to talk about it as you go along. What are you enjoying and why? What is disappointing you and what would make it better? Is there anything you need to know? If you set aside a regular time and place to talk, communication will be more comfortable. Do this every week or two as the relationship first becomes serious. Never let more than a month or two go by without one of these talks—even if all you have to say is that things are going great.

Most relationships change significantly when they turn into long-distance romances. Many students arrive at college carrying a torch for someone back home or at another school. College is an exciting scene with many social opportunities. If you restrict yourself to a single absent partner, you may miss out on a lot; and cheating or resentment can be the result.

Our advice for long-distance relationships: Keep seeing each other as long as you want to, but with the freedom to pursue other relationships, too. If the best person for you turns out to be the person from whom you are separated, this will become evident and you can reevaluate the situation in a couple of years. Meanwhile, keep your options open.

Becoming Intimate

Sexual intimacy inevitably adds a new and powerful dimension to a relationship. We suggest the following:

- **Don't hurry into it.**
- **If sexual activity would violate your morals or values, don't do it.** And don't expect others to violate theirs. It is reasonable to explain your values so that your partner will understand your decision, but you do not owe anyone a justification, nor should you put up with attempts to argue you into submission.
- **If you have to ply your partner with alcohol or other drugs to get the ball rolling, you aren't engaging in sex—you are committing rape.** Read Chapters 18 and 19 about acquaintance rape and information on alcohol and other drugs.
- **A pregnancy will certainly curtail your youth and social life.** Conception can occur even when couples take precautions. Data based on real-life use indicate that students who are sexually active for five years of college and use condoms for birth control all five years have around a 20 to 50 percent chance of a pregnancy (depending on how carefully and consistently they use condoms).

Here are some warning signs that should concern you:

- **Having sex when you don't really want to.** If desire and pleasure are missing, you are doing the wrong thing.
- **Guilt or anxiety afterward.** This is a sign of a wrong decision—or at least a premature one.
- **Having sex because your partner expects or demands it.**
- **Having sex with people to attract or keep them.** This is generally short-sighted and unwise. It will almost surely lower your self-esteem.
- **Becoming physically intimate when what you really want is emotional intimacy.**

When passions run high, physical intimacy can feel like emotional intimacy, but sex is an unsatisfying substitute for love or friendship. Genuine emotional intimacy is knowing, trusting, loving, and respecting each other at the deepest levels, day in and day out, independent of sex. Establishing emotional intimacy takes time—and, in many ways, more courage. If you build the emotional intimacy first, not only the relationship but also the sex will be better.

An interesting question is whether sex actually adds to your overall happiness. Believe it or not, a thorough review of the literature on happiness finds no evidence that becoming sexually active increases your general happiness. If you are expecting sex to make you happy, or to make your partner happy, the fact is that it probably won't for long. Sex relieves horniness, but it doesn't make happiness. Loving relationships, on the other hand, are powerfully related to happiness.

If you want sexual activity, but don't want all the medical risks of sex, consider the practice of "outercourse": mutual and loving stimulation between partners that allows sexual release but involves no exchange of bodily fluids. This will definitely require direct and effective communication, but it is an option that can be satisfying and fun in its own way.

Getting Serious

You may have a relationship you feel is really working. Should you make it exclusive? Don't do it just because being only with each other has become a habit. Ask yourself why you want this relationship to be exclusive. For security? To prevent jealousy? To build depth and trust? As a prelude to permanent commitment? An exclusive relationship is a big commitment. Before you make the decision to see only each other, make sure it is the best thing for each of you and for the relationship. You may find that you treat each other best and appreciate each other most when you have other opportunities.

Although dating more than one person can help you clarify what you want, multiple sexual relationships can be dangerous. Besides the health risks involved, it's rare to find a good working relationship where the partners had sex with others as well. Sexual jealousy is very powerful and can arouse insecurities, anger, and hurt.

Being exclusive provides the chance to explore a relationship in depth and get a taste of what marriage might be like. But if you are seriously considering marriage, consider this: Studies show that the younger you are, the lower your odds of a successful marriage. It also may surprise you to learn that trial marriage or living together does not decrease your risk of later divorce.

Above all, beware of what might be called "the fundamental marriage error": marrying before both you and your partner know who you are and what you want to do in life. Many 18- to 20-year-olds change their outlook and life goals drastically. The person who seems just right for you now may be terribly wrong for you within five or ten years. Why not wait to make a permanent commitment until you feel very centered and secure by yourself?

**SEE EXERCISE 15.1
INTERNET ACTIVITY**

If you want to marry, the person to marry is someone you could call your best friend—the one who knows you inside and out, the one you don't have to play games with, the one who prizes your company without physical rewards, the one who over a period of years has come to know, love, and respect who you are and what you want to be.

■ BREAKING UP

Change can be scary to think about and painful to create, but that doesn't make it less necessary. When you break up, you lose not only what you had, but also everything you thought you had, including a lot of hopes and dreams. No wonder it hurts. But remember that you are also opening up a world of new possibilities. You may not see them right away, but sooner or later you will.

If it is time to break up, do it cleanly and calmly. Don't be impulsive or angry. Explain your feelings and talk them out. If you don't get a mature reaction, take the high road; don't join someone else in the mud. If you decide to reunite after a trial separation, be sure enough time has passed for you to evaluate the situation effectively. If things fail a second time, you really do need to forget it.

What about being "just friends"? You may want to remain friends with your partner, especially if you have shared and invested a lot. You can't really be friends, however, until you have both healed from the hurt and neither of you wants the old relationship back. That usually takes at least a year or two.

If you are having trouble getting out of a relationship or dealing with its end, get help. Expect some pain, anger, and depression. Your college counseling center has assisted many students through similar difficulties. It is also a good time to get moral support from friends and family. There are good books on the subject, including *How to Survive the Loss of a Love* (see "Suggestions for Further Reading").

■ MARRIED LIFE IN COLLEGE

Both marriage and college are challenges. With so many demands, it is critically important that you and your partner share the burdens equally; you can't expect a harried partner to spoil or pamper you. Academic and financial pressures are likely to put extra strain on any relationship, so you are going to have to work extra hard at attending to each other's needs.

If you are in college but your spouse is not, it is important to bring your partner into your college life. Share what you are learning in your courses. See if your partner can take a course, too—maybe just to audit for the fun of it. Take your partner to cultural events—lectures, plays, concerts—on your campus. If your campus has social organizations for students' spouses, try them out.

Relationships with spouses and children can suffer when you are in college because you are tempted to take time you would normally spend with your loved ones and put it into your studies instead. You obviously will not profit if you gain your degree but lose your family. It's very important to schedule time for your partner and family just as you schedule your classes, and keep to the schedule just as carefully.

SEE EXERCISE 15.2

■ YOU AND YOUR PARENTS

If you are on your own for the first time, your relationship with your parents is going to change. Home will never be as you left it, and you will not be who you were before. So how can you have good relationships with your parents during this period of major change?

A first step in establishing a good relationship with your parents is to be aware of their perceptions. The most common perceptions are as follows:

- **Parents fear you'll harm yourself.** You may take risks that make older people shudder. You may shudder, too, when you look back on some of your stunts. Sometimes your parents have reason to worry.

- **Parents think their daughter is still a young innocent.** And yes, the old double standard (differing expectations for men than women, particularly regarding sex) is alive and well.

- **Parents know you're 20 but picture you as 10.** Somehow, the parental clock always lags behind reality. Maybe it's because they loved you so much as a child, they can't erase that image.

- **Parents mean well.** Most love their children, even if it doesn't come out right; very few are really indifferent or hateful.

- **Not every family works.** If your family is like the Brady Bunch, you are blessed. If it is even halfway normal, you will succeed. But some families are truly dysfunctional. If love, respect, enthusiasm, and encouragement just are not in the cards, look around you: Other people will give you these things, and you can create the family you need.

DOLLARHIDE/MONKMEYER PRESS PHOTO

If you are married or have children, take steps to involve your loved ones in your college life.

With your emotional needs satisfied, your reactions to your real family will be much less painful.

- **The old have been young, but the young haven't been old.** Parental memories of youth may be hazy, but at least they've been there. A younger student has yet to experience their adult perspective.

To paraphrase Mark Twain, when you are beginning college, you may think your parents rather foolish; but when you graduate, you'll be surprised how much they've learned in four years. Try setting aside regular times to update them on how college and your life in general are going. Ask for and consider their advice. You don't have to take it. Finally, realize that your parents are not here forever. Mend fences whenever you can.

SEE EXERCISE 15.4

■ FRIENDS

You are who you run with—or soon will be. Studies show that the people who influence you the most are your friends. Choose them carefully.

If you want a friend, be a friend. Learn to be an attentive listener. Give your opinion when people ask for it. Keep your comments polite and positive. Never violate a confidence. Offer an encouraging word and a helping hand whenever you can. You'll be amazed how many people will respect your opinions and seek your friendship.

Your friends are usually people whose attitudes, goals, and experiences are similar to your own. But in your personal life, just as in the classroom, you have the most to learn from people who are different from you. To enrich your college experience, try this. Make a conscious effort to make at least one good friend who is someone:

of the opposite sex	of another race
of another nationality	of a different sexual orientation
with a physical disability	on an athletic scholarship
of a very different age	from a very different religion
with very different politics	

These friendships may take more time and effort, but you will have more than just nine new friends; you will have learned to know, appreciate, and get along with a much wider variety of people than before.

ROOMMATES

Adjusting to a roommate on or off campus can be very difficult. Roommates range from the ridiculous to the sublime. You may make a lifetime friend or an exasperating acquaintance you wish you'd never known. A roommate doesn't have to be a best friend—just someone with whom you can share your living space comfortably. Your best friend may not make the best roommate. Many students have lost friends by rooming together.

If you are rooming with a stranger, establish your mutual rights and responsibilities in writing. Many colleges provide contract forms that you and your roommate can use. If things go wrong later, you will have something to point to.

If you have problems, talk them out promptly. Talk directly—politely but plainly. If problems persist, or if you don't know how to talk them out, ask your residence hall counselor for help; he or she is trained to do this.

Normally, you can tolerate (and learn from) a less than ideal situation; but if things get serious, insist on a change—your residence counselor will have ways of helping you.

SEE EXERCISE 15.5

SEE EXERCISE 15.6

CAMPUS INVOLVEMENT

Almost every college has numerous organizations you may join. Usually, you can check them out through activity fairs, printed guides, open houses, web pages, and so on. Organizations help you find friends with similar interests. Together you can try things you've never tried before. And remember, new students who become involved with at least one organization are more likely to survive their first year and remain in college.

To Greek or not to Greek? Fraternities and sororities can be a rich source of friends and support. Some students love them; others find them philosophically distasteful, too demanding of time and finances, or too constricting. Fraternities and sororities are powerful social influences, so you'll probably want to take a good look at the upper-class students in them. If what you see is what you want to be, consider joining. If not, steer clear.

Greek organizations are not all alike, nor are their members. If Greek life is not for you, a residence hall is one of the easiest places to make new friends.

SEE EXERCISE 15.7

Another good place to make friends is on the job, but avoid starting romantic relationships on the job. Dating someone who works over you or under you creates problems in a hurry. Even if you are on the same level, you may feel awkward or miserable if the relationship ends but the two of you must still work together. A special kind of job opportunity available at many schools is called co-op placement. These programs place you in temporary, paid positions with organizations that hire graduates in your major. Not only will you get excellent firsthand experience working in your field, but you also will make contacts that may help after graduation.

You are here for your education, but relationships are an integral part of it and can consume up to two-thirds of your waking hours. Whether you're a traditional-age new student or a returning student with family responsibilities, be sure to approach your relationships with the same effort and planning as you would approach your course work. Take life as it happens, but try to make it happen the way you want to take it. Long after you have forgotten whole courses you took, you will remember relationships that began or continued in college.

Learning Through Service

Last year over 543,000 students in America served over 28 million hours in order to benefit the community and learn. Involvement in this nationwide service movement will enrich your college experience and help you develop skills for success.

SIX REASONS TO SERVE

1. **Improving the local community.** As a college student you are a member of two communities: the college community and the surrounding community. Through service you can help both communities improve the quality of life for everyone.

2. **Enriching and applying classroom learning.** Service is perhaps one of the best ways to learn. As a student you will constantly be asked to solve theoretical problems and to read texts that discuss different aspects of life. Service allows you to apply your classroom knowledge to real-world problems.

3. **Gaining leadership skills.** Leadership involves creativity, which is needed to alleviate and solve many of the social ills in today's communities. Your solutions might include writing grants and encouraging other students to get involved. Many colleges have leadership positions available for students who want to create service projects for other students.

4. **Exploring career opportunities.** Service exposes you to a wide variety of potential careers. Many students who perform service do so in order to determine their main career interests.

5. **Meeting new friends.** New students often feel disconnected from campus. Participation in service activities is a great way to make friends.

6. **Developing an appreciation for diversity.** Your engagement in service will expand your ability to empathize with others. Service places you in unique settings where you often interact with people of different ages and ethnicities.

FINDING A SERVICE OPPORTUNITY

- **See if your campus has a community service office that maintains a list of local volunteer opportunities.** Your campus career center may also be a repository of service opportunities.

- **Become familiar with a campus service organization.** Most student organizations perform service during the academic year. Check with your campus activities center. If a service organization does not exist, start one!

- **Contact knowledgeable local agencies.** Community agencies such as the United Way usually maintain databases of service opportunities. In addition, civic organizations such as the Rotary and Lions clubs can assist you in identifying service opportunities. YMCAs, churches, and local government offices also have information about service.

- **Search the web.** Many service opportunities are listed on the World Wide Web. The Corporation for National Service will sometimes describe service activities happening in different parts of the United States. Local web pages often list service projects.

DIFFERENT WAYS TO SERVE

- **Short-term programs.** Many colleges offer one-time service projects in which you can participate. These types of projects are easy to perform and take place in various settings. Some examples of projects are trips to local children's homes to play with kids, working on building a house for the poor during an afternoon, or spending time with the elderly.

Learning Through Service (continued)

- **Long-term programs.** Examples include tutoring a child once a week, becoming a literacy teacher to children or adults, mentoring a mentally or physically challenged child, and serving food in a shelter once a week. The Peace Corps offers international service opportunities for a minimum of two years, and VISTA (Volunteers in Service to America) arranges for people to serve in the United States for periods of a year or more.

- **Service learning.** Many instructors are beginning to incorporate service into their classes because it is a proven way to help students learn. Your teacher might provide you with a list of service options that you can perform as part of your grade.

MAKING TIME FOR SERVICE

- **If your day is packed with classes, try volunteering in the evening.** Many towns offer opportunities to serve almost twenty-four hours a day. Some colleges offer extended service projects during fall and spring break.

- **Even if service is not a requirement in your classes, you can still volunteer.** For example, you could help at a local shelter as the basis for writing an English essay. If you are taking biology, you might write about local environmental problems and how students can help solve them. Building a house for a poor family might help you design your own house in an architecture class. Some schools even allow you to earn additional credit if you perform service as part of a class.

- **You can also earn money for service.** Check with your college financial aid office to see what types of paid service projects are available. Many schools now participate in America Reads, a literacy project that pays students who have federal work-study awards to tutor children. If you don't have work-study, you may still qualify for a service scholarship.

—David Janes, University of South Carolina

Search Online!

INFOTRAC COLLEGE EDITION

Try these phrases and others for Key Words and Subject Guide searches: "college students and love," "college students and parents," "extracurricular activities and college."

Also look up:

Students think love conquers all. (college students) *USA Today* (Magazine) Dec 1993 v122 n2583 p15

The new generation speaks out; student leaders discuss racism, love, sex and the black male-black female thing. (includes student profiles) Nicole Walker. *Ebony* Nov 1997 v53 n1 p158

Earning and learning: are students working too much? (Column) Martin Kramer. *Change* Jan-Feb 1994 v26 n1 p6

Relationships and the Web

A Join a Mailing List

Discussion on the Internet often includes stories of happy couples who met on the Internet, as well as stories of people who have created fake identities. From one extreme to the other, the Internet provides numerous opportunities for social interchange.

Using the LISZT index of mailing lists (*http://www.liszt.com/*), locate a mailing list of interest to you.

Name of mailing list _____

Content _____

Address for joining _____

Join the mailing list. What kind of mail do you receive from the list? Is it helpful to you? What have you learned from it?

B Visit a Chat Group

Using the Yahoo index of chat groups (*http://www.yahoo.com/Computers_and _Internet/Internet/World_Wide_Web/Chat/*) locate a chat group of interest:

Interest area _____

Name of chat group _____

Address _____

Log on and see what is being discussed. Is this a chat group you would like to join? What would you gain from being part of it?

C Newsgroups

Scan the list of newsgroups available from your Internet provider.

- With Netscape Navigator 4.0, click on Window/Netscape News/Options/Show All Newsgroups
- With Internet Explorer 4.0, clock on Mail/Read News/News/Newsgroups

Both major browsers, in their enlarged versions, now allow you to read newsgroups with the same tool used for reading e-mail. Netscape Navigator 4.0 includes Netscape Messenger; Microsoft Internet Explorer includes Outlook Express.

- With Netscape Communicator, select Communicator/Collabra Discussion Group
- With Outlook Express, select Go/News

Locate a newsgroup of interest to you:

Area of interest _____

Name _____

Scan the recent postings _____

Make a list of the major topics that seem to be discussed.

D Connect with a Long-Distance Friend

Using the address *http://www.qucis.queensu.ca/FAQs/email/college.html*, locate the e-mail address of a friend or relative on another campus:

Name _____

College _____

e-mail address _____

Exchange e-mail.
(Go to *http://csuccess.wadsworth.com* for the most up-to-date URLs.)

EXERCISE 15.2

Balancing Relationships and College

A For personal writing and group discussion: If you are in a relationship, what are the greatest concerns you have about balancing your educational responsibilities with your responsibilities to your partner? What can you do to improve the situation? If the balance poses a serious problem for you, is there someone on campus you can seek for counseling? If you need counseling but aren't sure where to turn, ask your instructor to help you find that person.

B If you are married and have children, write a letter to your spouse and another to your children, explaining why you must often devote time to your studies instead of to them. Don't deliver the letters; read them first and keep revising them until they sound realistic and convincing. Attempt to strike a sensible balance between your commitments to family and to your future academic and professional growth. If there are other married students in your class, share letters and get reactions. Then decide whether it's prudent to actually share these thoughts with spouse and children.

EXERCISE 15.3

Gripes

A Student Gripes. In surveys, these are the most frequent student gripes about parents. Check off the ones that hit closest to home for you:

_____ Why are parents so overbearing and controlling, telling you everything from what to major in to whom to date?

_____ Why do parents treat you like a child? Why are they so overprotective?

_____ Why do parents worry so much?

_____ Why do parents complain so much about money?

_____ Why are parents so hard to talk to?

_____ Parents say they want to know what's going on in my life, but if I told them everything, they'd go ballistic and I'd never hear the end of it!

Reflect on the gripes you checked. Why do you think your parents are like that? How do your thoughts affect your relations with them?

B Parent Gripes. Looking at things from the other side, students report the following as the most common gripes their parents have about them. Check off those that ring true for your parents:

_____ Why don't you call and visit more?

_____ Why don't you tell us more about what is going on?

_____ When you are home, why do you ignore us and spend all your time with your friends?

_____ (if dating seriously) Why do you spend so much time with your boyfriend or girlfriend?

_____ Why do you need so much money?

_____ Why aren't your grades better, and why don't you appreciate the importance of school?

_____ Why don't you listen to us about getting into the right major and courses? You'll never get a good job if you don't.

_____ What have you done to yourself? Where did you get that (haircut, tattoo, style of clothes, and so on)?

_____ Why don't you listen to us and do what we tell you? You need a better attitude!

How do such thoughts affect your parents? What do you think they are really trying to tell you?

EXERCISE 15.4   Five over 30

Select five adults over 30 whom you respect. Ask each the following questions.

- What were the best decisions you made when you were 18 to 22?
- What were the biggest mistakes you made in those years?
- What advice would you give someone who is 18?

Are there common themes in what they say? How good is their advice? Write a summary, bring it to class, and be prepared to share it.

EXERCISE 15.5   Common Roommate Gripes

Housing authorities report that the most common areas of conflict between roommates are those listed below. Check those that are true for you.

_____ One roommate needs quiet to study; the other needs music or sound.

_____ One roommate is neat; the other is messy.

_____ One roommate smokes; the other resents smoke.

_____ One roommate feels free to bring in lots of guests; the other finds them obnoxious.

_____ One roommate brings in romantic bedmates and wants privacy—or goes at it right in front of the other; the other is uncomfortable with this and feels banished from the room that he or she paid for.

_____ One roommate likes it warm; the other likes it cool.

_____ One roommate considers the room a place to have fun; the other considers it a place to get studying done.

_____ One roommate likes to borrow; the other doesn't.

_____ One roommate is a morning person; the other is a night owl.

_____ One roommate wants silence while sleeping; the other feels free to make noise.

_____ One roommate wants to follow all the residence hall rules; the other wants to break them.

If you are rooming with someone, review this checklist and write about what you and your roommate(s) can do to improve the situation. If you live alone, which of these gripes would be reason for you to not want to share? How might you overcome such situations if they arose?

Roommate Roulette

Pick five persons of the same sex, with whom you could imagine sharing a room, and interview them using the list of common roommate conflicts in Exercise 15.5. See how many points of commonality and difference you would have. Try to determine whether an ideal roommate really exists.

For each of the differences that could become conflicts on the list, write down the best compromise solutions you can. Bring your solutions to class and be prepared to have your classmates—some of whom are probably facing these very problems—judge how well they might work.

EXERCISE 15.7

Connecting with Campus Organizations

Get a list of your campus organizations from your campus student center. Choose six in which you might enjoy participating. Find out more about each: Attend a meeting, talk to an officer, or obtain and read detailed information. Choose two with which you would like to get involved this term. Bring your list to class, and be prepared to discuss what you found and your reasons for the selections you made.

SUGGESTIONS FOR FURTHER READING

Bass, Ellen, & Kate Kaufman. *Free Your Mind: The Book for Gay, Lesbian, and Bisexual Youth—And Their Allies.* New York: HarperCollins, 1996.

Bellah, Robert, et al. *Habits of the Heart: Individualism and Commitment in American Life.* New York: Harper & Row, 1985.

Cosgrove, Melba, Harold Bloomfield, & Peter McWilliams. *How to Survive the Loss of a Love.* New York: Bantam, 1976.

Daloz, Laurent A. Parks, et al. *Common Fire: Lives of Commitment in a Complex World.* Boston: Beacon, 1996.

Fisher, B. S., & J. J. Sloan. *Campus Crime, Legal, Social and Policy Perspectives.* Springfield, IL: Charles Thomas, 1995.

Gaines, Stanley O. *Culture, Ethnicity, and Personal Relationship Processes.* New York: Routledge, 1997.

Hendricks, Gay, & Kathlyn Hendricks. *Conscious Loving: The Journey to Co-Commitment—A Way to Be Fully Together Without Giving Up Yourself.* New York: Bantam, 1990.

Hirsh, Sandra, & Jean Kummerow. *LifeTypes.* New York: Warner, 1989.

Kobrin, Michael, & Joanna Mareth. *Service Matters: A Sourcebook for Community Service in Higher Education.* Providence, RI: Campus Compact, 1996.

Menninger, K. *The Crime of Punishment.* New York: Viking, 1968.

Myers, David G. *The Pursuit of Happiness: Who Is Happy and Why.* New York: Morrow, 1992.

RESOURCES

Relationships are important throughout life, and the support you get from them can keep you going with confidence and strength, especially during times of transition—moving to a new place, starting college, changing jobs, changing life situations. During transition times you can feel all alone, with no one to really support you. You probably have more resources than you realize. Use this Resources page to create a map of the relationships in your life. (See the example. Add photos if you want, or transfer your map to a larger sheet of paper and make a collage of the important people in your life.) When you are feeling down, or stressed, or alone, take a minute to look at this page and see the connections you have with other people. Give someone a call, write a letter, drop by to visit, or simply remember the good feelings and times your relationships bring you.

Example:

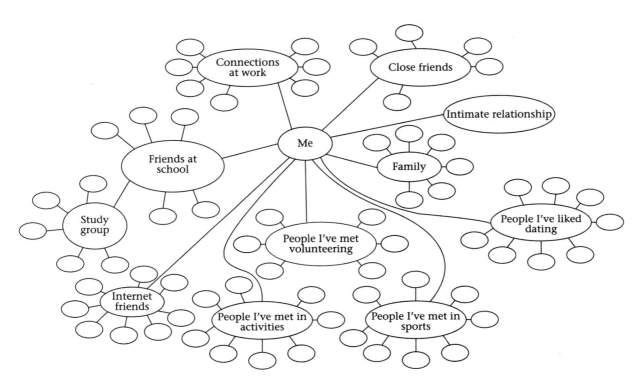

Create your map here:

JOURNAL

NAME _____

DATE _____

This chapter has covered a number of types of student relationships: friends, dating and intimate partners, marriage, parents, roommates, study groups, campus organizations, and jobs. Choose one of your relationships that needs help. Write your thoughts and feelings about the relationship, what you need from it, what you are willing to do to improve it, and what you hope the other person will be willing to do to make it better.

....

....

....

....

....

....

....

....

....

....

....

....

....

....

....

....

....

Your thoughts will probably be filled with emotion and written in free form, which is a good way to begin clarifying what is most important to you. Now, look back at what you've written, and use it to draft a letter that communicates in a more clear and logical way your needs and expectations about the relationship. You may want to revise your letter a few times to make sure that it says what you want it to say in a way that will support what you want to happen in the relationship. (For example, if you want to be treated with more care and compassion in the relationship, try to ask for that in a caring and compassionate way.) After you've finished your letter, wait a few days, then reread it, and decide whether or not you want to send or give it to the other person. (Sometimes, this process by itself can clarify your feelings about the situation.)

16

When Everyone Celebrates Diversity

CHAPTER OUTLINE

Cultural Pluralism

Expanding Our View of Diversity

A Diverse Campus Culture

Discrimination and Prejudice on College Campuses

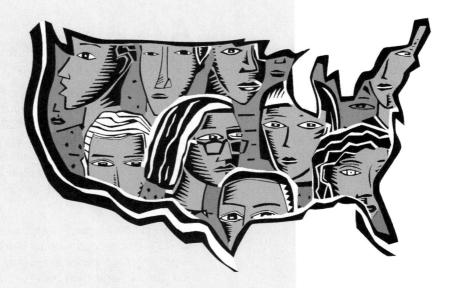

KEYS TO SUCCESS

- *Get to know at least one person on campus who cares about your survival.*

- *Get involved in campus activities.*

- *Take advantage of minority support services.*

- *Maintain connections with your home base, but be aware of the changes you may be going through and the impact of those changes on family and friends.*

- *Be proud of your heritage and culture.*

- *Immerse yourself in your culture as you learn to interact with people of other cultures.*

" I know diversity is in these days, but I'm not much into talking about it. I'm not even sure what it means. We had diversity celebration days in high school, but nobody took them very seriously. They seemed to separate us, not bring us together. I'm open to meeting other people, but I don't want to force anything. Live and let live. "

Ask almost any person in this country about his or her racial or ethnic background and you have the start of an interesting story:

My father is mostly Arab and part Kurdish. He always said that his strength and determination came from his Kurdish background. My mother's background is Scottish and English. She told me her mother's side of the family came over on the Mayflower. My parents met when my dad was a graduate student and my mother was an undergraduate. She was studying economics and he agreed to tutor her. I came to this country when I was 4 years old and I'm still figuring out what it means to be an Arab American.

—Baidah

My racial background is African American. The other thing I would add is that I see my background as Black and working class. Those two things go together for me; they are a part of my roots. How I grew up was kind of varied. On one hand I was born in California and on the other hand I was raised in Texas during segregation. Part of me grew up in a strongly segregated part of the South, and another part of me, as an adolescent, grew up in integrated California.

—Terrell

I'm American. I don't feel like I have a strong attachment to any particular group. My family is Italian, Polish, Irish, and French. On St. Patrick's Day, I say I'm Irish. If I go to an Italian restaurant, I pretend I'm Italian! I call one grandmother "Bapshee," and that's about how bilingual I am. Maybe I'm not anything.

—Eric

I'm Filipino American, and like most Filipinos I am also Catholic. Family values are stressed in my home. Outsiders might say that my culture is very patriarchal, but I grew up watching my parents share power equally. My mother was a very strong woman and the final decisions were always hers. I am the youngest of six children and am very opinionated, so no decision is ever easy in my household. In addition to family, education is heavily stressed. Attaining a college degree is a must—no, not a must, it just should happen—like breathing.

—Cristina

If you are like most students, you see college as the beginning of an exciting new stage in life, a time when you can learn a lot about yourself and the world as you prepare for the future. What is your responsibility to help create a campus environment in which all students can pursue these goals?

SEE EXERCISE 16.1

Figure 16.1 A Diversity Attitude Scale

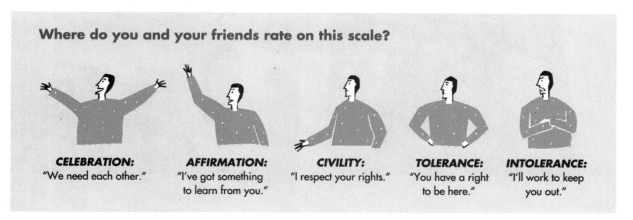

Where do you and your friends rate on this scale?

CELEBRATION:
"We need each other."

AFFIRMATION:
"I've got something to learn from you."

CIVILITY:
"I respect your rights."

TOLERANCE:
"You have a right to be here."

INTOLERANCE:
"I'll work to keep you out."

■ CULTURAL PLURALISM: REPLACING THE MELTING POT WITH VEGETABLE STEW

For years, students were taught that immigration created a melting pot—as diverse groups migrated to this land, their culture, religion, and customs mixed into this American pot to create a new society. The reality of what happened is more complex. Instead of melting into the pot, most immigrants were asked to adopt the culture of those already here, creating an Anglo-European soup. In order to get ahead, immigrants had to change their names to more Anglo-American spellings. They had to make sure their children learned English, and they had to do business the American way. Some groups could accomplish this more easily, although not without experiencing some discrimination. Today, members of different cultural groups may be more likely to see themselves as Eric does—"just American." At the same time, many European Americans have retained strong ethnic ties, while many non-European groups (for example, Africans, Japanese, and Chinese) found both laws and racial barriers impeding their integration into the culture at large.

As a result, many sociologists and educators have concluded that American society is less like a melting pot and more like a vegetable stew. Although each group has its own unique characteristics and flavor, all the groups together create a common broth. The dominant culture gradually has begun to acknowledge and affirm the diversity of cultures within its borders. After years of stressing almost exclusively commonalities, we are now focusing on our differences, too.

Cultural pluralism has replaced the melting pot theory. Under cultural pluralism, each group celebrates and practices its customs and traditions, while also participating in the general mainstream culture. "Unity in diversity" is the new rallying cry.

Whoever you are, in some ways you are part of that mainstream culture. In other ways, however, you probably feel that you are part of a smaller group, a microculture within society.

Cultural pluralism doesn't mean groups must remain isolated. In fact, as you learn more about another ethnic group's heritage, you may discover customs and traditions in which you would like to participate. Particular values stressed in one culture may appeal to you. For example, you may prefer the punctuality emphasized in European American cultures or the more relaxed time schedule of Arab Americans. You may value the sense of duty

SEE EXERCISE 16.2

PHOTO COURTESY OF EARLHAM COLLEGE

PHOTO BY ANGELA MANN

Most colleges make an effort to help students feel welcome, respected, and supported in every way that the students themselves feel is important.

and family obligation among Hispanic Americans or admire the sense of individual control and independence offered in the Anglo culture. Or your preferences may be directed toward the language, music, food, dress, dance, architecture, or religion of another culture.

If you are going to accept and affirm the differences of other groups, each group needs to be ready to listen to the other without criticism, instead of simply assuming that a different perspective is misguided, wrong, or backward.

■ EXPANDING OUR VIEW OF DIVERSITY

SEE EXERCISE 16.3

The concept of diversity has expanded to include sexual orientation. To make all students feel welcome, we must consider the needs and concerns of gay, lesbian, and bisexual students, as well as others.

Gary, a mass communications major in his junior year, decided to "come out" during the annual National Coming Out Day. He said:

> *I am tired of pretending I am someone I'm not. I need the community of other gay people to help me deal with the homophobia on campus, and I want to celebrate a part of me that I have come to accept and love. Believe me, my life would be a lot easier if I could accept the "normal" heterosexual lifestyle that society keeps shoving down my throat. What do I want from life? I want what most people want—the chance to go to school, have friends, get a job, and find someone to love.*

To create a welcoming environment for gay and lesbian students, most of us must first unlearn stereotypical notions. For example, you can't tell someone's sexual orientation just by looking at him or her. Being gay or lesbian is not always a choice. Each year, scientists find further evidence indicating that sexual orientation may be influenced by genetic as well as environmental factors. Last, most child molesters are White male heterosexuals—not homosexuals.

■ A DIVERSE CAMPUS CULTURE

SEE EXERCISE 16.4
INTERNET ACTIVITY
SEE EXERCISE 16.5

How diverse is your campus? Are you aware of the diversity that exists there? In what ways does your school encourage all students to feel welcome? How easy is it for students to express their culture and to learn about their culture or the cultures of others?

"I Know I Will Always Have a Cause I Am Fighting For"

It's been three years since I entered college. I was 18 and fresh out of high school when I journeyed to Hampton University.

I remember feeling scared and confused and thinking maybe this is not the right thing to do, then arriving at the beautiful campus and staring in awe at the old brick buildings. And the people, all the different Black faces. My apprehensions slowly fading.

I stayed at Hampton for two years and loved every day of it. However, the strain of tuition for a private university became too much. It was time for me to go back home.

I entered UC–Berkeley last fall. I felt I was really ready to battle and survive the competitiveness that I had heard so much about. I hung out in Berkeley when I was in high school. Yes, I was absolutely ready!

I knew I wanted to continue studying English, so I signed up for three classes: Shakespeare, American Literature, and an African American studies course. Shakespeare was great. I admit I was intimidated about taking the class with 300 students in a big auditorium. (At Hampton, my largest class was no more than 60 people.) Not to mention, I was one of about five African Americans in the class.

Shakespeare was a man before his time. He had a cause, I believe, to write about injustices he saw.

I was not as excited about my literature course. This was also a class of about 300 students, and again I was one of five. It's funny. When you're in a class that large, you begin to see how one can just fade away—our contributions, our struggle, our history. You almost forget you exist.

We read authors like T. S. Eliot, Virginia Woolf, and Henry James. I was not enthusiastic for this reason: Where are all the African American novelists? We did read Zora Neale Hurston's "Their Eyes Were Watching God," but that was all. This class focused on the modernist theme of "making it new"—authors from the late 1800s to the early 1960s. I can think of at least ten major African American writers who were pioneers then. We were "making it new" during the Harlem renaissance (the 1920s) with writers like Langston Hughes and Dorothy West. And we were around after that with Richard Wright, Ann Petry, and James Baldwin.

I asked my professor why we were only exploring European and American writers. She said African American writers of that time were mainly focused with writing the "protest novel," using literature to testify about the social and racial injustices African Americans endure. I struggled to understand why that was not as important and interesting as well.

I also took an African American studies course. I enjoyed it because I read authors from other ethnic cultures. I learned about Cesar Chavez and his efforts to organize Hispanic people to stand up for their rights. I learned about the migration of Korean families into America and the subhuman conditions they were forced to work under. Learning how similar all our struggles are sparked my interest and made me want to learn more.

At Berkeley I sometimes thought I was being watched and at any given moment one of the White students would come up and ask laughingly, "Do you really think you belong here?" I felt detached from social groups. Everything seemed different. It was hard to talk to my family about what I was going through.

I made it through the semester and—for whatever it is worth—academically, I did excellently. I also learned three valuable things. First, prestige has nothing to do with what a university can offer. Second, you are the only person responsible for making your educational experience all it can be. Third, grades don't mean a thing. It's what you learn and how you apply it that is important.

Recently I heard the writer and activist Amiri Braka say, "The conscious awareness of the need to struggle is priceless." I have not always understood why I have to constantly struggle. Becoming conscious of my struggle makes the issues much more personal! The challenge is understanding and fitting my people's fight within the greater circle.

My struggle has been to survive, just as those before me. And my mission is to pass on that courage to other young people like me, so that our spirit does not die.

—Monita A. Johnson
San Francisco Examiner, May 3, 1998
Used by permission.

One way to answer these questions is by completing Exercise 16.5 later in this chapter. For now, consider your campus diversity profile by looking at the extent of diversity among individuals on campus—by classes devoted in whole or in part to teaching you about the contributions of diverse individuals and societies, by diversity in organizations and residences, and by your institution's commitment to diversity:

A. Diversity in Numbers

1. In what ways are your student body, faculty, administrators, and staff diverse? What percentage of students, faculty, administrators, and staff come from different ethnic/racial groups?
2. What religious, linguistic, socioeconomic, gender, and geographic differences are there among students?

B. Diversity in the Curriculum

1. What are you learning about the contributions and concerns of people of color in your classes?
2. What courses or workshops are available if you want to increase your racial awareness and understanding?
3. Are courses offered that include the contributions and perspectives of gays and lesbians?

C. Diversity in Social and Residential Settings

1. What individuals or groups are reflected in the artwork, sculpture, and names of buildings on your campus?
2. What kinds of ethnic foods are served on a regular basis at the college dining facilities?
3. If your school has campus residences, does the residential life staff schedule ongoing discussions regarding sexual orientation, diversity, and tolerance? Who is in charge of these programs?
4. Do students from different ethnic groups have organizations and hold social events? Give some examples. Does your campus support a variety of diverse activities brought to campus? Give some examples.
5. Do gay and lesbian students have organizations and hold social events? Give some examples. Are there gay and lesbian support groups on campus? Who is in charge of these groups?
6. Where does cross-racial interaction exist on your campus? Is the atmosphere one of peaceful coexistence or resegregation? Where do students find opportunities to work, study, and socialize across racial/ethnic lines?

D. Institutional Commitment to Diversity

1. How does your college mission statement address cultural pluralism? (Your college mission statement may be printed in the catalog.)
2. What policies and procedures does your school have with regard to the recruitment and retention of students of color? Contact your admissions office for information.
3. What policies and procedures does your school have with regard to the recruitment and hiring of faculty and staff of color? Contact your affirmative action/equal opportunity office for information.
4. Does your school administration feel responsible for educating students about diversity? Or does it assume that students and faculty of color will do this?

Diversity is about more than racial or ethnic and religious backgrounds. It also encompasses gay, lesbian, bisexual, and transgender individuals who live in a world that is not always tolerant or accepting, much less affirming. All students grow when they learn to find pride in their own communities and to also accept the diverse groups around them.

© JONATHAN NOUROK/PHOTOEDIT

5. Does your school administration feel responsible for educating students about tolerance? Or does it assume that gay and lesbian organizations will do this?

■ DISCRIMINATION AND PREJUDICE ON COLLEGE CAMPUSES

Unfortunately, incidences of discrimination and acts of prejudice are rising on college campuses. Although some schools may not be experiencing overt racial conflict, tension may still exist; many students report having little contact with students from different racial or ethnic groups. Moreover, a national survey, "Taking America's Pulse," conducted for the National Conference of Christians and Jews, indicates that Blacks, Whites, Hispanics, and Asians hold many negative stereotypes about one another. The good news is that "nine out of 10 Americans nationwide claim they are willing to work with people of all races—even those they felt they had the least in common with—to advance race relations."*

In addition to being morally and personally repugnant, you should know that discrimination is illegal. Most colleges and universities have established policies against all forms of racism, anti-Semitism, and ethnic and cultural intolerance. These policies prohibit racist actions or omissions including verbal harassment or abuse that might deny "anyone his/her rights to equity, dignity, culture or religion." Anyone found in violation of such policies faces "corrective action including appropriate disciplinary action."

*"Survey Finds Minorities Resent Whites and Each Other," *Jet*, 28 March 1994.

SEE EXERCISE 16.6

SEE EXERCISE 16.7
INTERNET ACTIVITY

Search Online!

Try these phrases and others for Key Words and Subject Guide searches: "diversity and campus," "ethnicity and campus," "hate crimes and campus."

Also look up:

Back to square one: in California and Texas, two attempts to maintain campus diversity falter on race.
(includes related article on how preparatory courses for the law school exam can improve the chances minorities have of getting into law schools) Adam Cohen, Romesh Ratnesar. *Time* April 20, 1998 v151 n15

Reflections on affirmative action. (Facing the Future: The Status of Affirmative Action in the 21st Century) (Transcript). *American Behavioral Scientist* Oct 1997 v41 n2 p205

INFOTRAC COLLEGE EDITION

The New Majority

Why are institutions of higher learning so concerned about diversity on their campuses? One reason has to do with population figures. In 1990, 48 million Americans (about one-fifth of the total population) were identified as "minorities." By the year 2020 they will account for one-third of the population, and by the last quarter of the twenty-first century they will be a collective majority.*

The total U.S. population in 1990 was about 250 million according to the Bureau of the Census.† By 1998, it was projected to reach more than 269 million. As the general population has grown, so have the percentages of minority populations. Here are some of the groups currently considered minorities in the United States, although in some areas of the country they are actually in the majority.

AFRICAN AMERICANS

In 1990, African Americans made up about 12 percent (30 million) of the U.S. population. For 1998, the projection was 34 million and 12.7 percent. They come from diverse cultures and countries in Africa, the Caribbean, and Central and South America. Excluded from the mainstream White culture despite the end of slavery, they developed a system of historically Black colleges and universities dating from the mid-nineteenth century. These schools still award the majority of all bachelor's degrees received by African Americans.

ALASKAN NATIVE/AMERICAN INDIANS

About 2 million (0.8 percent) Americans identified themselves as (non-Hispanic) Eskimo, Aleut, and American Indian in 1990, from more than 300 tribes. Their heritage includes more

than 120 separate languages. By 1998 they were expected to reach 2.3 million, or 0.9 percent of the population.

ASIAN AMERICANS

Since discriminatory immigration laws ended in 1965, Asians have become one of our fastest-growing groups. In 1990 they numbered 7.5 million, or 3 percent. By 1998 they were projected to grow to 10.2 million, or 3.8 percent of the population. The largest of the many groups are Chinese, Japanese, Korean, Asian Indian, Filipino, and Vietnamese.

MEXICAN AMERICANS

All told, Hispanics in the United States were projected to reach 30 million or 11.2 percent of the population by 1998. Hispanics made up 9 percent of the U.S. population in 1990. The fastest-growing Hispanic group is Mexican Americans (almost 13 million). Mexican Americans have deep roots in the American Southwest from past centuries when that region belonged to Mexico and Spain. More than half of Mexican Americans live in Texas and California.

PUERTO RICANS AND CUBAN AMERICANS

Around 1990, Puerto Ricans living on the U.S. mainland numbered 2.3 million, and those living in Puerto Rico 3.3 million. All are U.S. citizens. There are more than a million Cuban Americans, mainly in Florida.

*Quality Education for Minorities Project, Education That Works. Cambridge: Massachusetts Institute of Technology, 1990.

†This and other figures come from the U.S. Bureau of the Census.

SEE EXERCISE 16.8

You don't have to wait for your school to take the lead in making your campus a more welcoming place. Everyone can work to create a community where diverse groups feel celebrated by "advocating for pluralism." For example, Cristina can stop laughing at her friends' racial jokes; Baidah can ask her English instructor to include some works by writers of color. Eric

SEE EXERCISE 16.9
SEE EXERCISE 16.10

and Terrell can attend the gay, lesbian, and allies support group on campus with Gary.

EXERCISE 16.1

Sharing Your Background

In the beginning of this chapter, Baidah, Eric, Cristina, and Terrell start to tell "their stories." Now it's your turn. Write a two-part essay. In the first part, describe the racial or ethnic groups to which you belong. Can you belong to more than one? Absolutely. Be sure to include some of the beliefs, values, and norms in your cultural background. How do you celebrate your background? What if you are like Eric and don't feel a strong attachment to any group? Write what you know about your family history and speculate on why your ethnic identity isn't very strong.

In the second part of your essay, discuss a time when you realized that your racial or ethnic background was not the same as someone else's. For example, young children imagine that their experiences are mirrored in the lives of others. If they are Jewish, everyone else must be too. If their family eats okra for breakfast, then all families do the same. Yet at some point they begin to realize differences. When did you realize that you were African American or Hispanic American or European American or Korean American or whatever?

Share your essays with other members of the class. In what ways are your stories similar? In what ways are they different?

EXERCISE 16.2

Creating Common Ground

Examine the items in the following chart. For each item, decide whether you would describe your preferences, habits, and customs as reflecting the mainstream (macroculture) or a specific ethnic microculture. Enter specific examples of your own preferences in the appropriate column (two examples are given). For a given item, you may enter examples under both macroculture and microculture, or you may leave one or the other blank. In filling out the chart, you may want to look back at the essay you wrote in Exercise 16.1.

Category	Macroculture	Microculture
Language		
Food	*hamburgers*	*sushi (Japanese)*
Music (for your peer group)		
Style of dress (for your peer group)		
Religion		
Holidays celebrated		
Heroes/role models		
Key values	*competition*	*cooperation (Native American)*
Lifestyle		
Personal goals		

Compare answers in a small group. Do most people in the group agree on what should be considered an example of the macroculture and what is an example of a microculture? Does anyone identify completely with the macroculture? Does anyone feel completely disconnected from the macroculture? What do you and others in your class regard as significant differences among you? In what areas do you share common ground?

EXERCISE 16.3   Hearing All Sides of a Story

This exercise involves forming caucus groups. A caucus group simply means any group in which you feel you automatically belong. For example, you might form caucus groups of commuters, learning-disabled students, Catholics, biracial students, gay and lesbian students, African American women, men, nontraditional students, and so on. First generate a list of possible caucus groups and then decide if there are enough potential members in the class to form a group of three or more members.

Join your caucus group. Meet to discuss the following questions: How does your group experience campus life? What are the major academic, residential, or social concerns of your group? How well does your college meet the needs of your group?

As a group, report on your discussion while other class members just listen. Afterward, listeners may comment or ask questions on what has been said, but they should refrain from challenging the perceptions of the group to which they are listening.

After all groups have reported, discuss what you learned from this exercise.

EXERCISE 16.4 INTERNET ACTIVITY   Questions About Homosexuality

Academic and professional associations are often sources of authoritative information, especially on controversial topics.

The American Psychological Association's "Answers to Your Questions About Sexual Orientation and Homosexuality" page provides answers to the following questions. First, write your responses to the following questions, and then look up the answers provided by the APA.

- Is sexual orientation a choice?
- Is homosexuality a mental illness or an emotional problem?
- Can lesbians and gay men be good parents?
- Can therapy change sexual orientation?

Now, compare your answers with the APA's answers, provided at: *http:// www.apa.org/pubinfo/orient.html.* (Go to *http://csuccess.wadsworth.com* for the most up-to-date URLs.)

EXERCISE 16.5   Getting the Diversity Facts on Your Campus

Consider campus diversity in a broader context—among the student body, faculty, administrators, and staff; in the curriculum; in social and residential settings; and at the institutional level (that is, the overall policies and procedures followed by the college).

In groups of three to five, investigate one of the areas in the list on page 250. Use the questions under each heading to help guide your research. Your instructor may be able to offer suggestions on where to locate relevant materials or appropriate people to interview. Each group should focus on two questions: (1) How easy is it for students to express their culture and to learn about their backgrounds or the backgrounds of others on this campus? and (2) In what ways does our school try to make all students feel welcome? Groups should report their findings to the class.

EXERCISE 16.6

Checking Your Understanding

How clear is your understanding of discrimination and prejudice? Check your knowledge by circling T (true) or F (false) for each of the following:

T   F   1. Positive stereotypes aren't harmful.
T   F   2. Prejudice is personal preference usually based on inaccurate or insufficient information.
T   F   3. The American Psychiatric Association lists homosexuality as a mental disorder.
T   F   4. Racism combines prejudice with power.
T   F   5. The problem of racism was solved years ago.
T   F   6. Racism hurts everyone.

(See page 256 for the answers.)

EXERCISE 16.7
INTERNET
ACTIVITY

Diversity in the Population and on Campus

Estimate the percentage of each group listed both in the total U.S. population and in the U.S. undergraduate student population.

General Population		Undergraduate Population
American Indian	_____	_____
Asian	_____	_____
Black	_____	_____
White	_____	_____
Hispanic	_____	_____

Compare your estimates with the U.S. Census national population projections (*http://www.census.gov/population/projections/nation/nsrh/nprh9600.txt*) and *Digest of Education Statistics 1997* (*http://nces.ed.gov/pubs/digest97/d97t207.html*). (Go to *http://csuccess.wadsworth.com* for the most up-to-date URLs.)

- How far off were you in estimating the general population statistics?
- What conclusions can you draw about your perception of society?
- How far off were you in estimating the student population statistics?
- What conclusions can you draw about your perception of the student population?
- Locate statistics for your own institution on your institution's home page.

EXERCISE 16.8

Combating Discrimination and Prejudice on Campus

What experiences have you had dealing with discrimination or prejudice on campus? Write briefly about the incident. Describe what happened and how you felt about it. Did you or anyone you know do anything about it? Did any administrator or faculty member do anything about it? Describe what was done. Do you think this was an effective way to deal with the incident? Explain.

If you have not experienced such problems, find out how your college would deal with acts of discrimination and prejudice. You may want to contact the campus affirmative action/equal opportunity office for information. Find out what steps students would need to take if they wished to follow up on an incident. Share your answers and information with other class members.

EXERCISE 16.9   Constructive Steps: Advocating for Pluralism

As a class come up with a list of steps that students could take at your school to "advocate for pluralism."

EXERCISE 16.10   Is Hate Speech Permitted on Your Campus?

In a small group, evaluate your campus policy on hate speech. Develop an argument for or against complete freedom of expression on Internet newsgroups accessible on campus computers. What values and what ideas about the nature of college or society does your argument reflect?

SUGGESTIONS FOR FURTHER READING

Bell, D. *Faces at the Bottom of the Well: The Permanence of Racism.* New York: Basic Books, 1992.

Boswell, J. *Same Sex Unions in Pre-Modern Europe.* New York: Villard, 1994.

DeVita, P. R., & J. D. Armstrong. *Distant Mirrors: American as a Foreign Culture.* Belmont, CA: Wadsworth, 1993.

Divoky, D. "The Model Minority Goes to School," *Phi Delta Kappan* (November 1988), 219–222.

Fisk, E. B. "The Undergraduate Hispanic Experience," *Change* (May/June 1988), 29–33.

Giovanni, N. "Campus Racism 101," *Essence* (August 1991), 71–72.

Halpern, J. M., & L. Nguyen-Hong-Nhiem, eds. *The Far East Comes Near: Autobiographical Accounts of Southeast Asian Students in America.* Amherst: University of Massachusetts Press, 1989.

Mathews, J. *Escalante: The Best Teacher in America.* New York: Holt, Rinehart & Winston, 1988.

Paley, V. G. *White Teacher.* Cambridge, MA: Harvard University Press, 1989.

Smith, S. G. *Gender Thinking.* Philadelphia: Temple University Press, 1992.

Stalvey, L. M. *The Education of a WASP.* Madison: University of Wisconsin Press, 1989.

Answers to Exercise 16.6:

1. *False.* Stereotypes, even if positive, assume that all members of a group are the same.

2. *True.* Racism reflects attitudes and actions rooted in ignorance.

3. *False.* The American Psychiatric Association removed homosexuality from its list of disorders in 1973.

4. *True.* Racism occurs when individuals use their prejudice to deny others their civil rights.

5. *False.* Check current newspapers, periodicals, and television reports for the latest incidents of racism.

6. *True.* Everyone benefits when all individuals are allowed to reach their full potential. A victim of racism might just be the person who could find a cure for AIDS.

RESOURCES

How many connections with diverse communities do you already have in your life? Look back at the relationships map that you made for the Resources in Chapter 15. Think about the different kinds of diversity and different communities discussed in this chapter.

Copy part or all of your relationship map below. Using different color markers, highlight all the people (including yourself) by gender, racial/ethnic background, sexual orientation, religious background, and so on. Make a key at the bottom of the map to show which color represents which group. (Keep in mind that most people will fall into several groups.)

After you acknowledge the diverse communities that you already have in your life, the next step is to educate yourself about communities you don't know as much about. For example, you may know a great deal about the contributions of Native Americans in U.S. history but know little about the role Asian Americans have played. You may know a lot about African American artists but little about classical music. Consider some specific activities that would further your knowledge and understanding. (For example, you could plan to attend a lecture that challenges your present thinking, interview a fellow student about his or her experiences on campus, switch the dial on your radio, or make a meal!)

List at least three activities that you plan to do this semester to expand your understanding of and appreciation for diversity.

JOURNAL

Reflect on your thoughts and feelings about your racial and ethnic background and about diversity issues on campus.

Comment on something that came up in one of the class discussions concerning diversity.

Which ideas or areas still present problems for you? What can you do about them?

CHAPTER

Managing Stress

17

KEYS TO SUCCESS

- *Learn what helping resources your campus offers and where they are.*
- *Take your health seriously.*
- *Never doubt your abilities.*

" Hey you! Yeah I said you! Watch where you're going. I mean, move and let me get by. I've gotta get to class, and I don't have time to hassle with you. What? Who are you tellin' to slow down? Hey, I was up till four studying . . . so maybe I'm a little edgy today. So chill! "

Stress is natural. To the extent it is a sign of vitality, stress is good. Yet unless we learn how to cope effectively with stress-producing situations, stress can overwhelm us and undermine our ability to perform. The primary way to manage stress is to modify the situation with something that enhances our feeling of control. For some, relaxation is also very important in counteracting stress. It's impossible to be tense and relaxed at the same time, and relaxation is a skill you can learn.

Did you realize you have actually *learned* to be tense in most stress-producing situations? Now you can learn how to identify the warning signs or symptoms of stress. And once you are aware of the warning signs, you can *choose* how you will react.

◼ A HEALTHY LIFESTYLE

The best starting point for handling stress is to be in good shape physically and mentally—by eating, sleeping, and exercising to reasonable degrees. If you are uncertain about what constitutes a healthy diet or whether yours is healthy, ask your campus health or counseling office for information, consult the library, or take a brief wellness course. Also, use the box on page 261 to determine how much caffeine you may be consuming on a regular basis.

In moderate amounts (50–200 milligrams per day), caffeine increases alertness and reduces feelings of fatigue, but even at this low dosage it may make you perkier during part of the day and more tired later and may give you headaches when you cut down. Consumed in larger quantities, it may cause nervousness, headaches, irritability, stomach irritation, and insomnia.

If starting college means a major change in your sleep habits, consider whether these are entirely necessary or due to a lifestyle choice that you may need to modify. Being rested makes you more efficient when you are awake. It also helps to make a lot of other activities more enjoyable and cuts down the likelihood that you'll succumb to annoying diseases, such as infectious mononucleosis.

Exercise regularly. The box "Start Healthy" suggests how. You may feel that you have no time for regular exercise, but even a daily regimen of stretches each morning can help lower stress, keep you looking and feeling trim, and enhance your energy.

Although competitive sports are fun and a great way to meet friends, and although weight training may be appealing, it's more beneficial to find an aerobic activity—swimming, jogging, brisk walking, cycling, or vigorous racquet sports—that strengthens your cardiovascular system and gives other physiological benefits. People who undertake aerobic exercise report more energy, less stress, better sleep, weight loss, and an improved self-image.

Start Healthy

GET ENOUGH REST

Aim for eight hours of sleep each night. Listen to your body, and rest more when you need to.

GET ENOUGH EXERCISE

1. **Mode.** Pick something you enjoy and will stick with. You can cross-train doing different exercises. Find exercise partners to help you keep going.

2. **Frequency.** Exercise at least three times weekly. For greater improvement, build gradually to four to six times weekly. Give yourself at least one day a week free of exercise so your body can recover.

3. **Duration.** Exercise for at least 20–30 minutes at a time, even at the beginning.

4. **Intensity.** Monitor the intensity of your workout. In order to get aerobic benefits, your heart must be beating at a target rate. To determine this rate, subtract your age from 220 and multiply by .60. Then subtract your age again from 220 and multiply this time by .75. These two answers are the high and low limits of what your heart rate (pulse) should be during exercise.

EAT FOR HEALTH

1. **Eat a balanced diet each day.**
2. **Watch your caffeine content.**

Item	Caffeine (milligrams)
1 cup brewed coffee	85
1 cup instant coffee	60
1 cup tea	30–50
12-ounce cola drinks	35–65
Many aspirin compounds	30–60
Various cold preparations	30
1 cup cocoa	2–10
1 cup decaffeinated coffee	3

3. **Eat when you are hungry.** Don't eat for comfort or distraction. Use food to fuel your body with energy. For emotional support or cheering up, try connecting with a good friend or exercising instead of eating.

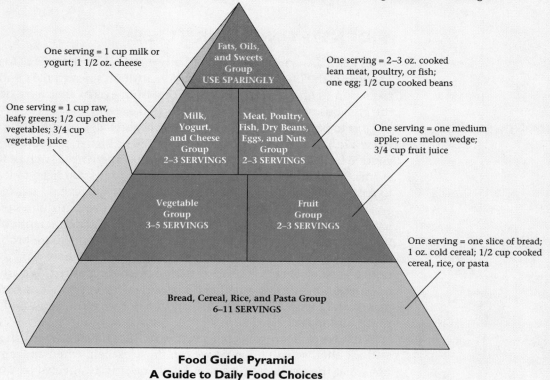

One serving = 1 cup milk or yogurt; 1 1/2 oz. cheese

Fats, Oils, and Sweets Group
USE SPARINGLY

One serving = 2–3 oz. cooked lean meat, poultry, or fish; one egg; 1/2 cup cooked beans

One serving = 1 cup raw, leafy greens; 1/2 cup other vegetables; 3/4 cup vegetable juice

Milk, Yogurt, and Cheese Group
2–3 SERVINGS

Meat, Poultry, Fish, Dry Beans, Eggs, and Nuts Group
2–3 SERVINGS

One serving = one medium apple; one melon wedge; 3/4 cup fruit juice

Vegetable Group
3–5 SERVINGS

Fruit Group
2–3 SERVINGS

One serving = one slice of bread; 1 oz. cold cereal; 1/2 cup cooked cereal, rice, or pasta

Bread, Cereal, Rice, and Pasta Group
6–11 SERVINGS

**Food Guide Pyramid
A Guide to Daily Food Choices**

■ WHAT HAPPENS WHEN YOU ARE TENSE

Signs of stress are easy to recognize and differ little from person to person. Basically your rate of breathing becomes more rapid and shallower; your heart rate begins to speed up; and the muscles in your shoulders and forehead, the back of your neck, and perhaps even across your chest begin to tighten. Probably your hands and perhaps your feet become cold and sweaty. There are likely to be disturbances in your gastrointestinal system, such as a "butterfly" stomach or diarrhea, vomiting, and frequent urination. Your mouth may become parched, your lips may dry out, and your hands and knees may begin to shake or tremble. Your voice may quiver or even go up an octave.

A number of psychological changes also occur when you are under stress. These changes are the result of your body and mind trying to "defend" you from some real or imagined threat. The threat could be from an actual situation, such as someone approaching you with a gun in hand. Or it could come from something that hasn't actually happened but that you are worried about. As a result, you're more easily confused, your memory becomes blocked, and your thinking becomes less flexible and more critical. If the situation persists, you may also find it difficult to concentrate, and you may experience a general sense of fear or anxiety, insomnia, early waking, changes in eating habits, excessive worrying, fatigue, and an urge to run away.

SEE EXERCISE 17.1

The urges to stand and fight or to run away are two of the human body's basic responses to stress. But many times both urges must be suppressed because they would be inappropriate. For instance, a person taking an exam may want to bolt from the exam room, but it probably would not help the grade to do so, and it's pointless to fight with a piece of paper. So we often find we must cope with a situation in a way that allows us to face it. This is where learning to manage stress can make a difference!

■ IDENTIFYING YOUR STRESS

Stress has many sources, but there are two prevailing theories as to its origin. The first is the life events theory, which attributes health risks and life span reduction to an accumulation of effects from events that have occurred in the previous twelve months of a person's life.

SEE EXERCISE 17.2

Turn to page 269 and complete the College Readjustment Rating Scale (Exercise 17.2). If you find that your score is 150 or higher, it would be good preventive health care to think about why you experienced each of the scored events. In addition, you might consider what skills you need to learn either to repair the damage that these events caused or to prevent their recurrence.

The other major theory about the sources of stress attributes our general level of stress to an overload of personal hassles and a deficit of uplifts or reliefs. This theory encourages us to evaluate our immediate problems but, while doing so, to focus on what's good about our lives and to strive to notice positive events instead of taking them for granted. We are all going to experience reversals, whether it's because we don't get along with a roommate, can't register for the course or time slot we want, can't find a parking space, and so on.

SEE EXERCISE 17.3

What we can control is our *reaction* to life's hassles. If we can adopt the attitude that we will do what we can do, seek help when appropriate, and not sweat the small stuff, we won't be as negatively affected by frustrations. It also helps to keep a mental tally of the positive things in our lives.

Physical activity, especially when it's fun, can serve as a remedy for stress.

PHOTODISC

■ A STRESS RELIEF SMORGASBORD

To provide yourself with a sense of relief, you need to do those things that help you to let go of stress or invigorate your mind and body. However, many of the traditional things that people do with the intention of relieving stress—such as drinking alcohol, taking drugs, oversleeping, or overeating—don't relieve stress and may actually increase it! There are many other ways of handling stress that actually work:

Get Physical

- **Relax your neck and shoulders.** Slowly drop your head forward, roll it gently to the center of your right shoulder, and pause; gently roll it backward to the center of your shoulders and pause; gently roll it to the center of your left shoulder and pause; gently roll it forward to the center of your chest and pause. Then reverse direction and go back around your shoulders from left to right.
- **Take a stretch.** In any situation, if you pause to stretch your body you will feel it loosen up and become more relaxed, so stand up and reach for the sky!
- **Get a massage.** Physical touch can feel wonderful when you are tense, and having someone help you relax can feel supportive.
- **Exercise.** Physical exercise strengthens both mind and body. Aerobic exercise is the most effective type for stress relief.

Search Online!

INFOTRAC COLLEGE EDITION

Try these phrases and others for Key Words and Subject Guide searches: "stress," "college and stress," "healthy diet," "how to relax."

Also look up:

Stressors of college: a comparison of traditional and nontraditional students. Patricia L. Dill, Tracy B. Henley. *The Journal of Psychology* Jan 1998 v132 n1 p25

Biofeedback: listen to the body. Carol J. Alexander, Lorraine Steefel. *RN* August 1995 v58 n8 p5

Road Warrior

A student who commuted 23 miles to school was tailgated just before arriving on campus one day. The accident was minor, but unfortunately she had been sipping coffee at the time of the collision, and it splashed all over her dress. She was so embarrassed that she didn't go to class. Unfortunately, that was a particularly important class, and her absence eventually cost her a full letter grade.

If you commute a long distance, carry a store of supplies. Leave your survival kit in your car if you drive, or in a locker at school if possible. Here are some things you should have in your kit. Talk with other students about other items that might be useful and add them to the list.

- emergency medical supplies
- flashlight
- one dollar in change
- some pencils and paper

- jumper cables
- local bus schedule
- rag or towel
- spare set of clothes
- _____
- _____
- _____
- _____

Get Mental

- **Count to ten.** Many people discount this method because it sounds too simple. Your purpose is to master self-control and gain a more realistic perspective or outlook. To give yourself time to gain that new outlook or to come up with a "better" way to handle the situation, count slowly while asking yourself, "How can I best handle this situation?"

- **Control your thoughts.** The imagination can be very creative—it can veer off in frightening directions if allowed to do so. To gain control of negative thoughts or worries, imagine yelling "Stop!" as loudly as you can in your mind. You may have to repeat this process quite a few times, but gradually it will help you shut out angry or frightening thoughts.

- **Fantasize.** Give yourself a few moments to take a minivacation. Remember the pleasure of an experience you enjoy, or listen to a child laugh, or just let your mind be creative. Make a list of some places or activities that make you feel relaxed and good about yourself. Next time you need to get away, refer to the list, close your eyes, and take a minibreak.

- **Congratulate yourself.** Give yourself pats on the back. No one knows how difficult a situation may have been for you to handle, or even how well you may have handled it, so tell yourself, "Good going."

- **Ignore the problem.** This may sound strange at first, but many problems just don't need to be dealt with or can't be solved right now. Forget about the problem at hand and do something more important or something nice for yourself.
- **Perform self-maintenance.** Stress is a daily issue, so the more you plan for its reduction, the more likely it will be reduced.

Get Spiritual

- **Meditate.** All that meditation requires is slow breathing and concentration. Look at something in front of you or make a mental picture while you gradually breathe slower and slower and feel the relief spread through your body and mind.
- **Pray.** You don't need to go through life feeling alone. Prayer can be a great source of comfort and strength.
- **Remember your purpose.** Sometimes it is very valuable to remind ourselves why we are in a particular situation. Even though it may be a difficult situation, you may need to remind yourself that you have to be there and to realize that the situation's importance outweighs its difficulty.

Use Mind and Body Together

- **Take a break.** If possible, get up from what you are doing and walk away for a while. Don't let yourself think about the source of the problem until after a short walk.
- **Get hug therapy.** We need at least four hugs a day to survive, eight hugs to feel okay, and twelve hugs to tackle the world. "Hugs" can come from many different sources and they can take many different forms. They can be bear hugs, smiles, compliments, or kind words or thoughts. If you have forgotten how to hug, ask a small child you know to teach you. Young children know that every time you give a hug, you get one back as a fringe benefit!
- **Try progressive relaxation.** Perform a mental massage of each muscle in your body from your feet up to your head. Take the time to allow each muscle to relax and unwind. Imagine that the muscles that were all knotted and tense are now long, smooth, and relaxed.
- **Laugh.** Nothing is so important that we must suffer self-damage. The ability to laugh at your own mistakes lightens your load and gives you the energy to return to a difficult task.
- **Find a pet.** Countless studies have demonstrated that caring for, talking to, holding, and stroking pets can help to reduce stress.

Develop New Skills

SEE EXERCISE 17.4

SEE EXERCISE 17.5
INTERNET ACTIVITY

- **Learn something.** Sometimes your problem is that you lack information or skills in a certain area. The sooner you remedy your deficiency, the sooner your distress will end.
- **Practice a hobby.** If you have one, use it; if you don't currently have one, then it's time that you did. A hobby can immerse you in an activity of your choice that provides you with a sense of accomplishment and pleasure.

The stress management habits that you are currently acquiring and practicing are likely to serve you for the rest of your life. Learning to handle stress in a healthy fashion is important not only to survive your first year and do well but to cope with the demands and opportunities of adulthood. A healthy adult is one who treats his or her body and mind in a respectful manner. When you do that, you communicate to all other adults that you are handling yourself well and don't need them to baby you or to tell you how to live your life.

▮STRESS AND CAMPUS CRIME

With all the stress you may be experiencing from relationships and your studies, one thing you certainly want to avoid is becoming a victim of crime. Danny E. Baker of the College of Criminal Justice, University of South Carolina, offers the following advice.

College and university campuses are not sanctuaries. Criminal activity occurs on campus on a regular basis. It is important to take proactive measures to reduce criminal activity on your campus.

The first step is to become familiar with how you can protect yourself as well as your personal property. Most campus crime involves theft. As students bring more valuable items to campus, such as computers, the opportunity for theft grows.

Personal Property Safety

Books can be stolen and sold at bookstores, and if not properly marked will never be recovered. Computers and other expensive items are stolen and traded for cash. To reduce the chances of such occurrences, follow these basic rules:

- Record serial numbers of electronic equipment and keep the numbers in a safe place.
- Mark your books on a preselected page with your name and an additional identifying characteristic such as your Social Security Number or driver's license number. Remember on which page you entered this information.
- Never leave books or bookbags unattended.
- Lock your room even if you are only going out for a minute.
- Do not leave your key above the door for a friend or roommate.
- Report lost or stolen property to the proper authority, such as the campus police.
- Don't tell people you don't know well about your valuable possessions.
- Keep your credit or bank debit card as safe as you would your cash.

Automobile Safety

- Keep your vehicle locked at all times.
- Do not leave valuables in your vehicle where they can be easily seen.
- Park in well-lighted areas.
- Maintain your vehicle properly so it isn't likely to die on you.
- Register your vehicle with the proper authorities if you park on

campus. This identifies your vehicle as one that belongs on campus and assists police when they patrol campus for unregistered vehicles belonging to potentially dangerous intruders.

Personal Safety

We cannot plan for every potential event that might cause injury. Each day we read about new tragedies: airplane crashes, accidental drownings, and violent crimes. We still fly and swim and we still go out at night, finding ourselves alone with individuals we do not know and experiencing other risky situations.

Here are some ways to increase your personal safety on campus:

- Find out if your campus has an escort service that provides transportation during the evening hours. Are you familiar with the hours and days of service? Use this important service if you must travel alone during evening hours.
- Write down the telephone number for your campus police. Are your police commissioned officers with the power to arrest? Do they receive special training in preventing crime in an academic community?
- If your campus has emergency call boxes, find out where they are and how to operate them.
- Be aware of dark areas on campus and avoid them, particularly when walking alone.
- Travel with at least one other person when going to the library or other locations on or near campus during evening hours.
- Let someone know where you will be and a phone number where you can be reached, particularly if you go away for the weekend. Sometimes parents call and become concerned when they can't reach you. An informed roommate can minimize the potential for parental concern.
- With the current passion for fitness, many students enjoy jogging—a great way to stay fit but also an opportunity for crime and injury. While jogging during the early evening and early morning, wear reflective clothing. And find a jogging partner so that you are not alone in situations where help is not readily available.

Your behavior both on and off campus should be proactive in terms of reducing opportunity. Remember the difference between fear and concern. Fear generally is an emotion that appears after a critical incident. However, responses to fear are short term and we soon return to old habits. Concern, on the other hand, allows us to make safety measures a part of our everyday routine. Be concerned.

Alcohol and Crime

The majority of violent crimes on or near college and university campuses have involved alcohol or drug use. Friends watch out for friends. Accordingly, pay attention to the "friends" with whom you socialize. Look out for one another.

A Word About Victims

Although crime prevention is proactive and attempts to minimize opportunity, crime does occur and ultimately some of us become victims. You may

A Relaxation Process

Get comfortable. Take a few moments to allow yourself to listen to your thoughts and to your body. If your thoughts get in the way of relaxing, imagine a blackboard in your mind and visualize yourself writing down all of your thoughts on the blackboard. By doing this, you can put those thoughts aside for a while and know that you will be able to retrieve them later.

Now that you are ready to relax, begin by closing your eyes. Allow your breathing to become a little slower and a little deeper. As you continue breathing slowly and deeply, let your mind drift back into a tranquil, safe place that you have been in before. Try to recall everything that you could see, hear, and feel back there. Let those pleasant memories wash away any tension or discomfort.

To help yourself relax even further, take a brief journey through your body, allowing all of your muscles to become as comfortable and as relaxed as possible. Begin by focusing on your feet up to your ankles, wiggling your feet or toes to help them to relax, then allowing that growing wave of relaxation to continue up into the muscles of the calves. As muscles relax, they stretch out and allow more blood to flow into them; therefore they gradually feel warmer and heavier.

Continue the process into the muscles of the thighs; gradually your legs should feel more and more comfortable and relaxed.

Then concentrate on all of the muscles up and down your spine, and feel the relaxation moving into your abdomen; as you do so you might also feel a pleasant sense of warmth moving out to every part of your body. Next focus on the muscles of the chest. Each time that you exhale, your chest muscles will relax just a little more. Let the feeling flow up into the muscles of the shoulders, washing away any tightness or tension, allowing the shoulder muscles to become loose and limp. And now the relaxation can seep out into the muscles of the arms and hands as your arms and hands become heavy, limp, and warm.

Now move on to the muscles of the neck—front, sides, and back—imagining that your neck muscles are as floppy as a handful of rubber bands. And now relax the muscles of the face, letting the jaw, cheeks, and sides of the face hang loose and limp. Now relax the eyes and the nose, and now the forehead and the scalp. Let any wrinkles just melt away. And now, by taking a long, slow, deep breath, cleanse yourself of any remaining tension.

not always use the best judgment, yet *no one* has the right to make you a victim. If you or a friend become the victim of a crime, report it to the authorities immediately. Never blame yourself! Reporting the crime quickly enables law enforcement officials to deal with it more effectively. If property is stolen, a quick report may help police recover and return the items.

Most institutions of higher learning are engaged in active crime prevention programs. If you live on campus, your residence advisor will be aware of crime prevention information and may sponsor crime prevention speakers as part of your residence hall programming.

GETTING HELP

Sometimes our problems are either too overwhelming or too complex for us to resolve by ourselves. If that is the case, you might benefit from checking out the services provided by your college counseling center. Counseling centers often offer individual or group sessions on handling difficult times or situations. The support and skills of a trained professional can help make difficult issues a lot more manageable.

EXERCISE 17.1   Your Signs of Stress

Recall your last troublesome experience. What signals from your mind or body (for example, worry, frightening thoughts, tense muscles, headache, stomach distress) let you know this was a distressing situation? How did you respond to those signals? What might you do next time to handle the situation more effectively?

EXERCISE 17.2   The College Readjustment Rating Scale

The College Readjustment Rating Scale is an adaptation of Holmes and Rahe's Life Events Scale. It has been modified for college-age adults and should be considered as a rough indication of stress levels and possible health consequences.

In the College Readjustment Rating Scale, each event, such as one's first term in college, is assigned a value that represents the amount of readjustment a person has to make as a result. In some studies, people with serious illnesses have been found to have high scores on similar scales. Persons with scores of 300 and higher have a high health risk. Persons scoring between 150 and 300 points have about a 50–50 chance of serious health change within two years. People scoring 150 and below have a 1 in 3 chance of a serious health change.

To determine your stress score, circle the number of points corresponding to the events you have experienced in the past six months or are likely to experience in the next six months. Then add up the circled numbers.

Event	Points
death of spouse	100
female unwed pregnancy	92
death of parent	80
male partner in unwed pregnancy	77
divorce	73
death of a close family member	70
death of a close friend	65
divorce between parents	63
jail term	61
major personal injury or illness	60
flunk out of college	58
marriage	55
fired from job	50
loss of financial support for college (scholarship)	48
failing grade in important or required course	47
sexual difficulties	45
serious argument with significant other	40
academic probation	39
change in major	37
new love interest	36
increased work load in college	31
outstanding personal achievement	29
first term in college	28
serious conflict with instructor	27
lower grades than expected	25
change in colleges (transfer)	24
change in social activities	22
change in sleeping habits	21
change in eating habits	19
minor violations of the law (for example, traffic ticket)	15

If your score indicates potential health problems, it would be to your benefit to seriously review the stress relief smorgasbord in this chapter and select and implement some strategies to reduce your stress.

Note: Adapted with permission from T. H. Holmes and R. H. Rahe, "The Social Readjustment Scale," in Carol L. Otis and Roger Goldingay, *Campus Health Guide*. New York: CEEB, 1989.

EXERCISE 17.3 Protection from Stress

A Feeling good about yourself can be an effective buffer against stress. Begin by identifying some of your personal strengths in writing. Expand this into a longer list of what you like about yourself, and keep the list in a private place. Every day, whether you feel the need or not, review your list and try to add a new positive thought about yourself.

B Likewise, it's important to eliminate unnecessary worries. Make a list of some of your current worries. Now write what you can do to eliminate some of them.

EXERCISE 17.4 Adding to and Using the Stress Reduction List

A Over your lifetime you've discovered some additional things that work to relieve stress for you. Write them down in a list. Expand your list by comparing notes with other students in the class.

B Try at least one stress relief technique suggested in this section for two weeks. Give it a good try. To help you change a stress habit to a control habit, recognize that you deserve to be a more relaxed, confident person.

EXERCISE 17.5 INTERNET ACTIVITY — Stress, Anxiety, and Relaxation

When you prepare for and take tests or give speeches:

do your hands get cold?	_____
does your breathing speed up?	_____
does your mouth go dry?	_____
do your muscles tense?	_____
do you sweat?	_____

If you said "yes" to any of the questions above, you are probably experiencing performance-related stress. Read "How to Master Stress" *(http://www.mindtools.com/smpage.html)*. What did you find to help manage your stress? (Go to *http://csuccess.wadsworth.com* for the most up-to-date URLs.)

SUGGESTIONS FOR FURTHER READING

Benson, H., & M. Z. Klipper. *The Relaxation Response*. New York: Morrow, 1976.

Glasser, W. *Positive Addiction*. New York: Harper & Row, 1979.

Hyatt, C., & L. Gottlieg. *When Smart People Fail*. New York: Simon & Schuster, 1987.

Kinser, N. S. *Stress and the American Woman*. New York: Ballantine, 1980.

Luks, A., & P. Payne. *The Healing Power of Doing Good*. New York: Ballantine, 1992.

Otis, C. L., & R. Goldingay. *Campus Health Guide*. College Entrance Examination Board, 1989.

Powell, J. W. *Campus Security and Law Enforcement* (2nd ed.). Boston: Butterworth-Heinemann, 1994.

Sapolsky, R. M. *Why Zebras Don't Get Ulcers*. New York: Freeman, 1994.

Seligman, M. *Learned Optimism*. New York: Knopf, 1991.

Viorst, J. *Necessary Losses*. New York: Fawcett, 1986.

RESOURCES

To control stress, you need to heed its warning signs. Use the charts below for one week to keep track of trouble-some experiences and your reactions and responses to them. Pay attention to times when you suddenly feel fatigued, tense, angry, upset, frightened, and so on. These are stress points in your day.

Event	Physical Signals	Emotional Signals
1.		
2.		
3.		
4.		
5.		
6.		

At the end of the week analyze the chart. Look for positive and negative patterns.

My Response	What I Would Do Differently Next Time
1.	
2.	
3.	
4.	
5.	
6.	

Based on this information, write a plan for stress management:

JOURNAL

NAME _____

DATE _____

Try one or more of the relaxation processes described in A Stress Relief Smorgasbord on page 263. Choose a day that has been especially stressful for you. When you have finished, relax for a few minutes. Then write about what it felt like to go through the processes.

....
....
....
....
....
....
....
....

It has been said that anticipating an important event (an exam, a new relationship, a move from home to a college residence hall) can often produce more stress than the actual happening. Is that true for you? Why do you think this is so? What were your biggest concerns just before you came to college? What are they now? If the list has changed, can you explain why?

....
....
....
....
....
....
....
....
....
....
....
....
....

CHAPTER

Sexual Decisions

18

KEYS TO SUCCESS

- *Learn what helping resources your campus offers and where they are.*

- *Get to know at least one person on campus who cares about your survival.*

- *Take your health seriously.*

- *Find faculty and staff support on campus.*

- *Develop peer support.*

" A few of my friends are always bragging about who they were with last night. I'm not into that. Some women around here turn me on, but I just don't want a sexual relationship right now. I have enough to deal with. Down the road a little, if I find the right person, who knows? "

We know from numerous studies that about 75 percent of traditional-age college students have engaged in sexual intercourse at least once. We will not judge your sexual decisions. But we will encourage you to know your options and to recognize that you have the right to choose what's comfortable for you. As a result, we hope you'll conclude that choosing to have sex also means choosing to protect yourself against unwanted pregnancy, unwanted sex, and sexually transmitted diseases.

■ SEXUAL DECISION MAKING

Not all first-year students are sexually active. However, college seems to be a time when recent high school graduates begin at least to think more seriously about sex. Perhaps this has to do with peer pressure or a sense of one's newfound independence, or maybe it's just hormones. Regardless of the reasons, it can be helpful to explore your sexual values and to consider whether sex is right for you at this time.

Although the sexual revolution of the 1960s and 1970s may have made premarital sex more socially acceptable, people have not necessarily become better equipped to deal with sexual freedom. There is an increase in the rate of sexually transmitted diseases (STDs) among college students, and unwanted pregnancies are not uncommon. More difficult to quantify is the degree to which young people may later regret decisions to have sex.

Why is it that otherwise intelligent people choose to take sexual risks? If you are 18 or so, you may feel you are invincible or immune from danger. Although you know certain risks exist, you may never have been sufficiently exposed to them personally to believe your own life could be touched. Although there are many pressures to become sexually active, certainly many factors may discourage sexual activity as well:

Encouragers	Discouragers
hormones	family values/expectations
peer pressure	religious values
alcohol/other drugs	sexually transmitted diseases
curiosity	fear of pregnancy
the media	concern for reputation
an intimate relationship	feeling of unreadiness
sexual pleasure	fear of being hurt or used

With such powerful pressures on each side, some people get confused and overwhelmed and fail to make any decisions. Or they may not feel comfortable enough with their decision to take responsibility for their actions—the "If I don't think or talk about it, then I can pretend I'm not really doing it" syndrome. This carries a risk: that sex will occur without the means to prevent pregnancy or STDs.

For your protection, try to clarify your own values and then act in accordance with them. Those who do this usually wind up happier with their decisions. Take a moment now to reflect on whether you plan to be sexually active. Whatever you decide, think about how you will reinforce your resolve to abstain from sex or only practice safer sex and how you plan to communicate that decision to your partner.

SEE EXERCISE 18.1

■ BIRTH CONTROL

One sexuality issue that heterosexual students need to be concerned about is preventing an unwanted pregnancy.

What is the best method of contraception? It is any method that you use correctly and consistently, each time you have intercourse. Table 18.1 compares the major features of some common methods, presented in descending order of effectiveness for pregnancy prevention.

Make sure whatever method you choose, you feel comfortable using it. Always discuss birth control with your partner so that you both feel comfortable with the option you have selected. For more information about a particular method, consult a pharmacist, your student health center, a local family planning clinic, the local health department, or your private physician. The main thing is to resolve to protect yourself and your partner every time you have sexual intercourse.

SEE EXERCISE 18.2

■ SEXUALLY TRANSMITTED DISEASES (STDS)

The problem of STDs on college campuses has been receiving growing attention in recent years as an epidemic number of students have become infected. The consequences of the most common STDs reach far beyond the embarrassment most students feel when diagnosed with a sexually related illness. The idea that nice young men and women don't catch these sorts of diseases is more dangerous and inaccurate than ever before. If you choose to be sexually active, particularly with more than one partner, exposure to an STD is a real possibility.

In general, STDs continue to increase faster than other illnesses on campuses today. Approximately 5–10 percent of visits to college health services nationally are for the diagnosis and treatment of STDs. For more information about any of these diseases, or others, contact your student health center, your local health department, or the National STD Hotline (1-800-227-8922).

CHLAMYDIA

The most common STD in the United States is chlamydia. Over 4 million new cases are diagnosed each year. Chlamydia is particularly threatening to women because a large proportion of women who are infected do not show symptoms, allowing the disease to progress to pelvic inflammatory disease (PID), now thought to be the leading cause of infertility in women. When chlamydia does produce symptoms in women, the symptoms may include mild abdominal pain, change in vaginal discharge, and pain and burning with urination.

Table 18.1 Methods of Contraception

ABSTINENCE (100%)*
What It Is
Choosing not to have intercourse.

Advantages
Only method that provides total protection against pregnancy and STDs.

Disadvantages
Does not allow for the benefits people look for from sexual intercourse.

Comments
Not an acceptable practice for many people.

NORPLANT (99.9%)
What It Is
Six matchstick-sized silicone rubber capsules inserted into a woman's arm, which continually release a very low dose of progesterone.

Advantages
Highly effective. Works for up to five years. Allows for sexual spontaneity. Low dose of hormones make this medically safer than other hormonal methods.

Disadvantages
Removal may be difficult. Very expensive to obtain initially.

Comments
Users may have typical side effects of hormonal methods, causing them to discontinue during the first year. This makes it somewhat risky due to the high initial cost.

DEPO-PROVERA (99.7%)
What It Is
A progestin-only method, administered to women by injection, every three months.

Advantages
Highly effective. Allows for sexual spontaneity. Relatively low yearly cost.

Disadvantages
A variety of side effects typical of progestin-type contraceptives may be present and persist up to 6–8 months after termination.

Comments
Method is easy and spontaneous, but users must remember to get their shots.

STERILIZATION (99.5%)
What It Is
Tubal ligation in women; vasectomy in men.

Advantages
Provides nearly permanent protection from future pregnancies.

Disadvantages
Not considered reversible and therefore not a good option for anyone wanting children at a later date.

Comments
Although this is a common method for people over age 30, most traditional-age college students would not choose it.

ORAL CONTRACEPTIVES (97–99%)
What They Are
Birth control pills.

Advantages
Highly effective. Allows for sexual spontaneity. Most women have lighter and shorter periods.

Disadvantages
Many minor side effects (nausea, weight gain), which cause a significant percentage of users to discontinue. Provides no protection against STDs.

Comments
Available by prescription only, after a gynecological exam.

INTRAUTERINE DEVICE (IUD) (98–99%)
What It Is
Device inserted into the uterus by a physician.

Advantages
Once inserted, may be left in for up to 10 years, depending on the type. Less expensive than other long-term methods.

Disadvantages
Increased risk of certain complications such as pelvic inflammatory disease and menstrual problems. Possible increased risk of contracting HIV, if exposed.

Comments
Women who have not had a child may have a difficult time finding a doctor willing to prescribe it.

CONDOM (88–98%)
What It Is
Rubber sheath that fits over the penis.

Advantages
Only birth control method that also provides good protection against STDs, including HIV. Actively involves male partner.

Disadvantages
Less spontaneous than some other methods because it must be put on right before intercourse. Belief of some men that it cuts down on pleasurable sensations.

Comments
Experts believe that most condom failure is due to lack of consistent use of condoms rather than misuse or breakage.

DIAPHRAGM (80–95%)
What It Is
Dome-shaped rubber cap that gets inserted into the vagina and covers the cervix.

Advantages
Safe method of birth control with virtually no side effects. May be inserted up to 2 hours prior to intercourse, making it somewhat spontaneous. May provide a small measure of protection against STDs.

Disadvantages
Wide variance of effectiveness based on consistent use, the fit of the diaphragm, and frequency of intercourse. Multiple acts of intercourse require use of additional spermicide.

Table 18.1 Methods of Contraception (continued)

Comments

Must be prescribed by a physician. Must always be used with a spermicidal jelly and left in for 6–8 hours after intercourse.

FEMALE CONDOM (80–95%)
What It Is

A polyurethane sheath that completely lines the vagina acting as a barrier between the genitals. Two rings hold it in place, one inside and one outside the vagina.

Advantages

Highly safe medically; does not require any spermicide. Theoretically provides excellent protection against STDs— almost perfectly leakproof and better than the male condom in this regard.

Disadvantages

Has not gained wide acceptance. Visible outer ring has been aesthetically displeasing to some potential users.

Comments

Although the effectiveness is not as high as for the male condom, this method has the advantage of offering good STD protection that is in the control of the woman.

CERVICAL CAP (80–90%)
What It Is

A cup-shaped device that fits over the cervix.

Advantages

Similar to diaphragm, but may be worn longer—up to 48 hours.

Disadvantages

Not widely available due to lack of practitioners trained in fitting them.

Comments

Longer wearing time increases risk of vaginal infections.

SPERMICIDAL FOAMS, CREAMS, AND JELLIES (80–90%)
What They Are

Sperm-killing chemicals inserted into the vagina.

Advantages

Easy to purchase and use. Provides some protection against STDs, including HIV.

Disadvantages

Lower effectiveness than many methods. Can be messy. May increase likelihood of birth defects should pregnancy occur.

Comments

As with condoms, it is suspected that failure is due to lack of consistent use. However, spermicides seem to work better in combination with other methods, such as the diaphragm.

NATURAL FAMILY PLANNING (80%)
What It Is

Periodic abstinence based on when ovulation is predicted.

Advantages

Requires no devices or chemicals.

Disadvantages

Requires a period of abstinence each month, when ovulation is expected. Also, requires diligent record-keeping.

Comments

For maximum effectiveness, consult a trained practitioner for guidance in using this method.

COITUS INTERRUPTUS (80%)
What It Is

Withdrawal.

Advantages

Requires no devices or chemicals and can be used at any time, at no cost.

Disadvantages

Relies heavily on the man having enough control and knowing when ejaculation will occur to remove himself from the vagina in time. Also may diminish pleasure for the couple.

Comments

Ejaculation must be far enough away from partner's genitals so that no semen can enter the vagina. Provides no protection against STDs.

*Percentages in parentheses refer to approximate effectiveness rates based on one year of using the method. Where two numbers are given, the lower percentage refers to the *typical* effectiveness, whereas the higher number refers to a *possible* effectiveness if used correctly and consistently.

In men symptoms are typically pain and burning with urination, and sometimes a discharge from the penis. Occasionally, the symptoms will be too mild to notice. Men who go without treatment may also become infertile, although this happens much more rarely than it does in women. In both sexes, symptoms usually appear one to three weeks after exposure. Even if symptoms are not apparent, an individual infected with chlamydia is still contagious and may transmit the disease to subsequent sexual partners. If detected, chlamydia is completely treatable with antibiotics.

GONORRHEA

Gonorrhea is a bacterial infection that produces symptoms similar to chlamydia. Although not quite as common as chlamydia, with approximately 2 million new cases nationwide per year, it still has a significant impact on the health of Americans. As with chlamydia, men will usually show symptoms, but women often do not. Gonorrhea is treatable with antibiotics, but in recent years new, more resistant strains of gonorrhea have made this process more difficult. Untreated gonorrhea, like chlamydia, can lead to more severe infections in men and women.

HERPES

A recent Centers for Disease Control study estimates that 45 million people are infected with genital herpes, a 30 percent increase since the late 1970s. The large majority of those testing positive for the virus were asymptomatic (showing no symptoms) and many were not aware they carried the virus. When those infected do have symptoms, the most obvious are usually blisters on the genitals, which are very similar to the cold sores and fever blisters people get on their mouths. In fact, oral and genital herpes are both caused by different strains of the same virus. (Both strains of the virus can be transmitted through oral sex.)

Symptoms appear on the genitals two days to two weeks after exposure in the form of small blisters or lesions that erupt into painful sores. Approximately 50 percent of those infected will never have another outbreak. The other 50 percent are likely to have outbreaks several times a year, particularly when they are under stress or their immune system is taxed by fatigue or illness.

Although there is no cure, the drugs Valtrex and Zovirax seem to reduce the length and severity of herpes outbreaks. People are most contagious after or right before lesions erupt, so it is important to abstain from any sexual contact at this time. It is difficult to determine exactly how contagious a person is at other times, but asymptomatic people can transmit herpes because the virus continues to live in the body indefinitely.

HUMAN PAPILLOMAVIRUS (HPV)

Although chlamydia may still be the most prevalent STD nationwide, HPV has become the leading STD affecting the health of college students. Some recent studies show that as many as 40–50 percent of sexually active college students may be infected.

HPV is the cause of venereal warts, which affect both men and women on their outer genitals and in the rectum of those who practice anal receptive intercourse. They may even grow inside a man's urethra or a woman's vagina. A typical incubation period for venereal warts is at least three months, though symptoms may not appear for many months or years after exposure. Genital warts may be small, flat, pink growths, or they may be larger, with a cauliflowerlike appearance. In either case they are rarely painful.

Because HPV is a virus, there is no cure, but treatment is available in the form of burning, freezing, chemical destruction, and, in severe cases, laser surgery. Wart removal often takes multiple treatments, which can be painful and perhaps disruptive. As with herpes, the virus remains in the body and may cause recurrences. Additionally, a person infected with HPV remains contagious to sexual partners for an indefinite period of time.

The major long-term health concern associated with HPV affects women. Certain strains of HPV don't cause the visible warts but invade the cervix. The subsequent cervical cell changes produce dysplasia, a precancerous condition that can lead to cervical cancer. In the past few years, the correlation between cervical cancer and HPV has become very strong, and most experts believe HPV is responsible for the large majority of cases of cervical cancer in our country today. The incubation period for these changes can take many years. Fortunately, if women are screened regularly with Pap smears, precancerous changes can be detected and treated before they lead to cervical cancer.

HEPATITIS B

Each year there are about 300,000 new cases of hepatitis B nationwide, most of them in adolescents and young adults. Hepatitis B is transmitted through unprotected sex and through contact with infected blood and is 100 times more infectious than HIV.

People who are infected with hepatitis B can have varying symptoms, and it's common to show no symptoms. When present, symptoms may include those similar to a stomach virus, in addition to yellowing of the skin and eyes. Occasionally, people become very ill and are disabled for weeks or months. Most people will recover completely, but some remain carriers for life. A small percentage of infected people go on to get chronic liver disease.

There is no cure for hepatitis B, and no treatment other than rest and a healthy diet. What is unique about this STD is that a vaccine is available to prevent it. The series of three shots is recommended by the Centers for Disease Control and the American Academy of Pediatrics for all young adults. The major drawback to the vaccine is that it's very costly, about $100 for the three shots.

HIV/AIDS

HIV/AIDS is very difficult to discuss briefly. We assume that you have already been exposed to a good deal of information on this STD. The main thing for you to know now is that the number of people with AIDS and the virus that causes it—HIV—continues to increase. During 1997, in the sixteenth year of the epidemic, the number of cases of AIDS had grown to over 600,000 in the United States. Although the rate of new cases has slowed, there's no doubt that there's been a steady increase in this disease over the years. The Centers for Disease Control estimate that at least 1 to $1^1/_2$ million people are infected with HIV. The routes of transmission for HIV are through blood, semen, vaginal fluids, and breast milk, or by being born to an HIV-infected mother.

Although intravenous drug users and men who have sex with other men still comprise the majority of AIDS cases, other groups have rapidly increasing rates of infection. In the late 1990s, those experiencing the greatest increases in new HIV infections and cases of AIDS were women, teens, heterosexuals, Hispanic Americans, and African Americans (who continue to be disproportionately represented among those with AIDS). Although we're discussing risk groups here, it's important to keep in mind that it's not who you *are*, but what you *do* that puts you at risk for contracting HIV.

By the mid-1990s, AIDS had become the number-one killer of men and women ages 25 to 44 in United States cities with 100,000 people or more. Considering the long incubation period for HIV to progress to full-blown AIDS, it is likely that those dying in their late twenties and early thirties contracted HIV during their college years.

Because other STDs are occurring at such a high rate, we know that many students obviously are engaging in the behaviors that put them at risk for all STDs, including HIV. In addition, having other STDs may predispose people to contract HIV more readily if they are exposed to the virus.

As with other STDs, abstinence, monogamy, and condoms (in that order) are the best ways to prevent the sexual spread of HIV. Get as much information as you can through your student health service, your local health department, or the National AIDS Hotline (1-800-342-AIDS).

Preventing STDs

Although the sexually transmitted diseases discussed here can be very serious and very scary, it's not all bad news. Good methods of protection are available, and you can choose what's right for you. The worst thing you can do is nothing.

ABSTINENCE

The first choice you always have is to abstain from sex. Even if three-quarters of college students are having sex, that still leaves a solid one-quarter who are not. If you currently fall in this group, congratulations! It can be difficult to choose a behavior when you're in the minority, but you are surely reaping benefits. One thing that can make the decision to abstain easier is realizing that abstinence doesn't have to mean a lack of intimacy, or even of sexual pleasure, for that matter. Abstinence (with a partner) encompasses a wide variety of behaviors from holding hands to more sexually intimate behaviors short of intercourse. These carry a lower risk of spreading disease, having an unwanted pregnancy, or possibly regretting sex than do vaginal or anal intercourse. Even if you've had intercourse in the past, you can become a "born again virgin" if you choose.

**SEE EXERCISE 18.3
INTERNET ACTIVITY**

MONOGAMY

Another very safe behavior, in terms of disease prevention, is having sex exclusively with one partner who is uninfected. However, having a long-term monogamous relationship is not always practical because many college students want to date and either aren't interested in becoming serious or just don't find the right person. And the love of your life this fall may not be the same next spring. A second reason is that it is hard to know for sure that your partner was not infected to begin with. Your chances of remaining healthy are better the more limited the number of your prior sexual partners and the longer you progress in the relationship disease-free.

CONDOMS

Lastly, there's the condom. As we enter the new century, the condom needs to be a given for those who are sexually active. Other than providing very good pregnancy protection it can help to prevent the spread of STDs, including HIV/AIDS. The condom's effectiveness against disease holds true for anal, vaginal, and oral intercourse. The most current research indicates that the rate of protection provided by condoms against STDs is similar to its rate of protection against pregnancy (90–99 percent). Not only has independent research supported this contention, but in 1993, the Centers for Disease Control endorsed condom use as a safe and effective method for STD/HIV prevention, when used correctly and consistently.

To some degree, however, this is easier said than done. The condom has long had a reputation of being a less spontaneous method and of diminishing pleasurable sensations. It may take some discussion to convince your partner that using condoms is the right thing to do. If he or she responds negatively to the suggestion, here are some comments that may help:

Almost no one finds it easy to talk about sex with a potential partner. That's no excuse. Express your needs and concerns. Be sure you understand the other person's feelings and concerns as well.

PHOTO BY HEATHER DUTTON

Your partner: Condoms aren't spontaneous. They ruin the moment.

You: If you think they're not spontaneous, maybe we're not being creative enough. If you let me put it on you, I bet you won't think it's interrupting anything!

Your partner: Condoms aren't natural.

You: What's not natural is to be uptight during sex. If we know we're protected, we'll both be more relaxed.

Your partner: I won't have sex with a condom on.

You: Well, we can't have sex without one. There are other things we can do without having intercourse. Why don't we stick to "outer-course" until we can agree on using condoms for intercourse?

SEE EXERCISE 18.4

■PERILOUS RELATIONSHIPS

In Love and Danger—Relationship Violence

Some individuals express their love in strange and improper ways, ways that should be reported to the authorities. It's called relationship violence—emotional, abusive, and violent acts occurring between two people who presumably care very much for each other. *First-year students are at particular risk because they are in a new and unfamiliar environment, may not realize the risks, want to fit in, and may appear to be easy targets.*

Approximately one-third of all college-age students will experience a violent intimate relationship. Almost every fifteen seconds, a woman in the United States is battered by her boyfriend, husband, or live-in partner. Women ages 16–24 (according to the March 1998 Justice Department report, *Violence by Intimates*) will experience the highest per capita rates of intimate relationship violence.

It's important to recognize the warning signs and know what to do if you find yourself in a violent relationship or know a friend in one.

Condoms

When selecting a condom, always consider the following:

1. **Use condoms made of latex rubber.** Latex serves as a barrier to bacteria and viruses, even those as small as HIV. "Lambskin" or "natural membrane" condoms are not as good for disease prevention because of the pores in the material. Look for "latex" on the package. For those allergic to rubber, there is a polyurethane condom on the market that also offers significant disease protection. Ask your pharmacist.

2. **Try different condoms until you find one that's comfortable and suits you.** Some men and women believe that condoms don't feel good. You have many options to choose from. Different brands and features have their own unique feel. If the first condom you select isn't totally desirable, don't give up on condoms altogether. Try another brand.

3. **Use a lubricant with a condom.** One of the main reasons condoms break is lack of lubrication. Check the list of ingredients on the back of the lubricant package to make sure the lubricant is water based. Do not use petroleum-based jelly, cold cream, baby oil, or cooking shortening. These can weaken the condom and cause it to break.

Source: Adapted from *Understanding AIDS: A Message from the Surgeon General*. HHA Publication No. (CDC) HHS-88-8404. Washington, DC: Government Printing Office.

- An abuser typically has low self-esteem, blames the victim and others for what is actually his or her own behavior, can be pathologically jealous of others who approach the partner, may use alcohol or drugs to manage stress, and views the partner as a possession.
- A battered person has low self-esteem, accepts responsibility for the abuser's actions, is passive but has tremendous strength, believes no one can help, and thinks no one else is experiencing such violence.

HOW TO TELL IF YOUR RELATIONSHIP IS ABUSIVE

Some classic telltale signs: You're frightened by your partner's temper and afraid to disagree. You apologize to others for your partner's behavior when you are treated badly. You avoid family and friends because of your partner's jealousy. You're afraid to say no to sex, even if you don't want it. You're forced to justify everything you do, every place you go, and every person you see. You're the object of ongoing verbal insults. You've been hit, kicked, shoved, or had things thrown at you.

WHAT TO DO IF YOUR RELATIONSHIP IS ABUSIVE

Tell your abuser the violence must stop. Say no firmly if you don't want sex. Have a safety plan handy: Call the police at 911, consult campus resources (women's student services, the sexual assault office, and so forth), call a community domestic violence center or rape crisis center, or call someone else on campus you can trust. Find a counselor or support group on campus or in the community. You can even obtain a restraining order through your local magistrate or county court. If the abuser is a student at the same institution, schedule an appointment with your campus judicial officer to explore campus disciplinary action.

Evidence indicates that violence tends to escalate once a person decides to make a break. Should you reach that point, it's wise to remove yourself from the other person's physical presence. This may include changing your daily patterns.

For further advice, go to your counseling center to find out about restraining orders, listing the abuser's name at the front desk, changing your locks, securing windows, and other precautions.

HOW TO SUPPORT A FRIEND WHOSE RELATIONSHIP IS ABUSIVE

Be there. Listen. Help your friend recognize the abuse. Be nonjudgmental. Help your friend contact campus and community resources for help. If you become frustrated or frightened, seek help for yourself as well.

Avoiding Sexual Assault

Anyone is at risk for being raped, but the majority of victims are women. By the time they graduate, an estimated 1 out of 4 college women will be the victim of attempted rape, and 1 out of 6 will be raped. Most women will be raped by someone they know, a date or acquaintance, and most will not report the crime. Alcohol is a factor in nearly three-quarters of the incidents. Whether raped by a date or a stranger, the victim can suffer long-term traumatic effects.

Tricia Phaup of the University of South Carolina offers this advice on avoiding sexual assault:

- **Know what you want and do not want sexually.** When the issue comes up, communicate it loudly and clearly to a partner.
- **Go to parties or social gatherings with friends, and leave with them.** Sexual assaults happen when people get isolated.
- **Avoid being alone with people you don't know very well.** Do not accept a ride home with someone you just met or study alone in your room with a classmate.
- **Trust your gut.** If a situation feels uncomfortable in some way, don't take chances. Get out of it even if it means a few minutes of embarrassment.

Search Online!

INFOTRAC COLLEGE EDITION

Try these phrases and others for Key Words and Subject Guide searches: "sexual activity in college," "acquaintance rape," "birth control."
Also look up:

Attitudes toward marriage and premarital sexual activity of college freshmen. Connie J. Salts, Melissa D. Seismore, Byron W. Lindholm, Thomas A. Smith. *Adolescence* Winter 1994 v29 n116 p775

Exploring negative dating experiences and beliefs about rape among younger and older women. Michelle Kalra, Eileen Wood, Serge Desmarais, Norine Verberg, Charlene Y. Senn. *Archives of Sexual Behavior* April-May 1998 v27 n2

Beyond "no means no": outcomes of an intensive program to train peer facilitators for campus acquaintance rape education. Kimberly A. Lonsway, Elena L. Klaw, Dianne R. Berg, Craig R. Waldo, Chevon Kothari, Christopher J. Mazurek, Kurt E. Hegeman. *Journal of Interpersonal Violence* Feb 1998 v13 n1 p73

- **Be alert to unconscious messages you may be sending.** Although it in no way justifies someone taking advantage of you, be aware that if you dress in a sexy manner, spend the evening drinking together, and then go back to your friend's room, that person may think you want something.
- **Be conscious of how much alcohol you drink, if any.** It is easier to make decisions and communicate them when you are sober, and also easier to sense a dangerous situation.

If you are ever tempted to force another person to have sex:

- **Realize that it is *never* okay to force yourself sexually on someone.**
- **Don't assume you know what your date wants.** He or she may want a different degree of intimacy than you do in the same situation.
- **If you're getting mixed messages, also ask.** You have nothing to lose by stopping. If someone really wants you, he or she will let you know. And if he or she doesn't, then it's the right decision to stop.
- **Be aware of the effects of alcohol.** It makes it more difficult to understand the communication you're receiving, and it is more likely to instigate violent behavior.
- **Remember that rape is legally and morally wrong.** If you have the slightest doubt about whether what you're doing is right, it's probably not. Regardless of whether a victim chooses to report the rape to the police or get a medical exam, it is very helpful to seek some type of counseling to begin working through this traumatic event.

The following people or offices may be available on or near your campus to deal with a sexual assault: campus sexual assault coordinator, local rape crisis center, campus police department, counseling center, student health services, student affairs professionals, women's student services office, residence life staff, local hospital emergency rooms, and campus chaplains.

Relationships with Teachers

Entering into a romantic relationship with one of your teachers can swiftly lead to major problems. On most campuses, faculty and staff are prohibited from having such relationships with students. It is tempting fate to enter into a personal, romantic relationship with someone who has power or authority over you—as you may learn when the relationship goes bad and you receive a low grade in the course. For this reason, it is imperative to avoid such entanglements and report problems to the proper campus authorities.

When sex happens in ignorance, in haste, or without regard for the other party involved, it may leave emotional scars that are difficult to erase. When individuals who have genuine feelings for each other can agree on the degree of intimacy and involvement, be honest and candid with each other, take proper precautions, and show respect for each other's needs and feelings, that's a different matter entirely.

EXERCISE 18.1

Personal Reflection on Sexuality

A Ask yourself the following questions to prepare for part B: Have you taken time to sort out your own values about sexual activity? If you aren't willing to commit to a particular plan of action at this time, what keeps you from doing so? If you are sexually active, do your values take into account your own and your partner's health? If that's not a priority for you, what would it take to get you to a point where safer sex took priority over unsafe sex?

B Write down some of your thoughts and intentions about sexuality. This should be for you alone to read. The act of writing may help you organize your thoughts. Committing your values to paper may also help you live by them when faced with tough decisions.

EXERCISE 18.2

Which Birth Control Method Is Best?

If you're choosing to be sexually active and don't desire to have children at this time, it's time to choose a method of birth control. Both partners should be involved in this decision. Consider various factors to decide what's right for you, your partner, and your relationship. You can answer these questions on your own and then have your partner complete the exercise, with both of you keeping in mind a particular method you're considering. Or you can complete it together, discussing the issue as you go.

	Me	My Partner
1. Has a pregnancy ever occurred despite using this preferred method of birth control?	_____	_____
2. Will I have difficulty using this method?	_____	_____
3. If this method interrupts love-making, will I be less likely to use it?	_____	_____
4. Is there anything about my behavior or habits that could lead me to use this method incorrectly?	_____	_____
5. Am I at risk of being exposed to HIV or other STDs if I use this method?	_____	_____
6. Am I concerned about potential side effects associated with this method?	_____	_____
7. Does this method cost more than I can afford?	_____	_____
8. Would I really rather not use this method?	_____	_____

EXERCISE 18.3
INTERNET ACTIVITY

Speak of the Devil

The Internet can be a major source of information on topics you are too embarrassed to ask about in person. Not all of the information on the Internet, however, is either timely or accurate. One of the best sources for information on such topics as sex, abstinence, rape and sexual assault, sexual orientation, sexual dysfunction, and "101 Ways to Please Your Lover Without Doing It" is the Duke University "Healthy Devil" Online (*http://h-devil-www.mc.duke.edu/h-devil/sex/sex.htm*). See also the resources on pregnancy testing, options, and suggested resources (*http://h-devil-www.mc.duke.edu/h-devil/preg/preg.htm*). (Go to *http://csuccess.wadsworth.com* for the most up-to-date URLs.)

EXERCISE 18.4

What's Your Decision?

Although you might know about the strategies to keep yourself from contracting an STD, knowledge doesn't always translate into behavior. Use the following chart to brainstorm all the reasons you can think of that people wouldn't practice each of the prevention strategies: abstinence, monogamy, or condom use. In other words, think about the barriers to safer sex. Then go back over your list and consider whether the barrier would apply to you (yes, no, or maybe). In this way you can better evaluate where you stand on the issue of safer sex and determine what areas you may need to work on to ensure that you protect yourself—always!

Barriers   **Does This Apply?**

_____   _____

_____   _____

_____   _____

_____   _____

_____   _____

_____   _____

_____   _____

_____   _____

_____   _____

_____   _____

SUGGESTIONS FOR FURTHER READING

Elliott, Leland, Cynthia Brantley, & Cynthia Johnson. *Sex on Campus: The Naked Truth About the Real Sex Lives of College Students.* New York: Random House, 1997.

Lear, Dana. *Sex and Sexuality: Risk and Relationship in the Age of AIDS.* Newbury Park, CA: Sage, 1997.

Nevid, Jeffrey S. *Choices: Sex in the Age of STDs.* Boston: Allyn & Bacon, 1995.

Powell, Elizabeth. *Sex on Your Terms.* Boston: Allyn & Bacon, 1996.

Sanday, Peggy Reeves. *Fraternity Gang Rape: Sex, Brotherhood, and Privilege on Campus.* New York: New York University Press, 1992.

Tannen, Deborah. *You Just Don't Understand: Women and Men in Conversation.* New York: Ballentine, 1990.

Warshaw, Robin. *I Never Called It Rape.* New York: HarperPerennial, 1988, 1994.

RESOURCES

List some of the resources that will help you make sensible decisions about sex by filling in the names, addresses, and phone numbers for any of the following people or places you might use:

Personal doctor

Student health center

Name of physician to see

Planned parenthood chapter

Local AIDS foundation or project

Local gay/lesbian resource center

Counseling center

Spiritual advisor/pastor/rabbi

Friends or relatives

Campus sexual assault coordinator

Local rape crisis center

Campus police

Women's student services office

In case a friend of yours shares with you a tale of relationship violence or sexual assault, be prepared. List steps you can take to provide assistance.

1. Let the person talk as much as she/he needs to.

2. Try to find out what actually happened.

3.

4.

5.

6.

Note: If you are not sure of what steps to take, ask your instructor to find a speaker from the sexual assault office, student health center, or another related group to help you complete this exercise.

JOURNAL

NAME _____

DATE _____

What effects may the issues in this chapter have on your present and future success in college?

....

....

....

....

....

....

....

....

Which of these issues concerns you the most? Why? Which of these issues angers you the most? Why?

....

....

....

....

....

....

....

....

What steps can you and your friends take to avoid negative or unwanted sexual encounters?

....

....

....

....

....

....

....

CHAPTER 19

Making Informed Choices About Alcohol and Other Drugs

CHAPTER OUTLINE

KEYS TO SUCCESS

- *Learn what helping resources your campus offers and where they are.*

- *Get to know at least one person on campus who cares about your survival.*

- *Take your health seriously.*

" When I got to the party last night, I felt uncomfortable. Like, I'm not used to drinking, but everyone else was doing it, so I had a beer, then another, and suddenly I began feeling great. I even made a pass at a girl. She was drinking vodka, so I joined her. But later that night I was sick as a dog. I'm not feeling very good this morning, either. I've already missed my 9 o'clock exam and I don't think I'll make my other classes today. "

The messages you hear about alcohol are innumerable and confusing. If you're just out of high school, you may have seen widespread alcohol use among parents and mentors. You probably want to belong to a social group, have friends, and relax. And because the social scene commonly includes alcohol as an accompaniment, you may feel pressured to partake. You are repeatedly tantalized by advertisements, movies, and television shows that tend to normalize, glamorize, and romanticize alcohol. You rarely know of anyone who gets seriously hurt or sick from alcohol. Yet you hear about tragedies on college campuses, and you may hear official messages about how dangerous alcohol can be. It's no surprise that you pay little attention to most of these messages, particularly when the allure of a great party confronts you each weekend.

At the same time you're struggling with such decisions, college campuses have been drawn into the national limelight for being associated with tragedies from alcohol abuse. Negative publicity has heightened concern among administrators, faculty, parents, and alumni about alcohol use on the college campus, prompting calls to action from all sides.

Yet many students remain angered by intrusions on their right to have fun and socialize. Colleges are torn between wanting to do the right thing—curbing abusive drinking on campuses—and listening to protests from students who want to preserve their right to drink.

■WHY DO COLLEGE STUDENTS DRINK?

The factors influencing drinking behaviors are very complex. However, the fundamental influences fall into six categories:

1. **Experiences prior to college.** Many students have grown up in a family environment that regularly includes alcohol consumption as a part of social celebrations. Some students may be children of alcoholics or chronic substance abusers—a factor known to affect use of alcohol and other drugs by those children.
2. **Normal human development.** Maturing from adolescence to adulthood may include experimentation and a quest for independence. Drinking is one of many expressions of the normal developmental phenomenon of breaking away from the family and establishing your self-identity.

Parents frequently worry that their children will rebel and experiment. Most of them just hope and pray no damage occurs during the process.

3. **Desire for pleasure and escape from the stresses of daily living.** Human emotions are powerful driving forces in behavior, and the pleasure and relaxation afforded by alcohol are clearly major contributing factors to its use—even though alcohol is a risky, albeit expedient, means of temporarily checking out of reality.

4. **Desire to develop personal relationships and to belong to peer groups.** Perhaps the most crucial influences on behaviors are those that result in the development of human relationships, particularly among peers. Everyone has an inherent desire to be accepted as part of a social group. We tend to engage in activities that feel normal and place us in the mainstream with others. Because alcohol has become a dominant feature of the social scene, both students and adults find themselves in settings where alcohol consumption is expected.

5. **Influence of mass media.** Commercial marketers have learned that associating sex appeal, the outdoors, and healthy-looking young people with their products catches your attention and creates a perception of normal behavior. Such perceptions bombard you daily through music, advertising, television, and social events. Ads in your student newspaper may advertise happy hours. Alcoholic beverage companies may sponsor athletic events and concerts. Glossy, alluring beer ads associate the product with sun, fun, and sex. Such messages may make it impossible for you to understand the reality of alcohol use among your peers.

6. **The campus culture.** Social clubs, Greek organizations, alumni bashes, and campus events focused around the consumption of alcohol (including drinking rituals and games) can contribute significantly to your perception of normal and acceptable behavior. A college administration that turns its back on the illegal underage drinking that occurs in these settings is creating a permissive environment that tacitly endorses illegal and abusive consumption. Campuses with limited access to recreational or alternative social events provide few options for students to spend their leisure time pursuing activities not associated with alcohol.

■ THE TRUTHS, NOT THE PERCEPTIONS

The truth is that underage drinking is punishable by law. The truth is that, although drinking is widespread on campus, a sizable minority of students choose not to drink. The truth is that binging or drinking just to get drunk, which we will address in a moment, is a destructive behavior—not only to the individual, but to others.

And, of course, the truth is that many people *do* drink. If they are of legal age, if they don't depend on alcohol to get them through the day, if they avoid drinking and driving, and if they drink in moderation, most likely they are in little danger of harming themselves, their friends, and their families.

Oddly enough, even alcohol and drug education programs may inadvertently create an image of "everybody's doing it." According to A. D. Berkowitz, "This misperception can alienate and marginalize the majority of students who use responsibly or who do not use at all by leading them to feel that it's their more responsible behavior which is deviant."

Yet because one's perception of what constitutes normal behavior is frequently not what is really happening, many students may think that the frequency and intensity of drinking is much higher than it actually is. The facts are often quite different from the perceptions. According to research, college students who choose to drink consume an average of five drinks in a week, whereas if you ask college students what they think their peers consume, it may be one-and-a-half to two times that amount. Simply knowing that actual consumption is lower may help you decide to consume at the lower rate.

You need not feel defensive or ashamed for letting things influence you, but you shouldn't choose to do something just because you believe everybody's doing it. It could be—as we shall soon discover—that everybody's not.

■ BINGE DRINKING

Light to moderate drinking may carry few risks, but there is one form of drinking that is potentially very dangerous. Abusive, high risk, or binge drinking is an important public health and safety issue on campus. Gaining an understanding of the prevalence and consequences of this pattern of drinking is important.

For males, binge drinking, as recently redefined, occurs when an individual consumes five drinks at one social occasion. For females, whose lower body weight makes them more susceptible to the effects of alcohol, consuming four drinks is considered binging in some studies, while others use the same number used for males.

Binge drinking is a pattern that not only places people at a particular risk of injury, illness, and even death, but has a negative impact on academic and social situations. Because binge drinking has resulted in numerous college student deaths in recent years, it has received massive media attention.

The academic, medical, and social consequences of binge drinking can seriously endanger one's quality of life. Research based on surveys conducted between 1992 and 1994 by the Core Institute at Southern Illinois University (see Internet reference in Suggestions for Further Reading) provides substantial evidence that binge drinkers have significantly greater risk of adverse outcomes, as listed in Table 19.1.

Among other problems, the data identify increased risk of poor test performance, missed classes, unlawful behavior, violence, memory loss, drunk driving, regretful behavior, and vandalism among binge drinkers, compared with all drinkers and all other students. At the same time, college health centers nationwide are reporting increasing trends in the serious medical conditions associated with alcohol use:

- alcohol poisoning causing coma and shock
- respiratory depression, choking, and respiratory arrest
- head trauma and brain injury
- lacerations
- fractures
- unwanted or unsafe sexual activity causing STDs and pregnancies
- bleeding intestines
- anxiety attacks and other psychological crises
- worsening of underlying psychiatric conditions such as depression

"The Police Got Me Drunk. Honest."

Recently I went on a ride-along with Master Police Officer Kyle Harris of the Norman Police Department. He's a drug recognition expert who patrols a special RID (removing intoxicated drivers) unit. Officer Harris had invited me to participate in officer alcohol training. I would be one of eight people volunteering to become intoxicated so the officers could practice field sobriety tests on me. I reluctantly agreed.

Because I'm not much of a drinker and terrified of losing control, it was hard to show up for training that day. I was a little worried what my peers and future employers might think. But it was for training purposes, and I would be in a controlled environment, so I decided to go.

I showed up early and sat in on the classroom training. I even practiced the tests, still sober, during breaks. The rest of the drinkers showed up just before 5 P.M. I didn't know any of them. I was shy and nervous. We took a breathalyzer before we had anything to drink, just to make sure we were clean.

We had to fill out an agreement that promised we wouldn't drive for 12 hours after drinking. We also had to give our names, addresses, body weights, and booze of choice. After the officers asked about our drinking history, it became clear that I was one of the most inexperienced drinkers there.

I started with a rum and Coke. About halfway through, I was everybody's friend. After I finished the drink, I had a buzz. Most of the other drinkers were finishing their second drink about the time I started mine.

A drink-and-a-half later, my neck and face were bright red. I was encouraged to drink more, but the last thing I wanted was to get out of control or sick. I nursed a third drink for about 45 minutes to maintain my level of intoxication. I was drunk. I was definitely one of the most impaired people there. Besides being talkative and flushed, I was wobbly. I had to watch the chair to make sure it didn't move on me before I could sit down. I had to keep my feet apart and my knees bent so that I wouldn't fall on my face. My attention level was zero. If I'd have been driving, I'd have been all over the road.

We stopped drinking and took another breathalyzer test. The officers wouldn't let us see what our blood alcohol content was. I knew mine was high. I thought I was probably over .10, the legal limit to be driving under the influence. If I would have blown a .06 to .09, I would have been charged with driving while impaired and could be sent to jail.

I failed all three field sobriety tests with all seven groups of officers. I had practiced and knew what they were looking for, but I couldn't fake it. Every group would have booked me in jail. If I'd have been driving, I'd have a criminal record right now.

The last thing the officers did was reveal how many ounces of liquor we had and what our blood alcohol content was. Not only did I have the least to drink, my blood alcohol content was the lowest. I only blew a .03. Legally, I could have driven a car, but I was too drunk to shift gears or buckle my seat belt.

I don't think people realize that everyone is affected differently when they drink. Depending on several things, you could feel blitzed, as I did, at .03 or feel okay at .15. I know you'd fail the test if you had a blood alcohol content that high, even if you felt okay to drive. People who feel okay are the most deadly drivers on the road.

I believe it only takes a second to change a life forever. Don't drink and drive, no matter how much you've had to drink. That changed life could be your own.

—Michelle Sutherlin. *The Oklahoma Daily*, October 30, 1997. Reprinted by permission.

Table 19.1 Annual Consequences of Alcohol and Other Drug Use (all students = 44,319; all drinkers = 26,247; all bingers = 16,908)*

Consequences	% Experiencing Consequence		
	All Students	All Drinkers	All Bingers
Had a hangover	59.7	81.1	89.5
Performed poorly on a test	21.8	31.4	40.8
Trouble with police, etc.	11.7	17.4	23.7
Property damage, fire alarm	7.8	11.8	16.5
Argument or fight	29.5	42.0	52.2
Nauseated or vomited	47.1	63.9	73.5
Drove while intoxicated	32.6	47.0	57.3
Missed a class	27.9	40.9	52.9
Been criticized	27.1	37.2	45.3
Thought I had a problem	12.3	16.4	21.6
Had a memory loss	25.8	37.3	48.0
Later regretted action	35.7	49.8	60.4
Arrested for DWI, DUI	1.7	2.4	3.3
Tried, failed to stop	5.8	8.1	10.6
Been hurt, injured	12.9	18.8	25.2
Taken advantage of sexually	11.4	15.9	19.9
Took sexual advantage of someone	6.1	9.0	11.9
Tried to commit suicide	1.6	1.9	2.6
Thought about suicide	5.1	6.7	8.2

Source: Adapted from Presley, C. A., Meilman, P. W., Cashin, J. R., & Lyerla, R. Alcohol and Drugs on American College Campuses: Use, Consequences, and Perceptions of the Campus Environment, Volume IV: 1992–94. Carbondale, IL: The Core Institute, Southern Illinois University.

Table 19.2 Correlation of Drinks Consumed in One Week with GPA

Number of Drinks Per Week	Grade Point Average
3.4	A
4.5	B
6.1	C
9.8	D and F

Source: Adapted from Presley, C. A., Meilman, P. W., Cashin, J. R., & Lyerla, R. Alcohol and Drugs on American College Campuses: Use, Consequences, and Perceptions of the Campus Environment, Volume IV: 1992–94. Carbondale, IL: The Core Institute, Southern Illinois University.

Although binge drinking in particular has been associated with adverse consequences, even those students who drink without binging are likely to see an inverse effect on their grades, depending on the number of drinks they consume weekly. In fact, all Core Institute surveys conducted since the early 1990s consistently have shown a negative correlation between grades and the number of drinks per week. Findings are similar for both two-year and four-year institutions, as shown in Table 19.2.

Binge drinking is somewhat more prevalent among college students than among other young adults. The University of Michigan study showed that in 1996, 38.3 percent of college students engaged in binge drinking in the preceding two weeks, compared with 34 percent of young adults the same age (see *Monitoring the Future Study* in "Suggestions for Further Reading").

SEE EXERCISE 19.1

© MATTHEW MCVAY/ALLSTOCK/PNI

Not all college students drink frequently and in excess or even at all. There are many enjoyable activities and events that do not need alcohol to make them fun.

Secondary Effects of Binge Drinking

Students who binge drink harm not only themselves but also others around them. Statistics from the 1995–96 survey from the Core Institute demonstrate the percentage of students who experience adverse effects as a result of others' drinking:

study interrupted	29%
space messed up	25%
felt unsafe	22%
unable to enjoy events	19%
interfered with in other ways	32%

In general, breaches of institutional codes of conduct and commission of campus crimes frequently have alcohol abuse as a common denominator.

Not Everybody's Doing It

Educators have tended to focus mainly on the negatives and perhaps overemphasize the consequences of excessive drinking. This creates a notion that everyone is drinking all the time. But it is important to understand that not every college student is drinking frequently or in excess. In fact, statistics indicate that a majority of college students do *not* drink excessively on a regular basis.

The Core Institute has been conducting nationwide surveys of drinking behaviors of college students since the early 1990s that provide important insights about drinking and its consequences. The most recent information was collected during 1995 and 1996.

Researchers surveyed 89,874 randomly selected college students from 171 two- and four-year colleges in the United States. Year in college (such as, first-year, sophomore, graduate student), gender, and ethnicity indicated a

SEE EXERCISE 19.2
INTERNET ACTIVITY

Table 19.3 Core Alcohol and Drug Survey

Used alcohol at least once in the preceding year	82.8%
Average number of drinks per week*	5.1
Binged at least once in the two weeks prior to completing the survey.	41.7%
Students under the age of 21 using alcohol at least once in the preceding 12 months	82.4%
Students under 21 using alcohol within the preceding 30 days	68.8%
Students not engaging in binge drinking in preceding two weeks	58.3%

*For all students. A drink is defined as a bottle of beer, a glass of wine, a wine cooler, a shot glass of liquor, or a mixed drink.

Source: Presley, C. A., and Leichliter, J. S. Recent Statistics on Alcohol and Other Drug Use on American College Campuses: 1995–96. Carbondale, IL: The Core Institute, Southern Illinois University.

representative sample of college students. Fifty-three percent of the sample were under 21 years of age, 41 percent were male, and 59 percent lived off campus. Table 19.3 lists some of the key findings of the survey.

In a 1998 update of its 1993 data, the Harvard School of Public Health College Alcohol Study indicates a sharp rise in the percentage of those who "drink to get drunk," offset somewhat by a corresponding rise in the number of nondrinkers. See Table 19.4.

The study also revealed that 19.8 percent of students surveyed had experienced five or more different alcohol-related problems (driving after drinking, damaging property, getting injured, missing classes, and getting behind in school work), an increase of 22 percent since 1993. And 35.8 percent of those surveyed reported drinking after driving, a 13 percent increase since the 1993 study.

Four out of five students who were not binge drinkers and who lived on campus experienced at least one secondhand effect of binge drinking, such as being the victim of an assault or an unwanted sexual advance, having property vandalized, or having sleep or study interrupted.

■WHAT SHOULD YOU DO?

You face challenging decisions about the use of alcohol. But fortunately, you have choices and you are ultimately the one in charge. When confronting the decision to use alcohol, you need to understand and accept the positive and negative consequences. You can make wise decisions. You can choose to abstain. You can also choose to consume. If you choose to consume, know the difference between high risk or abusive drinking and safe and responsible drinking. It can make a major difference in your life.

Chronic alcoholism or addiction is a commonly cited consequence of abusive drinking. Evidence indicates that teens who engage in heavy alcohol use before they reach 17 are at increased risk of alcoholism (Grant & Dawson, 1998).

Our advice? Give your use of alcohol some thoughtful reflection. Consider your family and religious values and recognize their influence. Reconcile the obvious moral and ethical conflicts before choosing to consume alcohol when it remains illegal or in violation of campus policy to do so.

Table 19.4 Harvard School of Public Health College Alcohol Study (1998)

	1993	1997
Drink to get drunk	39%	52%
Binge drinkers	44.1%	42.7%
Frequent binge drinkers	19.5%	20.7%
Don't drink	15.6%	19%

Source: H. Wechsler, G. W. Dowdall, G. Maenner, J. Gledhill-Hoyt, & H. Lee. "Changes in Binge Drinking and Related Problems Among American College Students Between 1993 and 1997." Results of the Harvard School of Public Health College Alcohol Study. *Journal of American College Health 47* (1998): 57–68.

Reducing the Risks

Beyond the legal context, recognize that aberrant patterns of drinking, such as binging, put you at particularly high risk of injury, illness, and negative academic or social consequences and that avoiding these behaviors can minimize your risks. The following suggestions probably won't cut down on your fun (in fact, you may have more fun because you're still awake) but can make a big difference in making your fun safer:

- **Maximize the amount of time you spend with a drink.** Avoid drinking more than one or two drinks in less than an hour.

- **Combine your alcohol consumption with food.** Food tends to absorb alcohol in the stomach and slows its absorption into the bloodstream.

- **Consider alternating nonalcoholic drinks with alcoholic beverages.** Simply having alcohol every other drink will fill the time while reducing the total number of alcohol beverages consumed.

- **Assign designated drivers and use them.** Never drive when you're drunk, and never ride with a driver who has been drinking.

- **Avoid participating in drinking games.** Chugging contests and other ritualistic drinking games encourage rapid consumption of large amounts of alcohol and are highly associated with significant risk of illness or injury. Drinking to get drunk is a form of Russian roulette and places you at greater risk of becoming a chronic user or abuser aside from the obvious acute risks of injury and illness.

- **Familiarize yourself with information about the actual level of drinking among your peers.** If your campus does not have information on drinking norms among your student population, study the information available in the national studies cited here. You'll probably be surprised to find that most students drink much less frequently and imbibe fewer drinks than you expected.

SEE EXERCISE 19.3

A Choice Not to Drink

You certainly have the choice not to consume alcohol. By doing so, you become a part of a group of students who value this course of action. This is a responsible, legal, and healthy decision you may want to advocate in the classroom, in the residence halls, and in social settings.

Undoubtedly you already know of other ways to experience pleasure and reduce stress. A game of basketball, shooting pool, a movie, a walk in the woods, or a stroll through a museum can do a lot to reduce stress without putting you at significant risk of injury or illness. Pursuing healthy escapes from life's stresses through outdoor recreation, intellectual pursuits, music, or the creative arts will benefit you for years to come. What's more, alcohol and other drugs are only temporary stress relievers and offer no other compensations. When you wake up, your problems are still going to be there and may seem all the worse because of your consumption the night before.

SEE EXERCISE 19.4

Your Rights

You have a right to a safe, clean, and secure academic and living environment. If drunk students are depriving you of this, consider rallying the support of others to prevent the secondary effects of abusive use of alcohol in your campus environment. Use your student government, student organizations, residence hall staff, or student life administration to influence policy development and to enforce the rights of other students.

Finally, insist that campus leaders apply the same standards of conduct for faculty, staff, campus visitors, and students. A campus demanding that students comply with existing drinking laws has difficulty gaining credibility if alumni, faculty, and athletic ticketholders repeatedly ignore state and local laws regarding consumption of alcohol.

■ OTHER DRUGS

Alcohol is the cause of the vast majority of health and societal problems among college students. Illegal recreational drugs, such as marijuana, cocaine, ecstasy, LSD, and heroin, are used by a much smaller number of college students and far less frequently. These drugs are significant public health issues for college students, however, and we hope that the comparative statistics shown in Table 19.5 and the brief additional information given below will provoke further reading and discussion.

The reasons college students use illicit drugs are similar to the reasons they use alcohol. Although it may be less likely that family or societal environments condone illicit drug use, the developmental need for experimentation, the relentless search for pleasure and escape, the influence of peer pressure—all coupled with subtle messages from the media and music industries—are major contributing factors to illicit drug use.

All drugs listed in Table 19.5, with the exception of alcohol, are illegal, and the penalties associated with their possession or use tend to be much more severe than those associated with underage alcohol use. None of these drugs is considered safe or innocuous by the medical community. In contrast to earlier recommendations regarding the potential for moderate and lower risk consumption of alcohol, we cannot offer similar advice for illicit drugs (except to never share drug needles). Side effects include the potential for long-term abuse, addiction, and severe health problems.

Additionally, athletic departments, potential employers, and government agencies do routine screenings for many of these drugs. Future employability, athletic scholarships, and insurability may be compromised if you have a positive drug test for any of these substances.

A brief summary of two of the most prevalent drugs follows.

Table 19.5 Usage of Alcohol and Other Drugs on College Campuses

Drug	Percentage Using at Least Once in Preceding Year	Percentage Using During Previous 30 Days
Alcohol	83	70
Marijuana	31	19
Cocaine	3.9	1.6
Amphetamines	6.9	3.1
Designer drugs (ecstasy)	3.6	1.3

Source: Presley, C. A., and Leichliter, J. S. Recent Statistics on Alcohol and Other Drug Use on American College Campuses: 1995–96. Carbondale, IL: The Core Institute, Southern Illinois University. Used by permission.

Marijuana

A single puff of marijuana has a half-life in the body of between three and seven days, depending on the potency and the smoker. Consider how a number of these potential effects could affect your academic performance:

- chronically slowed reaction time
- impaired hand-eye coordination
- altered perception of time (slow motion)
- impairment of depth perception and recent memory
- apathy, loss of drive, unwillingness or inability to complete tasks

Long-term use carries the same risks of lung infections and cancer that are associated with smoking tobacco. Some experts believe that marijuana may be a gateway to more potent and dangerous drugs.

Cocaine

Cocaine, whether snorted, injected, or smoked as crack, produces an intense experience that heightens senses. A crack high lasts only a few minutes; then the good feelings are gone. During the crash, the user may feel tired and unmotivated and find it impossible to sleep. Cocaine in any form can lead to a staggering number of physical, mental, and emotional problems, both short- and long-term. Sudden death has resulted from cardiac arrest.

Search Online!

INFOTRAC COLLEGE EDITION

Try these phrases and others for Key Words and Subject Guide searches: "binge drinking," "illegal drugs in college," "alcohol and health." Also try the names of other drugs about which you want more information (such as "methamphetamines").

Also look up:

College students' binge drinking at a beach-front destination during spring break. George L. Smeaton, Bharath M. Josiam, Uta C. Dietrich. *Journal of American College Health* May 1998 v46 n6 p247

Alcohol and drug use in UK university students. (United Kingdom) E. Webb, C.H. Ashton, P. Kelly, F. Kamali. *The Lancet* Oct 5, 1996 v348 n9032 p922

Tobacco—The Other Legal Drug

Tobacco use is clearly the cause of many important and serious medical conditions, including heart disease, cancer, and lung ailments. Over the years, tobacco has led to the deaths of hundreds of thousands of individuals.

Unfortunately, cigarette smoking is on the rise among college students, jumping 28 percent in four years. "The rise in this group is really an alarming sign," said Henry Wechsler of Harvard University. Wechsler compared surveys of more than 14,000 students at 116 colleges in 1993 and again in 1997 and found a 28 percent increase over those four years.

Because more women than men now smoke, the rate of cancer in women is rapidly approaching or surpassing rates in men.

Chemicals in tobacco are highly addictive, making discontinuation of smoking difficult. Although young people may not worry about long-term side effects, increased numbers of respiratory infections, worsening of asthma, bad breath, and stained teeth should be motivations to not start smoking at all.

■MAKING DECISIONS, FINDING HELP

The vast majority of college students have chosen not to drink abusively, not to use illegal drugs, and not to use tobacco. Still, those who use these substances abusively endanger their health and hopes for the future as well as endangering the well-being of others.

If you need help with that decision, or already have an alcohol or drug problem, one thing you might do is contact your campus counseling or health center, personal physician, or clergy. Unless your behavior is considered dangerous to yourself or to others, most counselors and physicians are required by their professional codes to respect the confidentiality of your visit and to try to help you with your problems. Before taking such a step, it's wise to check state and local laws on confidentiality, because they vary widely across the country.

SEE EXERCISE 19.5

SEE EXERCISE 19.6

If you are a responsible drinker, one who causes no harm to yourself or to others, we hope you won't be goaded into becoming a problem drinker. If you don't drink at all, we hope this chapter has assured you that it's okay. And if you do have an alcohol or drug problem, we urge you to seek appropriate professional care before things get any worse. College is a time for growing up, for discovering your talents, for preparing to succeed in life. Why let something as potentially damaging as alcohol or other drugs put a kink in those plans?

Why Students Binge

List the three most important reasons you think students binge drink. Explain why each reason is important. If you had the task of modifying drinking behaviors at your institution, what would you do?

The Core Alcohol and Drug Survey

A Use the Internet to access the Core Alcohol and Drug Survey results. Identify at least three data tables from the latest study that are applicable to your institution and student demographics. Review the data and explain how these findings are relevant to students at your institution.

B The use of drugs by athletes is one of the more controversial issues of drug use. Consider which of the following seven statements about athletes and drugs you believe to be true or false. Then check your answers at *http://www.sportserver.com/newsroom/sports/oth/1998/oth/mor/feat/archive/042598/mor74645.html* or *http://www.sportinggreen.com/SG/fbo/fbc/news/news/980424.980424.df026.html*. (Go to *http://csuccess.wadsworth.com* for the most up-to-date URLs.)

1. Drug use is highest in Division I.
2. Drug use is highest among African American student athletes.
3. Football has the highest use of anabolic steroids.
4. The majority of college athletes feel they must take drugs to "keep up with their competition."
5. Marijuana is the most commonly used recreational drug among college athletes.
6. Ephedrine is mainly used as a recreational drug by student athletes.
7. Supplements are rarely used by college athletes.

Survey of Alcohol Usage

Using data from the Core Institute and Harvard studies in this chapter, as well as any other information you can find, interview three to five students about their beliefs regarding alcohol and other drugs. Some questions you might ask:

- How can students have a social life without drinking?
- What influence do advertising, movies, and television have on your desire to drink or use other drugs? Explain your answer.
- Is there any situation where it is safe to drive when you're drunk? Describe the situation(s).
- For students who drink, what do you think is the average number of drinks per week? (Tell them it's 5.1.) What's your reaction to that?
- Can you give me a definition of binge drinking? (Tell them it's drinking five drinks in one social setting for men, or four for women.)
- Why do you think college students binge drink?

Use your notes to discuss your findings with others in the class. Employ the critical thinking process to arrive at a comprehensive portrait of attitudes toward alcohol and drug use on your campus. Then brainstorm to find ways to change that attitude if it needs changing.

EXERCISE 19.4   A Safe Stress Antidote

In groups of three to five, make a list of activities that can be used by students at your institution as an antidote for stress. In other words, brainstorm activities that can be extremely pleasurable and can relieve the stress of daily living. The only caveat is that these activities should be safe and fun. Share your list with other groups in the class.

EXERCISE 19.5   Advice to a Friend

If you could make only three recommendations to a friend about partying safer, what would they be? Explain how each would help your friend enjoy the party without putting himself or herself at risk.

EXERCISE 19.6   Lower the Drinking Age?

The national drinking age has been 21 since 1988. Data suggest that nearly 17,000 to 20,000 traffic deaths have been prevented as a result of raising the legal drinking age. Knowing this, can you or your classmates come up with any positive reasons for lowering the drinking age to 18?

SUGGESTIONS FOR FURTHER READING

Berkowitz, A. D. "From Reactive to Proactive Prevention: Promoting an Ecology of Health on Campus." In *Substance Abuse on Campus. A Handbook for College and University Personnel*. Westport, CT: Greenwood Press, 1997.

Core Alcohol and Drug Survey, Core Institute, Center for Alcohol and Other Drug Studies, Student Health Programs, Southern Illinois University at Carbondale, 62901*: *http://www.siu.edu/coreinst/*

Grant, B. F., & D. A. Dawson. "Age of Drinking Onset Predicts Future Alcohol Abuse and Dependence." *Journal of Substance Abuse*, 9 (1998):103–110.

Haines, Michael. *A Social Norms Approach to Preventing Binge Drinking at Colleges and Universities*. (1996). The Higher Education Center for Alcohol and Other Drug Prevention. Education Development Center, Inc., 55 Chapel Street, Newton, MA 02158-1060: *http://www.edc.org/hec/pubs/socnorms.txt* or *http://www.edc.org/hec/pubs/socnorms.pdf*

Monitoring the Future Study. The Inter-University Consortium for Political and Social Research, the University of Michigan, Institute for Social Research, P.O. Box 1248, Ann Arbor, MI 48106-1248: *http://www.isr.umich.edu/src/mtf/index.html*

Presidents Leadership Group. *Be Vocal, Be Visible, Be Visionary: Recommendations for College and University Presidents on Alcohol and Other Drug Prevention*. (1997). The Higher Education Center for Alcohol and Other Drug Prevention. Education Development Center, Inc., 55 Chapel Street, Newton, MA 02158-1060: *http://www.edc.org/hec/pubs/plgvisionary.htm*

Rosenburg, Bai, & Claudia Kalb. "Drinking and Dying." *Newsweek*, October 13, 1997.

Werner, M. J., L. S. Walker, & J. W. Greene. "Screening for Problem Drinking Among College Freshmen." *Journal of Adolescent Health, 15* (1994): 303–310.

Winerip, M. "Binge Nights." *The New York Times,* Education Life Section, January 4, 1998.

Wright, S. W., & C. M. Slovis. "Drinking on Campus. Undergraduate Intoxication Requiring Emergency Care." *Archives of Pediatric Medicine, 150* (1996): 699–702.

*Go to *http://csuccess.wadsworth.com* for the most up-to-date URLs.

RESOURCES

Whether or not to drink, smoke, or use drugs are decisions you must make for yourself. It's smart to know the consequences. Here are some ways to gather such information.

Visit your campus alcohol and drug office. If you don't know where to find it, ask your instructor or call the student services division. Chat with someone in the office about what tactics he or she uses to educate students on the use of these substances. Mention that research indicates that anti-drinking campaigns may actually tempt students to drink. Summarize what you learned.

Conduct an Internet search using "binge drinking" as a key phrase. Find at least two articles that add to the coverage of this topic in the chapter. Summarize what you learned.

Find copies of current or recent magazines that are targeted to a young audience (18–25). Go through them and note the ads for alcohol products and cigarettes. Explain what you believe are the tactics the advertiser is using to make the reader buy the product.

JOURNAL

NAME _____

DATE _____

How does the culture of your campus encourage the drinking behavior of students?

How does the campus culture discourage drinking behavior?

If you are a smoker, explain why you choose to smoke. If you are not a smoker, or have quit, describe what it's like to be in a room with smokers.

This chapter offers a number of reasons for binge drinking. Based on your own observations, can you furnish other reasons? If you disagree with any of the reasons in this chapter, tell why you feel this way.

CHAPTER

Managing Money

20

KEYS TO SUCCESS

- *Learn what helping resources your campus offers and where they are located.*

- *If you're a full-time student, try not to work more than 20 hours a week.*

- *Try to have realistic expectations.*

> ❝ *Money's no problem for me. Either I have it or I don't. If I have it, I spend it. Once it's gone, I stop. By the way, can you lend me fifty bucks until I get paid next week?* ❞

If you are putting yourself through school, you probably have more expenses and less income than you had in the past. If your parents are helping you pay for college, you are probably responsible for making and spending more money now than you ever were before.

Our aim is to help you take control of your money so that you can worry less about it and focus more on your education. The first part is about managing what you have. The second part is about making up the difference if your budget doesn't balance.

Money management boils down to three primary activities: analysis, planning, and budgeting.

■ ANALYSIS

Analyze your finances by identifying and comparing your expenses with your resources. Unless you know what your costs are and how much you have available, you are not going to be in control of anything. Think in terms of your academic year (August or September through May or June).

EXPENSES

Start by making a list of all the expenses you can think of, under two main categories of costs: educational and noneducational. Educational expenses are those you incur because you are a student, including tuition, fees, books, supplies, lab equipment, and so on. Noneducational expenses include all your other costs: housing, food, transportation, and miscellaneous and personal needs.

Be especially careful as you identify noneducational expenses because these costs are often hard to estimate. For example, it is easy to determine how much your tuition and fees are going to be, but it is not so easy to estimate utility bills or food and transportation costs. Be as methodical as you can. If you are careless, you may end up being nickeled and dimed to debt.

SEE EXERCISE 20.1

Table 20.1 shows most of the types of costs you will face. If you have other expenses, add them to the list.

RESOURCES

Next, identify your resources. Again, list your sources of financial support by category (savings, employment, financial aid, parents, spouse, and so on). Be realistic—neither overly optimistic nor too pessimistic—about your resources. Table 20.2 lists some common types of monetary support. List any additional sources.

SEE EXERCISE 20.2

COMPARING EXPENSES WITH RESOURCES

Once you have identified your expenses and resources, compare the totals. Remember that this is a tentative tally, not a final evaluation. This is especially important to note if your costs exceed your resources.

SEE EXERCISE 20.3

To bring your finances in focus, you must now complete the third step of

Table 20.1 Typical Expenses (academic year)

Educational Expenses

Tuition and fees	$3,100
Books and supplies	635
Subtotal educational expenses	$3,735

Noneducational Expenses

Housing and food	$4,400
Personal	900
Phone	200
Transportation	400
Clothing	600
Social/entertainment	500
Savings	400
Subtotal noneducational expenses	$7,400
Total educational and noneducational expenses	$11,135

Table 20.2 Typical Resources (academic year)

A. Parents/Spouse	
Cash	$ 2,000
Credit union loan	2,500
B. Work	
Summer (savings after expenses)	1,500
Part-time during year	2,000
C. Savings	
Parents	0
Your own	500
D. Financial Aid	
Grants	900
Loans	1,500
Scholarships	0
E. Benefits	
Veterans	0
Other	0
F. Other	
ROTC	900
Relatives	0
Trusts	0
Total	$11,800

your analysis: setting priorities and revising. To do this, classify your expenses as fixed or flexible. Fixed expenses are those over which you have no control; flexible expenses are those you can modify (flexible does not usually mean completely avoidable). Tuition, fees, and residence hall costs are generally fixed, because the institution requires you to pay specific amounts. Food may be fixed or flexible, depending on whether you are paying for a residential board plan or cooking on your own.

Table 20.3 shows some typical new-student costs divided into fixed and flexible expenses. The flexible expenses are listed in order of importance. If the total of your costs exceeds your resources, you can start revising your flexible costs, such as telephone, clothing, and entertainment. Although cutting wardrobe and entertainment costs may be less than enjoyable, good money management means maintaining control and being realistic.

SEE EXERCISE 20.4

■PLANNING

Having analyzed your costs and resources, you now have a good overall perspective on your financial situation. Next you need to plan how you will manage your money. Focus on timing, identifying when you will have to pay for various things, and when your resources will provide income.

For planning, you will need an academic schedule for your school (look in your college catalog or bulletin) and a calendar, preferably organized on an academic schedule such as August through July. First, review your institution's academic schedule for its overall time frame and specific dates. Determine your school's registration and payment schedules. When is the latest you can pay your housing deposit if you live on campus? What is the deadline for tuition and fees? What is the school's refund policy and schedule? Enter these critical dates on your own planning calendar for the entire year. Find out if your school accepts credit cards for tuition payments.

Table 20.3 Typical Expense Priorities (academic year)

Fixed Expenses

Tuition and fees	$ 3,100
Books and supplies	635
Housing	2,000
Subtotal fixed expenses	$ 5,735

Flexible Expenses

Food	$ 2,400
Transportation	400
Clothing	600
Personal	900
Phone	200
Social/entertainment	500
Savings	400
Subtotal flexible expenses	$ 5,400
Total fixed and flexible expenses	$11,135

Table 20.4 Sample Monthly Budget (September)

Resources

Summer savings	$1,500
Parents/spouse	1,850
Financial aid	500
ROTC	100
Part-time job	400
Total	$4,350

Fixed Expenses

Tuition and Fees	$1,550
Books and supplies	300
Dorm room	2,000
Total	$3,850

Flexible Expenses

Food (meal cash card)	$ 200
Supplies	50
Personal	50
Phone	22
Transportation	50
Social	60
Total	$ 432

Summary

Total resources	$4,350
Less total expenses	4,282
Balance	$ 68*

*Carried forward to October. Note that room is paid for entire term and will not be an item in October budget.

Then turn your attention to other important dates that are not institutionally related. For example, if you pay auto insurance semi-annually, when is your next big premium due?

After you have recorded the important dates of your major expenditures, do the same thing for your revenue. This knowledge is essential for planning, because you can't very well plan how you're going to pay for things if you don't know when you'll have the money. For example, financial aid is typically disbursed in one lump sum at the beginning of each academic term, whereas paychecks come in smaller, more frequent installments.

Are there going to be points at which your costs exceed your cash? If there are, you must adjust either when you must pay or when your income will arrive. If you will be a bit strapped paying all of your tuition and fees at the start of the term, see if your school has an installment plan that will let you stretch out the payments or if you can reschedule semi-annual payments (such as car insurance premiums) as monthly payments. Many schools also allow payment by credit card, but be careful about overloading your cards. This is a major reason students drop out of college.

SEE EXERCISE 20.5

Once you have determined the critical dates of income and expenses, planning becomes very simple. But keep in mind that most significant of all destroyers of planning, the dreaded Murphy's law: If something can go wrong, it will—and at the worst moment. For example, you might leave the

The Perils of Plastic

Believe it or not, credit card debt by first-year students has contributed significantly to the dropout rate for this group. You may have already received letters from banks and other businesses offering credit cards or other types of charge cards. Their goal is to lend you money so that you will pay high interest rates in return. They may also charge you annual or monthly fees. In 1998, the interest rates for such student accounts were generally around 18 percent. Rates often go as high as 20 percent, which is much higher interest than you would pay for many student loans.

At the same time, credit cards and other charge cards are sometimes very convenient. Before you decide to use a credit card or which card to choose, consider this advice:

1. **Don't accept or keep cards that you don't really need.**

2. **Choose the right card.** Before you accept a card, be able to answer these questions:

   a. Is there an annual or monthly fee or any other charge apart from interest you may have to pay? What are these fees?

   b. What is the interest rate?

   c. Is there a grace period (the time between making a purchase and paying off the charge, before you will be charged interest)? How long is it?

   d. Does the card allow cash advances? What fees and interest rates apply? (Cash advances are generally the most expensive way to borrow money.)

   e. Are there any fringe benefits to the card that would clearly be valuable to you or your family? Some cards offer a lower rate on phone calls, small cash rebates, or credit miles on frequent flyer programs. Usually the benefits are not significant unless you are charging large amounts.

3. **If you accept a card, sign it right away.** Keep a separate record of the card's number and expiration date and the number to call if it is lost or stolen.

4. **Destroy carbons or incorrect slips that have not been processed.**

5. **Save your charge slips so that you can be certain you have been correctly charged.**

6. **Never lend your card or tell its number to anyone except when necessary for a transaction.** If someone uses your number, you are not responsible for these charges, but you may go through a lot of trouble trying to show the bank which charges were yours and which were fraudulent.

7. **If the card is lost or stolen, you will probably have to pay no more than $50 of any charges made with the stolen card.** Report any loss of the card or other problems immediately by phone.

cap off your car's radiator and accidentally crack the engine block. Or a roommate might suddenly split for Bali, leaving you with higher expenses.

How can you prepare for and minimize the damage caused by unscheduled calamities? Frankly, you can't do everything, but you can prepare to some extent by being emotionally ready to deal with such things when they happen, by building up an emergency fund (even a small one), and by not departing from your money management plan.

Having completed the process of planning your expenditures, you should feel much more in control of your finances. This in turn can alleviate much potential stress.

■BUDGETING

The last step in developing a sound money management plan is budgeting. Budgeting takes self-discipline. Develop both a monthly budget and an academic year budget.

The budgeting process overlaps with the financial planning you did when you identified the timing of your "big ticket" items and income. The academic year budget transforms what you have on your academic calendar into a scheme that also includes your smaller, less dramatic ongoing expenses.

The monthly budget is a specific plan for each month's income and outgo—the final details necessary to make your management system work. It eliminates any confusion about what you must do in the near future, within a manageable block of time. It is also your method for maintaining continual control over your finances. Because it coincides with the cycle of your checking account, it also facilitates monthly balancing and scheduling.

To develop your monthly budget, put your expenses and income together on one sheet, as shown in Table 20.4 on page 308. After listing your fixed expenses, your flexible expenses, and your resources, subtract expenses from resources to create a summary for the month. Settle your fixed outlays and revise the flexible ones as necessary to achieve a reasonable balance. The September budget shown in the table happens to include the major start-up costs for tuition, fees, and so on. Make sure your budget is comprehensive and keeps track of how you spend what you spend.

You may want to consider investing in a financial program for your computer, one that will allow you to keep an on-screen checkbook and show you your assets and liabilities at a glance.

SEE EXERCISE 20.6

■INCREASING RESOURCES

Once you're doing everything to manage your current finances well, you may still need more money. How you acquire more aid has both immediate and long-term implications.

If you are going to be able to deal with your college expenses, it is essential that you see them realistically. Only by knowing how much your education is going to cost can you go about planning how to pay for it. If it is clear that you or your family cannot handle all of the costs, you should certainly apply for financial aid.

Financial Aid

SEE EXERCISE 20.7

SEE EXERCISE 20.8

This chapter will not go into detail about applying for financial aid because it is a complex process that varies from school to school and may change from year to year. What we will do is help you get started thinking about how financial aid works and about what questions you might ask at your school's financial aid office.

Financial aid refers to any type of funding you receive to assist yourself in paying for college. Most financial aid money is given on the basis of need, often according to "demonstrated financial need." Demonstrated financial need is eligibility determined by some specific financial scale, most commonly the federal needs analysis system called the "congressional methodology." Other types of financial aid awards may not depend on this type of eligibility.

Financial aid is categorized as either gift or self-help assistance. Gift assistance is that which does not have to be repaid. Self-help assistance requires you to do something in return, such as work or repay the money. An academic scholarship is gift assistance; a student loan is self-help assistance.

The basis upon which financial aid is awarded varies, but typical criteria are academic merit, financial need, or some combination of the two. The large federal aid programs and most state programs are based on financial need and acceptable progress toward a degree.

Financial aid can be further categorized into two types of gift assistance—grants and scholarships—and two types of self-help assistance—loans and work opportunities.

GRANTS

Grants are gift assistance and so do not have to be repaid. Most institutions offer numerous grants programs, the largest funded by the federal and state governments. Generally, grants are aimed at students with the greatest financial need. Students can often receive more than one type of grant simultaneously, but institutions do place limits on the total amount of grant assistance awarded to any one individual because such funds are limited. Most schools want to spread grants out among as many students as possible.

SEE EXERCISE 20.9 INTERNET ACTIVITY

SCHOLARSHIPS

Scholarships are awarded on the basis of superior academic achievement or merit, although financial need may also be a criterion. Most colleges and universities have scholarships for new students as well as for continuing students. Thousands of scholarships are also available from hundreds of national foundations, organizations, state and federal agencies, businesses, corporations, churches, and civic clubs.

The best way to find scholarship opportunities is to start with your institution and work your way out. Check the availability of scholarships from groups and organizations in your home region. Review information from the primary education-related agency or organization in your state. Go to the library or financial aid office at your school to ask for assistance and to review publications listing scholarships. Our best advice is, ask, ask, ask.

LOANS

Over the past fifteen years, long-term, low-interest educational loans have become the major means for financing college. A number of public and private

Search Online!

INFOTRAC COLLEGE EDITION

Try these phrases and others for Key Words and Subject Guide searches: "budgeting," "credit cards," "managing money."

Also look up:

The "I hate to budget" budget. (Forecast '95) Gregory Spears.

Kiplinger's Personal Finance Magazine Jan 1995 v49 n1 p63

Playing the credit card game to win: how to keep your interest rate low—and avoid those exasperating fees.

(Managing Money: Family Finances) Stephanie Gallagher. *Kiplinger's Personal Finance Magazine* June 1998 v52 n6 p50

student loan programs allow extended repayment periods (up to ten years, depending on the amount borrowed) and very reasonable rates (5–10 percent). Though the practice is not recommended unless absolutely necessary, it is possible to receive assistance from more than one loan program at a time.

The large federal student loan programs are based primarily on need. In addition to student loans there are also federally sponsored loans that do not require demonstrated need. The interest rate for this program can be as high as 12 percent, and repayment generally begins shortly after the loan is made. This program has become popular among parents whose dependents do not qualify for need-based aid.

Student loans are an extremely valuable component of the total financial aid picture, but it is important to remember that they are exactly what they are called: loans. They must be repaid. Failure to repay a student loan can have very negative consequences, including damaged credit, garnishment of wages, confiscation of income tax refunds, and litigation. Be very careful in assuming loan indebtedness during college because a sizable monthly loan repayment can become a heavy burden. Take out student loans only to the extent that they are absolutely necessary for you to stay in school. Otherwise, the student loan that seems like such a boon now may be a tremendous bane later.

WORK OPPORTUNITIES

Part-time work is a valuable type of self-help aid. The College Work–Study Program is a federal student aid program based on need that lets you earn some of the aid for which you may be eligible through employment, generally on campus. In addition, many schools have their own programs through which students earn money or in-kind support such as board. This type of assistance has two advantages. First, you are not indebted after graduation. Second, you may be able to work in areas related to your major, thereby gaining an edge in later job hunting.

Cooperative education (co-op) programs are another great opportunity for students at many institutions. These programs provide employment off campus in public and private agencies, business, and industry. Work may parallel education (part-time course load, part-time work) or alternate with it (full-time study one term, full-time work the next). This type of experience can also be invaluable when you look for that first job after graduation. Many graduates are offered permanent full-time positions as a result of co-op experience.

SEE EXERCISE 20.10 INTERNET ACTIVITY

■THE FINANCIAL AID PROCESS

The largest financial aid programs are those based upon need and regulated by state and/or federal agencies. For these programs, most institutions require at least two basic documents: a needs analysis document and an institutional application/information form. Another typical financial aid form is the scholarship application. Such forms vary widely depending on the scholarship sought and the organization awarding it, but they usually gather information about past performance, honors, leadership, and so on.

The Needs Analysis Document

The term *needs analysis* is sometimes used to refer to the general process of analyzing a student's financial resources in order to determine whether the student needs any further assistance to attend college. Frequently, however, it refers specifically to the federal system that provides a consistent national standard for deciding who will get federal financial aid. At best, needs analysis is simply a relative measure comparing a given family's ability to pay for a college education with that of other families.

To operate this system, the federal government requires certain basic information for determining eligibility, which you must provide on a needs analysis document. The federal form you are most likely to use is referred to by its acronym—the FAFSA. Before you fill one out, however, ask the financial aid office at your school if this is the proper form to use. You can find the FAFSA form on the Internet, along with other information about federal loans, at *http://www.ed.gov/prog_info/SFA/StudentGuide/1998-9/index.html*. (Go to *http://csuccess.wadsworth.com* for the most up-to-date URLs.)

The Institutional Application/Information Form

Many institutions have their own financial aid forms in addition to the needs analysis document. These forms typically ask for different information than is requested in the needs analysis.

Applying for Financial Aid

When you apply for financial aid, remember to:

1. **Plan ahead.** Find out what is available at your institution, how to go about applying, and when you must apply. You need to determine what information will be required, and you need to allow enough time to gather it.

2. **Allow sufficient time for the process to work.** The financial aid application process is often slow. (Summer is the peak season, so allow extra time in the summer.) After you have submitted your initial application, you may be asked to provide additional information to support or clarify it. Be prepared to do this promptly.

3. **Keep copies of everything.** Maintain a file with copies of everything you complete or send, including the date it was completed or sent. This will help you avoid confusion or costly delays due to miscommunication or things getting lost in the mail.

You are responsible for helping to finance your college education. Aside from working to help earn some of what you need, you can contribute in two other ways.

First, stretch your dollars. Be as frugal as possible in areas where you can be flexible, such as personal expenses. Think twice before you spend your money. Is what you're spending it on necessary, or can you live without it?

Second, be serious about your education. By applying yourself to the best of your abilities, managing your time wisely, keeping up in your classes, and not having to repeat courses because of poor grades, you will get the most value for your investment.

If you need more resources to pay for college, first consult your parents or anyone else who is helping you pay for college. Then visit your school's financial aid office and talk with a financial aid counselor. Then use the goal-setting process in Chapter 1 to line up additional resources.

EXERCISE 20.1

Listing Your Expenses

If you're doing the exercises in this chapter on paper, be sure to use a pencil so that you can revise your numbers as you go. Better yet, use a computer word processing or spreadsheet program. Creating your own budget is a great way to learn how to use a simple computer spreadsheet.

1. Spend a few minutes writing down all the types of expenses you can think of that will apply to you during this term or academic year. Then compare your list with the list in Table 20.1.

2. Using Table 20.1 as a rough model, list your expenses. Find the total. If you have trouble deciding how much to put down for a category such as clothing or personal items, try listing specific items you will need and estimate a cost for each. Use the estimates to help decide on a dollar total for the category.

EXERCISE 20.2

Listing Your Resources

1. Spend a few minutes writing down all the types of resources you will have during this academic year. Then compare your list with the list in Table 20.2.

2. Using Table 20.2 as a model, list your resources. Find the total.

 **EXERCISE 20.3**

Comparing Resources with Expenses

1. Subtract your total expenses from your total resources (or resources from expenses). Do you have more money than you need (a positive balance)? Or do you have less (a negative balance)? Is the difference large enough to worry about?

2. If you have more money than you need, check your expenses to be sure that you are not underestimating anything. Change any numbers that should be changed and recompare totals. If you still have more money than needed, increase the amount you plan to save so that your expense total equals your resources.

 EXERCISE 20.4

Setting Priorities

Note: Do this exercise if Exercise 20.3 showed that your expenses are significantly higher than your resources.

1. Using Table 20.3 as a model, create a list that separates your costs into fixed versus flexible expenses. Then focus on the flexible costs; which of them can be reduced? Change your figures to improve the balance of costs and resources, but be realistic. Don't lower expenses that cannot be lowered.

2. If your expenses are still greater than your resources, continue reading the chapter to see how you might add more to the resource side. Then come back and rework your figures to achieve a balance.

 EXERCISE 20.5

Timing Income and Expenses

Get the academic schedule for your school and any monthly calendar that is convenient.

1. On the academic schedule, find the due dates for your school's registration fees, room and board, and other charges. Record these amounts on the calendar. Look over your expenses to see whether there are any other dates when large payments may be due for things such as automobile insurance,

license fees, and required course materials. Record these amounts also on the calendar.

2. Now look at your list of resources and record the dates and amounts on your calendar when portions of your resources will be available.

3. Are there any points in the term when your resources won't cover your expenses? Use the goal-setting process in Chapter 1 to solve the problem.

EXERCISE 20.6

A Monthly Budget

Create a sample monthly budget to plan your income and expenses on a monthly basis.

Note that Table 20.4 includes tuition, books, fees, and other expenses that may be paid in one lump sum at the beginning of the term. This means that your budget for the first month may be very different than for later months. For this reason, you may want to use the second or third month of the term for your sample monthly budget.

Once you have done this for a month or two, you will probably have a good idea of how things are going and will not need to go through such a formal process again, except in months when you foresee unusual expenses.

EXERCISE 20.7

Applying Critical Thinking to the Money Management Process

Write a critical analysis of your current approach to managing money. You will need to consider your expenses, resources, budgeting, priority-setting, planning, and timing of income and expenses. Try to be as objective as you can. How do you assess the logic and appropriateness of your most important financial decisions? Can you identify any alternative strategies you might consider? Discuss these.

EXERCISE 20.8

Monitoring the Media

For a week or so, keep track of advertisements you see on television, hear on radio, or read in newspapers or magazines that not only hype credit cards but also suggest you need to own certain material things in order to be successful and happy. Subject these to a critical analysis. How do the positive outcomes depicted square with the impact of credit cards on your life? What essential facts, truths, and realities do these ads fail to portray? How would your life be different if credit cards or some other forms of borrowing money did not exist?

EXERCISE 20.9
INTERNET
ACTIVITY

Pell Grants

Many students who cannot afford college expenses may be eligible for federal Pell grants. Unlike loans, Pell grants do not have to be paid back.

Eligibility for Pell grants (as well as for many other federal programs) is based on your financial need. Your financial need is based on your expected family contribution (EFC), the amount you and your family are expected to contribute toward your education (see *http://www.ed.gov/prog_info/SFA/StudentGuide/1998-9/index.html*). Your financial aid administrator calculates your cost of attendance (COA) and subtracts your EFC and any financial aid you have already to determine your financial need.

Using the information collected in the previous exercises, calculate your financial need for federal aid. You may want to consider other options for federal aid presented in *The Student Guide to Financial Aid 1998–1999*, of the U.S. Department of Education (*http://www.ed.gov/prog_info/SFA/Student Guide/1998-9/index.html*). (Go to *http://csuccess.wadsworth.com* for the most up-to-date URLs.)

EXERCISE 20.10
INTERNET
ACTIVITY

Myths About Financial Aid

Which of the following statements about college financing are true?

_____ 1. Large amounts of private-sector aid go unclaimed each year because students don't know where to look.

_____ 2. Some scholarship search services have as high as a 96 percent success rate.

_____ 3. It isn't worth saving money for college, because the more money you have, the less financial aid you will receive.

_____ 4. Financial aid is charity.

_____ 5. Financial aid is only available for the poor.

_____ 6. When you apply for federal student financial aid, your financial information becomes public knowledge.

Check your answers at Finaid's "Myths about Financial Aid" page (*http://www.finaid.org/finaid/overview/myths.html*) and Scholarship Scam Alert (*http://www.finaid.org/finaid/scams.html*). (Go to *http://csuccess.wadsworth.com* for the most up-to-date URLs.) What did you learn?

SUGGESTIONS FOR FURTHER READING

Adams, Janelle P., ed. *The A's and B's of Academic Scholarships.* Alexandria, VA: Octameron Associates. Published yearly.

Chany, Kalman A., & Geoff Martz. *The Student Access Guide to Paying for College.* New York: Villard. Published yearly.

College Check Mate: *Innovative Tuitions Plans That Make You a Winner.* Alexandria, VA: Octameron Associates. Published yearly.

The College Costs and Financial Aid Book. Princeton, NJ: College Board Publications. Published yearly.

Directory of Special Programs for Minority Group Members, 4th ed. Garrett Park, MD: Garrett Park, 1986.

Earn and Learn: Cooperative Education Opportunities with the Federal Government. Alexandria, VA: Octameron Associates. Published yearly.

Financial Aid Fin-Ancer: Expert Answers to College Financing Questions. Alexandria, VA: Octameron Associates. Published yearly.

Kennedy, Joyce, & Herm Davis. *The College Financial Aid Emergency Kit.* Cardiff, CA: Sun Features. Published yearly.

Paying Less for College. Princeton, NJ: Peterson's. Published yearly.

Schlacter, Gail A. *Directory of Financial Aids for Women.* Santa Barbara, CA: Reference Service Press. Published biannually.

Schlacter, Gail A., & David R. Weber. *Directory of Financial Aids for Minorities.* Santa Barbara, CA: Reference Service Press. Published biannually.

Student Consumer Guide. Washington, DC: Government Printing Office. Published yearly.

RESOURCES

One key in managing your finances is finding sources of income. Use this page to list major sources of money that you could tap into to help finance your education.

Go to your campus or academic department's scholarship office. If there isn't a specific office, there may be a person (ask your academic advisor) who knows about scholarships and grants.

Make a list of scholarships you are eligible for:

....

....

....

....

....

Make a list of grants you are eligible for:

....

....

....

....

....

Consider applying for one or more of these (make sure to add the application deadlines to your calendar).

Go to your campus financial aid office. Get information on work–study programs and loans.

Make a list of work–study jobs and loans you are eligible for:

....

....

....

....

....

....

If your finances get out of control, consider using the following resources:

The National Foundation for Consumer Credit (for help with debt management): 800-388-2227

Experian (to get a copy of your credit report): 800-682-7654

JOURNAL

How well are you controlling your finances at this point?

....

....

....

....

....

....

....

....

What challenges do you face controlling your finances?

....

....

....

....

....

....

....

....

....

What can you do now to improve your current money management and financial situation in the near future?

....

....

....

....

....

....

....

....

....

Glossary/Index

Collaborative learning, 23–25, 27. *See also* Study groups
note-taking, 25, 90–91, 95, 179
College education
benefits of, 4–5
reasons for choosing, 15
College Readjustment Rating Scale, 262, 269–270
Commuter students students who live off campus and have to commute, or travel, to campus each day. Includes about 80 percent of all U.S. college students today. 9
Companionate love, 231
Computers, 144–158. *See also* Databases; E-mail; World Wide Web
accessing, 146, 153
applications, 148–149, 154
assistance, 144, 147, 153
disaster prevention, 147–148, 154
ethics, 151, 156
etiquette, 151
exercises, 152–156
Internet, 61, 149–151, 194
journal, 158
keyboarding, 146
as key to success, 7
and math/science courses, 181
and note-taking, 91–92, 147
personal resources, 157
and returning students, 10
self-assessment, 152
strategies, 145–146
support services, 9
and test preparation, 117
and time management, 51
and writing, 41, 148, 154–155
Condoms, 276, 280–281, 282
Conventional personality type, 198, 199
Cooperative (co-op) education programs that provide an opportunity to work in academic major-related settings off campus in public and private agencies, as well as in business and industry, either by parallel scheduling (going to school part-time and working part-time) or by alternate scheduling (staying out of school for an academic term and working full-time). 312
Counseling a wide variety of services to which students are entitled based on their payment of tuition. Most campuses provide confidential professional counseling and referral services in numerous different offices, including admissions, financial aid, residence halls, career planning, placement, veterans' affairs, study skills, academic

advising, and counseling. 9, 233, 268, 300. *See also* Academic advising; Support services
Courses. *See* Class participation; Classroom learning; **Majors**
Cover letters, 201, 202, 212
Creative thinking, 38, 39–40
Credit cards, 309
Crime, 266–268
Critical thinking careful observation of a problem or phenomenon followed by thoughtful, organized analysis resulting in a logical, reasoned response. 36–39
and essay tests, 121
exercises, 44, 46
habits, 43
journal, 48
as key to success, 7
and math/science courses, 175
and money management, 315
and note-taking, 95
personal resources, 47
and reading, 107
and time management, 57
and values, 219
and World Wide Web, 138
Criticism, 7, 22, 223
Cultural pluralism a concept of the integration of various cultures into a larger society that envisions continuing individual adherence to and general respect for separate cultural traditions. 247–248, 256. *See also* Diversity
Cuseo, Joseph, 23

Daily plans, 55, 63
Daly, William T., 37, 44
Databases computer application programs for categorizing, storing, and manipulating large amounts of data. 11, 136, 149
Date rape. *See* **Acquaintance rape**
Dawson, D. A., 296
Deadlines, 27, 51
Definitional notes, 90
deLisser, Peter, 88
Demonstrated financial need the eligibility for financial aid you are determined to have based on need; most commonly determined through the federal needs analysis system (the congressional methodology). 310–311
Depo-Provera, 276
Diaphragm, 276–277
Digest of Education Statistics, 14
Disabilities, students with, 9
Discrimination, 251–252
Discussion classes, 89–90
Distractions, 56

Diversity a reference to the growing variety of college students and faculty bodies, which include men, women, minorities, foreign students, and other groups that have been underrepresented on college campuses in the past. 4, 246–258
and campus culture, 248, 250–251, 254
and cultural pluralism, 247–248, 256
and discrimination, 251–252, 255, 256
exercises, 253–256
journal, 258
and learning styles, 74, 79
and minority students, 8
personal resources, 257
and sexual orientation, 248
and study groups, 24, 74
and time management, 50
and values, 218
Dropping a course most colleges allow students to drop (or quit) a course without penalty during specified periods of time. When dropping a course, you must follow the proper procedures, which include completing certain forms and obtaining official signatures. If you're receiving financial aid, your status may change if you drop a course. 29
Drugs, 298–300, 303
See also Alcohol

E-mail electronic mail. Various systems by which computers are linked so that personal computers can be used to send and receive messages and information. 21, 150–151
and connecting with teachers, 26, 32
exercises, 155–156
and relationships, 239–240
See also Internet
Emergencies, 116, 309
Employment
during college, 8, 236, 312
effects of college education on later, 4–5, 184
Encyclopedias, 133–134
Engel, Eliot, 29
Enterprising personality type, 198, 199
Escort services, 267
Essay tests, 121–122, 126
Ethics, 151, 156
Etiquette, computer, 151
Examinations. *See* Test preparation; Tests

Exercise
  and safety, 267
  and stress, 260, 261, 263
  and test preparation, 114
  and time management, 55
Expectations, 8
Explanatory writing, 40
Exploratory writing, 39–40
Extracurricular activities. *See* Campus activities
Extroverted learning style, 70, 71

Fact notes, 90
Family
  relationships with, 8, 234–235, 240–241
  and returning students, 10
  and values, 225
Fantasizing, 264
Feeling learning style, 70, 72, 73
Female condom, 277
Feynman, Richard, 174
Finances. *See* Money management
Financial aid student scholarships, grants, and loans. Some forms of financial aid are gifts, but others are loans that must be repaid with interest. Some aid is offered only to new first-year students, while other sources of financial aid are available to all students. To determine your eligibility for any aid, see your financial aid counselor. The application process for financial aid for a fall semester usually begins during the preceding January. 8, 9, 310–313
Flaming highly emotional, highly critical messages via e-mail. 151
Flash cards, 120
Flexibility, 106–107
Forgetting, 84–85, 92
Fraternities/sororities, 236
Freedom, 4
Free time, 55
Freewriting, 40, 45
Friendship, 235
  and breaking up, 233–234
  and minority students, 8
  and values, 218, 225
  See also Relationships

Gardner, Martin, 184
Gay/lesbian/bisexual students, 248, 254
Gender differences, 193
Gift assistance any type of financial aid that does not have to be repaid. 311. *See also* Financial aid
Goal-setting, 11–12
  and academic honesty, 222
  and career planning, 206–207

exercises, 15, 16, 60–61
  as key to success, 7
  and time management, 60–61
Gonorrhea, 277–278
Grades most schools use the A-F system. A is the highest grade, and F means failure. A-D are passing grades for which you will earn points and credits. If you transfer colleges, however, the D grades may not transfer. Most colleges require a minimum 2.0 GPA, or C average, for graduation; in addition, you might lose financial aid, housing, and other benefits when your GPA falls below a certain level. Bad grades and low GPAs also may lead to dismissal or suspension. Some schools have pass/fail grades (P/F or S/U) and an incomplete grade (I), the latter representing work not completed during the term it was taken.
  and academic honesty, 221
  dissatisfaction with, 29
  math/science courses, 178–179
Grant, B. F., 296
Grants a type of financial assistance that does not have to be repaid. 311. *See also* Financial aid
Graphics/presentation software, 149
Grasha-Riechmann instrument, 69
Grasha, Tony, 69
Greeks. *See* Fraternities/sororities
Groups. *See* Campus activities
GUIDE checklist, 162–165

Hate speech, 256
Health, 8, 9, 114
  See also Drugs; Sexuality; Stress
Hepatitis B, 279
Herpes, 278
High school-college contrasts
  active learning, 20, 26
  exercises, 30
  freedom, 4
  and keys to success, 6
  time management, 51
  values, 219
HIV/AIDS acquired immune deficiency syndrome; a sexually transmitted disease for which there is currently no known cure. As the disease progresses, it gradually breaks down the body's immune system and thus lowers its defense mechanisms, making it impossible for the body to function normally or properly. 279–280
Hobbies, 265
Hogan/Champagne Personal Style inventory, 75

Holland, John, 197–199
Homework
  completing on time, 6
  math/science courses, 175, 182
  and note-taking, 91
  and time management, 52–53
Homosexual students. *See* Gay/lesbian/bisexual students
Housing office, 9
How to Solve It (Polya), 182
HPV. *See* Human papillomavirus
Hug therapy, 265
Human papillomavirus (HPV), 278–279

Impromptu speaking, 167–168, 169
Indexes, periodical, 135–136
Information. *See* Computers; Library research
InfoTrac, 11
Internet a worldwide system of telecommunication connections and procedures that lets computer users exchange messages and information via computer. 61, 149–151, 194
  See also E-mail; World Wide Web
Intimacy. *See* Sexuality
Intrauterine device (IUD), 276
Introverted learning style, 70, 71
Intuitive learning style, 70, 71, 73
Investigative personality type, 198
IUD. *See* Intrauterine device

Jobs. *See* Career planning; Employment
Journal, 18
  active learning, 21, 34
  alcohol/drug use, 303
  career planning, 213
  computers, 158
  critical thinking/writing, 48
  diversity, 258
  introduction to, 13
  learning styles, 82
  library research, 142
  math/science courses, 190
  money management, 318
  note-taking, 98
  public speaking, 172
  reading, 112
  relationships, 244
  sexuality, 288
  stress, 272
  test preparation, 128
  time management, 66
  values, 228
Judging learning style, 70–71, 72
Jung, Carl, 70, 230

Keirsey Temperament Sorter, 79
Keyboarding, 146
Kolb Learning Style inventory, 75

Spirituality, 265

Spreadsheets computer application program used mainly for budgeting, financial planning, and other tasks requiring calculations based on lists of numerical information. 148–149

SQ3R study method, 107–108

STDs. *See* Sexually transmitted diseases

Sterilization, 276

Stress, 2, 260–272
  and alcohol, 291, 302
  and crime, 266–268
  exercises, 269–270
  journal, 272
  and lifestyle, 260–261
  personal resources, 271
  relief methods, 263–266, 268, 270
  returning students, 10
  signs of, 262, 269
  sources of, 262, 269–270
  and test preparation, 115

Stretching, 263

Strong Interest Inventory, 198, 199

Study groups
  and active learning, 20, 21, 23–25
  exercises, 30
  as key to success, 7
  and learning styles, 74
  math/science courses, 179–180
  personal resources, 97
  and reading, 103
  returning students, 10
  self-assessment, 125
  and test preparation, 25, 114, 116, 125, 179

Study skills, 7, 95. *See also* Classroom learning; Note-taking; Reading; Study groups; Test preparation
  and distractions, 56, 57
  returning students, 10
  SQ3R method, 107–108

Styles. *See* Learning styles

Subject encyclopedias, 133–134

Success, keys to, 6–8, 10

Summaries, 119, 125

Support services, 8, 233. *See also* **Academic advising**
  and alcohol/drug use, 300
  career counseling, 7, 9, 199
  and personal safety, 267
  and stress, 268

Sutherlin, Michelle, 293

Syllabus one or more pages of class requirements that an instructor gives out on the first day of a course. The syllabus acts as a course outline, telling when you must complete assignments, readings, and so on. 26, 51

Systematic thinking, 39

Task words, 121–122, 126

Teachers. *See also* Teachers, out-of-class interaction with
  and academic freedom, 27–28
  and active learning, 26–29
  choice of, 7
  connecting with, 26, 32, 114, 178
  and intellectual values, 219
  as job references, 200
  journal, 34
  personal resources, 33
  problems with, 29
  responsibilities of, 31
  teaching styles, 74–75, 79–80

Teachers, out-of-class interaction with
  and active learning, 20, 26, 27
  as key to success, 7
  and math/science courses, 180–181
  and note-taking, 89
  sexual relationships, 284
  and study groups, 25

Teaching assistants, 181

Teaching styles, 74–75, 79–80

Term assignment preview, 51, 52–53

Term papers, 51

Test preparation, 114–120
  and emergencies, 116
  exercises, 124–126
  and health, 114
  journal, 128
  and learning styles, 75, 117
  math/science courses, 178–179
  memory aids, 119–120, 125
  mind mapping, 117–118, 119–120
  personal resources, 127
  self-assessment, 124
  and stress, 115
  and study groups, 25, 114, 116, 125, 179
  summaries, 119, 125
  and time management, 51, 114

Tests, 120–121. *See also* Test preparation
  essay, 121–122, 126
  matching, 123
  multiple-choice, 123
  true-false, 123

Textbooks. *See* Reading

Thinking learning style, 70, 72, 73

Thought control, 264

Time management, 50–66
  and academic honesty, 222
  and critical thinking, 57
  daily plans, 55, 63
  and diversity, 50
  exercises, 58–64
  journal, 66
  as key to success, 7

  master plans, 51
  and math/science courses, 175
  personal resources, 65
  and priorities, 50, 58–60
  procrastination, 56–57, 64, 148
  sample timetable, 54
  term assignment preview, 51, 52–53
  and test preparation, 51, 114
  weekly plans, 61–63

Tobacco, 300

Tolerance, 218

Treisman, Uri, 175

True-false tests, 123

Tutoring, 117

Typing. *See* Keyboarding

Uncertainty, 27

Understanding Mathematics (Alfeld), 185

Values, 216–228
  academic honesty, 219–222
  challenges to, 218
  choosing, 222–223
  defined, 216
  exercises, 224–226
  intellectual, 218–219
  journal, 228
  personal resources, 227
  self-assessment, 217–218, 224–225

Venereal warts, 278

Visual aids, 165

Visualization, 120

Vocabulary, 108

Voice, and public speaking, 167

Voting, 220

Walster, Elaine, 231

Wechsler, Henry, 300

Weekly plan, 61–63

Word processing, 148, 154–155 *See also* Computers

Work. *See* Employment

World Wide Web, 14, 136–138
  exercises, 140
  and reading, 109
  and relationships, 239–240

Writing, 39–43
  and computers, 41, 148
  exercises, 45–46
  habits, 43
  journal, 48
  as key to success, 7
  personal resources, 47
  support services, 9, 42

Zen and the Art of Motorcycle Maintenance (Pirsig), 41

Zinsser, William, 39, 45

WE'D LIKE TO HEAR FROM YOU

Thank you for using *Your College Experience,* 4th Edition. We care a lot about how you liked this book and how useful you found it. Please let us know how we can improve the next edition by returning this page with your comments, using the postage-free label on the other side. Or send us an e-mail message to *csuccess@wadsworth.com.* Either way, we'd like to hear your thoughts.

Overall, how valuable was the book as part of the course? Why? _____

_____

_____

_____

Which parts or exercises were particularly helpful? Why? _____

_____

_____

_____

Which parts or exercises should be changed? Why? _____

_____

_____

_____

Are there any topics not covered in the book that you think should be added? _____

_____

_____

How else can we improve *Your College Experience*? _____

_____

_____

_____

Thanks and good luck!

John Gardner

Jerry Jewler

Your name _____ School _____

Your address _____

City/State _____ Zip _____

Your instructor's name _____

May Wadsworth quote you, either in promotion for *Your College Experience* or in future publishing ventures?

Yes _____ No _____

FOLD HERE

TEAR PAGE OUT

FOLD HERE

NO POSTAGE
NECESSARY
IF MAILED
IN THE
UNITED STATES

BUSINESS REPLY MAIL
FIRST CLASS   PERMIT NO. 34   BELMONT, CA

POSTAGE WILL BE PAID BY ADDRESSEE

John N. Gardner / A. Jerome Jewler
Your College Experience, 4th Edition
℅ College Success Editor
Wadsworth Publishing Company
10 Davis Drive
Belmont, CA 94002-9801